LINCOLN'S WAR

❧ THE LOCHLAINN SEABROOK COLLECTION ❧

Everything You Were Taught About the Civil War is Wrong, Ask a Southerner!
Everything You Were Taught About American Slavery is Wrong, Ask a Southerner!
Lincoln's War: The Real Cause, the Real Winner, the Real Loser
Confederate Flag Facts: What Every American Should Know About Dixie's Southern Cross
Give This Book to a Yankee! A Southern Guide to the Civil War For Northerners
Women in Gray: A Tribute to the Ladies Who Supported the Southern Confederacy
The Unholy Crusade: Lincoln's Legacy of Destruction in the American South
Honest Jeff and Dishonest Abe: A Southern Children's Guide to the Civil War
Confederacy 101: Amazing Facts You Never Knew About America's Oldest Political Tradition
Slavery 101: Amazing Facts You Never Knew About America's "Peculiar Institution"
The Great Yankee Coverup: What the North Doesn't Want You to Know About Lincoln's War!
Confederate Blood and Treasure: An Interview With Lochlainn Seabrook
A Rebel Born: A Defense of Nathan Bedford Forrest - Confederate General, American Legend (winner of the 2011 Jefferson Davis Historical Gold Medal)
A Rebel Born: The Screenplay
Nathan Bedford Forrest: Southern Hero, American Patriot - Honoring a Confederate Icon and the Old South
The Quotable Nathan Bedford Forrest: Selections From the Writings and Speeches of the Confederacy's Most Brilliant Cavalryman
Give 'Em Hell Boys! The Complete Military Correspondence of Nathan Bedford Forrest
Forrest! 99 Reasons to Love Nathan Bedford Forrest
Saddle, Sword, and Gun: A Biography of Nathan Bedford Forrest For Teens
Nathan Bedford Forrest and the Battle of Fort Pillow: Yankee Myth, Confederate Fact
Nathan Bedford Forrest and the Ku Klux Klan: Yankee Myth, Confederate Fact
Nathan Bedford Forrest and African-Americans: Yankee Myth, Confederate Fact
The Quotable Jefferson Davis: Selections From the Writings and Speeches of the Confederacy's First President
The Quotable Alexander H. Stephens: Selections From the Writings and Speeches of the Confederacy's First Vice President
The Alexander H. Stephens Reader: Excerpts From the Works of a Confederate Founding Father
The Quotable Robert E. Lee: Selections From the Writings and Speeches of the South's Most Beloved Civil War General
The Old Rebel: Robert E. Lee As He Was Seen By His Contemporaries
The Articles of Confederation Explained: A Clause-by-Clause Study of America's First Constitution
The Constitution of the Confederate States of America Explained: A Clause-by-Clause Study of the South's Magna Carta
The Quotable Stonewall Jackson: Selections From the Writings and Speeches of the South's Most Famous General
Abraham Lincoln: The Southern View - Demythologizing America's Sixteenth President
The Unquotable Abraham Lincoln: The President's Quotes They Don't Want You To Know!
Lincolnology: The Real Abraham Lincoln Revealed in His Own Words - A Study of Lincoln's Suppressed, Misinterpreted, and Forgotten Writings and Speeches
The Great Impersonator! 99 Reasons to Dislike Abraham Lincoln
Encyclopedia of the Battle of Franklin - A Comprehensive Guide to the Conflict that Changed the Civil War
Carnton Plantation Ghost Stories: True Tales of the Unexplained from Tennessee's Most Haunted Civil War House!
The McGavocks of Carnton Plantation: A Southern History - Celebrating One of Dixie's Most Noble Confederate Families and Their Tennessee Home
Jesus and the Law of Attraction: The Bible-Based Guide to Creating Perfect Health, Wealth, and Happiness Following Christ's Simple Formula
The Bible and the Law of Attraction: 99 Teachings of Jesus, the Apostles, and the Prophets
Christ Is All and In All: Rediscovering Your Divine Nature and the Kingdom Within
Jesus and the Gospel of Q: Christ's Pre-Christian Teachings As Recorded in the New Testament
Seabrook's Bible Dictionary of Traditional and Mystical Christian Doctrines
The Way of Holiness: The Story of Religion and Myth From the Cave Bear Cult to Christianity
Christmas Before Christianity: How the Birthday of the "Sun" Became the Birthday of the "Son"
Autobiography of a Non-Yogi: A Scientist's Journey From Hinduism to Christianity (with Amitava Dasgupta)
Britannia Rules: Goddess-Worship in Ancient Anglo-Celtic Society - An Academic Look at the United Kingdom's Matricentric Spiritual Past
The Book of Kelle: An Introduction to Goddess-Worship and the Great Celtic Mother-Goddess Kelle, Original Blessed Lady of Ireland
The Goddess Dictionary of Words and Phrases: Introducing a New Core Vocabulary for the Women's Spirituality Movement
Princess Diana: Modern Day Moon-Goddess - A Psychoanalytical and Mythological Look at Diana Spencer's Life, Marriage, and Death (with Dr. Jane Goldberg)
Aphrodite's Trade: The Hidden History of Prostitution Unveiled
UFOs and Aliens: The Complete Guidebook
The Caudills: An Etymological, Ethnological, and Genealogical Study - Exploring the Name and National Origins of a European-American Family
The Blakeneys: An Etymological, Ethnological, and Genealogical Study - Uncovering the Mysterious Origins of the Blakeney Family and Name

Five-Star Books & Gifts From the Heart of the American South

❧ SeaRavenPress.com ❧

LINCOLN'S WAR

THE REAL CAUSE, THE REAL WINNER, THE REAL LOSER

Illustrated by the author, Colonel

LOCHLAINN SEABROOK

JEFFERSON DAVIS HISTORICAL GOLD MEDAL WINNER

Diligently Researched for the Elucidation of the Reader

Sea Raven Press, Nashville, Tennessee, USA

2016

LINCOLN'S WAR

Published by
Sea Raven Press, Cassidy Ravensdale, President
The Literary Wing of the Pro-South Movement
PO Box 1484, Spring Hill, Tennessee 37174-1484 USA
SeaRavenPress.com • searavenpress@gmail.com

1st SRP paperback edition, 1st printing: December 2016, ISBN: 978-1-943737-37-6
1st SRP hardcover edition, 1st printing: December 2016, ISBN: 978-1-943737-38-3

ISBN: 978-1-943737-38-3 (hardcover)
Library of Congress Control Number: 2016958871

Lincoln's War: The Real Cause, the Real Winner, the Real Loser, by Lochlainn Seabrook.
Includes an index, endnotes, and bibliographical references.

Front and back cover design and art, book design, layout, and interior art by Lochlainn Seabrook.
All images, graphic design, graphic art, and illustrations copyright © Lochlainn Seabrook.
Cover image: Fort Moultrie, Charleston, South Carolina, April 1865
Cover image & design copyright © Lochlainn Seabrook.
Portions of this book have been adapted from the author's other works

The views on the American "Civil War" documented in this book are those of the publisher.

The paper used in this book is acid-free and lignin-free. It has been certified by the Sustainable Forestry
Initiative and the Forest Stewardship Council and meets all ANSI standards for archival quality paper.

PRINTED & MANUFACTURED IN OCCUPIED TENNESSEE, FORMER CONFEDERATE STATES OF AMERICA

Dedication

TO THE COURAGEOUS EARLY AMERICAN MEN AND
WOMEN—FROM THOMAS JEFFERSON AND CATHERINE MOORE
BARRY TO JEFFERSON DAVIS AND MILDRED LEWIS
RUTHERFORD—WHO STOOD UP FOR THE CONSERVATIVE
VALUES OF THE U.S. AND CONFEDERATE FOUNDING FATHERS.

Epigraph

"Lee's shrine at Lexington, not Lincoln's tomb, will be
the shrine of American patriotism when once history is
told correctly."

Dr. Littlefield, Needham, Massachusetts

Lee Chapel, Lexington, Virginia.

CONTENTS

SEA RAVEN PRESS

THE WORLD'S #1 SOUTH-FRIENDLY BOOK PUBLISHER

Restoring Dixie's honor
Defending traditional Southern culture
Preserving authentic Confederate history
One book at a time!

Nashville, Tennessee

SeaRavenPress.com

NOTES TO THE READER

THE TWO MAIN POLITICAL PARTIES IN 1860

☛ In any study of America's antebellum, bellum, and postbellum periods, it is vitally important to understand that in 1860 the two major political parties—the Democrats and the newly formed Republicans—were the opposite of what they are today. In other words, the Democrats of the mid 19th Century were Conservatives, akin to the Republican Party of today, while the Republicans of the mid 19th Century were Liberals, akin to the Democratic Party of today.[1]

In fact, the modern Republican Party—a political descendant of the progressive 18th-Century Federalist Party—was founded in 1854 by liberals (then sometimes known as "fusionists") familiar with communist Karl Marx,[2] who along

The author's cousin, Confederate Vice President and Democrat Alexander H. Stephens: a Southern Conservative.

with various types of socialists, radicals, and revolutionaries, wrote its platform, served as delegates at the 1860 Republican convention, zealously campaigned for Lincoln, and were instrumental in getting him into the White House.[3]

In essence then the Confederacy's Democratic president, Jefferson Davis, was a Conservative (with libertarian leanings); the Union's Republican president, Abraham Lincoln, was a Liberal (with socialistic leanings). This is why, in the mid 1800s, the conservative wing of the Democratic Party was known as "the States' Rights Party,"[4] it is why Lincoln idolized the radical leaders of the European socialist revolution of 1848,[5] and it is why the radical left members of the Republican Party agreed with socialists and communists that the American "Civil War" was a "revolutionary movement" (Marx), a "radical revolution" (Thaddeus Stevens), and a "social revolution" (James A. Garfield).[6]

Hence, the Democrats of the Civil War period referred to themselves as "conservatives," "confederates," "anti-centralists," or "constitutionalists" (the latter because they favored rigorous adherence to the original Constitution—which tacitly guaranteed states' rights—as created by the Founding Fathers), while the Republicans called themselves "liberals," "nationalists," "centralists," or "consolidationists" (the latter three because they wanted to nationalize the central government and consolidate political power in Washington, D.C.).[7] Due to the 19th-Century Republicans' (Liberals') hatred of the Constitution (which they derogatorily referred to as a "scrap of paper"),[8] Democrats (Conservatives) of that era called them "radicals,"[9] or more accurately, the "Anti-Constitutional Party."[10]

Since in our post-truth political world these facts are new to most of my readers,[11] let us further demystify them by viewing them from the perspective of the American Revolutionary War. If Davis and his *conservative* Southern constituents (the Democrats of 1861) had been alive in 1775, they would have sided with George Washington and the American colonists, who sought to secede from the tyrannical government of Great Britain; if Lincoln and his *liberal* Northern constituents (the Republicans of 1861) had been alive at that time, they would have sided with King George III and the English monarchy, who sought to maintain the American colonies as possessions of the British Empire. It is due to this very comparison that Southerners often refer to the "Civil War" as the Second American Revolutionary War.

Thus in the early 20th Century former Confederates spoke of 18th-Century Federalist Alexander Hamilton as a big government or centralizing Liberal, while acknowledging that Thomas Jefferson and the Republicans were "now Democrats," the Conservatives of the Civil War period,[12] men committed to states' rights and a literal and strict interpretation of the Constitution.[13] This is made more clear by the fact that in his day Conservative Jefferson was a member of the

U.S. President William McKinley, in 1896 the first Conservative Republican since the party's inception in 1854.

"Democratic-Republican Party," which, after his death, "dropped the name 'Republican' which it had borne during his life, and assumed the name 'Democrat.'"[14] Writes Elizabeth Avery Meriwether:

> Not until 1854 did the [politically liberal] men of the Federal and Whig persuasion unite and organize a party and take the name "Republican." The Republican [Liberal] party of the 1860s was the legitimate offspring of the old New England Federalists [big government Liberals], and inherited all its

progenitor's faiths, hopes, hates and purposes, viz: Passion for power, fear and hate of Democracy [here meaning conservatism], hate of the Union . . . and the strong persistent determination to break the Union asunder and form of the Northeast section a Northeastern Confederacy. All these ideas belonged to the old Federalists [Liberals] of New England, and were handed down to the Republican [Liberal] party in 1854.[15]

These party designations were particularly evident in the so-called "New South" shortly after Lincoln's War, as historian Holland Thompson notes:

William Jennings Bryan, in 1896 the first Liberal to win the presidential nomination of the Democratic Party, and the first progressive to add a populist plank to the party's platform since its inception in 1828.

The political organization [the Democrats] to which allegiance was demanded was generally called the Conservative party, and the Republican [Liberal] party was universally called the Radical party. The term Conservative was adopted partly as a contrast, partly because the peace party had been so called during the War, and especially because the name Democrat was obnoxious to so many old Whigs [antebellum Liberals]. It was not until 1906 that the term Conservative was officially dropped from the title of the dominant party in Alabama [the Democratic Party].[16]

Finally, it is important to note here that the conservative Republican Party and the liberal Democratic Party that we are so familiar with today, did not arise until 1896, when the then *liberal* Republican Party switched to a *conservative* platform and nominated Conservative capitalist William McKinley of Ohio (who was supported by conservative former Confederate soldiers)[17] as its presidential nominee. That same year the then *conservative* Democratic Party switched to a *progressive* platform, nominating the Liberal "fusion candidate" William Jennings Bryan of Illinois as its presidential nominee,[18] whose populist platform Conservatives charged rested on a cornerstone of "chartered communism."[19] This major developmental change in American politics is why the Border States (Delaware, Maryland, West Virginia, Kentucky, and Missouri) did not begin to be carried by Republican candidates until 1896,[20] and it is why the election of 1896 has been called "the most important in U.S. history since Lincoln's War."[21]

Without a basic understanding of these facts, the American "Civil War" will forever remain incomprehensible.

THE TERM "CIVIL WAR"

☞ As I heartily dislike the phrase "Civil War," its use throughout this book (as well as in my other works) is worthy of an explanation.

Today America's entire literary system refers to the conflict of 1861 using the Northern term the "Civil War," whether we in the South like it or not. Thus, as all book searches by readers, libraries, and retail outlets are now performed online, and as all bookstores categorize works from this period under the heading "Civil War," book publishers and authors who deal with this particular topic have little choice but to use this term themselves. If I were to refuse to use it, as some of my Southern colleagues have suggested, few people would ever find or read my books.

The American "Civil War" was not a true civil war as Webster defines it: "A conflict between opposing groups of citizens of the *same* country." It was a fight between two individual countries; or to be more specific, two separate and constitutionally formed confederacies: the U.S.A. and the C.S.A.

Add to this the fact that scarcely any non-Southerners have ever heard of the names we in the South use for the conflict, such as the "War for Southern Independence"—or my personal preference, "Lincoln's War." It only makes sense then to use the term "Civil War" in most commercial situations, distasteful though it is.

We should also bear in mind that while today educated persons, particularly educated Southerners, all share an abhorrence for the phrase "Civil War," it was not always so. Confederates who lived through and even fought in the conflict regularly used the term throughout the 1860s, and even long after. Among them were Confederate generals such as Nathan Bedford Forrest, Richard Taylor, and Joseph E. Johnston, not to mention the Confederacy's vice president, Alexander H. Stephens.

In 1895 Confederate General James Longstreet wrote about his military experiences in a work subtitled, *Memoirs of the Civil War in America.* Even the Confederacy's highest leader, President Jefferson Davis, used the term "Civil War,"[22] and in one case at least, as late as 1881—the year he wrote his brilliant exposition, *The Rise and Fall of the Confederate Government.*[23] Authors writing for *Confederate Magazine* sometimes used the phrase well into the early 1900s,[24] and in 1898, at the Eighth Annual Meeting and Reunion of the United Confederate Veterans (the forerunner of today's Sons of Confederate Veterans), the following resolution was proposed: that from then on the Great War of 1861 was to be designated "the Civil War Between the States."[25]

CLARIFICATION
☛ To assist the reader in keeping track of the often confusing two-party political system referenced by early Americans writers and speakers before, during, and after Lincoln's War, I have inserted brackets identifying Victorian party affiliations—as well as additional notes and comments—where I deem appropriate. My words are always set in full justification and at normal font size. When I cite others their words are indented and set in a smaller font.

PRESENTISM
☛ As a historian I view *presentism* (judging the past according to present day mores and customs) as the enemy of authentic history. And this is precisely why the Left employs it in its ongoing war against traditional American, conservative, and Christian values. By looking at history through the lens of modern day beliefs, they are able to distort, revise, and reshape the past into a false narrative that fits their ideological agenda: the liberalization *and* Northernization of America, the strengthening and further centralization of the national government, and total control of American political, economic, and social power, the same agenda that Lincoln championed.

This book, *Lincoln's War: The Real Cause, the Real Winner, the Real Loser*, rejects presentism and replaces it with what I call *historicalism*: judging our ancestors based on the values of their own time. To get the most from this work the reader is invited to reject presentism as well. In this way—along with casting aside preconceived notions and the erroneous "history" churned out by our left-wing educational system—the truth in this work will be most readily ascertained and absorbed.

LEARN MORE
☛ Lincoln's War on the American people and the Constitution can never be fully understood without a thorough knowledge of the South's perspective. As this book is only meant to be a brief introductory guide to these topics, one cannot hope to learn the complete story here. For those who are interested in additional material from the South's perspective, please see my comprehensive histories listed on page 2.

THE NORTH IS STILL LYING ABOUT LINCOLN'S WAR

1

THE REAL CAUSE OF LINCOLN'S WAR

IF OUR MAINSTREAM HISTORY BOOKS are correct, the direct cause of the American "Civil War" was "slavery." Most people have read and heard this old Yankee chestnut so many times that they never give it a second thought. But anything put out by the Liberal establishment, which is where nearly all of our school textbooks and history books come from, should always be questioned.

C.S. President Jefferson Davis: Democrat and small government Conservative.

Why? Because politically correct leftists operate from feelings rather than facts, making their perception of history not just inaccurate, but dangerous. For them, their "warm and fuzzy" sociopolitical theories of "higher law" and "social justice" are more important than common sense, jurisprudence, or even the Constitution. This essentially liberalistic worldview completely colors and biases their articles, books, blogs, TV shows, and films against America and her traditions, including Christianity, conservatism, and especially the traditional South and the

Confederacy—the favorite whipping post of the Far Left.

One of the results of this subjective, emotional, theoretical, and unhistorical approach to history has been the myth that "the cause of the Civil War was slavery," the same one that was taught to you by our government, and which is now being taught to your children, and which will one day be taught to your grandchildren.

This myth was invented and promulgated by 19th-Century progressives, among whom was Union President Abraham Lincoln. Those familiar with my books are aware that the platforms of the two major parties were reversed in 1860, making Lincoln and the Republicans at the time *Liberals* (often with strong socialistic leanings) and Jefferson Davis and the Democrats of the day *Conservatives* (often with strong libertarian leanings). This is precisely why communists and socialists eagerly offered to serve under Lincoln while none evinced any interest in Davis or the Southern Cause.

U.S. President Abraham Lincoln: Republican and big government liberal.

Without knowing and understanding this one simple fact, the American "Civil War" is inexplicable. Thanks to the Left's ubiquitous revisionist history books—which fill our schools, libraries, and bookstores—this fact is indeed literally unknown to the majority of Americans. Thus we have the bizarre phenomenon of both uninformed Liberals and Conservatives adopting the communist view that the conflict was a "war over slavery."[26]

But was it?

Of course not! And the political and military leaders of both the Confederacy and the Union said so, as we will now see.

Let us begin with the most important individual of the Great War of 1861, C.S. President Jefferson Davis, who made the following comment on the subject:

The truth remains intact and incontrovertible, that the existence of African servitude was in no wise the cause of the conflict, but only an incident. In the later controversies that arose, however, its effect in operating as a lever upon the passions, prejudices, or sympathies of mankind, was so potent that it has been spread like a thick cloud over the whole horizon of historic truth.[27]

The leader of the Union, U.S. President Abraham Lincoln, also strongly denounced the idea that the cause of the War was connected to slavery. Indeed, he made this clear from his very first day in office, when, on March 4, 1861, in his First Inaugural Address, the new U.S. commander-in-chief drove home his policies on slaves ("property") and slavery. Said Lincoln:

> Apprehension seems to exist among the people of the Southern States that by the accession of a Republican administration their property and their peace and personal security are to be endangered. There has never been any reasonable cause for such apprehension. Indeed, the most ample evidence to the contrary has all the while existed and been open to their inspection. It is found in nearly all the published speeches of him who now addresses you. I do but quote from one of those speeches when I declare that *'I have no purpose, directly or indirectly, to interfere with the institution of slavery in the States where it exists. I believe I have no lawful right to do so, and I have no inclination to do so.'* Those who nominated and elected me did so with full knowledge that I had made this and many similar declarations, and had never recanted them.[28]

Many of his own constituents did not agree with Lincoln, and continued to claim that the War was one of abolition. Angered, in the midst of the conflict he released the following statements:

> *My enemies* pretend I am now carrying on this war for the sole purpose of abolition. So long as I am President, it shall be carried on for the sole purpose of restoring the Union. . . . If there be those who would not save the Union unless they could at the same time destroy slavery, I do not agree with them. My paramount object in this struggle is to save the Union, and is not either to save or to destroy slavery. If I could save the Union without freeing any slave I would do it.[29]

Mainstream historians and the liberal media like to gloss over these important words, so let us repeat them here in order to establish the truth once and for all: *if Lincoln were alive today, he would consider those who claim that his War was fought over slavery his "enemies."*

If this is not clear enough, early on Lincoln's Secretary of War Simon Cameron wrote the following to Union General Benjamin F. Butler:

> President Lincoln desires the right to hold slaves to be fully recognized. The war is prosecuted for the Union, hence no question concerning slavery will arise.[30]

The U.S. Congress was of the same mind as its president, asserting that the Civil War had no relationship to slavery. On July 22, 1861, it issued the following resolution:

> . . . this war is not waged upon our part in any spirit of oppression, nor for any purpose of conquest or subjugation, nor purpose of overthrowing or interfering with the rights or established institutions [that is, slavery] of those States; but to defend and maintain the supremacy of the Constitution and to preserve the Union with all the dignity, equality, and rights of the several States unimpaired; that as soon as these objects are accomplished the war ought to cease.[31]

The Union's highest military officer, Ulysses S. Grant, agreed, offering this comment on the topic of slavery and the cause of the War:

> The sole object of this war is to restore the union. Should I be convinced it has any other object, or that the government designs using its soldiers to execute the wishes of the Abolitionists, I pledge to you my honor as a man and a soldier, I would resign my commission and carry my sword to the other side.[32]

Grant, a slave owning Yankee Liberal who was soon to become our eighteenth president, states here that he would sooner fight for the Confederacy than fight for the Union against slavery!

And why, Mildred Lewis Rutherford rightly asked, if the Union was fighting to destroy slavery and the Confederacy was fighting to preserve slavery, was Grant, a slaveholder and an anti-abolitionist,[33] put in command of the Union army, while Lee, a non-slave owner and an abolitionist, was put in command of the Confederate army? The argument is even more absurd when we consider that at the start of Lincoln's War in the Spring of 1861 there were 315,000 slave owners in the Yankee military, but only 200,000 in the South's military.[34] Even Southern foe Daniel Webster of Massachusetts readily acknowledged that all of the leading men of the South regarded slavery as "an evil, a blight, a scourge, and a curse," that needed to be abolished as soon as was practicable.[35]

If it was not to destroy slavery, why then did the North wage war against the South?

As we can see from some of the foregoing statements, Lincoln and his administrators claimed that it was to "preserve the Union." And this was allegedly based on the liberal's political theory that there is a "higher law" than the Constitution, that "law" being the arbitrary and purely subjective concept of "social justice."[36]

But what American leader would assume dictatorial powers; trample over the Constitution; declare war and increase the size of the army and navy without congressional approval; institute an illicit naval blockade; unlawfully suspend *habeas corpus*; illicitly create an unsupported paper currency; kill hundreds of thousands of his own countrymen (including women and children of all races); unlawfully seize and redistribute Southern private property and wealth to Northerners; rob, steal, and plunder ordinary citizens (the North confiscated some $200 million from Southern planters and merchants[37]—the equivalent of $4 billion today); despotically suppress free speech by shutting down over 300 newspapers (for printing articles he did not like); illegally imprison the entire legislatures of various states; and burn hospitals, universities, and libraries to the ground in order to "preserve the Union"?[38]

Liberal Union General Ulysses S. Grant of Ohio.

The very idea is not only irrational and even insane, but runs counter to everything the Founding Fathers intended to establish: a "*voluntary union of friendly states*,"[39] known even by early American Liberals, like Alexander Hamilton, as a "Confederate Republic."[40]

Additionally, if the War had been an abolitionary one, why did it not end on September 22, 1862, when Lincoln issued his Preliminary Emancipation Proclamation? Or at least on January 1, 1863, the day he issued his Final Emancipation Proclamation? Yet the conflict continued for over two more years. Why, if the slaves had been "freed"?

In 1863 Confederate President Jefferson Davis answered the question about why the South went to war:

> The people of the States now confederated became convinced that the Government of the United States had fallen into the hands of *a sectional majority, who would pervert that most sacred of all trusts to the destruction of the rights which it was pledged to protect.* They believed that to remain longer in the Union would subject them to a continuance of a disparaging discrimination, submission to which would be inconsistent with their welfare, and intolerable to a proud people. They therefore determined to sever its bonds and establish a new Confederacy for themselves.
>
> The experiment instituted by our revolutionary fathers, of a voluntary Union of sovereign States for the purposes specified in a solemn compact, *had been perverted by those who, feeling power and forgetting right, were determined to respect no law but their own will. The Government had ceased to answer the ends for which it was ordained and established.* To save ourselves from a revolution which, in its silent but rapid progress, was about to place us under the despotism of numbers [that is, a democracy; very different than a republic], and to preserve in spirit, as well as in form, a system of government we believed to be peculiarly fitted to our condition [that is, a confederate republic], and full of promise for mankind, we determined to make a new association, composed of States homogenous in interest, in policy, and in feeling.
>
> *True to our traditions of peace and our love of justice, we sent commissioners to the United States to propose a fair and amicable settlement of all questions of public debt or property which might be in dispute. But the Government at Washington [that is, Lincoln], denying our right to self-government, refused even to listen to any proposals for a peaceful separation. Nothing was then left to do but to prepare for war.*[41]

Thus, Davis asserted, the South was forced to take up arms against the North, not over slavery, but to vindicate the political rights, the freedom, equality, and State sovereignty which were the heritage purchased by the blood of our revolutionary sires.[42]

Texas Governor Joseph D. Sayers likewise later declared:

. . . it may be insisted, without danger of successful contravention, that it was for the strict and faithful observance of the constitution, as understood, and for the right of local self-government under such interpretation, that the South made contention, and upon that issue mainly was the war fought by it.[43]

After Lincoln's War, Southerner Lyon Gardiner Tyler, the son of America's tenth President, John Tyler,[44] put the matter this way:

The emancipation of slaves [in 1863] by the late war is the best evidence that the South never fought for slavery, but *against a foreign dictation and a sectional will*. Within the Union slavery was probably secure for many years to come. The war was nothing more than the outcome of a tyranny exerted for seventy-two years by the North over vital interests of the South.[45]

Conservative Confederate General Nathan Bedford Forrest of Tennessee.

The common Rebel soldier knew exactly why he was defending Dixie, even if his description was not as elegant as Tyler's. A Yankee officer once asked a filthy, ragged, barefoot Confederate prisoner why in the world he was fighting. Looking him squarely in the eyes, Johnny Reb said: "Because y'all are down here."[46]

One Confederate officer who felt the same way was the beloved military genius General Nathan Bedford Forrest. On April 12, 1864, during the Battle of Fort Pillow, the by now famous Forrest came upon a Yankee soldier.

"What in hell are you doing down here?" he asked the terrified Federal, as minié balls whizzed by their ears. "I should kill you right here and now!" he continued. "If you goddamned Yanks had stayed home and minded yer own business, the war would have been over a long time ago!"[47]

As we have seen, as for the North itself, Lincoln stated in no uncertain terms that he took up arms against the South to "preserve the Union," a position from which he never wavered. And it should be clear by now that abolition was merely one of the many results of the War, not the cause;[48] a means by which Liberal Lincoln could achieve his goal of installing big government—not the end itself.[49]

Evidence of this fact took place at the Hampton Roads Conference on February 3, 1865. Here, Lincoln demanded restoration of the Union, while the Southern peace commissioners demanded independence. Neither side would budge and the War continued for another two months. If the conflict had been over slavery, as Northern mythology repeatedly tells us, then it would have ended that day,[50] for Davis had already decided to emancipate Southern slaves and enlist them in the Confederate army (this decision was made official by the Confederate Congress just a few weeks later, in March).[51]

Finally, as Patrick J. Buchanan points out, at the time Lincoln declared war on the South, the vast majority of slave owners and their slaves were still part of the U.S. On April 12, 1861, the day the Battle of Fort Sumter began, Virginia, for example, one of the largest slave-holding states, had not yet seceded and was still in the Union. Obviously then, Lincoln's attack on the South was not an attack on slavery.[52]

In short, the "Civil War" was not a "crisis of abolition." It was what objective historians call a "crisis of constitutionalism."[53]

Thus we can be sure that the idea that the North waged a violent four year war to "preserve the Union" was just another smokescreen to conceal its true liberal agenda, which, as we will discuss in more detail shortly, was to install big government, then known as the "American System," in Washington.[54]

Why then did the South take up arms against the North? Was it not to "preserve slavery"?

This is indeed what our leftist mainstream historians tell us. But as we have seen, the writings of progressives are inherently suspect, and nearly always false, for they are based on emotion and opinion rather than objectivity and facts. Let us then listen to what the Confederacy's highest officials had to say on the topic.

Confederate Vice President Alexander H. Stephens declared that the South seceded for one reason and one reason only: to "render our liberties and institutions more secure" by "rescuing, restoring, and re-establishing the Constitution." As for the War, the South took up arms, he noted, for no other reason than a "desire to preserve constitutional liberty and perpetuate the government in its purity."[55]

According to Robert E. Lee, the South's highest ranking military officer:

> All the South has ever desired was that the Union as established by our forefathers should be preserved; and that the government as originally organized should be administered in purity and truth.[56]

The common soldier, on *both* sides, heartily agreed that they were not fighting to either preserve slavery or destroy it. White Union soldiers were near universal in their agreement on this score. How do we know this? Because they so often openly voiced their disdain for the black man. White Union troops who served under Yankee General Ambrose E. Burnside, for instance, declared that they would not be "caught in the company of niggers,"[57] a common refrain throughout the Northern ranks.

Such remarks were exacerbated by the issuance of the Emancipation Proclamation on January 1, 1863. After being told of the edict, along with Lincoln's new black enrollment policies, the great majority of his white soldiers, who vociferously described themselves as "anti-abolitionist," hissed and booed, and officers reported widespread "demoralization" among their men.[58] Rhode Island's war governor, William Sprague, noted sourly:

> We had to take a lot of abuse in return for an endorsement of Abraham Lincoln's Emancipation Proclamation. We were hissed in the streets and denounced as traitors.[59]

In January 1893 historian and Lincoln devotee Ida Tarbell wrote:

> Many a [Northern] man deserted in the winter of 1862-1863, because of Lincoln's Emancipation Proclamation. The [Union] soldiers did not believe that Lincoln had the right to issue it, and they refused to fight.

Lincoln knew that hundreds were deserting.[60]

Many "prominent" Union officers simply did not want "niggers" in their lines and "sneered at the idea of negroes fighting . . ."[61] One of the most demoralized of Lincoln's commanders was Yankee General Joseph "Fighting Joe" Hooker,[62] who sent the president a scathing letter about his Emancipation Proclamation, reporting that much of the Union army was solidly against it. Wrote Hooker:

> At that time . . . a majority of the officers, especially those high in rank, were hostile to the policy of the Government in the conduct of the war. The emancipation proclamation had been published a short time before, and a large element of the army had taken sides antagonistic to it, declaring that they would never have embarked in the war had they anticipated the action of the Government.[63]

Even in those troops where a smidgen of abolition sentiment existed, the average Yankee soldier was hesitant to interfere with slavery, an institution that he was used to and which he knew to be legal under the Constitution. So accepted was slavery among most Union officers that they nearly always allowed Southern slaveholders into their lines to search for runaway slaves.[64]

Another disgruntled Yankee general, the infamous Fitz John Porter,[65] wrote that Lincoln's Emancipation Proclamation was

Liberal Union General Fitz John Porter of New Hampshire.

widely jeered throughout the Union army, inducing disgust, dissatisfaction, and words of infidelity toward the U.S. president that were very close to treasonous.[66]

Shortly after the Battle of Sharpsburg, one of the president's Yankee soldiers wrote that Lincoln's proclamation was denounced by most men of the Northern army, for "none wanted to fight for the black man, but only to preserve the Union." "Subdue the Rebs first, talk about the civil rights of the nigger afterward," they fumed.[67]

In July 1862 a Yankee soldier from New York remarked that just about everyone in the U.S. army was infuriated with Lincoln and the "negro issue," and that most wanted nothing more than to put a noose around the neck of Northern abolitionist and socialist Horace Greeley.[68] Another Union soldier said, "I really don't care what happens to the nigger, and I'm certainly not going to risk my life for him. I'd rather fight him than Johnny Reb." Yet another U.S. serviceman wrote: "No doubt the ideal way to solve the dilemma of the negroes would be to shoot all of 'em."[69] One of the many thousands of Yankees who defected over to the Confederate side announced: "I'd just as soon live with Satan in Hell than lift a finger to free the slaves."[70]

In early 1863, not long after Lincoln issued his Emancipation Proclamation, a Yankee soldier from his home state, Illinois, expressed the following sentiment: "I have suffered long and hard through this war, all for the 'poor nigger.' Yet I see no evidence that my suffering has helped him in anyway."[71] Not atypical was the comment of a New England Union soldier. In 1863, while stationed in New Orleans, he wrote to his brother: "I was out walking today and came upon a small black baby crawling along. My first instinct was to crush the horrid thing to death, there and then."[72]

In the summer of 1862 some of Union General George B. McClellan's staff "seriously discussed" marching to Washington to "intimidate the president," in the hopes that he would refrain from interfering with slavery and simply bring the War to a quick and peaceful close. Union General John Pope noted that among the Army of the Potomac there were frequent comments made about Lincoln's flaws and the possibility of replacing him with someone more able.[73]

The fact that the Union military was not fighting for abolition, and that it even nearly fell apart when Lincoln issued his Emancipation Proclamation, is so obvious and well-known in scholarly circles that even our most entrenched pro-North, pro-Lincoln historians have had to acknowledge it. In 1907, one of these, James H. Wilson, for example, made the following comment about the notorious document:

> It is worthy of remark that it never received the active support of the [U.S.] army, in whose ranks the love of the Union, and the

determination to save it, rather than the hatred of slavery, were always the controlling sentiments.[74]

If the North did indeed fight to abolish the "peculiar institution," one has a right to wonder why, for the first two years of his War, Lincoln barred blacks from joining his armies, and why a black Union recruiting office in Cincinnati, Ohio—no doubt under orders from the Lincoln administration—was shut down by police, who told the Northern African-Americans who had lined up to enlist: "This is the white man's war, and you damned niggers are not needed or wanted!"[75]

Intelligent people will also be curious as to why, when he finally allowed African-Americans to enlist (the *real* purpose of the Emancipation Proclamation, as that document itself states), Lincoln used many of his new black recruits as shock troops: sent into battle first, they spared white lives by absorbing the brunt of the attack.[76]

The result of these racist policies was inevitable. By the end of the War 38,000 black Yankee soldiers had been killed,[77] making the mortality rate among Lincoln's African-American servicemen 40 percent higher than for his white soldiers.[78] Apparently, this was just how Lincoln planned it. As he himself once said:

> I thought that whatever negroes can be got to do as soldiers, leaves just so much less for white soldiers to do in saving the Union.[79]

Liberal Iowa Governor Samuel J. Kirkwood.

This included, of course, taking cold Confederate steel.

Others in Lincoln's party put it more bluntly. Samuel J. Kirkwood, Iowa's governor, said that he would rather sacrifice the lives of "niggers" than the lives of the nation's white sons.[80] Another man from Lincoln's party, Illinois Senator John A. "Black Jack" Logan, a Yankee general in the War, stated publicly that he would rather that "six niggers" be killed than a single white man.[81] In the winter of

1864, the London *Telegraph* stated what the North has still yet to find the courage and honesty to acknowledge: not once did Lincoln ever consider enlisting and arming Negroes on his own. It was only when he could not afford to lose anymore white soldiers that the decision came.[82]

If some of my readers require more proof that the North did not fight to end slavery, consider the following.

Even after exploiting "freed" African-Americans for little more than cannon fodder and servile labor, Lincoln continued to issue racist policies that not only discouraged his black soldiers, but hurt his own war effort. One of the more egregious of these was the order to racially segregate all Union troops,[83] with black troops to be led by white officers[84]—an order followed closely at conflicts like the Battle of Nashville.[85]

Another one of Lincoln's racist military policies concerned pay. After earlier promising equal pay,[86] Lincoln's order (via the Militia Act of July 17, 1862)[87] that black soldiers receive half the pay of white soldiers,[88] infuriated both blacks and abolitionists.[89] This was a "necessary concession" to white Northern racism,[90] Lincoln explained to a furious Frederick Douglass in the summer of 1863.[91] Many of Lincoln's black soldiers were *never* paid. Former African-American servant Susie King Taylor wrote:

> I was the wife of one of those men who did not get a penny for eighteen months for their services, only their rations and clothing.[92]

There was also the issue of white recruitment: Lincoln and his cabinet feared that granting equal pay to black soldiers would discourage Northern whites from enlisting,[93] most who made it clear that they did not want to fight next to blacks anyway, however noble the Union cause.[94]

Adding fuel to the fire, black Yankee officers, those rare few that existed,[95] were paid the same as white Yankee privates.[96] Yet when the Confederacy also finally officially enlisted blacks, March 23, 1863, they were immediately integrated and given equal pay and equal treatment with white soldiers.[97]

Lincoln himself was no abolitionist, for he often said he hated the entire movement and believed that abolition was worse than slavery. Indeed, this is why he stalled the Emancipation Proclamation for several years, was a leader in the racist Northern-founded "American Colonization Society," had slaves complete the construction of the White House, implemented (as we have seen) extreme racist military policies, used profits from Northern slavery to fund his War, often referred to blacks as "niggers" (both privately and publicly), said he was willing to allow slavery to continue in perpetuity if the Southern states would come back into the Union (the Hampton Roads Conference, February 3, 1865), pushed nonstop for the deportation of blacks, defended slave owners in court, and continually blocked black enlistment, black suffrage, and black citizenship.[98]

Liberal Ohio Representative Thomas Corwin.

And it was Lincoln who had no social welfare plan for those African-Americans he intended to free with the Emancipation Proclamation, and who were to simply be turned loose on the streets of America without jobs, education, homes, food, or clothing. When asked what would be done to smooth their transition into free white society, he said with a devilish grin: "Let 'em root, pig, or perish!"[99]

These represent but a fragment of his racist and anti-black deeds.

Without question the second most obvious reason we know Lincoln did not go to war over slavery—after promising not to interfere with slavery in his First Inaugural Address—was his support, in the same speech, of the proposed 1861 proslavery amendment to the Constitution, the Corwin Amendment, named after Yankee Representative Thomas Corwin of Ohio. The measure read:

"No amendment shall be made to the Constitution which will authorize or give to Congress the power to abolish or interfere, within any State, with the domestic institutions thereof, including that of persons held to labor or service by the laws of said State."[100]

Its meaning is clear: the Corwin Amendment would have allowed slavery to continue in perpetuity without any interference from the national government.[101] With the required two-thirds vote[102] it was passed by the U.S. House of Representatives on February 28, 1861, and by the U.S. Senate on March 2, 1861, two days before Lincoln's presidential inauguration[103]—during which, as noted, he publicly mentioned the "proposed amendment" in his First Inaugural Address on March

Liberal black civil rights advocate Frederick Douglass of Maryland.

4. "I have no objection to its being made express and irrevocable," he stated emphatically before the country that day.[104]

By this time three states had actually ratified the Corwin Amendment, and certainly the rest would have as well, if given the chance. However, the act was dropped with the start of the Battle of Fort Sumter, on April 12, 1861. Had hostilities not exploded between the South and the North that Spring day, what can only be called "Lincoln's proslavery amendment" would have been signed into law, and American slavery would have continued indefinitely.[105] Unfortunately, the War would have taken place regardless, for, as this chapter proves, slavery was not the issue at its center.

There are a thousand other reasons we know Lincoln's War was not fought over the "peculiar institution," from the fact that he was a leader in the racist Yankee organization called the American Colonization Society (which sought to deport all blacks in order to make the U.S. "white from coast to coast"), to his support of a program that would have corralled all African-Americans into their own all-black state[106]—or at least would have thoroughly segregated them from the white population.[107] His apathy toward the black race was well-known, prompting Frederick Douglass' infamous statement. "When it comes to African-Americans," said the celebrated black civil rights leader, "President Lincoln lacks the genuine spark of humanity."[108]

Does any of this sound like a man who would send thousands to their deaths, nearly bankrupt the U.S. treasury, and risk destroying his own reputation as America's sixteenth president just to rid our country of slavery, an institution that Southerners had never wanted to begin with and which they had been trying to abolish since the 1700s?[109]

Still, Lincolnites and other uneducated members of the Church of "Honest Abe" assert that his War was founded on "the principle of abolition."

Much of the confusion over where Lincoln stood regarding slavery comes from the fact that he purposefully sowed bewilderment on the matter in an attempt to procure votes for his reelection in 1864. The ultimate demagogue, he always said whatever he thought his particular audience wanted to hear, a habit that he was roundly criticized for. Of this particular characteristic Conservative Illinois Senator Stephen Arnold Douglas, the "Little Giant," stated:

> Lincoln has a fertile genius in devising language to conceal his thoughts. . . . He is to be voted in the south a proslavery man, and he is to be voted in the north as an abolitionist . . . for he can trim his principles any way in any section, so as to secure votes.[110]

Thus, as has often been noted about the duplicitous Liberal leader:

> Mr. Lincoln was an adroit politician. When dealing with the [conservative] South, he said: "I have no Constitutional right to free your slaves, and no desire to do so."
> When dealing with the [conservative] Border States, he said: "Slavery is not to be interfered with."
> When dealing with the [liberal] Republican party, he said: "This country cannot remain half slave and half free."
> When dealing with the [liberal] Abolitionists, he said: "This war is against slavery."
> When dealing with [monarchical and socialist] Foreign Nations, he said: "The slaves must be emancipated."[111]

Yet Lincoln's racist beliefs were never far from the surface. On July 17, 1858, he made the following comment before an enthusiastic *liberal* audience at Springfield, Illinois:

What I would most desire would be the separation of the white and black races.[112]

In September 1859, at the time diametrically opposed to black civil rights, Lincoln made this remark—a mere one year before he was elected president:

Negro equality! Fudge!! How long, in the Government of a God great enough to make and maintain this universe, shall there continue [to be] knaves to vend and fools to gulp, so low a piece of demagoguism as this?[113]

Liberal Union General Benjamin F. Butler of New Hampshire.

This is the same Lincoln who Liberals, like his Secretary of War, Edwin M. Stanton, fondly referred to as "the most perfect ruler of men that ever lived"![114]

Though Lincoln worshipers maintain that their "god" changed his racist views on black deportation and eventually rejected the American Colonization Society, evincing a love and acceptance for the merging of blacks into American society, the facts show a starkly different reality.

According to the memoirs of Union General Benjamin F. "the Beast" Butler (like Lincoln, also despised in the South for war crimes against humanity), in early April 1865, the president invited him to the White House to discuss his latest deportation plans to ship all blacks out of the country. This was just days before Lincoln was killed by John Wilkes Booth, a disillusioned Confederate supporter from Maryland. Of his last meeting with Lincoln in April, Butler writes:

A conversation was held between us after the negotiations had failed at Hampton Roads [February 3, 1865], and in the course of the conversation he said to me: —

"But what shall we do with the negroes after they are free? I can hardly believe that the South and North can live in peace, unless we can get rid of the negroes. Certainly they cannot if we don't get rid of the negroes whom we have armed and disciplined and who have fought with us, to the amount, I believe of some one hundred and fifty thousand men. I believe that it would be better to export them all to some fertile country with a good climate, which they could have to themselves.

"You have been a staunch friend of the race from the time you first advised me to enlist them at New Orleans. You have had a good deal of experience in moving bodies of men by water,—your movement up the James was a magnificent one. Now we shall have no use for our very large navy; what, then, are our difficulties in sending all the blacks away?"[115]

Butler responded by discussing his own idea of how to "send all the blacks away." The solution was simple: settle a colony for them in the Isthmus of Darien (modern Panama). To this Lincoln agreed, replying: "There is meat in that, General Butler; there is meat in that."[116]

These types of comments could be multiplied almost indefinitely.

Can we still really believe that Lincoln and his soldiers "fought to destroy slavery"?

What members of the anti-South movement never ask themselves is why millions of Southerners and Northerners, including men, women, and children, would support a war and risk their lives for the mere 5 percent of the Southern population who owned slaves? Why would they be willing to hazard everything for an institution that was already on its way out, in a region, the South, that had been pressing for abolition since the very formation of the U.S. in 1776? In other words, why would any sane human being put his life, family, home, and business in jeopardy to either save or destroy slavery?

The answer is that no one would. This fact is so obvious that it is entirely glossed over by even the most well-read intelligent individuals, solely because of the overwhelming indoctrination they have received from our Liberal government-run schools and media.

I have said for many years, and I will say it again: it is absurd to think

Liberal abolitionist Wendell Phillips of Massachusetts.

that men would gamble life and limb to either preserve or wipe out slavery. Slavery was nothing more than an ancillary issue regarding Lincoln's War—and authentic history supports this. Even the most diligent global study of slavery reveals that not a single country ever went to war against its own people for the purpose of abolishing slavery. Not for one day, not for a week, and certainly not for four years, as Lincoln did.

This is why America's slaves were not freed until eight months *after* his death and the War ended, with the passage of the Thirteenth Amendment. This marked the official end of slavery in the U.S., for Lincoln's Emancipation Proclamation had been illegal and unenforceable, and thus largely ignored. In fact, not a single slave was *legally* freed by it,[117] which is why, according to abolitionist Wendell Phillips of Massachusetts, "Lincoln acknowledged that the Emancipation Proclamation was the greatest folly of his life,"[118] one that only further united the South and further divided the North.[119] Of Lincoln's illicit edict Rutherford writes:

> Not a negro in the States that did not secede [that is, the North] was freed by Lincoln's Proclamation and it had no effect even in the South as it was unconstitutional and Lincoln knew it. Many in the North resented it, and Lincoln was unhappy over the situation as [his friend Ward Hill] Lamon testified. The negroes were freed by an amendment [the Thirteenth] offered by a Southern man, John Brooks Henderson of Missouri. Emancipation did not become a law until after Lincoln's death. It is really a farce for negroes to celebrate Emancipation Day, and give Lincoln the credit.[120]

Of course, as Lincoln himself said on numerous occasions, the Emancipation Proclamation was not meant to free the slaves for humanitarian reasons, but was merely a tool to help him win his War. This is why he repeatedly referred to it not as an "abolitionary measure," but as a "*war measure*"; not as a "civil rights emancipation," but as a "*military emancipation.*"[121]

In a letter dated August 26, 1863, Lincoln reveals the real reasoning behind the Emancipation Proclamation. It is a response to a group of "unconditional Union men" from Illinois who were angry that he had issued the document. Said President Lincoln:

> I have neither adopted nor proposed any measure which is not consistent with even your view, provided you are for the Union. I suggested compensated emancipation, to which you replied that you did not wish to be taxed to buy Negroes. But I have not asked you to be taxed to buy Negroes, except in such way as to save you from greater taxation, to save the Union exclusively by other means. You dislike the Emancipation Proclamation, and perhaps would have it retracted. I think that the Constitution invests the Commander-in-Chief with the law of war in time of war. The most that can be said, if so much, is, that the slaves are property. Is there, has there ever been, any question that by the law of war, property both of enemies and friends may be taken when needed? And is it not needed, whenever taking it helps us, or hurts the enemy? Armies, the world over, destroy enemies' property when they cannot use it; and even destroy their own to keep it from the enemy.[122]

Lincoln was either lying or completely ignorant of ethics and international law, both which forbid the destruction, or even the disturbance, of "private property" during civilized warfare. Of course, like many Liberals today, big government leftist Lincoln was not civilized when it came to his enemies, particularly his *Southern* enemies, which is one of the means by which he was able to outlast the Southern armies and suppress states' rights.[123] For his many outrages and illegalities, Lincoln will forever be considered a war criminal in Dixie.[124]

Of our sixteenth president's use of the Emancipation Proclamation as a "military emancipation," Confederate Surgeon General C. H. Tebault wrote:

> This Emancipation Proclamation was . . . clearly not a humanitarian

act, but a military measure, and so acknowledged. The platform on which President Lincoln was nominated and elected recognized African slavery and stands of record.

In this respect, over all other national platforms it is most distinctly, emphatically and pronouncedly unique.

At the celebrated Hampton Roads Conference, held on the 30th of January, 1865, between President Lincoln and Hon. Mr. Seward, Secretary of State of the United States, on the Federal side, and Vice-President A. H. Stephens, Hon. Robt. M. T. Hunter and Judge John A. Campbell of the Confederate States, on the side of the South, Mr. Stephens asked Mr. Lincoln what would be the status of that portion of the slave population in the Confederate States, which had not then be come free under his Proclamation; or in other words, what effect that Proclamation would have upon the entire "Black Population?" Would it be held to Emancipate the whole, or only those who had, at the time the war ended, become actually free under it?

Conservative Confederate diplomat Judge John A. Campbell of Georgia.

Mr. Lincoln said that was a judicial question. How the Courts would decide it, he did not know, and could give no answer. *His own opinion was that as the Proclamation was a war measure and would have effect only from its being an exercise of the war power, as soon as the war had ceased, it would be inoperative for the future. It would be held to apply only to such slaves as had come under its operation while it was in active exercise.* This was his individual opinion, but the Courts might decide the other way, and hold that it effectually emancipated all the slaves in the States to which it applied at the time. So far as he was concerned he would leave it to the Courts to decide. He never would change or modify the terms of the Proclamation in the slightest particular.

. . . Mr. Seward . . . said, it might be proper to state to us, that Congress, a day or two before, had proposed *a Constitutional Amendment [the Thirteenth]* for the immediate abolition of slavery throughout the United States, which he produced and read to us from a newspaper. *He said this was done as a war measure. If the war were then to cease, it would probably not be adopted by a number of States, sufficient to make it a part of the Constitution;* but presented the case in such light as clearly showed his object to be, to impress upon the minds of the Commissioners that, if the war should not cease, this, as a war measure, would be adopted by a sufficient number of States to become a part of the Constitution, and without saying it in direct words, *left the inference very clearly to be perceived by the Commissioners that his opinion was, if the Confederate States would then abandon the war they could themselves defeat this amendment, by voting it down as members of the Union. The whole number of States, it was said, being thirty-six, any ten of them could defeat this proposed amendment.*[125]

Here, according to Lincoln, the Emancipation Proclamation was merely a war measure, one that would thus become inactive when the conflict came to an end. After that, said our sixteenth president, as long as the Southern states rejoined the Union (and paid their taxes) they could continue to practice slavery if they so chose. He did not care either way. For he was never against slavery itself, but merely against the *extension*\ and *spread* of the institution outside the South, particularly into the Northern states and still undeveloped Western states (the "Territories"). After all, curbing its spread, not ending slavery, was the main reason the Republican Party was formed in 1854 to begin with.[126]

As always with the racist Liberal president, this was not for the benefit of blacks, but for the benefit of whites: he did not want a flood of emancipated Southern negroes pouring North, stampeding defenseless Yankees and taking over their towns. Here is how he phrased it during a September 16, 1859, speech at Columbus, Ohio. If slavery is allowed to spread across the U.S., said the negrophobic chief executive:

They will be ready for Jeff Davis and [Alexander H.] Stephens and other leaders of that company, to sound the bugle for the revival of the slave-trade, for the second Dred Scott decision, for the flood of slavery to be poured over the Free States, while we shall be here tied down and helpless, and run over like sheep.[127]

Lincoln and his bigoted constituents need not have feared a "flood" of freed Southern slaves coming North. Most Southern blacks had no interest in leaving beautiful sunny Dixie and their homes, friends, and families for the frigid gray environs of Yankeedom, with its equally cold people and strict racist "black codes." Nonetheless, his comments leave no doubt as to where he stood regarding African-Americans, a people he openly regarded as an "inferior race."[128]

Liberal Union Secretary of War Salmon P. Chase of New Hampshire.

Lincoln's own Secretary of War, Salmon P. Chase, said of our sixteenth president's views on slavery and the Western Territories:

Not war upon slavery within those limits, but fixed opposition to its extension beyond them. Mr. Lincoln was the candidate of the people, not for abolition but as opposed to the extension of slavery.[129]

In 1854 Lincoln himself stated: "I now do no more than oppose the extension of slavery."[130] This was to be done, according to a speech he gave on May 29, 1856, not by national abolition, but in this manner:

> Let us draw a cordon, so to speak, around the slave states, and the hateful institution, like a reptile poisoning itself, will perish by its own infamy.[131]

Pro-North historians claim that Lincoln later changed his views from wanting to merely limit slavery to the South to wanting nationwide abolition. It is true that over time he altered his *public* statements to reflect sociopolitical trends (in an effort to procure votes and remain in power). *Privately*, however, he never wavered from the idea that whites must be accommodated by restricting slavery to where it already existed. Here is what the venerable *Encyclopedia Britannica* says on this topic:

> [Checking the extension of slavery] was the key-note to his thought *ever after*, both in regard to the territories and in regard to the preservation of the Union. *He admitted frankly that his overmastering concern was the welfare of the free poor people of the white races.*[132]

Let us once again let Lincoln speak for himself on the matter. On December 15, 1860, a little over a month after he had been elected president, he wrote a letter to North Carolinian John A. Gilmer, in which the uttered the following words:

> You [Conservatives] think slavery is right and ought to be extended;[133] we [Liberals] think it is wrong and *ought to be restricted*. For this neither has any just occasion to be angry with the other. As to the State laws, mentioned in your sixth question, I really know very little of them. I never have read one. *If any of them are in conflict with the fugitive-slave clause, or any other part of the Constitution, I certainly shall be glad of their repeal . . .*[134]

A week later, in a similar letter to Conservative Alexander H. Stephens (the upcoming Confederate vice president), this one dated December 22, 1860, Lincoln writes:

Do the people of the South really entertain fears that a Republican [Liberal] administration would, directly or indirectly, interfere with the slaves, or with them about the slaves? If they do, I wish to assure you, as once a friend, and still, I hope, not an enemy, that *there is no cause for such fears. The South would be in no more danger in this respect than it was in the days of [George] Washington.* I suppose, however, this does not meet the case. You think slavery is right and ought to be extended, while we think it is wrong and *ought to be restricted. That, I suppose, is the rub. It certainly is the only substantial difference between us.* [135]

This, of course, was merely a continuation of the racist-based views Lincoln had held all along, from the beginning of his political career: if slavery was allowed to spread outside the South, it would take jobs, land, and homes away from whites, he and other Liberals claimed. For example, just two years earlier, on October 15, 1858, he made this statement at Alton, Illinois, during his seventh and final joint debate with Judge Stephen A. Douglas:

Now, irrespective of the moral aspect of this question as to whether there is a right or wrong in enslaving a negro, I am still in favor of our new [Western] Territories being in such a condition that *white men* may find a home—may find some spot where they can better their condition—where they can settle upon new soil, and better their condition in life. I am in favor of this not merely (I must say it here as I have elsewhere) *for our own people* who are born amongst us, but as an outlet for *free white people* everywhere, the world over—in which Hans, and Baptiste, and Patrick, and all other men from all the world, may find new homes and better their condition in life. [136]

Lincoln's left-wing compatriots were of the same mind. In 1846 Liberal Congressman David Wilmot of Pennsylvania introduced his "Wilmot Proviso" to try and prevent the spread of slavery into Western lands acquired by the U.S. from Mexico during the Mexican-American War (1846-1848). Again, his proposition was not for the sake of blacks, however. It was solely for whites. [137] In the winter of 1847, the Yankee politician articulated the motivations behind his notorious document this way:

I have no squeamish sensitiveness upon the subject of slavery, no morbid sympathy for the slave. I plead the cause and the rights of white freemen. I would preserve to free white labor a fair country, a rich inheritance, where the sons of toil, of my own race and own color, can live without the disgrace which association with negro slavery brings upon free labor. I stand for the inviolability of free territory. It shall remain free, so far as my voice or vote can aid in the preservation of its free character. . . . The white laborer of the North claims your service; he demands that you stand firm to his interests and his rights, that you preserve the future homes of his children, on the distant shores of the Pacific, from the degradation and dishonor of negro servitude. *Where the negro slave labors, the free white man cannot labor by his side without sharing in his degradation and disgrace.*[138]

Liberal Congressman David Wilmot of Pennsylvania.

Wilmot, who once commented that he had spent much of his adult life fighting against Northern Abolitionists,[139] later remarked to a colleague:

> By God, sir, men born and nursed of white women are not going to be ruled by men who were brought up on the milk of some damn Negro wench![140]

In 1860, the man who was to become Lincoln's Secretary of State, New Yorker William H. Seward, described the African race as a

foreign and feeble element, like the Indians, incapable of assimilation
. . . it is a pitiful exotic unwisely and unnecessarily transplanted to our
fields . . .[141]

Lincoln could not have agreed more with Seward and Wilmot, and
in fact, according to his own statement, he voted for the anti-black, pro-
white Wilmot Proviso "as good as forty times."[142]

On October 16, 1854, during a speech at Peoria, Illinois, the true
white supremacist was revealed, along with the one of the real reasons
he was against slavery (and its extension). Said Lincoln:

> Whether slavery shall go into Nebraska, or other new Territories, is
> not a matter of exclusive concern to the people who may go there.
> *The whole nation is interested that the best use shall be made of the Territories.*
> *We want them for homes of free white people.* This cannot be, to any
> considerable extent, if slavery shall be planted within them.[143]

It is here that we finally uncover the reason Lincoln himself was not
a slave owner like Grant and thousands of other Yankees. It is here that
we come to the very foundation of his antislavery views and of his
Emancipation Proclamation: it was not so much slavery itself that
bothered him. It was that the institution brought whites and blacks into
close proximity with one another, the latter "degrading" the former by
race-mixing, or what was then called "amalgamation." As the prejudiced
president put it during a public debate with Stephen A. Douglas in
Chicago on July 10, 1858, "the inferior race bears the superior down."[144]
Thus to keep America white (one of Lincoln's stated lifelong goals),
slavery would first have to be abolished (emancipation), then blacks
would have to be deported to a foreign land (colonization).[145]

Lincoln, like the black racists, black separatists, and black
colonizationists who came before and after him,[146] felt a deep repugnance
toward those of other races. Speaking from his own Caucasian point of
view, he summed up his feelings on the matter:

> There is a natural disgust in the minds of nearly all white people, at the
> idea of an indiscriminate amalgamation of the white and black races.[147]

Based on Lincoln's own words and actions, it is obvious that he included himself in the category of "nearly all white people."[148]

Later, others in his party would concur: "America's Western Territories (soon to become the Western states) should remain as white as New England!" they declared.[149] One of these men, Senator Lyman Trumbull, was certainly speaking for his good friend, neighbor, and fellow American Colonization Society supporter Abraham Lincoln when he said publicly:

> *I, for one, am very much disposed to favor the colonization of such free negroes as are willing to go in Central America. I want to have nothing to do either with the free negro or the slave negro. We, the Republican [Liberal] party, are the white man's party.* [Great applause] We are for free white men, and for making white labor respectable and honorable, which it never can be when negro slave labor is brought into competition with it. [Great applause]
>
> *We wish to settle the Territories with free white men, and we are willing that this negro race should go anywhere that it can to better its condition, wishing them God speed wherever they go. We believe it is better for us that they should not be among us. I believe it will be better for them to go elsewhere.*[150] . . . *When we say that all men are created equal, we do not mean that every man in organized society has the same rights. We do not tolerate that in Illinois.*[151]

Trumbull made great efforts to reassure the public that neither he, Lincoln, or their Liberal Party (the Republicans) advocated the idea of Negro equality. As he said at a political debate:

> I by no means assent to the doctrine that negroes are required by the Constitution of the United States to be placed on an equal footing in the States with white citizens.[152]

Both being from ultra Negrophobic Illinois, Trumbull and Lincoln had strong feelings about blocking the spread of slavery, not only from their state, but also from the Western Territories, for Illinois itself was considered a Western state at the time.[153] On October 16, 1854, during a speech at Peoria, Illinois, for example, Lincoln could not have been more explicit:

Let it not be said I am contending for the establishment of political and social equality between the whites and blacks. I have already said the contrary. . . I am . . . arguing against the extension of a bad thing, which where it already exists, we must of necessity, manage as best we can.[154]

This is precisely why leftist Lincoln had been against the Mexican-American War:[155] unable to see it for what it actually was (a land war to expand U.S. territory; i.e., an aspect of Manifest Destiny),[156] he viewed it as an intentional ploy by Conservatives to spread slavery westward.[157] He was dead wrong of course. But this did not stop him from pushing his white supremacist views; views, as with modern racist Liberals, he hoped to impose upon the entire North American continent.[158]

Just a few years later, Trumbull, and by extension his boss, Lincoln, noted that

There is a very great aversion in the West—I know it to be so in my State [of Illinois]—against having free Negroes come among us. Our people want nothing to do with the Negro.[159]

Thus, when it came to slavery, racially bigoted Lincoln was at heart not an abolitionist (a group he had always loathed),[160] but an anti-expansionist, which means, in turn, that his War could not have been about destroying slavery in the South.

There are a number of other reasons we know that Lincoln did not inaugurate his war to defeat slavery, all which are glossed over or suppressed by anti-South historians.

Let us begin with the Emancipation Proclamation.

The careful reader must ask why, if

Liberal Senator Lyman Trumbull of Connecticut.

lawyer Lincoln desired the destruction of slavery in Dixie, he carefully worded his emancipation so that it was active only in the Confederacy, the Southern states, where he had no legal power? The C.S.A. was a sovereign foreign nation at the time, and thus outside the judicial bounds of the U.S.A. Here, from the proclamation, is his exact wording concerning *where* slavery was to be outlawed:

> Now, therefore I, Abraham Lincoln President of the United States, by virtue of the power in me vested as Commander-in-Chief, of the Army and Navy of the United States in time of actual armed rebellion against the authority and government of the United States, and as a fit and necessary war measure for suppressing said rebellion, do on this first day of January, in the year of our Lord one thousand eight hundred and sixty-three, and in accordance with my purpose so to do publicly proclaimed for the full period of one hundred days, from the day first above mentioned, order and designate as the States and parts of States wherein the people thereof, respectively, are this day in rebellion against the United States, the following, to wit: Arkansas, Texas, Louisiana (except the parishes of St. Bernard, Plaquemines, Jefferson, St. John, St. Charles, St. James, Ascension, Assumption, Terrebonne, Lafourche, St. Mary, St. Martin, and Orleans, including the City of New Orleans), Mississippi, Alabama, Florida, Georgia, South Carolina, North Carolina, and Virginia (except the forty-eight counties designated as West Virginia, and also the counties of Berkeley, Accomac, Northampton, Elizabeth City, York, Princess Ann, and Norfolk, including the cities of Norfolk and Portsmouth); and which *excepted parts are for the present left precisely as if this proclamation were not issued.*[161]

Even a casual perusal reveals something quite stunning about this document, one that is widely and wrongly held to have "ended slavery across America": Lincoln's Emancipation Proclamation says nothing about freeing the 500,000 to 1,000,000 slaves who still lived and worked in the "abolitionist North"[162] (there were 315,000 Yankee slaveholders serving in the Union military alone at the time),[163] or in Southern areas occupied by Northern troops, such as several Louisiana parishes, where servitude was still legal and practiced.[164] It does not even mention Tennessee, though it was still a loyal member state of the Confederacy. The reason?

Tennessee was largely under Yankee domination by January 1863 (the state's capital city, Nashville, had been captured a year earlier on February 23, 1862),[165] and was well on her way to being forced back into the Union.[166] Indeed, the last state to secede (on June 8, 1861),[167] after the War the Volunteer State would be the first Confederate state to be reunionized (on July 24, 1866),[168] and was thus largely passed over by Reconstruction in 1867.[169]

In short, Lincoln left slavery intact in Tennessee, as well as in numerous counties and parishes in other states. He literally says that these *"excepted parts are for the present left precisely as if this proclamation were not issued."*

Was all of this a simple mistake, an error of judgment, a memory lapse, or lack of knowledge of geography on Lincoln's part? Hardly. In Missouri he did the same thing: after illegally invading the state and illegally putting it under martial law, he issued an illegal emancipation proclamation to illegally free Missouri's slaves. But not all of them. *Only those belonging to supporters of the Confederacy.* Those slaves who belonged to supporters of the Union were allowed to remain in perpetual servitude.[170]

And herein lies a vital clue as to Lincoln's true motivations.

Liberal Union General David Hunter of New York.

It is apparent by omitting the Confederate state of Tennessee from his Emancipation Proclamation, along with all other Northern-held Southern regions, that he overtly and purposefully intended to allow slavery to continue in these areas. Why else would he activate the illegal decree *only* in those regions engaged in "hostile acts" against the United States?[171] The edict was, in the end, as even left-leaning historians admit, not an abolitionary document, but simply a "military punishment."[172]

Another notable piece of Lincolnian history that has been whitewashed from our history books is that our sixteenth president often countermanded the emancipation of slaves by his cabinet members and military officers. Such men included: Simon Cameron,[173] John W. Phelps,[174] John C. Frémont,[175] Jim Lane,[176] and David Hunter.[177] Why prevent abolition if abolition was the purpose of the War?

Further evidence of Lincoln's true feelings toward slavery is supplied by his "Ten Percent Plan," issued on December 8, 1863.[178] Here, a Confederate state could be "readmitted" to the Union if just 10 percent of its citizens took an oath of allegiance to the U.S.[179] Afterward, that state could reestablish slavery if it so desired.[180] In 1864, according to Confederate Secretary of State Judah P. Benjamin, far from demanding complete and immediate abolition, Lincoln let it be known that he was willing to let the issue be decided on by a general vote in both the South and the North.[181]

It was just such duplicitous politics that prompted New England abolitionist Lysander Spooner to rightly call Lincoln and his cabinet imposters and con-artists,[182] "double-faced demagogues" who were trying to "ride into power on the two horses Liberty and Slavery."[183]

If Lincoln's War was a contest to end slavery, why did members of his own party constantly criticize him for not making slavery the central issue of the War from the beginning?[184]

Liberal Union General George B. McClellan of Pennsylvania.

Lincoln's indifference toward black civil rights and his public offer to allow the Southern states to continue practicing slavery indefinitely (the Corwin Amendment, his Ten Percent Plan, etc.) angered many of his military officers as well. One of them was Yankee General George B. McClellan, with whom Lincoln had a long and rancorous relationship. Not only would they run against each other in the 1864 presidential election, but at one point, in late 1862, there was so much animus between them that the two had spies sent out to investigate one another.[185]

Ultimately, just as Lincoln never advocated either social or political equality for blacks,[186] he never insisted on complete and permanent emancipation. In fact, as we have seen, he said his proclamation would terminate as soon as the War ceased.[187] Clearly, he was not only in no hurry to abolish slavery, he also had little concern about its continuance:

in his own personal five-part emancipation plan he included a clause for allowing the Southern states nearly another fifty years, until the year 1900 specifically, to abolish the institution[188]—slyly passing the issue onto future generations to deal with.

Many of our greatest and most objective historians, such as Louis M. Hacker, acknowledge that the real Lincoln was completely apathetic when it came to the topic of slavery, and that during the 1860 election his party was totally "silent on the issue." Indeed, Lincoln went out of his way to assure the American people, both North and South, that he had no intention of doing anything that might disturb the Union—including interfering with slavery[189]—just as he did during his First Inaugural Address, March 4, 1861.[190]

For delaying, even ignoring, emancipation, "Honest Abe" was vigorously castigated by fellow Yanks, who referred to him variously as "Simple Susan,"[191] "the slow coach at Washington,"[192] the "tortoise President",[193] "the baboon at the other end of the avenue," and "that damned idiot in the White House."[194] Liberal Indiana Representative George W. Julian, a member of Lincoln's own party, as just one example, offered the following review of the president's actions to a governmental committee on February 7, 1865:

> . . . it was that the President, instead of striking at slavery as a military necessity, and while rebuking that policy in his dealings with Hunter and Frémont, was *at the same time so earnestly espousing chimerical projects for the colonization [deportation] of negroes, coupled with the policy of gradual and compensated emancipation, which should take place some time before the year 1900, if the slaveholders should be willing.* . . . Hence it was that for nearly two years of this war the government, while smiting the rebels with one hand, was with the other guarding the slave property and protecting the constitutional rights of the men who had renounced the Constitution . . . *[Lincoln's] purpose to crush the rebellion and spare slavery was found to be utterly suicidal to our cause.*[195]

This does not sound like a man who was interested in abolition, let alone someone who would start a full scale war in order to destroy it.

Those who are still having difficulty abandoning the belief that Lincoln started the War for the welfare of blacks and the abolition of slavery, will be interested in his well-known public reply to Yankee abolitionist Horace Greeley.

On August 19, 1862, the New England socialist published an open letter to Lincoln in his New York newspaper, the *Tribune*. Entitled "The Prayer of Twenty Millions,"[196] it assaulted the president's abysmal civil rights record and accused of him of prolonging the war by refusing to abolish slavery. Those who voted for you, Greeley, began impatiently,

> are sorely disappointed and deeply pained by the policy you seem to be pursuing with regard to the slaves of the rebels. . . *We think you are strangely and disastrously remiss in the discharge of your official and imperative duty with regard to the emancipating provisions of the new Confiscation Act.* . . . Had you, sir, in your Inaugural Address, unmistakably given notice that . . . you would recognize no loyal person as rightfully held in slavery by a traitor, we believe the rebellion would therein have received a staggering, if not fatal blow.[197]

Socialist newspaperman Horace Greeley of New Hampshire.

Four days later, on August 22, 1862, an immovable Lincoln responded to the withering public attack with his own. "Dear Mr. Greeley," he wrote defensively to the celebrated antislavery advocate:

> If there be those who would not save the Union unless they could at the same time save slavery, I do not agree with them. If there be those who would not save the Union unless they could at the same time

destroy slavery, I do not agree with them. *My paramount object in this struggle is to save the Union, and is not either to save or destroy slavery. . . . If I could save the Union without freeing any slave, I would do it . . . What I do about slavery and the colored race, I do because I believe it helps save the Union . . .*[198]

This letter was written exactly one month before he issued his Preliminary Emancipation Proclamation (in which he calls for deporting all blacks out of the U.S.), and just four months before issuing his Final Emancipation Proclamation (in which he refers to his edict, not as a civil rights measure, but as a temporary "war measure").[199]

Despite antiblack statements like the ones he made to Greeley, oddly Lincoln continues to be known globally as the "Great Emancipator." Yet the perceptive and enlightened perceive him more correctly as the most cunning, shrewd, tricky, secretive, and racist politician in American history.[200]

On those rare occasions when Lincoln did speak out against slavery, his venom was always directed, of course, at *white* slave owners. Like modern enemies of the South (in particular, reparationists), Lincoln conveniently disregarded the reality of America's tens of thousands of *black* slave owners.[201]

Indeed, one of the first slave owners in the American colonies was a black servant by the name of Anthony Johnson. After his arrival in 1621, he quickly worked off his term of indenture and began purchasing human chattel.[202] The Virginia slaver from Angola (Africa), who owned both black *and* white slaves, actually helped launch the American slave trade by forcing authorities to legally define the meaning of "slave ownership."[203] In 1652 his son John Johnson imported and bought eleven white servants, who worked under him at his plantation, located on the banks of the Pungoteague River.[204]

Johnson and his family were just the first of countless thousands of American black slave owners and traders.[205]

In 1830, in the Deep South alone, nearly 8,000 slaves were owned by some 1,500 black slave owners (about five slaves apiece). In Charleston, South Carolina, as another example, between 1820 and 1840, 75 percent of the city's free blacks owned slaves. Furthermore, *25 percent of all free American blacks owned slaves, South and North*.[206] Let us note here that in 1861, the South's 300,000 white slave owners made up only 1 percent of the total U.S. white population of 30,000,000 people.[207] Thus, while only one Southern white out of every 300,000 owned slaves (1 percent), one black out of every four blacks owned slaves (25 percent). In other words, far more blacks owned black (and sometimes white) slaves than whites did.

Due to poor census taking, we can be sure that there were thousands of additional black slave owners who were never counted, making the figure of 25 percent a gross underestimate. As an example, one calculation concludes that at least 50 percent of the black slave owners of Charleston, South Carolina, were left out of the 1860 Census.[208]

Liberal U.S. President Abraham Lincoln of Kentucky, and later, Illinois.

Lincoln, however, could have cared less how many blacks owned slaves in 1860, or at any other time. Indeed, he completely disregarded black as well as Native-American and *white Northern* slave owners. He only focused on *white Southern* slave owners. Why? Because his interest was never abolition. As he made patently clear over and over, his main agenda—the dream of every Liberal, Socialist, and Communist—was always the "preservation of the Union," which, in liberal-speak, means the realization of the American System: installing big government and centralizing all power at Washington, D.C.

Unfortunately for Lincoln, he could not achieve this goal if the Southern states were allowed to secede. For their split from the Union meant that states' rights was a legal constitutional right, a right that would undermine the empire Lincoln and his left-wing supporters planned on building in our country's capital city. To help insure success Lincoln released his Emancipation Proclamation. Not as an "abolitionary measure" or a "civil rights emancipation," but as what he revealingly and specifically called a "war measure" and a "military emancipation." The main hope behind the edict was, after all, to instigate slave insurrections across the South and thereby help bring down the Confederacy (this never occurred: there was not a single slave revolt during the War).

If nothing else does, the above facts alone prove, once and for all, that Lincoln did not wage war against the South over slavery.[209]

And yet there is more!

American slavery, both in the North and in the South, was already well on its way to extinction in 1860. The Founding Fathers certainly understood this, which is one reason they did not use the words "slave" or "slavery" when they wrote out the U.S. Constitution.[210] Lincoln himself admitted it.[211] Why, then, fight an expensive bloody war to try and end it?

The South—where the first voluntary emancipation in North America took place in 1655, and where the American abolition movement itself began in the 1700s—never wanted or asked for the institution. It had been pushed on the North by England and then forced on the South by the North when it became unprofitable (due to long cold winters, short summers, hilly terrain, and rocky, sandy soil), and when white Yankees realized that they did not want to live among blacks. Notable Southerners, like George Washington and Thomas Jefferson, were campaigning for abolition from the very founding of the United States, and later, Confederate officers like Patrick R. Cleburne and Robert E. Lee supported abolition and enlistment of African-Americans well before the end of the War.[212]

On November 7, 1864, Conservative Confederate President Jefferson Davis began advocating the idea of the military impressment of slaves, with *emancipation at the time of discharge*,[213] while just two months later, in January 1865, he was discussing and calling for *full Southern abolition*. This was nearly a full year prior to the issuance of the Thirteenth Amendment in the North.[214] Thus even many Yankees understood that trying to coerce the South into abolition was a fool's errand. Charles Francis Adams Jr. of Massachusetts, for example, the grandson of U.S. President John Quincy Adams, wisely wrote:

> Had the South been allowed to manage this question unfettered the slaves would have been—ere this—fully emancipated and that without bloodshed or race problems.[215]

Finally, if the entire conflict was merely about the Confederacy wanting to "maintain slavery," all the Southern states had to do was remain in the Union where it was still fully protected.[216] In his First Inaugural Address a month before the War started, Lincoln was ready to sign the Corwin Amendment into law, while clearly and emphatically stating that he had no desire to interfere with slavery, and no legal right to do so.[217] And, as we have just seen, as late as February 1865 Lincoln was promising the seceded Southern states that, as far as he was concerned, if they would return to the Union they could keep slavery, asserting that the Emancipation Proclamation was merely a "war measure" and would cease to be active when the conflict terminated.[218]

Liberal Union Brigadier General Charles F. Adams Jr. of Massachusetts (far left).

Thus we have hammered the final nail into the coffin of the old Liberal myth that the "Civil War" was about the destruction of the "peculiar institution." Slavery was not the direct or even the indirect cause of the conflict. It was merely an ancillary issue that brought the debate between states' rights (conservatism) and big government (liberalism) to the forefront.

In 1918 we find a reprint of an article contributed by James Callaway to *The Macon Telegraph*. Entitled "The Constitution and Slavery," it is highly relevant to the subject of this chapter, and so I have included it here:

In much of the literature of Northern magazines and newspapers is still seen a disposition to impress the thought that the South fought to perpetuate slavery and that nothing else was behind the war. When we aver that our soldiers drew their swords in what they believed the cause of liberty and State Self-government, the reply is that it was slavery only that inspired the fight on our part. This view does a grievous injustice to half a million patriotic soldiers who were animated by as pure a love of liberty as ever throbbed in the bosom of man and who made as splendid exhibition of self-sacrifice as any soldiers who ever fought on any field of battle.

In his book, *A Soldier's Recollections*, Dr. Randolph H. McKim, of the Army of Northern Virginia, now rector of the Church of the Epiphany, Washington, D. C., replies to this criticism of Northern friends in the following words:

"If slavery was the corner stone of the Southern Confederacy, what are we to say of the Constitution of the United States? That instrument as originally adopted by the thirteen colonies contained three sections which recognized slavery, Article 1, Sections 2 and 9, and Article 4, Section 9. And whereas the Constitution of the Southern Confederacy prohibited the slave trade, the Constitution of the United States prohibited the abolition of the slave trade for twenty years. And if the men of the South are reproached for denying liberty to three and a half millions of human beings at the same time they professed to be waging a great war for their own liberty, what are we to say of the revolting colonies of 1776 who rebelled against the British crown to achieve their liberty while slavery existed in every one of the thirteen colonies undisturbed?

"*Cannot those historians who deny that the South fought for liberty because they held the blacks in bondage see that upon the same principle they must impugn the sincerity of the signers of the Declaration of Independence? We ask the candid historian to answer this question: If the colonists of 1776 were freemen fighting for liberty, though holding the blacks in slavery in every one of the thirteen colonies, why is the title of liberty denied the Southern men of 1861 because they too held the blacks in bondage?*

"*Slavery was an inheritance which the people of the South received from the fathers, planted in the colonies by the common law of England; and if the States of the North within fifty years after the*

Revolution abolished the institution, it cannot be claimed that the abolition was dictated by moral consideration, but by differences of soil, of climate, and of industrial interests.

"The sentiment in favor of emancipation was rapidly spreading in the South in the first quarter of the nineteenth century. Wilson acknowledges that *there was no avowed advocacy of slavery in Virginia at that time. In the year 1826 there were one hundred and forty-three emancipation societies in the United States, and of these one hundred and three were in the South.* The Virginia Legislature, under the advice of Thomas Jefferson, so strong was the sentiment for emancipation, in 1832 came near passing a law for gradual emancipation, and under the growing sentiment would have passed it the next session but for an unfortunate reaction created by *the fanatical agitation of the subject by the abolitionists led by William Lloyd Garrison.* Garrison and his followers resorted to such violent abuse of the Southern people that the Virginia Legislature postponed action. A Massachusetts writer, George Lunt, says: '*Virginia, Kentucky, and Tennessee were engaged in practical movements for gradual emancipation, and this movement was arrested by the violent aggression of the abolitionists.*'

Anti-South Liberal, busybody, and abolitionist William Lloyd Garrison of Massachusetts.

"These facts are beyond dispute: (1) That *from 1789 to 1837 slavery was almost universally considered in the South as an evil*; (2) that public opinion there underwent a revolution on this subject in the decade 1832 to 1842. What produced the fateful change? Not the invention of the cotton gin, as is often asserted, for that took place in 1793. No; but *the abolition crusade launched by William Lloyd Garrison January 1, 1831. Its violence and virulence produced the result that such abuse does. It angered the South. It stifled discussion. It checked a movement on its way to gradual emancipation.* At Farmington, Massachusetts, *Garrison before a great multitude burned the Constitution, declaring it a 'league with the devil and a covenant with hell.' Vile literature was sent out among the negroes of the South advocating insurrection and the torch.* It was so incendiary in character that President [Andrew] Jackson in his message to Congress in 1835 called attention to the transmission through the mails [by Liberals] 'of inflammatory appeals addressed to the passion of the slaves, in prints, magazines, and various sorts of publications, *calculated to stimulate them to insurrection and to produce [the] horrors of a servile race war.*'"

So we see that, *but for the fanatical movement to accomplish results by violence and coercion, emancipation would probably have come [in the South].* What a disappointment that would have been, for there was such longing to plunder the eleven Southern States, and they did it, even to the Kaiser's taste! Dr. McKim says:

"*Not the Southern people, but the government of Great Britain, must be held responsible for American slavery.* The colony of Virginia protested time and again against sending slaves to her shores. In 1760 South Carolina passed an act prohibiting the further importation of slaves, but England rejected the act of the Carolina colony with indignation. *Virginia was the first of all the States to prohibit the slave trade, and Georgia was the first to incorporate such a prohibition in her Constitution. Virginia abolished the slave trade thirty years before New England was willing to consent to its abolition.*"

Dr. McKim continues:

"The Southern soldiers were not thinking of their slaves; only a few owned any when they cast their all in the balance."

No. It was a fight for the sacred right of self-government. It was a defense of their homes and firesides; they fought to repel invasion and resist a war of subjugation. Not one soldier in ten was interested in slavery. Why, in February, 1861, Mr. Davis wrote to his wife: 'In any case our slave property will be eventually lost.'"

The fact is, the South expected peaceable secession and failed to recognize the "revenue" question involved. *"If we let the South go," said Mr. Lincoln, "from whence shall we derive our revenue?"*[219]

Liberal abolitionist Lysander Spooner of Massachusetts.

Here we have evidence that, for Lincoln at least, the root of the American "Civil War" was money and the power it bought—not slavery. Much of the Yankees' money, of course, derived from the high tariffs it imposed on the South, which is why Southerners, like Robert Barnwell Rhett of South Carolina, had always contended that the South's number one grievance with the North was the tariff.[220]

Since Lincoln's War clearly had a strong economic component, let us look at this topic more closely for a moment.

At the time the national tariffs amounted to 95 percent of the federal revenue, of which *70 percent was derived from the South* to finance the cost of the central government in Washington.[221] In plain English what this means is that an independent South would have spelled financial doom for the North, and Lincoln was not about to let this occur. He and his Northern business associates, the "Wall Street Boys," were thick as thieves, and together they were committed to recapturing the goose that laid the golden egg: the seceded Southern states.[222]

Yankee abolitionist, individualist, and natural rights advocate, Lysander Spooner, saw right through Lincoln's tragicomedy, correctly referring to the president's Wall Street Boys as the "lenders of blood money." As Spooner saw it:

. . . these lenders of blood money had, for a long series of years previous to the war, been the willing accomplices of the slave-holders in perverting the government from the purposes of liberty and justice, to the greatest of crimes. They had been such accomplices *for a purely pecuniary consideration*, to wit, a control of the markets in the South; in other words, the privilege of holding the slave-holders themselves in industrial and commercial subjection to the manufacturers and merchants of the North (who afterwards furnished the money for the [Civil] war). And these Northern merchants and manufacturers, these lenders of blood money, were willing to continue to be the accomplices of the slaveholders in the future, for the same pecuniary considerations. But the slaveholders, either doubting the fidelity of their Northern allies, or feeling themselves strong enough to keep their slaves in subjection without Northern assistance, would no longer pay the price these Northern men demanded. And *it was to enforce this price in the future—that is, to monopolize the Southern markets, to maintain their industrial and commercial control over the South—that these Northern manufacturers and merchants lent some of the profits of their former monopolies for the [Civil] war, in order to secure themselves the same, or greater, monopolies in the future. These—and not any love of liberty or justice—were the motives on which the money for the [Civil] war was lent by the North.*[223]

By subduing the South and forcing her to return to the Union, Lincoln was able to continue imposing high tariffs on his southern neighbors which, in turn, created huge corporate profits for Yankee businessmen—which included scores of Northern slave traders, some of his biggest and most important financial backers. For not only did they finance both his 1860 campaign and his 1864 campaign, but, as is clear from Spooner's observations above, they also funded the War itself.[224] It was a self-serving symbiotic relationship that the wily Lincoln crafted and managed with the skill and finesse of a surgeon.

Besides tariffs Lincoln's subjugation of the South benefitted the North financially in another way: Dixie's 3,549 miles of coastline, her innumerable port towns, inlets, rivers, immense fertile farmlands, abundant agricultural products, and her hardworking people, were all vital to Northern economic growth and stability. The South's major seaports alone—New Orleans, Louisiana; Mobile, Alabama; Pensacola, Florida; Fernandina, Florida; Savannah, South Carolina; Charleston,

South Carolina; Wilmington, Delaware; New Bern, North Carolina; and Norfolk, Virginia—were worth untold billions of dollars to the North.[225]

The South's 817,674 square miles (compared with the Northeast's paltry 217,622 square miles)[226] was so abundant in natural and manmade resources that in 1860, just prior to the start of Lincoln's War, not only was she far richer than the North,[227] but her economy was the third largest of any region or country in either Europe or the Americas.[228] As far as wealth, the Confederate States were the fourth richest nation in the world,[229] more affluent than any European country except England. Modern Italy, for instance, did not reach the level of per capita income the antebellum South enjoyed until the beginning of World War II.[230]

Additionally, between 1840 and 1860, the per capita income of the South grew at an average annual rate of 1.7 percent, and was a third higher than in the North. This is a sustained long-term growth rate that has been achieved by few nations.[231] And though the South possessed only 30 percent of America's population, 60 percent of America's wealthiest men were Southerners, a group that owned twice as much property as moneyed Northerners.[232]

The C.S.A. was much wealthier than the U.S.A. in 1860, just one of the many reasons Lincoln would not let the South go.

In 1860, of the 7,000 U.S. families who possessed wealth of $111,000 or more, 4,500 of them (nearly 65 percent) lived in the South, while of the richest percentile that same year, 59 percent were Southerners.[233] So wealthy was the Confederacy that if she had been allowed to develop without interference from Lincoln, she would have become one of the world's major international powers, with a standing army many times bigger than the North's[234]—and this with a far smaller population than the North.[235]

The greedy, materialistic, commercially-minded North could not ignore such riches, power, and potential. For the Southern states, in essence, were seen by Yankees as vital elements in the creation of a nationwide domestic market that was to be controlled at the North;[236] a massive "indivisible nation" that would please both their socialist and communist constituents[237] and the Northeast's rich and powerful businessmen—many who were tied, directly or indirectly, to the 250 year old Yankee slave trade.[238]

Based on economics alone then, Lincoln was not going to allow the Southern states to secede; and if they did, they would be forced back, at the tip of a gun barrel if need be—which is precisely what occurred.

For Northern Liberals the American "Civil War" was indeed, in great part, a conflict built around business and finance. While modern Yankee mythologists have tried hard to obscure this fact, Lincoln knew it and so did nearly everyone else, including many foreigners. In 1862 English novelist Charles Dickens exposed the truth behind America's "War Between the States":

> *The Northern [Liberals'] onslaught upon slavery is no more than a piece of specious humbug disguised to conceal its desire for economic control of the United States. Union means so many millions a year lost to the [Conservative] South; secession means loss of the same millions to the North.* The love of money is the root of this as many, many other evils. *The quarrel between the North and South is, as it stands, solely a fiscal quarrel.*[239]

As we have seen, the South was rich in countless manmade and natural resources. Therefore her "economic control" was absolutely vital to Northern interests. It is easy to see then why Lincoln and his Wall Street Boys considered Dixie the ultimate money prize, one they could not afford to lose.[240]

On July 1, 1861, in his Message to Congress, Lincoln drove the point home: the South *must* be forced to return to the Union, otherwise the North would suffer tremendous loss financially. Said the president:

> What is now combated, is the position that secession is consistent with the Constitution—is lawful, and peaceful. It is not contended that there is any express law for it; and nothing should ever be implied as law, which leads to unjust, or absurd consequences. *The nation purchased, with money, the countries out of which several of these States were formed. Is it just that they shall go off without leave, and without refunding? The nation paid very large sums, (in the aggregate, I believe, nearly a hundred millions) to relieve Florida of the aboriginal tribes. Is it just that she shall now be off without consent, or without making any return? The nation is now in*

debt for money applied to the benefit of these so-called seceding States, in common with the rest. Is it just, either that creditors shall go unpaid, or the remaining States pay the whole? A part of the present national debt was contracted to pay the old debts of Texas. Is it just that she shall leave, and pay no part of this herself?

Again, if one State may secede, so may another; and when all shall have seceded, none is left to pay the debts. Is this quite just to creditors? Did we notify them of this sage view of ours, when we borrowed their money? If we now recognize this doctrine, by allowing the seceders to go in peace, it is difficult to see what we can do, if others choose to go, or to extort terms upon which they will promise to remain.[241]

Money was clearly front and center in Lincoln's mind when he initiated war against Dixie: in this same speech he asked Congress for $400 million (in today's currency about $10 billion) to pay for the men and supplies necessary to physically coerce the South back into the Union.[242] This had to be one of the most preposterous plans ever laid before Congress, for if enacted it would only put the U.S. further in debt (the national debt was one of Lincoln's chief complaints to begin with). Additionally, if in the future the North were to be

Like most Britons English novelist Charles Dickens sympathized with the Confederacy.

victorious and the South was forced to pay back this sum, it would surely bankrupt her. Northern deficit, Southern insolvency, and all for what purpose?[243] Another example of "Liberal logic"!

In any event, did Lincoln really believe that the South would willingly rejoin the Union after waging a bloody war against her, after bombing her into rubble, after exterminating nearly 25 percent of her population, after humiliating and occupying her, then bankrupting her? Diplomacy was certainly not one of his strong points.[244]

Despite the extreme irrationality of Lincoln's congressional request,

Northern pro-Lincoln journalists, magazine editors, and newspapers were quick to support his concerns over the potential loss of the South and her abundant wealth and resources. A month before the War, on March 2, 1861, the New York *Evening Post*, enunciated Lincoln's concerns perfectly, saying that the revenue from duties must be collected at the Southern ports, otherwise the sources that supply the treasury would dry up. This would leave the government without money. Unable to function, the *Evening Post* ranted on, it would go bankrupt, leaving nothing for the U.S. army, navy, or their officers' salaries.[245]

Lincoln's Wall Street Boys—many who, as mentioned, were still involved in the Yankee slave trade, and who, as Spooner noted, helped fund Lincoln's two elections using profits from that tainted business—were also on board, of course, as were the Boston elite—the latter group, in particular, making it known that it was quite willing to grant huge concessions to the South in the interest of making money.[246]

In short, in early 1861, when the threat of secession and war came, the average Yankee was thinking about the same thing his modern day descendants are: the economy. Only a few radical liberals, abolitionists, socialists, and communists had any interest in abolishing slavery; and in fact, the tiny "Northern abolition movement" was hated and reviled by most Yanks, including Lincoln, who once remarked that he hoped to never be "tarred with the abolitionist brush."[247] In January 1861, Fernando Wood, the mayor of New York City, for example, stated that if the South seceded, his city should secede with it in order to preserve business and trade. As a result, 200 of the New York's wealthiest and most influential citizens were planning to "throw off the authority of the Federal and State governments" and seize the forts, navy yards, and war vessels in the harbor, and then declare New York a "free city.[248] No Yankee talk of destroying slavery; only of preserving the economy.

In such an environment it is not surprising that abolitionists like Lewis Tappan, Theodore Weld, and William Lloyd Garrison were repeatedly stoned, egged, spit on, and had their lives threatened by fellow Northerners. Ohio abolitionist Elijah Lovejoy was shot and killed by an angry Yankee mob for publishing anti-slavery articles,[249] just one more piece of evidence that the North did not go into the War to destroy slavery, but rather to subjugate the South in an attempt to "collect the revenue."

In our investigation into the real cause of Lincoln's War we have come full circle without finding even a hint that the conflict was based around slavery. Yes, on March 21, 1861, Confederate Vice President Alexander H. Stephens declared that "slavery is the cornerstone" of the Confederate Constitution. But when he made this statement he was merely repeating the words of a *Yankee* judge, Associate Justice of the U.S. Supreme Court, Henry Baldwin of Connecticut who, 28 years earlier, in 1833, had said:

> Slavery is the corner-stone of the [U.S.] Constitution. The foundations of the Government are laid and rest on the rights of property in slaves, and the whole structure must fall by disturbing the corner-stone.[250]

As Richard M. Johnston noted later in 1884, all Stephens did during his "Cornerstone Speech" was accurately point out the fact that

> on the subject of slavery there was no essential change in the new [Southern Confederate] Constitution from the old [U.S. Constitution].[251]

Conservative C.S. and U.S. statesman Alexander H. Stephens of Georgia.

In other words, decades before the formation of the Southern Confederacy, Yankees widely regarded slavery as the cornerstone of the Union.[252]

It would be far more accurate to say then that *slavery was the cornerstone of the Union*, for not only would New England, the founder of American slavery, have gone bankrupt without it,[253] it was the North's Wall Street Boys (Yankee financiers, merchants, stock traders, and industrialists) who made the most money from the institution and who were thus the most interested in keeping it alive.[254] Taking Vice President Stephens' remarks out of context, as enemies of the South do, does not change these facts.[255]

We have irrefutably proven and permanently established that Lincoln's War was a contest between *liberalism* (whose constituents wanted the national government to control the states) and *conservatism* (whose constituents wanted the state governments to control themselves). Why is this not better known? Because the "Civil War" has been ignorantly disguised and commonly misrepresented by Liberals and uninformed Conservatives as a fight between "the North and the South," "the Blue and the Gray," "the Union and the Confederacy," "the Free States and the Slave States," "Abolitionists and Slaveholders." These catchphrases only serve to conceal and distort the reality behind the War, which was the very intention of their originators.

Let us end this chapter with the final death blow to this tired old myth; an irrational fiction that was cunningly invented and perpetuated by Northern radicals, socialists, and communists with a fiery hatred for facts and a passionate love for falsehood. On May 30, 1861, Mrs. R. L. Hunt of New Orleans, Louisiana, sent a letter to her brother, Salmon P. Chase (at the time a Liberal), Lincoln's Secretary of the Treasury, from which I have extracted the following comments. "Dear brother," she began in defense of the South:

> *Do not delude yourself or others with the notion that war can maintain the Union.* Alas, I say it with a heavy heart, the Union is destroyed; it can never be restored.[256] If, indeed, the federal government had frowned upon the first dawning of disunion, things might have been different. But the United States suffered South Carolina to secede without opposition, and with scarcely a murmur of disapprobation. . . . All the Southern States, with the exception of Kentucky, Missouri, and Maryland, have joined in the secession, and have formed themselves into a powerful confederacy of States, with a government possessing all the usual powers of sovereignties, exercising entire and exclusive sway, legislative, executive, and judicial, within the limits of those States, and dissolving all connection with the United States. Having thus by a revolution hitherto almost bloodless assumed and exercised the right of self-government, *the Confederate States are now threatened with war and desolation if they do not abjure the government they have formed, and renounce forever the right of altering or abolishing that government—no matter how oppressive or despotic it may become.*
>
> The time has passed for a discussion about the territories and fugitive slaves and the constitutional right of a State to secede.

Secession has proved to be a revolution, the overthrow of the Constitution,[257] the dissolution of the Union.[258] Still secession is *un fait accompli*. Disunion is a fixed fact. It is worse than useless to deny or attempt to evade this truth.

The question, then, to be determined is not, Shall the Union be maintained? but, Shall the Confederate States be allowed to govern themselves? And *this is a question of liberty and free government.*

And how do the statesmen of the North, how do you, my dear brother, who should recognize facts as they are, propose to deal with this question? With sword and buckler, the rifle, the bayonet, and the musket, the cannon, and all the dread instruments of war, with infantry and cavalry and ships and navies and armies!

With these you propose to subjugate the entire free people of the South, while you mock them with the declaration that your object is to maintain a Union which no longer exists. Is this wise, just, quite in keeping with the spirit of Christianity and of liberty, and with the lofty character of the United States? Would you desire a union of compulsion, a union to be maintained by the bayonet, a union with hatred and revenge filling the hearts of the North and of the South? I hope you would not. But if you would, the thing is impossible. You can never subjugate the South—never. Her people are high-spirited, martial, and intelligent. Educated in the school of American liberty, they value the right of self-government above all price. . . . They view the attempt to conquer them and to compel them to submit to the government of their victors as an effort of high-handed tyranny and oppression. You may for the moment have an advantage in wealth and numbers. But . . . *the North is fighting for subjugation and domination, the South for liberty and independence. It is precisely like the great revolutionary struggle of 1776 against the tyranny of Great Britain—a struggle for liberty on one side and for despotism on the other. How can you expect victory in such a cause?* . . . Surely eight millions of people, *armed in the holy cause of liberty* in such a country as they possess are invincible by any force the North can send against them.

The South is now united to a man. There is no division among the people here. There is but one mind, one heart, one action. Do not suffer yourself to be misled with the idea that there are Union men in the South. There is not a man here who will not resist the arms of the North. The [unconstitutional] action of Mr. Lincoln and his cabinet has made them all of one mind.

I will tell you what I see here in the city. Every night the men are drilling. Young and old, professional men and laborers, lawyers, doctors, and even the ministers are all drilling. The shops are closed at six that the clerks may go to their drilling. The ladies hold fairs, make clothes, lint, etc., for the army, and animate the men by appeals to their chivalry and their patriotism *to resist the enemy to the death.* What is seen in New Orleans pervades the whole South. Never were a people more united and more determined.[259]

What would prompt such courage, resistance, and unification among the 8 million European-Americans in the South, and what would inspire them to go up against the formidable North, which possessed a population of 22 million European-Americans, and thus three times the financial backing, weaponry, and soldiery?

Not a single soldier on either side of Lincoln's War fought over slavery. To think otherwise is absurd, illogical, and unhistorical.

Slavery? The very idea is laughable! Only a few hundred thousand Southerners actually owned slaves, less than five percent of the total population.[260]

In the letter cited above Mrs. Hunt, who lived with her husband in the deep South and was thus well versed in Southern sentiment, only refers to the word "slave" once and this is in relation to the Fugitive Slave Law—any discussion of which, she pleads, is now pointless, since secession and the formation of the Confederate States of America have already taken place. More importantly, there is no mention of the Southern people trying or even wanting to "preserve slavery," "save slavery," or "maintain slavery." Why? Because this was never part of the Southern Cause—no matter how many times the overly emotional, uninformed, opinionated, politically correct enemies of the South say otherwise.

Mrs. Hunt's entire focus is on the fact that Liberals (mainly in the North) are fighting to "subjugate and dominate" Conservatives (mainly in the South), who are fighting for "liberty and independence." This is why, "to a man," American Conservatives at the time—whether they were from the South, the North, the East, or the West—had only one battle cry: "States' rights, and death to those who make war against them!"[261]

THE REAL WINNER
OF LINCOLN'S WAR

W HO WON THE "CIVIL WAR"? Unless you were born of educated and enlightened pro-South parents, you were inevitably taught the same nonsense as the rest of America: the victor, according to popular opinion, was the "righteous" North, headed by "Honest Abe," who "freed the slaves" and "saved the Union."

Like every other article of history put out by our leftist mainstream media, however, this too is just another fairy tale, ingeniously woven to hide the truth while degrading the conservative, traditional, Christian South and glorifying the liberal, progressive, atheistic North. And here we arrive at the truth about why the War was fought and who actually won.

We have seen that the "Civil War" did not concern slavery, that neither side said it was fighting for abolition. Instead both the North and the South maintained that their goal was to "preserve the Union." How can this be? How could both sides be fighting for the same objective?

Victorian Americans, as always, divided down party lines, held that there were two different ideas of what the Union was and what it should be. This was just as true then as it is today.

The first was the original Union as established on conservative principles by the Founding Fathers. The second was a new Union that

Liberals intended to construct on top of the first, and which was to be based on leftist even socialistic and communistic ideologies.

Naturally Jefferson Davis and the conservative South took up arms to preserve the *first* Union, that of the Founding Fathers, with its tacit promise of states' rights and its wide ranging restrictions on governmental power (see the Ninth and Tenth Amendments). The liberal North, however, took up arms to preserve the *second* Union, the one promised by incoming president and big government proponent Abraham Lincoln and his radical leftist, socialist, and communist followers; a "union" purposefully designed to overthrow states' rights and centralize all political power in an omnipotent national government at Washington, D.C. It was *this*, the second Union—the one proposed by Liberals—that the South "rebelled" against, not the original Union, as the anti-South movement maintains.

Clement L. Vallandigham, an Ohio Copperhead who, in 1862, coined the Conservative slogan: "To maintain the Constitution as it is, and to restore the Union as it was."

Though in 1860 Dixie was predominately Conservative, that is, it backed the Democratic Party (the Conservative Party), there *were* Southern Liberals—for example, Republican politician William G. Brownlow of Virginia; and though Yankeedom was predominately Liberal, that is, it backed the Republican Party (the Liberal Party), there *were* Northern Conservatives—for example, Democrat Representative Clement L. Vallandigham of Ohio. Thus the "Civil War" was in reality *not* a contest between North and South. *It was one between conservatism and liberalism.*

Though today's left-wing historians would rather you not know this, and have in fact done everything they can to conceal it from you, it has long been known and discussed by intelligent, intellectually curious people. One of these was Confederate Vice President Alexander H. Stephens, who repeatedly stated that the War was a battle between what were then called "Consolidationists" or "Centralists" (that is, Liberals who wanted to consolidate or centralize power in the federal government) and "Constitutionalists" (that is, Conservatives who wanted to maintain states' rights and the constitutional separation of powers).[262]

This is why, as I discuss in "Notes to My Readers," the Democrats of the Civil War period referred to themselves, not just as "constitutionalists," but also as "Conservatives," "confederates," and "anti-Centralists," while the Republicans called themselves not just "consolidationists," but also "Liberals," "nationalists," and "Centralists."[263]

Antifederalist Conservative U.S. President Thomas Jefferson of Virginia.

These terms were used by both parties right up to the election of 1896, when, for the first time, the Democrats switched to a liberal platform (with progressive presidential nominee William Jennings Bryan) and the Republicans changed over to a conservative platform (with capitalist presidential nominee William McKinley).[264]

To put all of this into sharper focus we can say that, in essence, the Civil War was a battle between two different systems of social and economic life, which gave birth to two different systems of political theory: a conservative one and a liberal one. It was, then, a contest between two entirely different and opposing civilizations:[265] Southern agrarianism and Northern industrialism;[266] the farming and commerce capitalism of the South and the finance and industry capitalism of the North;[267] Southern free trade and Northern protective tariffs;[268] Southern traditionalism and Northern progressivism; Southern ruralism (the countryman) and Northern urbanism (the townsman); the South's desire to maintain Thomas Jefferson's small government Confederate Republic and the North's desire to change it into Alexander Hamilton's big government Federal Democracy.[269] In 1906 pro-North, Lincoln-worshiping historian Francis Newton Thorpe correctly put the matter this way:

> The war was a conflict between two civilizations, two incompatible ideas, two conceptions of Republican government, the one embodied

in the word *nation* [which is a liberal-progressive-socialist concept], the other, in the word *confederacy* [a conservative-traditional-capitalist concept].[270]

Shorn of Yankee myth and anti-South propaganda, Lincoln's War was nothing more than a political clash that pitted liberal, progressive, industrialists (mainly Northerners) who disliked the Constitution and wanted to federalize power, against conservative, traditional, agriculturalists (mainly Southerners) who were strict constitutionalists and wanted to localize power.[271]

The real winner of the War then was not the North. It was Liberalism, which early Americans referred to as the "American System."

Let us look at this left-wing political theory more closely.

Devised and promoted by Lincoln's political hero, slave owner Henry Clay[272]—a man Old Abe called "my *beau ideal* of a statesman, the man for whom I fought all my humble life"[273]—the American System was a nationalist program in which there was to be a single sovereign authority, the president, who was to assume the role of a kinglike ruler with autocratic powers.[274]

Likewise, the government at Washington, D.C. was to be federated, acting as a consolidated superpower that would eventually control the money supply, offer internal improvements,[275] intervene in foreign affairs, nationalize the banking system,[276] issue soaring tariffs, grant

Liberal, slave owner, and U.S. statesman Henry Clay of Virginia, Lincoln's lifelong idol.

subsidies to corporations, engage in protectionism, and impose an income tax,[277] all hints of Lincoln's coming empire.[278]

In essence, what the American System proposed was a federated government that was the polar opposite of a confederated government. In the late 1700s, under the Liberals' proposed federation, its proponents, the Federalists, Monarchists, or Hamiltonians (named after Liberal Alexander Hamilton), as they were variously called,[279] not only sought to create a large, domineering, all-powerful, nationalized government to which all interests (from private to business) were subordinate,[280] but they also proposed that the states be largely stripped of their independence and authority, then placed in an inferior role. Hamilton himself wanted to get rid of the states completely.[281] Jeffersonianism was to be

Federalist, monarchist, centralist, and big government Liberal Alexander Hamilton.

abolished and replaced with the Hamiltonian or American system.[282]

Naturally everything about Clay's American System was repugnant to traditional Southerners and Northerners—a group that we will call the Confederalists (those who were against federalism),[283] but one that referred to itself as the Antifederalists or Jeffersonians (after Thomas Jefferson).[284] Conservative Southerner John C. Calhoun prophetically referred to the American System as "a dangerous and growing disease,"[285] one that would someday bring about the ruin of our delicately designed republic.[286]

Why was the American System anathema to the Jeffersonians? Because it went counter to the conservative ideas set forth by the Founders in their formation of the U.S. Confederacy (nicknamed "The Confederate States of America"),[287] the system of government favored by the South. Jefferson, for instance, a man who put his faith in ordinary people rather than in institutions,[288] had intended for America to be built on the innately individualistic farmer,[289] its economy on agriculture, and its government on republicanism (a constitutional government in which supreme power resides in the body of its citizens).[290] He distrusted the world of manufacturing, banking and foreign trade, believing that it led to class divisions, economic chaos, and mob rule.[291] Instead, he preferred an agrarian economy built around a simple equalitarian republic, even if it meant slowing the growth of the national economy.[292]

The Hamiltonians, on the other hand, wanted to replace the farmer with the merchant, agrarianism with industrialism, republicanism with socialism.[293] Their emphasis was on capitalism, even if it meant "economic inequality" in American society.[294] They also wanted to dilute sectional differences between North and South and establish a strong permanent national army, both hostile ideas in the South.[295]

Lincoln was a political descendant of Hamilton and the early American Federalists, monarchists, and consolidationists, which is why, like modern day Liberals, he did not like the Constitution.[296] His own supporters called it a "scrap of paper" and a "covenant with death and a league with hell."[297] Some 150 years later, big government Liberal Barack Hussein Obama followed in Lincoln's footsteps, referring to the Constitution as "an imperfect document," while his anti-American followers eagerly campaigned to throw out the *entire* document, calling it "old, outdated, and useless."[298]

As a Liberal, Lincoln was no different than Obama and every other progressive on this particular score. In February 1861, while meeting with a Southern peace commission at Willard's Hotel in Washington, D.C., the president-elect was asked by New York businessman William E. Dodge what he was going to do to prevent war with the South. Lincoln's response is chilling. When I get to the Oval Office, he said,

> I shall take an oath to the best of my ability to preserve, protect, and defend the Constitution. This is a great and solemn duty. With the support of the people and the assistance of the Almighty I shall undertake to perform it. I have full faith that I shall perform it. *It is not the Constitution as I would like to have it*, but as it is that is to be defended.[299]

Reading between the lines, it is obvious that even prior to becoming president, Lincoln was plotting to alter, and even destroy, the Constitution of Washington, Jefferson, Madison, Franklin, Mason, Pinckney, and the other Founders.

This crime was to be just the most recent of untold hundreds that Liberals (mainly in the North) had been perpetuating against Conservatives (mainly in the South) since the turn of the 19th-Century, violating both the Constitution and the decisions of the Supreme Court. These leftist outrages against the conservative, traditional, Christian South stretched into the Civil War period (1861-1865) and went on long after, through Reconstruction (1865-1877) and the Grant administration

(1869-1877)—a period known even to North-leaning historians as one of the most corrupt and "deplorable" Liberal presidencies in U.S. history; the "nadir of national disgrace."[300] A partial list of unconstitutional acts committed by American Liberals includes:

"1. The Missouri Compromise, 1820. Slave territory restricted and no Constitutional authority for it.

"2. The Tariff Acts of 1828 and 1833. The Constitution says the tariff must be uniform—one section must not be discriminated against in favor of another.

"3. Violation of the Fugitive Slave Law. Article 4, Section 2, Clause 3.

"4. Coercion in 1861. Article 4, Section 4.

"5. Laws of neutrality, Trent Affair. Article 6, Clause 2—Violation of International Law.

"6. Writ of *Habeas Corpus* suspended. Article 1, Section 9, Clause 2.

"7. War was declared without the consent of Congress, 1861. Article 1, Section 8, Clauses 11, 12.

"8. Emancipation Proclamation. Article 4, Section 3, Clause 2.

"9. West Virginia made a State. Article 4, Section 3, Clause 1.

"10. The Hanging of Mrs. [Mary] Surratt. Amendments—Article 5.

"11. The Execution of [Confederate Captain] Henry Wirz. Amendments—Article 6.

"12. [Issuance of] the Fourteenth and Fifteenth Amendments. Article 5. [Note: These two "Civil War Amendments" were anti-Conservative in character and intention.]

"13. The Seizure without compensation of property after surrender. Amendments—Articles 4 and 6.

"14. Squatter Sovereignty. It allowed a territorial government to exclude slavery.

"15. The liberty of the press taken away. Amendments—Article 1. [Note: For example, during his administration Lincoln illegally shut down over 300 Conservative and pro-South newspapers in the North.]

"16. The Freedom of Speech Denied. [Clement L.]

Vallandigham imprisoned in Ohio. Amendments—Article
1.
"17. Blockading ports of States that were held by the Federal
Government to be still in the Union."[301]

Under such circumstances it is little wonder that the conservative,
Constitution-loving Southern states wanted to secede, that they did
secede, and that they fought back so forcefully during Reconstruction (the
second phase of the Liberals' war on the conservative South) forming such
conservative groups as the pro-Constitution Ku Klux Klan (which was not
in any way connected to the modern KKK).[302]

Many have asked me what proof I have that Lincoln was a Liberal with
leftist tendencies. Besides those already discussed, let us count the ways.

National socialist Adolf Hitler of
Austria, one of Lincoln's
greatest admirers.

To begin with, our anti-Confederacy
sixteenth president surrounded himself with
political revolutionaries,[303] was supported
by thousands of radical European socialists
called the "Forty-Eighters,"[304] was adored by
socialists and communists alike, and has
always been honored by nationalists,
dictators, revolutionaries, humanists, and
communists from around the world.[305]
These would include national socialists like
Adolf Hitler,[306] Marxist socialists like Karl
Marx, European socialists like George Julian
Harney,[307] American socialists like Horace
Greeley,[308] radical socialists like Alexander
Ivanovich Herzen,[309] and Christian socialists
like Francis Bellamy (author of America's *Pledge of Allegiance*).[310] Lincoln
has even been supported by anarchists like Mikhail Bakunin.[311] Marx, the
founder of modern communism, was so enamored by "Honest Abe" that
he wrote him a personal letter supporting his election.[312]

Lincoln's progressiveness is also the reason that, in the 1930s,
American communists formed a military organization called "The
Abraham Lincoln Battalion," and it is why the 1939 Communist Party
Convention in Chicago, Illinois, affectionately displayed an enormous
image of Lincoln over the center of its stage, flanked by pictures of

Russian communist dictators Vladimir Lenin on one side and Joseph Stalin on the other.[313]

Lincoln's deep-seated liberalism is also why he himself was an enthusiastic supporter of revolutions, revolutionary ideas, and revolutionary leaders, such as those who headed the 1848 socialist revolts in Europe;[314] it is why, in July 1861, he specifically asked European revolutionary Giuseppe Garibaldi to head the Union army;[315] it is why he gave well-known Forty-Eighter Reinhold Solger a post in the U.S. Treasury Department;[316] it is why he selected socialists for his administration, men such as the notorious radical Charles A. Dana[317] (managing editor of socialist Horace Greeley's New York Tribune[318]—both who were personal friends of Karl Marx),[319] who served as Lincoln's Assistant Secretary of War (under Edwin M. Stanton);[320] it is why he employed socialists to aid his election campaigns, men like Casper Butz, Friedrich Kapp (a presidential elector for Lincoln), and Friedrich Karl Franz Hecker, the latter a Union officer who helped found the Republican Party and later promoted the election of Lincoln in 1860.[321]

It is also why Lincoln was worshiped by socialistic radicals in the Republican Party, "enemies of the Constitution"[322] like Wendell Phillips, James A. Garfield, and Thaddeus Stevens—the same men who called for the execution of Southern slave owners (Conservatives), seizure of their plantations, and the redistribution of their property to other Liberals, progressives, and socialists.[323]

Lincoln's entrenched progressive views are also why he enlisted so many left-wing officers in his armies, men such as communist Union General Joseph Wedemeyer (a personal friend of Marx and

Socialist Charles A. Dana of New Hampshire served as Assistant Secretary of War in the Lincoln administration.

Engels),[324] communist Union General August Willich, communist Union Lieutenant Fritz Jacobi, communist Union Major Robert Rosa,[325] socialist Union General Max Weber,[326] socialist Union General Francis Channing Barlow,[327] communist Union Colonel Fritz Anneke,[328]

German socialist Friedrich K. F. Hecker helped found the Republican Party in 1854, worked for Lincoln's election in 1860, and served as a Union officer during Lincoln's War.

communist Union Adjutant Anselm Albert,[329] socialist Union Colonel Charles Zagonyi,[330] socialist Union General (under General John C. Frémont) Alexander Sandor Asboth,[331] socialist Union Colonel George Duncan Wells,[332] socialist Union General Alexander Schimmelfennig,[333] socialist Union Captain Isidor Bush,[334] socialist Union General Franz Sigel,[335] socialist Union Captain Gustav Von Struve,[336] socialist Union Chief Topographical Engineer (under Frémont) Johan Fiala,[337] socialist Union General Albin Francisco Schoepf,[338] socialist Union Colonel Henry Ramming,[339] socialist Union General Peter Joseph Osterhaus,[340] socialist Chief of the Ohio Army's Secret Service (under Union General George B. McClellan) Allan Pinkerton,[341] and socialist Union General Friedrich Salomon,[342] among countless others.

A number of these anti-American European progressives were instrumental in organizing Union regiments, such as Yankee Generals Julius Stahel and Ludwig Blenker (who together set up the First German Rifles or Eighth New York Infantry).[343] The most famous socialist in Lincoln's army was no doubt the German-American revolutionary Carl Schurz, who not only rose to the rank of general,[344] but who campaigned for Lincoln in 1860 and later served as a Missouri Senator, U.S. Minister to Spain,[345] and U.S. Secretary of the Interior.[346] Naturally big government Liberal Lincoln and big government socialist Schurz considered themselves "good friends."[347]

The depth of passion socialists have always had for big government Liberal Lincoln can be seen in the following May 1869 letter from the General Council of the International Labor-Union to the National Labor Union. Among the many statements it contained were the following:

In our address of felicitation to Mr. Lincoln on the occasion of his reelection to the presidency of the United States, we expressed *our conviction that the civil war would prove as important to the progress of the working class as the War of the Revolution had been for the progress of the bourgeoisie.*

And actually the victorious termination of *the antislavery war* has inaugurated a new epoch in the annals of the working class. In the United States an independent labor movement has since sprung into life, which is not being viewed with much favor by the old parties and the professional politicians.[348]

Here we have confirmation from the Left that Lincoln's War was indeed a contest between Conservatives or capitalists (which, generally speaking, Victorian socialists referred to as the "bourgeoisie") and Liberals (which they called the "proletariat" or laborers), and that these same socialists viewed the conflict as an "antislavery war."

Next time you hear someone say that Lincoln's War was "a battle over slavery," remember that it was 19th-Century socialists and communists—men and women who hated both the South and the concept of states' rights, and who would stop at nothing to destroy both—who most enthusiastically promoted this false idea. And why did they detest states' rights? Because they could not turn the U.S. into one large "indivisible nation" if the individual states were considered little "nations" unto themselves, with the power to ignore or overturn the decisions and activities of the central government.[349] This, in turn, is why early American liberals, socialists, and communists loathed the conservative South—and still do.

American communists closely associate Lincoln with Russian communist dictator Joseph Stalin.

Was Lincoln himself a socialist? Not technically speaking, for he owned private property (for example, his Greek Revival house in Springfield, Illinois) and businesses (for example, the German newspaper, the *Illinois Staats-Anzeiger*),[350] both "deadly sins" in the Church of Socialism.

However, his left-wing followers correctly saw his overall big government politics as progressive and at the least very sympathetic with many of their socialistic causes. Hence, for them the "Civil War" was seen as a class struggle between the bourgeoisie (middle class) and the proletariat (working class), with even the Emancipation Proclamation counting as a socialist program—one not for the benefit of black civil rights, but for the benefit of the socialists' agenda, which needed free men to help advance the communist revolution and build its utopian democratic society.[351]

Thus in 1863 British statesman Benjamin Disraeli could say that the conflict in the U.S. was a "great revolution" that would completely alter America,[352] while the *Springfield Republican* (of Massachusetts) championed the emancipatory edict as "the greatest social and political revolution of the age."[353] In 1892 socialists went as far as to write that "socialism triumphed over statecraft [that is, states' rights] within a month, when Abraham Lincoln signed the Emancipation Proclamation."[354] They even bragged that New England socialist Wendell Phillips went about

the land telling his fellow-citizens that the chattel slaves having been freed, next in order was the emancipation of the wage slaves—as had been demanded over thirty years before by the originators of the [socialist] movement.[355]

Not surprisingly, Lincoln and his socialist devotees worked closely together during his entire presidency. One of them, the tireless socialist campaigner Carl Schurz—who even his own party members considered "irregular"[356]—helped write the 1860 Republican platform (successfully injecting a number of his ideas into the program),[357] while another, Robert Dale Owen (son of famed Welsh-American utopian socialist Robert Owen),[358] helped inspire Lincoln's illegal and fake Emancipation Proclamation. According to socialist writer Morris Hillquit:

[Owen's] letter to President Lincoln is said to have been a potent factor in bringing about the President's proclamation abolishing chattel slavery.[359]

In plain English, Lincoln's Emancipation Proclamation was inspired by socialists.

Other socialists—as well as those who "were favorably disposed toward Fourierism"[360]—who admired or even loved Lincoln, were Ralph Waldo Emerson, Nathaniel Hawthorne, Parke Godwin, Theodore Parker, George Ripley, William Henry Channing, Margaret Fuller, George W. Curtis, Henry David Thoreau, and Amos Bronson Alcott.[361] Why would such esteemed left-wing Americans idolize and support Lincoln if he was not, in one way or another, in sympathy with their goals, beliefs, and ideologies?

Lincoln's most famous socialist friend was German revolutionary Carl Schurz, who helped write the 1860 Republican platform, campaigned for Lincoln, and went on to become a Union general. After the War Schurz continued to spread his anti-American socialist ideas as a Missouri Senator, U.S. Minister to Spain, and U.S. Secretary of the Interior.

Scores of other socialists, radicals, and freethinkers, many of them foreign, either aided Lincoln in his 1860 campaign or actually worked in his administration; in many cases, both. Some began assisting him as early as 1854, the year the Republican (Liberal) Party was founded to limit, not abolish, slavery.[362] Individuals from these groups included: Frederick Hassaurek (Lincoln's minister to Ecuador),[363] Nicholas J. Rusch (a Union captain, Lieutenant Governor of Iowa, and Commissioner of German Emigration),[364] George Schneider (the "voice of the Forty-Eighters" and Lincoln's consul at Elsinore, Denmark),[365] Herman Kreismann (Secretary of the Legation at Berlin, Germany), Gustav Körner (Union colonel of volunteers and, after Schurz, Minister to Spain),[366] Theodore Canisius (business partner and consul to Vienna, Austria),[367] Johann Bernhard Stallo (an anti-Bible, anti-Christian),[368] Heinrich Börnstein (Union military commander and consul to Bremen, Germany),[369] Carl Rotteck (a prominent Forty-Eighter),[370] and Wilhelm Hoffbauer (another conspicuous Forty-Eighter).[371]

At least 42 of Lincoln's delegates at the 1860 Chicago Republican Convention were native Germans, many, if not most, who were socialists. Lincoln's pre-convention group was also packed with Forty-Eighters, European ultra-liberals who supported his progressive ideas;

men such as: Adolf Douai, Johannes Gambs, Elias Peissner, Heinrich Vortriede, Adolph Wiesner, Karl Dänzer, August Becker, Jakob Müller, Hermann Kiefer, Bernhard Domschke, Johannes Georg Günther, Robert Blum, and Karl Röser.[372]

Like moths to a flame, Left-wingers, revolutionaries, humanists, Marxists, anarchists, radicals of all sorts, even fascists, have long been drawn to Lincoln, resulting in numerous books on the president's "socialism" and "communism." In 1936, for example, communist Earl Browder came out with his book *Lincoln and the Communists*, writing admiringly:

> If the [communist] tradition of Lincoln is to survive, if his words shall play a role in political life today, this will be due not to the Republicans nor the Democrats, but to the modern representatives of historical progress, the *Communists*. Today, it is left to the Communist Party to revive the words of Lincoln.[373]

The cover of Earl Browder's 1936 pro-communist, pro-Lincoln book: *Lincoln and the Communists*, published in New York City.

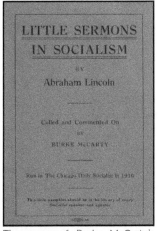

The cover of Burke McCarty's 1910 pro-socialist, pro-Lincoln book: *Little Sermons in Socialism by Abraham Lincoln*, a Chicago print.

Twenty-six years earlier, in 1910, socialist Burke McCarty penned *Little Sermons in Socialism by Abraham Lincoln*. In it McCarty writes:

We do not claim that Abraham Lincoln was a Socialist, for the word had not been coined in his day.[374] We do not claim that he would, if he had lived, been a Socialist to-day, for we do not know this.

We do claim, and know, however, that Abraham Lincoln was in spirit to the hour of his death, a class conscious working man, that his sympathies were with that class, that he voiced the great principles of the modem constructive Socialism of to-day, and that *had he lived and been loyal and consistent with these principles which he always professed, he would be found within the ranks of the Socialist Party*.[375]

As an example, McCarty notes that one of the socialist's credos is the unification of workers worldwide, and records the following words by Lincoln, uttered November 21, 1864, before a working men's association:

The strongest bond of human sympathy outside the family relation should be one *uniting all working people* of all nations, tongues and kindreds.[376]

Lincoln's dislike of capitalism was evident early on, as McCarty points out, citing one of the future president's political speeches from 1837:

These *capitalists generally act harmoniously and concert, to fleece the people*, and now that they have got into a quarrel with themselves, we are called upon to appropriate the people's money to settle the quarrel.[377]

In November 1864, again, as McCarty shows, Lincoln toed the socialist party line by speaking out against corporations and the wealthy class who owned them:

As a result of the war, corporations have been enthroned and an ear of corruption in high places will follow, and the money power of the country will endeavor to prolong its reign by working upon the prejudices of the people, *until all wealth is aggregated in a few hands, and the Republic is destroyed!*

I feel at this moment more anxiety for the safety of my country than ever before, even in the midst of war. God grant that my suspicions may prove groundless![378]

Without question the ultimate proof of Lincoln's radical leftist political views comes from the fact that not only did he have much in common with Hitler (including a hatred of states' rights),[379] he actually borrowed (or assimilated) many of his wartime ideas from the Communist Manifesto, written by Marx and Engels in 1848. From my own study and research into this issue I would include the following:

1. Communist Manifesto: "A heavy progressive or graduated income tax."[380] Lincoln was the founder of what would become the IRS.[381]

2. Communist Manifesto: "Confiscation of the property of all rebels."[382] Lincoln ordered the seizure of the property of Southerners (especially wealthy ones), and after the War this property was given away or sold to carpetbaggers, Northern radicals, and industrialists.[383]

3. Communist Manifesto: "Centralization of credit in the hands of the State, by means of a national bank with State capital and an exclusive monopoly."[384] Lincoln was instrumental in pushing for the establishment of a national banking system,[385] which began on February 25, 1863, under the new National Bank Act.[386]

4. Communist Manifesto: "Centralization of the means of communication and transport in the hands of the State."[387] Lincoln was associated with enlarging the postal service, granting railroad contracts, and setting up the Bureau of Printing and Engraving.[388] The conservative South was, of course, opposed to this kind of "government liberality," but the U.S. Congress under Lincoln forged ahead regardless.[389]

German revolutionary Karl Marx, founder of modern communism and a zealous Lincoln devotee.

5. Communist Manifesto: "The bringing into cultivation of wastelands, and the improvement of the soil generally in

accordance with a common plan."[390] The Department of Agriculture was founded during the Lincoln Administration.[391]

6. Communist Manifesto: "Gradual abolition of the distinction between town and country, by a more equable distribution of the population over the country."[392] One of Lincoln's chief goals was the Northernization of the South, to be remade into the industrial likeness of the Northeast. As Lincoln once coldly said to Interior Department official T. J. Barnett: "The entire South needs to be obliterated and replaced with new businessmen and new ideas."[393]

7. Communist Manifesto: "Free [that is, tax-payer/government-sponsored] education for all children in public schools."[394] Lincoln's Morrill Act, passed by Congress in 1862, gave 20,000 acres of public lands to each representative in Congress. The proceeds from the sale of these lands were used to establish the first land-grant colleges, which focused on agricultural, mechanical, scientific, military, and classical arts and subjects.[395]

Let us note that Lincoln also opposed organized religion and was a self-admitted anti-Bible, anti-Christian "infidel,"[396] which aligns him with anti-religious liberals, socialists, and communists, like Marx and Engels, the world over.[397]

We must also consider the fact that leftists who came after Lincoln imitated *him* specifically, not Conservative Jefferson Davis. In 1867, for instance, under the auspices of the left-leaning Democrat (Conservative at the time) President Andrew Johnson (a rare Southerner who remained loyal to the Union during Lincoln's War), the intrusive, expensive, cumbersome, unnecessary, and unconstitutional Department of Education was founded. Strengthened from the 1950s

German socialist Friedrich Engels, cowriter of the Communist Manifesto and friends with many of Lincoln's socialist and communist supporters, administrators, and military officers.

onward and greatly expanded in 1979 by ultra Liberal President Jimmy Carter, today it has grown into a massive propaganda machine, one of whose main purposes is to inculcate our youth with socialist, progressive, communist, anti-American ideas and doctrines. This, of course, perfectly accords with the motivations of the early American socialists and communists who promoted documents like the Communist Manifesto.[398]

Proof that the Lincoln's Republican Party was a liberal body hell bent on destroying not slavery but the Constitution, and that Davis' Democratic Party was a conservative body fighting to save not slavery but the Constitution, can be seen in the remarks made by those living in the mid 1800s.

Let us start with Southern author Elizabeth Avery Meriwether, who wrote under the pseudonym "George Edmonds." In the following material she uses the word "monarchy" for what we now call *liberalism*, and the word "democracy" for "republicanism" or "Americanism"—or what we now call *conservatism* (the Democrats had, up until recently, been Conservatives).[399] Let us note here that the U.S. is not now and never has been a democracy: a political body that is *ruled by majority*. The Founding Fathers intentionally set up the U.S. as a (confederate) republic: a political body that is *ruled by law*. Meriwether comments:

> The underlying cause of every conflict between man and man, tribe and tribe, country and country, has been on the one side a craving for power, on the other side an effort to escape that power. The nascent spirit of one is Monarchy [liberalism], of the other Democracy [conservatism]. *These two principles are inherently and eternally antagonistic, and underlie nearly, if not every, war fought on earth. Stratas of superficial causes usually overlay and cover up the real causes of war, as they did in the war on the South.*
>
> The seven years' war which severed the seceded Colonies from British rule was an open, undisguised fight between Monarchy and Democracy. *The four years' war between the Southern and Northern States was a fight between the same old enemies. Monarchy and Democracy, though the astute Republican [Liberal] party, while heart and soul Imperialistic [left-wing], concealed and covered up that principle under loud declarations of Freedom and blatant professions of humanitarianism. Under these hypocritical cloaks, the Monarchic [Liberal] principles had full swing for four years, and*

committed every species of crime and outrage peculiar to enraged Monarchists [Liberals]. When the [British] soldiers of Monarchy [Liberalism] in 1783 took ships and sailed Eastward to their kingly country [England], the soldiers of Democracy [conservatism] fondly hoped they had driven their ancient enemy forever from this New Continent. The snake was scotched, but not killed. Nor was it banished. It remained here in our midst with veiled features and softened voice, biding its chance to up and regain its former power.

Alexander Hamilton was the head and front of American Monarchists [Liberals]. He wanted to make this Government a pure Monarchy [as defined here in our terms, a federalized socialist nation]. Hamilton advocated a "strong centralized Government," of imperial policy. Gouverneur Morris, a contemporary and friend of Hamilton, said:

> "Hamilton hated Republican [Conservative] Government, and never failed on every occasion to advocate the excellence of and avow his attachment to a Monarchic [dictatorial] form of Government."

From the formation of the Union, the Federalists [Liberals] of New England hated and feared Democratic [Conservative] principles. Their great leader, Hamilton, made no secret of this feeling. In his speech at a New York banquet Hamilton, in high opposition to [Thomas] Jefferson's Democracy, cried out: "The People! Gentlemen, I tell you the people are a great Beast!" In 1796 [Liberal] Gov. [Oliver] Walcott, of Connecticut, said: "I sincerely declare that I wish the [liberal] Northern States would separate from the [conservative] Southern the moment that event (the election of [Conservative] Jefferson) shall take place."

William Plumer of Massachusetts, another early American Liberal who believed in the right of secession.

Congressman [William] Plumer [of New Hampshire], a Federalist [big government Liberal] and an ardent Secessionist, in 1804 declared that "All dissatisfied with the measures of the Government looked to a separation of the States as a remedy for grievances."

As early as 1796 men of Massachusetts began to talk of New England seceding from the Union. It was declared that if [Liberal John] Jay's negotiation closing the Mississippi for twenty years could not be adopted, it was high time for the New England States to secede from the Union and form a Confederation by themselves.

The Monarchic [liberal/dictatorial] principles did not thrive under Hamilton's lead. Hamilton was too plain spoken. *The Republican [Liberal] party became more astute. In 1861, while making loud professions of desiring the largest freedom for the people, that party was making ready to rob them of every liberty they possessed.* "At the formation of this Union," says [Liberal journalist] E. P. [Edward Payson] Powell, "Hamilton laid before the Constitutional Convention of 1787 eleven propositions, which he wished to make the basis of the Union, but they were so Monarchistic [liberalistic] in tone they received no support whatever."

Ultra Liberal, socialistic radical, South-hating U.S. President James A. Garfield of Ohio.

The Republican [Liberal] war on the South stood solidly on Monarchic [dictatorial] principles. The [conservative] principles of 1776 were set aside in the 1860s, but not for years after the [conservative] South was conquered did Republicans [Liberals] openly admit they were inspired by the spirit of Monarchy [socialism, centralization, and empire building]. During [Conservative U.S. President William] McKinley's last campaign, Hamilton was loudly lauded and Jefferson decried as a visionary, a French anarchist. Hamilton Clubs were organized and Republican [Liberal] novelists set to writing romances with [left-wing] Hamilton as the hero. During [Liberal James A.] Garfield's campaign, a Republican [liberal] paper, the Lemars, Iowa, *Sentinel*, said:

> "Garfield's rule will be the transitory period between State Sovereignty [conservatism/traditionalism] and National Sovereignty [liberalism/socialism]. The United States Senate will give way to a National Senate. State Constitutions and the United States Senate are relics of State Sovereignty [states' rights] and implements of treason. Garfield's Presidency will be the Regency of Stalwartism [partisan devotion]; after that—Rex [that is, King]."

Fate used the hand of an insane "Stalwart" to impede, if not estop, the Monarchic plans of that time. The New York *Sun*, July 3rd, 1881, quoted President Garfield as saying:

> "The influence of [Thomas] Jefferson's Democratic [conservative] principles is rapidly waning, while the principles of Hamilton [liberalism] are rapidly increasing. Power has been gravitating toward the Central Government."

Power did not gravitate, it was wrenched at one jerk to the Central Government by Lincoln's hand. Not until after Hamilton and Jefferson had passed away did the followers of Jefferson drop the name "Republican" which they had borne during his life, and assume the name "Democrat."

Democracy—the rule of the people—is more expressive of Jefferson's doctrines. *Not until 1854 did the men of the Federal and Whig persuasion [Liberals all] unite and organize a party and take the name "Republican." The Republican party of the 60s was the legitimate offspring of the old New England Federalists, and inherited all its progenitor's faiths, hopes, hates and purposes, viz: Passion for power, fear and hate of Democracy, hate of the Union, belief in States' Rights, in States' Sovereignty, in Secession, and the strong persistent determination to break the Union asunder and form of the Northeast section a Northeastern Confederacy. All these ideas belonged to the old Federalists of New England, and were handed down to the*

Republican [Liberal] party in 1854.

Wendell Phillips, New England's tongue of fire, speaking of the inherent purposes of his party, said: "The Republican [Liberal] party is in no sense a national party. It is a party of the North, organized against the [Conservative] South."

The Republican [Liberal] party was organized against the South, organized to fight the [Conservative] South in every possible way; to fight as its progenitors, the Federalists [early American Liberals], had fought from 1796 to 1854, with calumnies, vituperations, false charges, every word and phrase hate could use, until the time came to use guns, bayonets, bullets, cannon balls and shells; and faithfully did that party carry out the ignoble and cruel purpose of its organization.

The war on the South was begun by the Federalists [Liberals] of New England in 1796. In 1814 a work of some four hundred and fifty pages, called *The Olive Branch*, was published in Boston, which throws electric light on certain almost forgotten events in New England's history. *The Olive Branch* contains extracts from a series of remarkable productions called the "Pelham Papers," which appeared in the Connecticut *Courant* in the year 1796. The *Courant* was published by Hudson and Goodwin, men of Revolutionary standing. The Pelham Papers were said to have been the joint production of men of the first talent and influence in the State.

Commenting on these papers of 1796, *The Olive Branch* of 1814 says:

> "A Northeastern Confederacy has been the object for a number of years. They (the [Liberal] politicians of New England) have repeatedly advocated in public print, separation of the States. *The project of separation was formed shortly after the adoption of the Federal [U.S.] Constitution.* The promulgation of the project first appeared in the year 1796, in these Pelham Papers. At that time there was none of that catalogue of grievances which since that period, have been fabricated to justify the recent attempt to dissolve the Union."

This refers to the efforts made in 1804 and 1814 to get the New England States to secede from the Union, so they might be separated from the Democratic [conservative] Southern and Western States. *The Olive Branch* continues:

> "At that time there was no 'Virginia Dynasty,' no 'Democratic [conservative] Madness,' no 'war with Great Britain.' The affairs of the country seemed to be precisely according to New England's [Liberals'] fondest wishes. Yet at that favorable time (1796) New England was dissatisfied with the Union and begun to plot to get out of it. The common people, however, were not then ready to break up the Union. The common people at that time had no dislike of the [conservative] Southern States.
>
> Then [liberal] New England writers, preachers and politicians deliberately began the wicked work of poisoning their minds against the [conservative] Southern States. *To sow hostility, discord and jealousy between the different sections of the Union was the first step New England took to accomplish her favorite object, a separation of the States.* Without this efficient instrument, all New England's efforts would have been utterly unavailing. Had the honest yeomanry of the Eastern States continued to respect and regard their Southern fellow-citizens as friends and brothers, having one common interest in the promotion of the general welfare, it would be impossible to have made them instruments in the unholy work of destroying the noble, the splendid Union."

But for the unholy work of having taught the common people of [liberal] New England to hate the [conservative] people of the South, the cruel war of the 1860s would never have been fought. "For eighteen years," continues *The Olive Branch* (the eighteen years from 1796 to 1814),

> "the most unceasing endeavors have been used to poison the minds of the people of the [liberal] Eastern States toward, and to alienate them from, their fellow-citizens of the [conservative] Southern States. The people of the South have been portrayed as 'demons incarnate,' as destitute of all the 'good qualities which dignify and adorn human nature.' Nothing can exceed the virulence drawn [by Yankee Liberals]

of the [conservative] South's people, their descriptions of whom would more have suited the ferocious inhabitants of New Zealand than a polished, civilized people."

. . . Mr. A. K. Fiske, a distinguished Republican [Liberal], throws some light on the relationship of the two parties, Hamilton's and Jefferson's; in other words, the party favoring Monarchy [liberalism] and the party favoring Democracy [conservatism], the rule of the people. "Hamilton and Jefferson," says Fiske in April 1879,

"represent the two opposing ideas which prevailed at the time our Government was formed, and which, with some variations, have been the basis of our political divisions into parties ever since, and have been involved in all the contests and controversies in our constitutional career. [Liberal] Hamilton embodied the tendency to a centralization of power in the national Government. There is no doubt that he would have preferred a monarchy. [Conservative] Jefferson, on the other hand, represented the demand for a complete diffusion of sovereignty among the people, and its exercise locally and in the States, and the confining of national functions as closely as possible under the most restrictive interpretation of the Constitution."

The U.S. Capitol has often been under socialist and even communist influence, particularly during the Lincoln and Grant administrations.

Mr. Fiske admits that Hamilton, the monarchist, represented the [Liberal] party which opposed the sovereignty of the people. A writer in the St. Louis *Globe-Democrat*, a staunch [liberal] advocate of Hamilton's strong government doctrines, in that paper, March 6, 1898, made this significant comment:

"The resemblance between [Liberal] Hamilton and [Liberal] Lincoln is so close no one can resist it. Hamilton is dwarfed by no man. A just parallel of Hamilton and Lincoln will show them alike in many ways. They were alike almost to the point of identity. Hamilton's

work made Lincoln's possible."

Hamilton's monarchic principles certainly made Lincoln's work possible. *Lincoln put in practice what Hamilton had advocated. Hamilton made no concealment of his monarchic principles; he preferred a monarchy such as England has, but failing that he wanted a President for life and the Governors of States appointed by the President. Until seated in the White House, Lincoln talked Democracy [conservatism] and affected great esteem for Jefferson's Democratic [conservative] principles.*

As soon as he held in his grip the machinery of government, he schemed for absolute power, and as soon as he was commander in chief of nearly 3,000,000 armed men, no imperial despot in pagan time ever wielded more autocratic power than did Abraham Lincoln, and Republican [Liberal] writers of today [1904, the year of this writing] are so imbued with imperialism they laud and glorify Lincoln for his usurpation of power.

Although [today, 1904,] well informed Republicans [Liberals] know that the war on the South was waged neither to save the Union nor to free slaves, it does not suit that party to be candid on this subject. Now and then, however, some Republican [Liberal] forgets *the party's policy of secrecy* and tells the truth. That boldly imperialistic Republican [Liberal] journal, the *Globe-Democrat*, of St. Louis, in its issue of April 9, 1900, had an article which uncovers facts, even to the foundation stones, on which rested the war of the 1860's. Consider the following:

> "Lincoln, Grant and the Union armies gave a victory to Hamiltonism (Monarchy) [liberalism] when it subjugated the Confederates (Democrats) [Conservatives] in the South. (This is strictly true; it was a victory over Democracy [conservatism] by Monarchy [liberalism].) The cardinal doctrines of Democracy [conservatism] are the enlargement of the power of the States [that is, states' rights]. All the prodigious energies of the war could not extinguish these. The lesson of the war was extreme and extraordinary, and yet in a sense ineffective."

Ineffective, because it did not crush out the very life of Democracy [conservatism]. Monarchists [Liberals] always appear to be ignorant of the fact that there is a streak of divinity in Democracy [conservatism] which cannot be killed. Monarchy [liberalism] a thousand and ten thousand times has fancied it has forever put an end to Democracy [conservatism], but sooner or later it rises up, fronts and fights for the rights of humanity with all its power.

"The Democrats [Conservatives]," continues the *Globe-Democrat*, "have been since the war more strenuous than before in insisting on the preservation of the power of the States."

The cardinal doctrine of the Democratic [Conservative] party has not been, since the formation of the Union, the enlargement of State power, but has been the preservation of the power reserved to the States by the Constitution. The cardinal power of the Republican [Liberal] party, since the day Mr. Lincoln assumed the Presidency, has been the enlargement of executive power. No well-informed man can deny this.[400]

Here are some more samples from those who lived in the Victorian Era, eyewitnesses to the right-wing policies of the American Conservative Party, the Democrats, and the left-wing policies of the American Liberal Party, the Republicans:

Abraham Lincoln, big government Liberal with socialistic proclivities. He will always be known in the South as "Dishonest Abe."

The Republican [Liberal] party is in no sense a National party; it is a party pledged to work for the downfall of Democracy [conservatism], the downfall of the [Founding Father's voluntary] Union, and the destruction of the United States Constitution. The religious creed of the party was hate of Democracy [conservatism], hate of the [original] Union, hate of the Constitution, and hate of the Southern people. . . . The Republican [Liberal] party is the first sectional party ever organized in this country. It does not know its own face and calls itself National, but *it is not National, it is sectional. It is the party of the North pledged against the South. It was organized with hatred of the Constitution.*

The Republican [Liberal] party that elected Abraham Lincoln is pledged to the downfall of the [Founders'] Union and the destruction of the United States Constitution. *William Lloyd Garrison believed in the Constitutional right to hold slaves, and said the Union must be dissolved to free them. He believed in the Constitutional right of secession, so was willing to publicly burn the Constitution to destroy that right and called it 'a compact with death and a league with hell.'* — Wendell Phillips of Massachusetts.[401]

"Mr. Lincoln assumed the dictatorship, *overthrew the government as it was formed by issuing a military edict or decree which changed the fundamental law of the land*, and declared that he would maintain this by all the military and naval power of the United States." — R. G. Horton, Northern author.[402]

"Mr. Lincoln, finding a geographical party in the process of formation, allowed himself to be placed at its head, and encouraged its action by *that sectional declaration, 'I believe this government cannot permanently endure half slave and half free.'* That expression gave hope to the abolitionists, and defeated Stephen Douglas." — George Lunt of Massachusetts.[403]

"I do not blame the [conservative] people of the South for seceding, for the men of that [Liberal] party about to take the reins of government in their hands are her mortal foes, and stand ready to trample her institutions under feet." — Benjamin F. Wade from Ohio, a confirmed South-loather.[404]

Radical Liberal Senator Benjamin F. Wade of Massachusetts.

"The Republican [Liberal] party is a conspiracy under the form, but in violation of the [conservative] spirit of the Constitution of the United States to exclude the [conservative] citizens of slaveholding States from all sharing in the government of the country, and to compel them to adapt their institutions to the opinions of the [liberal] citizens of the free [Northern] States." — Judge William A. Duer of New York.[405]

"The nomination of Mr. Lincoln was purely accidental, and that he was a sectional candidate upon merely sectional grounds none can deny and for the first time in the history of the republic, a candidate was thus presented for the suffrages of its citizens." — George Lunt of Massachusetts.[406]

"Many Republicans [Liberals] desire a dissolution of the Union and urge war as a means of accomplishing dissolution. . . . The leaders of the Republican party are striving to break up the Union under pretense of unbounded devotion to it. Hostility to slavery on the part of the [left-wing] disunionists is stronger than fidelity to the Constitution." — Stephen A. Douglas of Illinois.[407]

Liberal U.S. Representative William Alexander Duer of New York.

"I shall stress that this war was not waged by the [liberal] North to preserve the Union, or to maintain Republican [here meaning conservative] institutions, but to destroy both. It will be seen that the war changed the entire character and system of our government, overthrew the rights of States, and forced amendments against the action of the people. . . . At the very time the abolitionists [Liberals] were preaching a mad crusade against the Union, and *educating a generation to hate the government of our fathers*, Southern men, the great [Conservative] leaders of the South, were begging and imploring that the Union might be preserved." — R. G. Horton, Northern author.[408]

"Republican [Liberal] hate has blasted the fair heritage of our fathers. The prediction made two years before Daniel Webster's death has literally come true. He said: *'If these [left-wing] fanatics (abolitionists) ever get the power in their own hands they will override the Constitution, set the Supreme Court at defiance, change and make laws to suit themselves, lay violent hands on them who differ in opinion, or who dare question their fidelity, and finally deluge the country with blood'.*" — The *Cincinnati Enquirer*, January 15, 1881.[409]

If this sounds exactly like the Liberal Party of today, that is because it is! They are one and the same, the Liberal 21st-Century Democratic party being the direct descendant of the Liberal 19th-Century Republicans. How tragic that so few know this.

The Liberal version of the Civil War has indeed triumphed, for the average American is completely unaware of such facts, and worse, in many cases actually believes the opposite; that, for example, the Confederates were akin to totalitarian anarchists, radicals, and revolutionaries; that they were a kind of 19th-Century racist gestapo made up of white supremacists seeking to eliminate the black race and tear down both the U.S. Union and the government. Nothing could be further from the truth, of course, and, as part of our discussion on the Great War between conservative traditionalists and liberal progressives, we will now prove it.

The Left has long tried to compare Conservative Jefferson Davis and the Southern Confederacy with Nazi leader Adolf Hitler and the Third Reich. The opposite is true. Lincoln packed his administration and military with scores of socialists, just one reason national socialist Hitler wrote fondly of Lincoln's anti-states' rights policies in his biography, *Mein Kampf*.

In an attempt to permanently tarnish the conservative, traditional, Christian South, for over 100 years leftists, liberals, socialists, atheists, humanists, and communists have been comparing the Southern Confederacy to dictatorial Germany, and, after World War II, with Adolf Hitler and his socialist Nazi regime. Due to the general public's lack of knowledge of both American and world history, this ploy has been largely successful. If you ask 100 people on the street who was more similar to the early German socialists (and later Hitler), the South or the North, invariably most will say the former.

But, as this very book makes clear, the Southern Confederacy not only had nothing to do with socialism, the patriotic Americanism it espoused could not have been more different, for Americanism is conservative, socialism is liberal. Thus, this makes the Southern Confederacy identical to the Allied forces who were arrayed *against* Germany in the first half of the 20th Century. Evidence for this comes, in part, from the word Nazi itself.

Nazi is actually an acronym, one that therefore, technically, should be written in capital letters: NAZI. This acronym derives from the German term *Nationalsozialistische*, meaning "National Socialist," or more fully, the *Nationalsozialistische Deutsche Arbeiterpartei*, a phrase meaning the "National Socialist German Worker's Party." Though the Nazis were *national* socialists and today's American socialists are *democratic* socialists, nonetheless the two share many of the same ideas, beginning with the core doctrines of socialism. This is

Even anarchists are drawn to states' rights-hating Lincoln, one of whom was Russian revolutionary Mikhail Bakunin.

why, in the 1940s, Nazi socialists promoted the same basic themes that the modern American Socialist Party does: big government, anti-capitalism, social welfare, dependence on government, and a rigid even violent intolerance of outsiders and opposing views and groups.[410]

There is some confusion about Nazism because in Europe it is associated with fascism, dictatorship, autocracy, and totalitarianism, all which are considered (radical far) *right-wing* there, while here in the U.S.A. socialism is seen as a *left-wing* ideology.[411]

Whatever label we choose to give it, Nazism, and European socialism in general, could not be more dissimilar to the Southern Confederacy, which was a conservative republic, founded on conservative-libertarian principles. Unlike the big government-loving Nazis, for instance, the Confederacy emphasized a small limited central government. Unlike the states' rights-hating Nazis, Confederates saw states' rights as one of the most important of the constitutional freedoms (see Amendments Nine and Ten). Unlike the bigoted and racist Nazis,

19th-Century Southern Confederates were well-known for their hospitality, racial tolerance, universal Christian love, and humanitarianism[412]—all still true today.[413]

Thus, on the *American* political spectrum, the Nazis and the Confederates were located on the extreme ends from one another, with the German socialists on the far left side and the American Southern conservatives on the far right.[414]

This is not the first time the ignorant and the malicious have wrongly equated the right-wing Southern Confederacy with the left-wing faction of a major conflict. A generation earlier, in 1914, with the start of World War I, vengeful Liberals and uneducated Socialists, many even

from the South, began comparing the small government Confederates to the big government Germans, then an empire under the leadership of Emperor Wilhelm II—the man who led the "Central Powers" in a bid to take over Europe. To liken Conservative President Jefferson Davis and the Confederacy, a republic totally devoted to states' rights, personal liberty, and constitutional freedom, with a dictatorial European monarch and an imperialistic regime is ludicrous. Yet this is precisely what occurred in the early 20th Century.[415]

Conservative Sumner Archibald Cunningham of Tennessee.

In 1918, Sumner Archibald Cunningham, founder of *Confederate Veteran* magazine, made these comments on the topic:

Since the beginning of the great war in Europe the favorite pastime of many writers of this country has been *the comparison of Germany in this war to the South in the sixties, losing sight entirely of the reasons which led the Southern people to take up arms.* To our shame much of this unjust comparison has emanated from the South. What can we think of a Southern man who says that "the South had no more reason to fight for her rights in the territories than Germany has to fight for a place in the sun"? For the next hundred years tongue and pen will be busy fighting over the great battles of the World war, and we can but expect *those unfair comparisons of the South* to continue. *Ignorance as well as prejudice is responsible for much of it, and we should be able to combat that with knowledge of the real motive influencing our people in the War between the States.*[416]

These "prejudicial," "unfair comparisons," and the unending inherent South-shaming that goes along with them, continue into the present, and are part of the motivation behind this book.

Fortunately, many early Yankees refused to accept or believe the anti-South propaganda put out by Liberals regarding the Confederacy, Lincoln's War, and World War I. Matthew Page Andrews of Baltimore, Maryland, cites one of these intelligent, well-informed Northerners, Reverend A. W. Littlefield, in the following relevant article from 1918, entitled "Fighting For the Same Principle." It was written in the final year of "the War to End All Wars":

In view of the fact that *every newspaper and periodical in the North has in one way or another made some comparison between the Germany of to-day and the Southern Confederacy*, I feel sure that your readers will be particularly interested in seeing some extracts from a remarkable letter I received from Rev. A. W. Littlefield, of Needham, a loyal and liberal son of Massachusetts. He writes:

"Now, as evolution and growth are always likely to develop too far in any given direction unless restrained by opposing and complementary forces, the [liberal] North was sure to so overdevelop the issue of 'a perfect Union, one and inseparable,' that the States holding to 'consent of the governed, local self-government, and self-determination of sovereign States,' in this case the *[conservative] Southern States, were sure to array themselves against the [liberal] Northern States, which were the sponsors of Lincoln's view and that of the North generally.*

"Not only did the tendency of a principle to overdevelop itself show itself on our continent, but in Europe *Germany* has done this very thing to the fullest extent—viz, *carried federation to the complete extreme of imperialism.* And nothing but Allied success in this war can prevent the evolutionary process, unrestrained, from completely Romanizing (Prussianizing in this case) the whole world. And *nothing but the taking up of arms in 1861 by the South has prevented the imperializing of America,* in my judgment. I am not quite sure that Charles Francis Adams [Jr.] saw this fact. Certainly *most Americans are not in the least aware of it, if one may judge from history and current comment.* The mere A B C of evolutionary processes ought to teach people its tendency and its danger if restraining elements are not brought to bear. The [conservative] South furnished such restraint in America, and the [conservative] Allies are doing likewise in this world war.

"*If the South and the Allies occupy the same status in principle, why did not the South win? Not only because superior forces were arrayed against her, but because the North succeeded in convincing her people that the South was abjectly immoral, in that she 'held human beings in bondage.' This issue completely obscured the great politico-economic morality of the Southern people, the really true Americans.* That feeling, that the South should be crushed because of her 'iniquitous immorality,' was dominant in 1861 and still persists to-day.

"I surely believe that *had the North and England really understood that the South was fighting for precisely such principles as the Allies are fighting for to-day, there would have been no war against the South; and had that been the case, I also am of the opinion that the Anglo-Southern American principles would have so affected the world that Germany would never have gotten her start in her attempt to imperialize mankind.* But the evolutionary process was developing so fast in Europe and the seeming immorality of the South in holding human beings in bondage was brought so to the fore that the coalition of real Englishmen in the Old and the New World could not at that time be consummated. That union is now at hand, and there can be but one result.

"*I verily believe that in principle the new federation of the English-speaking peoples and their Latin allies could do no better when they come to draw up the constitution for world federation than to take for their model the Constitution of the Confederate States* with but very slight modifications. For unless such principles become the basis of this coming world federation, evolutionary processes, just because they constantly tend to over-development, will irresistibly carry world federation, even under Allied auspices, over the line into world imperialism, precisely as the Germans most desire and are so savagely fighting for."

Mr. Littlefield goes further to say that *the North was wrong in her contention and that might [physical force] triumphed because of the struggle of the South against undue centralization, great crushing combinations of business and provincialism, and commerce-killing high tariffs.* He adds "that *the so-called 'Lost Cause' is not dead, but has become the herald of the patriot dawn": that historically these things should be "settled right"; and that "the coming generation needs to realize these truths so that legislation may be modified away from imperialism back to true federalism [that is, confederalism] resting upon the true principles of consent of the governed, local self-government, and the self-determination of sovereign States."*[417]

The Conservative South fought for the Constitution and the government created by the Founding Fathers. The Liberal North fought against the Constitution and the government created by the Founding Fathers. It is clear, therefore, who was in the right and who was in the wrong.

THE REAL LOSER
OF LINCOLN'S WAR

IF WE ARE TO BELIEVE mainstream historians, "the South lost the Civil War," and thus this is what all of our schoolbooks, textbooks, and university press-published books tell us. But is this true?

The well-informed, the intellectually curious, and the naturally intelligent never accept "popular history" at face value. They know that in order to find the Truth they must dig below the surface of the mainstream media—that is, the liberalist propaganda, politically correct ideologies, socialistic theories, subjective emotionalism, overt revisionism, and baseless opinions that fill our history books. For Truth, in particular the historical Truth, will never be found in books written and published by uneducated individuals and biased organizations who detest the South and all that she stands for: American exceptionalism, tradition, patriotism, family values, and Christianity.

When we break through the glossy veneer of anti-South misinformation and disinformation regarding Lincoln's War and pry off the cover of the "Liberal Party's policy of secrecy,"[418] what do we discover? We find that the idea that "the South lost the Civil War," an article of faith in the anti-South movement, is nothing more than another Yankee myth; a simplistic fiction that, like every other leftist belief, is designed to mask reality while promoting progressive ideals.

The reality that the Left is concealing is this: The South did not lose the Civil War. *America, or rather all Americans, lost the Civil War.* For tragically, the Founders' agriculturally-based Confederacy, with its

small, weak central government, was overturned by Lincoln's industrially-based, federated American System, with its massive, all-powerful central government. And every American citizen, including the liberal-socialists who have always supported this type of large bloated federal entity, have been suffering ever since.

It is true that this liberalizing process toward empire was already well underway long before Lincoln. It was Lincoln, however, who attempted to finish the job using total war on the American people and the Constitution.

Liberal Union General Winfield Scott of Virginia.

"Right makes might," he once observed icily,[419] this despite the fact that many of his own cabinet members and constituents said that the Southern states should be allowed to secede "in peace." These included such Yankee luminaries as Winfield Scott, Henry Ward Beecher, and Horace Greeley.[420]

How tragic, for in the end Lincoln did not "preserve the Union" or "free the slaves,"[421] the very reasons he gave the American public for starting, waging, and prolonging his War.[422] As U.S. president, his only primary functions were to support the Constitution and enforce federal laws,[423] both jobs which he either flagrantly ignored or refused to do. Then, for political gain, he contaminated race relations in the South[424] (by artificially and self-servingly pitting the two races against one another).[425] Finally, he destroyed the concept of Union (a *voluntary* association of states) as laid down by the Founding Generation.[426]

Many in the South still consider America's deep-seated black and white racism to be the greatest legacy of Lincoln's War.[427] After all, the antebellum South, in comparison to the antebellum North, was relatively free of the type of racism found above the Mason-Dixon Line at the time.[428] As early as 1831 individuals like French aristocrat Alexis de

Tocqueville, who toured the South and the North that year, noticed that Southerners were "much more tolerant and compassionate" toward blacks than Northerners. This is why, while visiting America in the 1850s, Englishman Sir Charles Lyell observed that the Southern states justifiably "make louder professions than the Northerners of democratic principles and love of equality."[429]

After his tour of the states in 1831, Tocqueville summed up his observations this way:

> Whosoever has inhabited the United States must have perceived that in those parts of the Union in which the negroes are no longer slaves, they have in no wise drawn nearer to the whites. On the contrary, *the prejudice of the race appears to be stronger in the States which have abolished slavery than in those where it still exists; and nowhere is it so intolerant as in those States where servitude never has been known.*
>
> It is true that in the [liberal] North of the Union marriages may be legally contracted between negroes and whites; but *public opinion would stigmatize a man who should connect himself with a negress as infamous, and it would be difficult to meet with a single instance of such a union.* The electoral franchise has been conferred upon the negroes in almost all the States in which slavery has been abolished; but if they come forward to vote, *their lives are in danger.* If oppressed, they may bring an action at law, but they will find none but whites among their judges; and although they may legally serve as jurors, *prejudice repulses them from that office. The same schools do not receive the child of the black and of the European. In the theatres, gold can not procure a seat for the servile race beside their former masters; in the hospitals they lie apart; and although they are allowed to invoke the same Divinity as the whites, it must be at a different altar, and in their own churches with their own clergy.* The gates of Heaven are not closed against these unhappy beings; but their inferiority is continued to the very confines of the other world; *when the negro is defunct, his bones are cast aside, and the distinction of condition prevails even in the equality of death. The [Northern] negro is free, but he can share neither the rights, nor the pleasures, nor the labour, nor the afflictions, nor the tomb of him whose equal he has been declared to be; and he can not meet him upon fair terms in life or in death.*
>
> *In the [conservative] South, where slavery still exists, the negroes are less carefully kept apart; they sometimes share the labour and the recreations of the* whites; *the whites consent to intermix with them to a certain extent,* and although the legislation treats them more harshly, *the habits of the*

[Southern] people are more tolerant and compassionate. In the South the master is not afraid to raise his slave to his own standing, because he knows that he can in a moment reduce him to the dust at pleasure. *In the North the white no longer distinctly perceives the barrier which separates him from the degraded race, and he shuns the negro with the more pertinacity, since he fears lest they should some day be confounded together.*

French diplomat, traveler, and historian Alexis de Tocqueville.

Among the Americans of the South, Nature sometimes reasserts her rights, and restores a transient equality between the blacks and the whites; but in the North pride restrains the most imperious of human passions. The American of the Northern States would perhaps allow the negress to share his licentious pleasures if the laws of his country did not declare that she may aspire to be the legitimate partner of his bed; but he recoils with horror from her who might become his wife.

Thus it is, in the United States, *that the prejudice which repels the negroes seems to increase in proportion as they are emancipated, and inequality is sanctioned by the manners while it is effaced from the laws of the country.* But if the relative position of the two races which inhabit the United States is such as I have described, it may be asked why the Americans have abolished slavery in the North of the Union, why they maintain it in the South, and why they aggravate its hardships there? The answer is easily given. It is not for the good of the negroes, but for that of the whites, that measures are taken to abolish slavery in the United States.[430]

What Tocqueville refers to as "those States where servitude never has been known" is a reference to what were then called the Western Territories (today the Western states), at the time an area with the least number of blacks and where slavery had never been practiced. It was here that he found white racism toward blacks the strongest.

To emphasize these facts, the Frenchman goes on to point out that while slaves had been freed in the North and now had so-called "full equal rights," Northern white society continued to strongly discourage blacks, often with the threat of death, from voting, sitting on juries, or attending white schools or white churches. According to Tocqueville, blacks in the "liberal abolitionist North" were not even permitted to sit next to whites in theaters, take a sick bed next to them in Northern hospitals, or be buried next to them in death.[431]

Southern whites and blacks got along just fine—until nosy Northerners began to interfere in the early 1800s. What was the point of meddling? Southern abolition was already in full swing. It was South-hating, pushy, self-righteous liberalism, pure and simple.

As history clearly shows, it was only *after* Lincoln's War that race relations truly deteriorated in the South, and nearly all of this was instigated by Northern Liberals as part of so-called "Reconstruction." As one Southerner observed in the postbellum period, the whites of Virginia were much more prejudiced against blacks *after* the conflict than they had been before.[432] And here was one of the true tragedies of the Liberal's vindictive Reconstruction program, which even leftist historians now agree was a massive "political blunder and a social outrage"—"unconstitutional, revolutionary, and void," for it alienated the once harmonious Southern races, cutting blacks off from the only people who understood them and who would have been willing to help them: Southern whites.[433]

Such intolerance was not inherent to the South. It was the product of the Liberals' fictitious "race war," whose purpose during Reconstruction was to foment hatred and violence between the races (the same purpose for which Liberals use it today). A divided people are easier to control socially, economically, politically, and psychologically, which is the very foundation of liberalism. Hence, we find that a strong tendency toward racism, divisiveness, fear-mongering, graft, criminality, lying, and cheating, as well as an admiration for thugs and outlaws, was indeed endemic to the 19th-Century Liberal Party—as it still is. In 1920 Southern historian Mildred Lewis Rutherford wrote:

> *Before the [Eighteen-] Sixties, lynchings of negroes in the South were of very rare occurrence—there was no occasion for it—we had no incendiary literature distributed among the negroes until [Liberal South-hater] John Brown tried it and failed.* The incendiary literature is now largely responsible for present day conditions. *The South is the negro's friend. The South wants the negro to stay in the South.* The South has not encouraged immigration from [that is, to] the Latin States for fear of race antagonism [like Lincoln and his American Colonization Society did]. *All that the South asks is to be let alone in her management of the negro, so that the friendly relations may continue.*[434]

Thankfully, interracial relations have improved enormously since the Liberals' vengeful and disastrous Reconstruction programs ended and the last Yankee soldier was driven from the South in 1877. Left on their own, white and black Southerners have naturally gravitated back toward the open and affectionate relationships they had before Lincoln invaded their homeland.[435]

But Lincoln did accomplish what he actually truly set out to do in private: not "free the slaves," but stamp out both states' rights and the secession movement while instituting a liberal, socialistic form of government—in reality, a massive nanny

Like nearly all of the American chief executives before him, Conservative President Andrew Jackson correctly referred to the U.S.A. as a "Confederate Republic."

state, the Left-wing version of an empire—that has made political slaves of all Americans. In the process, he turned what U.S. Presidents George Washington, Thomas Jefferson, and Andrew Jackson all lovingly called a "Confederated Republic" (i.e., a "Confederacy")[436] into a nation, something the Southern Founders certainly never intended or envisioned. "Our government," postwar 19th-Century pundits later correctly observed, "is wholly perverted from its true design."[437] The Washington *Post* wrote on August 14, 1906:

> Let us be frank about it. The day the people of the North responded to Abraham Lincoln's call for troops to coerce sovereign States, *the Republic died and the Nation was born.*[438]

In Chief Justice John Marshall's day the U.S.A. was known as "the Confederacy," or more accurately, "The Confederate States of America," the name later intentionally adopted by the seceding Southern states.

As such, nation-building nationalist Lincoln must be considered nothing less than the "Great Federator": the creator of American big government for big business, with its big spending, Big Brother mind-set.[439] He is also either fully or partially responsible for the following: America's internal revenue program (the IRS), American protectionism, American imperialism, American expansionism, America's bloated military despotism, America's enormous standing army, America's central banking system, America's corporate welfare system (which Lincoln called "internal improvements"), America's nation-building agenda, and America's deeply entangled foreign alliances. (Lincoln apparently never read Thomas Jefferson's admonition that America's approach to foreign affairs should be: "Peace, commerce, and honest friendship with all nations, entangling alliances with none.")[440]

And here, politically at least, is Lincoln's greatest legacy, for big government opened the door to federal tyranny and its many dangers and horrors: the consolidation of governmental powers, the centralization of Executive power, unchecked presidential power, the growth of the nanny state, unlimited abuses and corruption, and the progressive, intrusive, oppressive, tax-and-spend government that American citizens now labor under, whether they are Lincolnian Liberals themselves, or Independent, Conservative, or Libertarian.[441]

In short, though Liberals Alexander Hamilton, John Marshall, and Daniel Webster had all helped further centralize the government before Lincoln came along,[442] it was Lincoln who was directly responsible for completely nationalizing America; that is, for "establishing the supremacy of the national government over the states."[443] This he did, not only through brutal warfare, but by creating a national army, national taxes, a national banking system, and a national currency, all which greatly extended and strengthened the power of the central government.[444] And all of this at the expense of individual civil liberties and states' rights.[445]

In 1903 celebrated Yankee historian James Ford Rhodes of Ohio, who referred to the Federal government that Lincoln created as a "dictatorship,"[446] made the following accurate prophecy:

> Mr. Lincoln assumed extra legal powers, at the same time trying to give to those illegal acts the color of legality. Lincoln has made a precedent which future rulers will imitate. What Lincoln excused and defended will be assumed as the right for rulers to follow.[447]

Victorian Southerners too predicted, with unerring accuracy, the course the U.S. would take if Lincoln's Liberal American System were adopted. In December 1866, not even two years after the War ended, Robert E. Lee wrote the following in a letter to Lord Acton:

> . . . I yet believe that *the maintenance of the rights and authority reserved to the States and to the people, not only essential to the adjustment and balance of the general system, but the safeguard to the continuance of a free government.* I consider it as the chief source of stability to our political system, whereas *the consolidation of the States into one vast republic, sure to be aggressive abroad and despotic at home, will be the certain precursor of that ruin which has overwhelmed all those that have preceded it.*[448]

As Lee anticipated, thanks in great part to Lincoln, the U.S. Federal government has continued to consolidate, growing more aggressive abroad and more despotic at home with each passing year.

Between the Depression years (1930s) and the World War II era (1940s), for example, tremendous governmental expansion occurred, particularly in the Executive Branch, with new committees, bureaus, agencies, boards, and administrations multiplying almost beyond imagination.[449] Between 1998 and 2008 alone the U.S. government grew 71 percent, a trend that continued unabated with the election of the Lincoln-worshiping radical, socialistic, and progressive Liberal, Barack Hussein Obama, to the presidency in 2008 and 2012.[450] During his first term alone he doubled the national debt—more than has been accumulated by *all* of our prior presidents, from George Washington to George W. Bush.[451] According to one authority writing in mid 2010:

> Since President Obama took office the national debt has increased by $3.7 trillion. To put that in perspective, it took the U.S. 216 years, from 1776 until 1992, to accumulate the same amount of debt that Obama has borrowed in 2.5 years. It's higher than any time in American history, equaling more than 95% of our entire economy. We are currently borrowing roughly 40 cents of every dollar we spend and sending the bill to our children and grandchildren.[452]

Following in the footsteps of big government Liberal Lincoln is what today's progressives and socialists call "progress."

In 1980 Ronald Reagan spoke for traditional Southerners, as well as for lovers of liberty everywhere, when he stated that many Americans now feel similar to what their colonial ancestors felt two centuries ago: encumbered, smothered, and even subjugated by a government that has become too big, too complex, too controlling, too impersonal, and too inefficient to work for the benefit of the average person.[453]

The outsized, gluttonous, power-hungry, political behemoth Reagan is referring to was the unrealized dream of nearly every Federalist, Whig, Liberal, progressive, centralist, and consolidationist between 1776 and 1860.

Conservative Confederate General Robert E. Lee: just one of millions of slavery-hating Southern abolitionists who believed in small government and states' rights.

In 1865, at Appomattox, it was Abraham Lincoln who finally made that Federalist dream come true:[454] on April 9 of that year, the doctrine of secession was finally suppressed, along with the constitutional view that the U.S. was a confederation of independent nation-states,[455] that is, "distinct nations."[456]

Now, under Lincoln's anti-South program of invasion, emancipation, confiscation, conflagration, extermination, occupation, penalization, and humiliation,[457] America's people were "irrevocably bound together"[458] in what his devoted communist followers approvingly called an "indivisible nation":[459] the states lost their sovereignty (not in reality, but only in the eyes of Liberals), and the U.S. became a single federated nation operating under an all-powerful, centralized big government[460]—more menacing and omnipotent than at any other time in American history up to that point.[461] The Old South died and the Yankee-inspired, so-called "New South" was born the day Lee stacked arms at Appomattox.

Sadly, as President Obama repeatedly did, American presidents (from both major parties) have been walking through the socialistic door Lincoln opened ever since, even committing many of the same crimes he did; but now without punishment or recrimination, often without notice or comment, and sometimes even with the blessings of a majority of the American people.[462]

One of the U.S. presidents who patterned his social legislation after Lincoln was Franklin Delano Roosevelt,[463] the man who launched the modern welfare state.[464] As with his Liberal "Civil War" predecessor, Roosevelt's "New Deal" programs and other policies led to growing concern over governmental centralization, American imperialism, interference with free enterprise, fears of socialism, and alarm that the U.S. was turning into an "international police power." Indeed, it was under Roosevelt, who was given dictatorial control over nearly all areas of human life (agriculture, industry, finance, and labor),[465] that the federal government first truly exploded in size, with the creation of countless "committees, bureaus, agencies, administrations and boards." And even though the U.S. government itself acknowledges that the result has been "great waste, inefficiency and expense," new, unnecessary federal agencies continue to be created into the present day.[466]

It is no surprise to learn then that the term "New Deal" was not an invention of the Roosevelt administration. Rather, it dates back to 1865, when it was coined to describe Lincoln's socialistic domestic policies,[467] many which were meant to continue the Liberals' unconstitutional plan to further embroil the government in non-governmental business.[468] A partial list of items from Lincoln's own New Deal program includes:

The Morrill Tariff (1861)
The First Income Tax (1861)
An Expanded Postal Service (1861)
The Homestead Act (1862)
The Morrill Land-Grant College Act (1862)
The Department of Agriculture (1862)
The Bureau of Printing and Engraving (1862)
Transcontinental Railroad land grants (1862, 1863, 1864)
The National Banking Acts (1862, 1863, 1864, 1865, 1866)
The position of Comptroller of the Currency (1863)
The National Academy of Science (1863)
Free Urban mail delivery (1863)
The Yosemite nature reserve land grant (1864)
The Contract Labor Act (1864)
The Office of Immigration (1864)
The Railway mail service (1864)
The Money order system (1864)[469]

With such a socialistic atmosphere surrounding the Lincoln administration, it is little wonder that 61 new trade unions were formed between the years 1863 and 1865 alone.[470]

How similar Lincoln and Roosevelt were! If the Lincoln years represent the Second American Revolution, then the Roosevelt years were truly the "Third American Revolution." For it was during this period that the concept of the national government underwent a complete transformation, from passive and aloof to aggressive and interventionist.[471]

Leftist New Deal Presidents Franklin D. Roosevelt and Abraham Lincoln had much in common.

With the ongoing and unrelenting erosion of her

Constitution and civil liberties, we have to wonder how much longer what was intended by the Founding Fathers to be the "States United"[472] will remain the "United States." We began as a conservative country of enlightened laws and standards, built on what was originally a republic with a confederated government (the Confederacy), held in place by a confederate constitution (the Articles of Confederation).[473] Our Constitution, in turn, was founded on the conservative ideas of inalienable natural rights, states' rights, self-government, the right of secession, a system of checks and balances, and, the very heart of the document, the separation of powers.[474] Without these, what will become of what was once the world's greatest confederacy, what Confederate Vice President Alexander H. Stephens rightly called "the best government the world ever saw"?[475] Our leaders have forgotten Thomas Jefferson's sagacious statement that "the people . . . are the ultimate guardians of their own liberty."[476]

More to the point, is the government we now "enjoy" the one the Southern Founders had in mind for 21st-Century America? Hardly. Throughout their lives, most, like Jefferson (author of the Declaration of Independence), James Madison (the "Father of the Constitution"), and George Mason (the inspiration behind the Bill of Rights), all ardently preached and warned against both the federating tendencies (empire building) of government and the very crimes and excesses that politicians like Lincoln repeatedly engage in. Will the American people ever reclaim their Ninth and Tenth Amendment rights, rights they once held precious but which were ripped from their grasp in 1865 by "Honest Abe"?[477] Our new President Donald J. Trump may hold the key.

It is for instituting big government, infringing on individual rights, and launching a needless and illegitimate War comprising some 10,455 bloody battles and skirmishes[478]—one that (according to Northern statistics) killed at least 3,000 people a week for 208 weeks (note: 25 percent of all Southern white men of military age and one of every nineteen white Southerners died)[479]—that Lincoln will always be remembered by liberty-loving Americans, wherever they are from or live.

In short, Lincoln's War was caused by the recklessness, inhumanity, and aggressiveness of its highest leader, a big government Liberal who could not tolerate the rival views of small government Conservatives.

And it was this same man who illegally called for 75,000 troops and ordered them to invade the South (where American conservatism has always been the most heavily concentrated). However, Northern states, like Maryland, who resisted Lincoln's unconstitutional, Nazi-like rulings, were also invaded, their state governments shut down, and their legislators illegally imprisoned.[480]

We will recall that many of the Union officers who led these unlawful campaigns against their fellow Americans were "Forty-Eighters," disgruntled foreign socialists and communists, radical immigrants who had come to the U.S. after their left-wing revolution failed in Europe in 1848. Naturally, all of them gravitated to Liberal Lincoln and the North, rightly viewing Conservative Davis and the South as the arch enemies of their ultimate plan: "the reconstruction of a social [that is, socialist] world" in America.[481]

By sheer numerical and economic superiority—along with the North's illegal and inhumane naval blockade, brutal "scorched earth" military policies, and disregard for both international law and established ethics—on April 9, 1865, Liberal Lincoln, the Liberal Party (then the Republicans), and the American Liberal movement, forced Conservative Davis, the Conservative Party (then the Democrats), and the American Conservative movement into surrendering many of their constitutional rights.

Conservative Confederate General Joseph Wheeler of Georgia knew the truth about the Southern Cause.

Despite his best efforts, along with those of his South-hating, Constitution-loathing, freedom-despising, anti-American socialist and communist supporters, Lincoln was not able to kill off the spirit that prompted the conservative South and her conservative Northern compatriots to take up arms. For, as we have made clear, the driving force behind the Southern Confederacy had nothing to do with slavery or the destruction of the Union, as our Yankee-slanted historically inaccurate "history" books tell us. It was a love of liberty, the U.S. Constitution, and self-government. This is why, in 1899, Conservative Confederate General Joseph Wheeler could say:

> When the South yielded, it was to numbers, battalions, artillery; to the unlimited resources of the Federal Government. The armies of the South laid down their arms, but not one iota of their belief in the truth and justice of their cause did they surrender.[482]

It is true that the U.S. flag, not the C.S. flag, now flies over the Southern states. What Lincoln did not defeat, however, was Dixie's soul: her sense of independence, her natural pugnaciousness, her "rebelliousness," her passion for freedom, her love of self-determination.[483] These traits were, after all, the real core of the Confederacy and her conservative citizens. And they still are. For the Confederacy was not a place, a region on a map that could be overthrown and subdued, as even some Northerners once recognized. In the late 1800s a wise man from Massachusetts wrote of the South:

> Such character and achievement were not all in vain; that though the Confederacy fell as an actual physical power, *it lives eternally in its just cause—the cause of constitutional liberty*.[484]

Southerners could not have agreed more.

On November 7, 1864, the same day he advocated the official start of Southern emancipation[485] and six months before the end of Lincoln's War, Conservative President Jefferson Davis stood before the Confederate Congress and said:

> . . . if the campaign against Richmond had resulted in success instead of failure; if the valor of the army, under the leadership of its accomplished commander, had resisted in vain the overwhelming masses which were, on the contrary, decisively repulsed; if we had been compelled to evacuate Richmond as well as Atlanta, the Confederacy would have remained as erect and defiant as ever. Nothing could have been changed in the purpose of its Government, in the indomitable valor of its troops, or in the unquenchable spirit of

its people. The baffled and disappointed foe would in vain have scanned the reports of your proceedings, at some new legislative seat, for any indication that progress had been made in his gigantic task of conquering a free people. *The truth so patent to us must ere long be forced upon the reluctant Northern mind. There are no vital points on the preservation of which the continued existence of the Confederacy depends. There is no military success of the enemy which can accomplish its destruction. Not the fall of Richmond, nor Wilmington, nor Charleston, nor Savannah, nor Mobile, nor of all combined, can save the enemy from the constant and exhaustive drain of blood and treasure which must continue until he shall discover that no peace is attainable unless based on the recognition of our indefeasible rights.*[486]

Conservative Confederate President Jefferson Davis admonished Liberals for trying to "conquer a free people" and their "indefeasible rights," but his warning went unheeded.

Davis' words, though 145 years old, explain why, to this day, traditional Southerners are "still fightin' the War." Not the "Civil War." But the war to reclaim America's true political heritage, the very one Lincoln destroyed on April 9, 1865, at Appomattox;[487] the one he promised *all* Americans in his Gettysburg Address on November 19, 1863; the same Jeffersonian heritage that, two years later, he overturned and caused to "perish from the earth"; namely, a constitutional government "of the people, by the people, for the people."[488]

Northerners created Lincoln, Northerners elected Lincoln, Northerners supported Lincoln, Northerners worshiped Lincoln, Northerners murdered Lincoln, and Northerners fabricated his mythology after his death. Perhaps then it takes a Northerner to truly get to the heart of the matter.

Here is what one of them, Maryland journalist, H. L. Mencken, had to say about Lincoln's most famous declamation:

> The Gettysburg speech was at once the shortest and the most famous oration in American history. . . the highest emotion reduced to a few poetical phrases. Lincoln himself never even remotely approached it. It is genuinely stupendous. But let us not forget that it is poetry, not logic; beauty, not sense. Think of the argument in it. Put it into the cold words of everyday. The doctrine is simply this: that the Union soldiers who died at Gettysburg sacrificed their lives to the cause of self-determination—that government of the people, by the people, for the people, should not perish from the earth. *It is difficult to imagine anything more untrue. The Union soldiers in the battle actually fought against self-determination; it was the Confederates who fought for the right of their people to govern themselves.*[489]

British journalist Alistair Cooke concurred, calling Lincoln's Gettysburg Address a classic work of oratory of highly questionable reasoning.[490]

The great irony of Lincoln is that during his lifetime he was voted America's worst president, and the direct cause of disunion, America's bloodiest and most expensive war, and the unnecessary deaths of untold thousands. He was also denounced as the leader of the Union's most corrupt and diabolical administration, and the man responsible for the loss of the Founding Father's Confederate government, the destruction of the original Constitution, increased racial strife, and the near annihilation of much of what was good, beautiful, noble, and unique about the South. Yet *after* death, thanks to the diligent and overly imaginative work of Lincoln hagiographers, eulogists, and mythologists, he was recast as the Nation's Healer, the Great Emancipator, the Great Peacemaker, the Great Preserver, the Greatest of all Presidents: "Honest Abe."[491]

However, only one of these two legacies can be authentic, not both. The traditional South will adhere to the former, for as true Americans we believe it is more important to be historically accurate than politically correct.[492]

This typical piece of artistic Northern propaganda portrays an impassioned Lincoln delivering his Gettysburg Address on November 19, 1863, to a spellbound teary-eyed audience—another piece of Yankee mythology. Lincoln himself later admitted that the speech fell on his listeners like a "wet blanket." "It was a flat failure," he bemoaned, and "the people are disappointed." Little wonder. It was all an overt lie; a part of what I call "The Great Yankee Coverup": the Northern concealment of the truth about Lincoln's War. Liberals are still hiding that truth today. And what is that truth? It was the conservative South that was fighting for "a government of the people, by the people, for the people." It was the liberal North that was trying to destroy it.

The so-called "Lost Cause" was not lost, as South-haters love repeating *ad infinitum*. They want to believe that it is was "lost" so they do not have to deal with it anymore, and so they can get about the business of enlarging the central government, social engineering America, and dividing and enslaving the people. Like other members of the Left-Wing, they cannot tolerate views that contradict their own, and so ideas that differ from theirs are either ignored, rewritten, demonized, or suppressed using fraud, defamation, and fear-mongering.

But this "Cause" cannot be swept away or forgotten, nor can it be revised into something that it was not. Why? Because the so-called "Southern Cause" or "Confederate Cause" was Americanism (conservatism) and the concomitant government known as a "confederacy," or what Montesquieu called a "confederate republic": a small nearly powerless central government headed by a chief executive with severely restricted powers, and comprised of sovereign nation-states in which supreme power resides in its citizens, who elect officers to represent them.[493] The "Rebel Cause" then was neither specifically Southern or even Confederate. It was American, rooted in the conservative ideals established by the Founding Generation and ensconced in our most sacred national document, the U.S. Constitution.

Ideas like conservatism cannot be "lost," they cannot be crushed, they cannot be suppressed, they cannot be deleted or shredded, and they cannot be destroyed by either law or war. They exist apart from human intervention, for they are of the mind and heart. And this is precisely where the worldwide love of national freedom, states' rights, and personal liberty reside. Out of reach of the Liberal's intolerance, arrogance, racism, and megalomania, conservatism burns like an eternal flame wherever the light of freedom shines. And it is burning today more brightly than ever before in human history. This is why *true* early conservatives never referred to the Southern Cause as the "Lost Cause." Rather they used phrases like the "Sacred Cause," the "Holy Cause," and the "Immortal Cause," for "principles never die."[494]

This is why Yankee Conservative Clement L. Vallandigham could say to his Liberal opponents during the War:

> You have not conquered the South; you never will. The war for the Union is in your hands a most bloody and costly failure. . . . Money you have expended without limit, and blood poured out like water. . . . Defeat, debt, taxation, and sepulchers—these are your only trophies.[495]

In 1918 Sam M. Gaines of Washington, D.C. penned the following article entitled, "The Fight, Not the Cause, Was Lost," which is germane to our discussion:

> Certain writers and speakers have industriously propagated the idea that in the result of the War between the States the Confederate cause was lost. They have taken much pains to fix in the public mind a distinct impression that the South's cause is a "lost cause." *This transparent fallacy* has found lodgment not only in the minds of the unthinking class in the South, by whom the phrase is frequently used to characterize the result of the war, but also in the minds of some Southerners whose intelligence should have prevented them from adopting this paradoxical term as a correct expression of the consequence of the war. In the latter class may be placed Mr. R. W. Townsend, the author of a volume of poetry entitled "The Passing of the Confederate." In this poem Mr. Townsend declares that "all for which we fought is lost."
>
> It will be necessary to set forth briefly what constituted the South's cause and the origin of it. *To say that the South's cause is a "lost cause" is a radically erroneous and misleading confusion of terms. The South's cause, the principles for which the Southern people stood, was in no manner affected by the war. The [conservative] political convictions of the people of the Southern States touching their right of self-rule constituted the South's "cause." Those convictions as to the fundamental principles of government which are essential to liberty and were made secure by the fathers in organic law were not changed, modified, or uprooted by the result of the armed conflict.*
>
> The conventions which framed the Articles of Confederation [1781] and the [U.S.] Constitution [1788] made a new departure in government. *They formed a system of government in which supreme authority was vested in the people as constituting distinct States, making government at all times subordinate to the people's will. The dominating purpose of the governments, State and Federal, was to secure the liberty of the individual and the right of the people to rule through the sovereignty of the body politic.* Community independence, based on law susceptible of change only in the prescribed legal mode, was the keystone of the State and Federal governments.
>
> For fifty years the people of the North and South were in general accord as to the nature and extent of the powers of the Federal government. The principles established by the fathers were avowed, confirmed, and sustained in practice for half a century by the people

of both sections. *The wildest political dreamer in those days never asserted that the Federal government possessed supreme authority over the people of the several States.*

Finally, discord between the sections was fomented and flagrantly aroused by *a [Liberal-Socialist] faction in the North which arbitrarily claimed the authority to regulate or destroy certain rights and institutions of the [Conservative] Southern people which had been recognized and guaranteed protection by the solemn compact between the States in 1787. This meddlesome interference with the private affairs of the people of the South was wholly unwarranted and lawless and destructive of the principles of the Union.*

The hostility thus aroused, for which the North was solely responsible, resulted [in 1854] in the organization of a political party [the Republican Party, then the Liberal Party] in the North which disavowed allegiance to the Constitution and fidelity to the principles of the government. (Yet in their own conceit they were not traitors.) *This party, led by Lincoln, proclaimed a doctrine at once new, revolutionary, and subversive of liberty; it asserted that the Federal government possessed sovereign authority and could enforce its decrees on the people of the Southern States by force, if necessary. This party came into control of the government in 1861, and thus was overthrown the beneficent system of free institutions which was conceived by the wisdom and consecrated by the blood of our forefathers. Thenceforward the Federal government was administered, not in accordance with the Constitution and the laws appertaining thereto, but in conformity to the autocratic and idiosyncratic theories of President Lincoln. For the first time in this country he substituted a personal government for a government of law.*

Both the conservative U.S. Founding Fathers and the conservative C.S. Founding Fathers based their form of government on what 18th-Century French judicial scholar Baron de Montesquieu called a "confederate republic."

In this crisis the Southern people [Conservatives] remained faithful to the traditional principles of the government, the principles which they had upheld from the beginning. They had lived all their lives in the rarified atmosphere of the ideals of the fathers. They prized liberty above all other earthly possessions. *They believed, and the doctrine is steeped in the wisdom of the ages, that the centralization of power is incompatible with*

*liberty; that freedom abides only where sovereign, inalienable power is inherent
in the people, constituting separate States. These principles incorporated into
law and approved by experience constituted the reason, the factors, and the
impelling purpose of, and justification of conscience for, the South's action
from 1860 to 1865, inclusive.*

Returning to the question under consideration, the fate of the
South's cause, did the result of the war change the convictions of the
Southern people as to the wisdom of the principles of government
established by the fathers or deprive them of those principles? The
political principles which composed the South's cause were as vital and
had as strong a hold on the minds and hearts of the Southern people
after the war as before it. *The administration of President Lincoln,
conducted in conformity to his assertion that a State occupied the same relation
to the Federal government that a county occupied to the State, and the
administrations of his successors who were in sympathy with his purpose to
abrogate the power of the States and thus to destroy self government by
consolidating all authority in the government at Washington brought to the
people of the South new and overwhelming evidence that the principles for
which they had fought were indispensable to the maintenance of popular rights.*

Another conclusive proof that the South's [conservative] cause is
not lost has been afforded by the [liberal] North. Within the last few
years the Northern States generally, realizing that all power was being
filched from them, have resumed the exercise of the rights established
by the founders. The people of the North have put into effective
operation within their respective States the principles of local
self-government, of State sovereignty, which the South has adhered to
in peace and contended for in war. The initiative, the referendum,
and the recall are some of the agencies being employed by the people
to restore government to its original foundations.

Moreover, it may be said parenthetically that *the discredited,
antiquated, and alien theories of government which President Lincoln put into
operation and attempted to engraft upon our system have been thoroughly
repudiated and abandoned by the people of the Northern and Northwestern
States.* The blinding passions of the war having subsided, a freer
intellectual atmosphere is abroad, and there is a general recrudescence
of sentiment favoring a return to the rule of the people. The people
of the several States have asserted their sovereign authority by taking
into their own hands the reins of government, thus putting into
operation the principles established by the founders of the republic.
Thus has been vindicated the enormous sacrifice of blood and treasure made by

the South in behalf of free institutions, and Jefferson Davis, vilified and traduced as a traitor, is seen in his true character, the patriot of patriots.

Mr. Townsend fails to differentiate between the Southern cause and the result of the war between the North and the South. They are entirely different things. The one is a question of principle, the other of physical and material strength. The South lost the fight and much of its property, but was not in any degree deprived of the principles for which it contended. The devotion of the Southern people to their principles and their adherence to them did not depend on their success in the war. Neither the vitality nor the justice of a cause lies in the physical strength of its supporters. War is a contest of brute force and cannot determine the truth or falsity of the principles adhered to on either side. The principles which the South avowed were not subjected to shot, shell, and blade. Those weapons were effective only in determining the comparative physical and material avoirdupois of the contending sections. The fact that the South proved the weaker did not lessen its devotion to its principles nor make its cause a "lost cause."[96]

The Confederate soldier loved the government and the Constitution created by the Founding Generation. Liberals under Lincoln were threatening to destroy both. The so-called "Southern Cause" was a conservative attempt to preserve them.

As is clear, in essence "the principles maintained by the South were essentially the same as those previously upheld by the North," that is, prior to Lincoln's War. The common charge then that "the cause of the South was an unworthy one," that it was "rebelliousness," "un-American," and even "treasonous," are all "misrepresentative and false in perspective and proportion."[497] Thus it was often said of the Confederate soldier:

> No more sacred principles ever inspired human hearts than thrilled the souls of these patriotic brothers, who bravely and conscientiously *fought for State independence, State sovereignty, and self-government in the defense of their beloved Southland, to repel from their homes an invading and relentless foe bent on pillage and subjugation.* Their love for the Southern cause [conservatism] was proverbial; it entered into the warp and woof of their beings. To live in the hearts of survivors is not to die. It is a memorial more enduring than bronze or granite. The going away of these noble brothers leaves vacancies in the ranks of the Confederate veterans, vacant seats in the sanctuary of God, and vacant chairs in the home circle. Hope inspired of love crowns them with blood-bought seats in the heavenly bivouac in the home of the soul.[498]

In 1918 former Confederate General Bennett H. Young echoed these sentiments:

> The cause that gave to the world Robert E. Lee, Stonewall Jackson, Joseph E. Johnston, Albert Sidney Johnston, Nathan Bedford Forrest, Joseph Wheeler, John H. Morgan, J. E. B. Stuart, Wade Hampton, and John B. Gordon cannot and will not be forgotten.
>
> If those who were actors in the conflict or descendants of those who made such marvelous record should fail or refuse to honor the Confederate cause and those who battled for the rights of the South, the world will and ought to reckon them as ingrates and cravens.
>
> The heroic memories that gather about Sharpsburg, Spotsylvania, Cold Harbor, Gettysburg, Petersburg, Perryville, Murfreesboro, Shiloh, Chickamauga, Galveston, and Wilson's Creek are immortal. They inspire brave men and women with grand conceptions of patriotism and courage. They stir the hearts of the men of every age who honor valor and true manhood . . .[499]

Let us read the most significant line from General Young's comments once again: "The cause that gave to the world Robert E. Lee cannot and will not be forgotten." And that patriotic cause was Americanism, or what was once known as Jeffersonianism and what is now called conservatism.

Thus, as Meriwether writes, there were three anti-American Liberals, Abraham Lincoln, William H. Seward, and Joseph Medill (owner of the *Chicago Tribune* and the man who, in 1854, proposed the name "Republican" for the newly founded Republican Party) who

were the chief conspirators against American liberty. They lived to see the triumph of their evil work. They lived to see the principles of Democracy [conservatism] trampled down into the bloody mire on a hundred battlefields. They lived to see the desolation of the [conservative] States they had hated for their adherence to [Thomas] Jefferson's principles [Jeffersonianism]. They lived to see the once free people of the States on the South Atlantic coast robbed of every liberty they had won by their swords from England's King. They lived to see the South's fair and fruitful fields desolate deserts, her homes heaps of ashes, her fertile land a wide waste; and if, during all that devilish work, one word of sympathy for the suffering people of the South, one word of pity for the anguish and agonies endured, ever passed the lips of either of these three men I have failed to find any record thereof. On the contrary, the more cruel officers and soldiers in the field, the more highly they were commended. It is related that the last utterance that fell from Lincoln's lips was a gibe at the crushed and conquered South. "Shall the orchestra play Dixie?" he was asked as he sat in his box in Ford's theatre that fatal night. "We have conquered the South," returned Lincoln gleefully, "we may as well take her music."[500]

Marylander John Wilkes Booth's attempt to end the Liberals' destruction of the Constitution by taking Lincoln's life was both immoral and pointless. Perverse political theories like liberalism cannot be expunged through violence. Only education can institute real lasting change.

A few moments later John Wilkes Booth pounced and our sixteenth president lie mortally wounded. He would perish the next day, April 15, 1865, from his injury.

But not before scoring a major victory for liberalism and a major loss for conservatism, the Constitution, and the American people; a debacle of national proportions that has reverberated down into the present day.

JEFFERSON DAVIS
ON LINCOLN'S WAR

SINCE THE LIBERAL VICTORS OF Lincoln's War, along with their revisionist left-wing historians, have so thoroughly distorted, perverted, edited, suppressed, and rewritten the facts about the conflict, one can never hope to uncover the truth from this group. This is why today the Liberal version of the War is a hopeless labyrinth of misinformation and disinformation. Even a cursory reading of the average left-wing Civil War book will leave the intelligent reader frustrated and confused, for the facts have been redacted so many times that all that remains is a perplexing, nonsensical, overly simplistic, and absurd fairy tale about the "evil slave-loving South" and the "righteous slave-hating North."

What is behind this diabolical phenomenon?

Liberal-created Civil War books, films, articles, and blogs all derive from the same destructive mental disorder: the leftist's, socialist's, and communist's unrelenting urge to make history accord with their own soul-destroying social ideologies, political theories, personal opinions, and over-inflamed emotions. This makes their version of the War historically inaccurate and unreliable, for it is based on fiction rather than reality.

To uncover the truth about the real cause of Lincoln's War, and in

Conservative Jefferson Davis: one of the greatest thinkers, most gifted writers, and most outstanding constitutional scholars in American history.

turn, the real winner and the real loser, we must turn to those individuals we can trust, and none are more trustworthy, and there are no greater authorities on the subject, than the Confederate Trinity. I am speaking here of the three highest officials in the Confederate government: President Jefferson Davis, Vice President Alexander H. Stephens, and General Robert E. Lee, three of the most conservative, brilliant, well educated, honest, ethical, moral, and godly men ever produced by America.

Let us begin with President Davis, who, naturally, had much to say about the cause of Lincoln's War, for it was Lincoln who started it, then blamed the South for "firing the first shot"! Davis, the most conservative chief executive in American history, penned the following statements in 1881, 16 years after the conflict had ended. Thus he had the benefit of hindsight, making his views even more equitable in perspective. Wrote Davis:

> [One of the main causes of the War surely was] the ravings of a [Liberal] party in the North, which denounced the Constitution and the Union, and persistently defamed their [Conservative] brethren of the South.[501]

> *Ignorance and credulity have enabled unscrupulous partisans so to mislead public opinion, both at home and abroad, as to create the belief that the institution of African slavery was the chief cause, instead of being a mere incident in the group of causes, which led to war.* In keeping with the first misrepresentation was that of the position assigned to the belligerent parties. Thus, *the North is represented as having fought for the emancipation of the African slaves, and the South for the increase and extension of the institution of African servitude as it existed in the Southern States. Therein is a twofold fallacy.*[502]

[Under Lincoln] the states and the people thereof had become consolidated into a national Union. . . . This was the usurpation. This lay at the foundation of the war. Every subsequent act of the Government was another step in the same direction, all tending palpably to supremacy for the Government of the United States, the subjugation of the States, and the submission of the people.[503]

This was the adversary with whom we had to struggle, and *this was the issue for which we fought. That we dared to draw our swords to vindicate the rights and the sovereignty of the people, that we dared to resist and deny all sovereignty as inherently existing in the Government of the United States, was adjudged an infamous crime, and we were denounced as "rebels."* It was asserted that those of us "who were captured should be hung as rebels taken in the act." Crushing the corner-stone of the Union, the independence of the States, the Federal Government assumed toward us a position of haughty arrogance, refused to recognize us otherwise than as insurrectionists and "rebels," who resisted and denied its *usurped sovereignty*, and who were entitled to no amelioration from the punishment of death, except such as might proceed only from the promptings of mercy.[504]

Under the power of Congress to levy duties on imports, tariff laws were enacted, not merely "to pay the debts and provide for the common defense and general welfare of the United States," as authorized by the Constitution, but, positively and primarily, for the protection against foreign competition of domestic manufactures. *The effect of this was to impose the main burden of taxation upon the Southern people, who were consumers and not manufacturers, not only by the enhanced price of imports, but indirectly by the consequent depreciation in the value of exports, which were chiefly the products of Southern States.* The imposition of this grievance was unaccompanied by the consolation of knowing that the tax thus borne was to be paid into the public Treasury, for the increase of price accrued mainly to the benefit of the manufacturer. Nor was this all: a reference to the annual appropriations will show that the disbursements made were as unequal as the burdens borne—the inequality in both operating in the same direction.

These causes all combined to direct immigration to the [liberal] Northern section; and with the increase of its preponderance appeared more and more distinctly *a tendency in the Federal Government to pervert functions delegated to it, and to use them with sectional discrimination against the [conservative Southern] minority.*[505]

[More proof that slavery was not the cause of the War comes from the Lincoln Government itself.] As late as the 22nd of April, 1861, Mr. [William Henry] Seward, United States Secretary of State, in a dispatch to [New Jersey Senator] Mr. [William Lewis] Dayton, Minister to France, since made public, expressed the views and purposes of the United States Government in the premises as follows. It may be proper to explain that, by what he is pleased to term "the revolution," Mr. Seward means the withdrawal of the Southern States; and that the words italicized are, perhaps, not so distinguished in the original. He says: "The Territories will remain in all respects the same, whether the revolution shall succeed or shall fail. *The condition of slavery in the several States will remain just the same, whether it succeed or fail.* There is not even a pretext for the complaint that the disaffected States are to be conquered by the United States if the revolution fails; for the rights of the States and *the condition of every being in them* will remain subject to exactly the same laws and forms of administration, whether the revolution shall succeed or whether it shall fail. In the one case, the States would be federally connected with the new Confederacy; in the other, they would, as now, be members of the United States; *but their Constitutions and laws, customs, habits, and institutions, in either case, will remain the same.*"[506]

Three generations: President Davis, his daughter Margaret Davis Hayes, and his grandchildren.

By the exclusion of the South, in 1820, from all that part of the Louisiana purchase lying north of the parallel of thirty-six degrees thirty minutes, and not included in the State of Missouri; by the extension of that line of exclusion to embrace the territory acquired from Texas; and by the appropriation of all the territory obtained from Mexico under the Treaty of Guadalupe Hidalgo, both north and south of that line, it may be stated with approximate accuracy that the [liberal] North had monopolized to herself more than three fourths of all that had been added to the domain of the United States since the Declaration of Independence. This inequality, which began . . . in the more generous than wise confidence of the [conservative] South, was employed to obtain for the North the lion's share of what was afterward added at the cost of the public treasure and the blood of patriots.[507]

Nor was this the only cause that operated to disappoint the reasonable hopes and to blight the fair prospects under which the original compact was formed. The effects of discriminating duties upon imports . . . favoring the manufacturing region, which was the [liberal] North; burdening the exporting region, which was the [conservative] South; and so imposing upon the latter a double tax: one, by the increased price of articles of consumption, which, so far as they were of home production, went into the pockets of the manufacturer; the other, by the diminished value of articles of export, which was so much withheld from the pockets of the agriculturist. In like manner the power of the majority section was employed to appropriate to itself an unequal share of the public disbursements. These combined causes—the possession of more territory, more money, and a wider field for the employment of special labor—all served to attract immigration; and, with increasing population, the greed grew by what it fed on.[508]

This became distinctly manifest when the so-called "Republican" [that is, the Liberal Party of that day] Convention assembled in Chicago, on May 16, 1860, to nominate a candidate for the Presidency. *It was a purely sectional body*. There were a few delegates present, representing an insignificant minority in the "border States," Delaware, Maryland, Virginia, Kentucky, and Missouri; but not one from any State south of the celebrated political line of thirty-six degrees thirty minutes. It had been the invariable usage with nominating conventions of all parties to select candidates for the Presidency and Vice-Presidency, one from the North and the other from the South; but this assemblage nominated Mr. Lincoln, of Illinois, for the first office, and for the second, Mr. [Hannibal] Hamlin, of Maine—both Northerners. Mr. Lincoln, its nominee for the Presidency, had publicly announced that the Union "could not permanently endure, half slave and half free." The resolutions adopted contained some carefully worded declarations, well adapted to deceive the credulous who were opposed to hostile aggressions upon the rights of the States. *In order to accomplish this purpose, they were compelled to create a fictitious issue, in denouncing what they described as "the new dogma that the Constitution, of its own force, carries slavery into any or all of the Territories of the United States"—a "dogma" which had never been held or declared by anybody, and which had no existence outside of their own assertion.* There was enough in connection with the nomination to assure the most fanatical foes of the Constitution that their ideas would be the rule and guide of the party.[509]

The resistance to the admission of Missouri as a State, in 1820, was evidently not owing to any moral or constitutional considerations, but merely to political motives; and the compensation exacted for granting what was simply a right, was the exclusion of the South from equality in the enjoyment of territory which justly belonged equally to both, and which was what the enemies of the South stigmatized as "slave territory," when acquired.[510]

The sectional policy then indicated brought to its support the passions that spring from man's higher nature, but which, like all passions, if misdirected and perverted, become hurtful and, it may be, destructive. The year 1835 was marked by the public agitation for the abolition of that African servitude which existed in the [conservative] South, which antedated the Union, and had existed in every one of the States that formed the [U.S.] Confederation [of 1781]. *By a great misconception of the powers belonging to the General Government, and the responsibilities of citizens of the [liberal] Northern States, many of those citizens were, little by little, brought to the conclusion that slavery was a sin for which they were answerable; and that it was the duty of the Federal Government to abate it.*[511]

Thus, by the activity of the propagandists of abolitionism, and the misuse of the sacred word Liberty, they recruited from the ardent worshipers of that goddess such numbers as gave them in many Northern States the balance of power between the two great political forces [conservatism and liberalism] that stood arrayed against each other; then and there they came to be courted by both of the great parties, especially by the Whigs [essentially the big government Liberals of the day], who had become the weaker party of the two. Fanaticism, to which is usually accorded sincerity as an extenuation of its mischievous tenets, affords the best excuse to be offered for the original abolitionists, but that can not be conceded to the political associates who joined them for the purpose of acquiring power; with them it was but hypocritical cant, intended to deceive. Hence arose the declaration of the existence of an "irrepressible conflict," because of the domestic institutions of sovereign, self-governing States—*institutions over which neither the Federal Government nor the people outside of the limits of such States had any control, and for which they could have no moral or legal responsibility.*[512]

These facts prove incontestably that the sectional hostility which exhibited itself in 1820, on the application of Missouri for admission into the Union, which again broke out on the proposition for the annexation of Texas in 1844, and which reappeared after the Mexican war, never again to be suppressed until its fell results had been fully accomplished, was not the consequence of any difference on the abstract question of slavery. *It was the offspring of sectional rivalry and political ambition. It would have manifested itself just as certainly if slavery had existed in all the States, or if there had not been a [single] negro in America. No such pretension was made in 1803 or 1811, when the Louisiana purchase, and afterward the admission into the Union of the State of that name, elicited threats of disunion from the representatives of New England. The complaint was not of slavery, but of 'the acquisition of more weight at the other extremity' of the Union. [As now, it] was not slavery that threatened a rupture in 1832, but the unjust and unequal operation of a protective tariff.*[513]

Davis at his Mississippi home, "Beauvoir," after the War.

The raid into Virginia under [Liberal psychopath] John Brown—already notorious as a fanatical partisan leader in the Kansas troubles—occurred in October, 1859, a few weeks before the meeting of the Thirty-sixth Congress. Insignificant in itself and in its immediate results, it afforded a startling revelation of the extent to which sectional hatred and political fanaticism had blinded the conscience of a class of [Liberal] persons in certain States of the Union; forming a party steadily growing stronger in numbers, as well as in activity.[514]

[Just prior to the 1860 presidential election, it] needed but little knowledge of the status of parties in the several States to foresee a probable defeat if *the Conservatives* [known as the Democrats at the time] were to continue divided into three parts, and *the aggressives* [that is, progressives: the Liberal pro-North candidates and their supporters] were to be held in solid column. But angry passions, which are always bad counselors, had been aroused, and hopes were still cherished, which proved to be illusory. *The result was the election, by a minority, of a President [that is, Lincoln] whose avowed principles were necessarily fatal to the harmony of the Union.*[515]

[Between 1850 and 1860] the progress of sectional discord and the tendency of the stronger section to unconstitutional aggression had been fearfully rapid. With very rare exceptions, there were none in 1850 who claimed the right of the Federal Government to apply coercion to a State. In 1860 men had grown to be familiar with threats of driving the [conservative] South into submission to any act that the Government, in the hands of a [liberal] Northern majority, might see fit to perform. During the canvass of that year, demonstrations had been made by quasi-military organizations in various parts of the North, which looked unmistakably to purposes widely different from those enunciated in the preamble to the Constitution, and to the employment of means not authorized by the powers which the States had delegated to the Federal Government.[516]

Well-informed men still remembered that, in the [1787] Convention which framed the Constitution, a proposition was made to authorize the employment of force against a delinquent State, on which *Mr. [James] Madison remarked that "the use of force against a State would look more like a declaration of war than an infliction of punishment, and would probably be considered by the party attacked as a dissolution of all previous compacts by which it might have been bound."* The Convention expressly refused to confer the power proposed, and the clause was lost. While, therefore, in 1860, many violent men, appealing to passion and the lust of power, were inciting the multitude, and preparing [liberal] Northern opinion to support a war waged against the [conservative] Southern States in the event of their secession, there were others who took a different view of the case. Notable among such was . . . [Yankee crusader and socialist Horace Greeley's] New York *Tribune*, which had been the organ of the abolitionists, and which now declared that, "if the cotton States wished to withdraw from the Union, they should be allowed to do so"; that "any attempt to compel them to remain, by force, would be contrary to the principles of the Declaration of Independence and to the fundamental ideas upon which human liberty is based"; and that, "if the Declaration of Independence justified the secession from the British Empire of three millions of subjects in 1776, it was not seen why it would not justify the secession of five millions of Southerners from the Union in 1861." Again, it was said by the same journal that, "sooner than compromise with the South and abandon the Chicago platform," they would "let the Union slide." Taunting expressions were freely used—as, for example, "If the Southern people wish to leave the Union, we will do our best to forward their views."[517]

That signs of coming danger so visible, evidences of hostility so unmistakable, disregard of constitutional obligations so wanton, taunts and jeers so bitter and insulting, should serve to increase excitement in the South, was a consequence flowing as much from reason and *patriotism* as from sentiment. He must have been ignorant of human nature who did not expect such a tree to bear fruits of discord and division.[518]

President Davis sitting in his favorite spot at "Beauvoir," circa 1880s.

5

ALEXANDER H. STEPHENS ON LINCOLN'S WAR

L ET US NOW EXAMINE THE words of Confederate Vice
President Stephens, noted constitutional scholar, outstanding
orator, upright Christian, prominent intellectual, lifelong
Conservative politician, and traditional Southern author. His views on
the cause of the War are identical to those of President Davis, while
reenforcing three of the most significant subjects pertaining to American
history: the authentic nature of the U.S. government, the facts about so-
called Southern "slavery," and the true instigator of the "Civil War."

The following material is presented in a question-and-answer
format, the questions being asked by a Liberal (a Republican at the time)
of Stephens, a Conservative (a Democrat at the time). First a brief
civic's lesson concerning American history by a *truthful* historian, with
Stephens providing an overview of the U.S. government:

[It was] from a violation of the organic principles of . . . the nature and
character of the Government of the United States [that] the [American
Civil] war had its origin. [I have shown] . . . that ours is a Federal
[Confederate] Government. In other words, we have seen that it is a

Government formed by a Convention, a *Fœdus*, or Compact between distinct, separate, and Sovereign States. . . . *This Federal or Conventional Government, so formed, possesses inherently no power whatever. All its powers are held by delegation only, and by delegation from separate States. These powers are all enumerated and all limited to specific objects in the Constitution. Even the highest Sovereign Power it is permitted to exercise—the war power, for instance—is held by it by delegation only. Sovereignty itself—the great source of all political power—under the system, still resides where it did before the Compact was entered into, that is, in the States severally, or with the people of the several States respectively. By the Compact, the Sovereign Powers to be exercised by the Federal Head were not surrendered by the States—were not alienated or parted with by them. They were delegated only.* The States by voluntary engagements, agreed only to abstain from their exercise themselves, and to confer this exercise by delegation upon common agents under the Convention, for the better security of the great objects aimed at by the formation of the Compact, which was the regulation of their external and inter-State affairs.[519]

Conservative Alexander H. Stephens, one of the greatest minds produced by the American South.

What type of government does the U.S. possess? Stephens answers the question this way:

Our system, taken altogether, is a peculiar one. The world never saw its like before. It has no prototype in any of all the previous Confederations, or Federal Republics, of which we have any account. It is neither a "Staaten-bund" [a Confederation of states] exactly, nor a "Bundesstaat" [a Federal state], according to the classification of Federal Republics by the German Publicists. It differs from their "Staatenbund" in this, that the powers to be exercised by the Federal Head are divided into three departments, the Legislative, Judicial, and

Executive, with a perfectly organized machinery for the execution of these powers within its limited sphere, and for the specific objects named, upon citizens of the several States without the intermediate act or sanction of the several States. In the "Staaten-bund," or "States' Confederation," according to their classification, the Federal Government can enact no laws which will operate upon the citizens of the several States composing it, until the States severally give them their sanction. Such was our Federal [Confederate] Union under the first Articles [of Confederation]. But our present system, as we have seen, went a step further, and introduced a new principle in Confederations. While, therefore, our system differs specifically in this particular from their "Staatenbund," or "States' Confederation," yet it agrees entirely with it in its essential Generic difference from their Bundesstaat, in this, that the States collectively constitute an international unit as regards third parties, but do not cease to be international units as regards each other.[520]

Next Stephens explains how the United States of America came to be described by the Founding Fathers as a "Confederate Republic":

[Our country] differs . . . generically from . . . [the Germans'] "Bundesstaat," or "Federative State," or what may properly be called "an incorporate Union," in this, that *no Sovereign Power whatever, under our system, is surrendered or alienated by the several States; it is only delegated.* The difference between our system and their "Staaten-bund," is, however, only specific, as we see. It is not Generic. They are both essentially the same. *Ours is a newly developed species of Government of their Genus "Staaten-bund."* This specific difference is what struck [Alexis] De Tocqueville as "a wholly novel theory, which may be considered as a great discovery in modern political science," and for which there was as yet no specific name. His language is:

"This Constitution, which may at first be confounded with the Federal Constitutions which have preceded it, rests, in truth, upon a wholly novel theory, which may be considered as a great discovery in modern political science. In all the Confederations which preceded the American Constitution of 1789, the allied States, for a common object, agreed to obey the injunctions of a Federal Government; but they reserved to themselves the right of ordaining and enforcing the execution of the laws of the Union. The American States, which combined in 1789, agreed, that the Federal Government should not only dictate, but should execute its own enactments. In both cases, the right is the same, but the exercise of the right is different; and this difference produced the most momentous consequences. . . . The new word, which ought to express this novel thing, does not yet exist. The human understanding more easily invents new things than new words, and we are hence constrained to employ many improper and inadequate expressions."

This new principle of so constituting a Federal [Confederate] Republic as to make us "one nation as to Foreign concerns, and to keep us distinct as to domestic ones," with a division of the delegated powers into Legislative, Judiciary, and Executive Departments, and with an organization and machinery in the Conventional Government, thus formed, for the full exercise of all its delegated and limited powers, similar to those of the separate States creating it, . . . was indicated as early as December 1786, by Mr. [Thomas] Jefferson in a letter to Mr. [James] Madison. This was the grand principle finally carried out. It was a grand step in progress in the science of Government. This was what so signalized our career for sixty years, and this is the peculiar specific difference between our Federal Republic and all others of similar general type, to which Lord [Henry] Brougham alludes when he says:

"It is not at all a refinement that a Federal Union should be formed; this is the natural result of men's joint operations in a very rude state of society. But the regulation of such a Union upon pre-established principles, the formation of a system of Government and legislation in which the different subjects shall be not individuals but States, the application of legislative principles to such a body of States, and the devising means for keeping its integrity as a federacy [Confederacy], while the rights and powers of the individual States are maintained entire, is the very, greatest refinement in social policy to which any state of circumstances has ever given rise, or to which any age has ever given birth."

From this exposition, we see clearly the proper solution of the vexed question, whether the United States constitute a Nation or not. We see clearly not only that they do constitute a Nation, but also what sort of a Nation it is. *It is not a Nation of individuals, blended in a common mass, with a consolidated Sovereignty over the whole; but a Nation the constituent elements, or members of which, are separate and distinct political organizations, States, or Sovereignties. It is a "Confederated Republic," as Washington styled our present Union. This is the same as if he had styled it a Confederated Nation. It is, in truth, a Confederated Nation [i.e., a Confederacy]. That is, it is a Nation of States, or in other words, a Nation of Nations. In this sense, these States, thus united, do constitute a Nation, and a Nation of the highest and grandest type the world ever saw!*[521]

How did Stephens define the terms "sovereignty," "ultimate sovereignty," and "paramount authority?" Here is his answer:

[The word sovereignty] . . . involves the idea of a divisibility of Sovereignty itself. It is essential that [one] . . . shall first clearly understand the real import of this word in its proper political sense.

I will therefore answer . . . first, by stating as distinctly as I can, what I mean by Sovereignty in this connection. . . . It is true, we have no very clear or accurate definition of it, by any political writer or publicist, that I have seen. Most of them have given their ideas of it by explanations and descriptions. By Sovereignty and Paramount authority I mean the same thing. If I were to undertake to express my ideas of it in regular formula, I should say that *Sovereignty or Paramount authority, in a proper political sense, is that inherent, absolute power of self-determination, in every distinct political body, existing by virtue of its own social forces, which, in pursuit of the well-being of its own organism, within the limitations of natural*

A young Alexander H. Stephens, known to his friends as "little Aleck."

justice, cannot be rightfully interfered with by any other similar body, without its consent. With this explanation . . . I have only to add, that Sovereignty, as I understand it, is that innate attribute of the Political Body so possessing it, which corresponds with the will and power of self action in the personal body, and by its very nature is indivisible;

just as much so as the Mind is in the individual organism.

This is the doctrine clearly taught by all writers of note on the subject, in both ancient and modern times. Hence, no Political Body can be absolutely Sovereign for any purpose, and not Sovereign for all purposes which lie within the domain of Sovereignty itself. Bodies-Politic may, by delegation, exercise certain Sovereign powers for some purposes and not for all. This is the case with all Conventional States. *We must, moreover, discriminate between the powers of Sovereignty and Sovereignty itself. Sovereign powers are divisible. The exercise of them in all good Governments has been and is entrusted by delegation to different hands; such as the Executive Power, the Legislative Power, the Judicial Power. These are all high Sovereign powers committed to separate and distinct hands. Sovereignty itself, however, from which they all emanate, remains meanwhile the same indivisible unit. This is the Trinity in Unity exhibited in all properly constituted Representative Governments.* Nor is the delegation to another of the right to exercise a power of any kind, whether Sovereign or not, an alienation of it. The fact of its being delegated, shows that the source from which the delegation proceeds continues to exist.

. . . In our system, or united systems, Sovereign powers are not only divided into the three great branches, as I have stated, both in the Federal Government and in the several State Governments; but they are also divided in like manner between these two systems of Governments. Some of the Sovereign powers are delegated to all the States to be exercised jointly by them in Congress assembled, as well as by special officers of the Federal Government; and some of them are delegated to the various officers of the several State Governments. Those delegated to each, being delegated by the Sovereign power of the people of the several States separately; and divided similarly in each case. There is no alienation of any portion of Sovereignty itself in either case. This continues to reside with the people of the several States as separate, integral units. I have only further to add in answer to [the Liberals'] . . . inquiry, that *by ultimate Sovereignty in this argument, I mean that original, inherent, innate and continually existing rightful Power, or Will of the several Bodies-Politic, or States of our Union—that source and fountain of all political power—which is unimpaired by voluntarily assumed obligations; and which at any time, within the terms stated, can rightfully resume all its delegated powers—those to the Federal Government as well as those to the several State Governments.*

These great and essential truths of our history [are now] thus forever established beyond question or doubt . . .[522]

Stephens now moves onto an important discussion concerning the South's institution of black "slavery" (as distinct from white, red, yellow, and brown slavery—which have also been extremely common throughout world history)[523] and the War for Southern Independence:

[I will now proceed to] the immediate and exciting question, which brought the organic principles of the Government into such terrible physical conflict in the inauguration of the war. This was . . . the question of negro Slavery, or more properly speaking that political and legal subordination of the black race to the white race, which existed in the Seceding States [as well as the Northern states].

I thus speak of Slavery as it existed with us, purposely. For . . . that *what was called Slavery with us, was not Slavery in the usual sense of that word, as generally used and understood by the ancients, and as generally used and understood in many countries in the present age. It was with us a political Institution. It was, indeed, nothing but that legal subordination of an Inferior race to a Superior one* [Note: Stephens is referring here to what he believed was the cultural, social, moral, and religious superiority of Anglo-Saxon society, just as the African has long considered his society culturally, socially, morally, and religiously superior to that of the European; L.S.] *which was thought to be the best in the organization of society for the welfare politically, socially, morally and intellectually of both races. The slave, so-called, was not in law regarded entirely as a chattel, as has been erroneously represented. He was by no means subject to the absolute dominion of his master. He had important personal rights, secured by law. His service due according to law, it is true, was considered property, and so in all countries is considered the service of all persons, who according to law are bound to another or others for a term, however long or short. So is the legal right of parents to the service of their minor children in all the States now considered as property. A right or property that may be assigned, transferred or sold.* [Alexander] Hamilton expressed the idea of this peculiar Institution, as it existed with us, clearly, when he said:

"The Federal Constitution, therefore, decides with great propriety on the case of our slaves, when it views them in the mixed character of persons and of property. This is in fact their true character. It is the character bestowed on them by the laws under which they live."

They [Southern black "slaves"] were so viewed and regarded by the

Constitutions and laws of all the States. The relation of master and slave under the Institution, as before said, was but one of "reciprocal service and mutual bonds." The view of them as property related to their services due according to law.

. . . This matter of negro subordination, I repeat, was the exciting question in 1860. There were, it is true, many other questions involving the same principles of the Government, which had agitated the public mind almost from the time it went into operation, still exciting the public mind to a greater or less degree: but this question of the status of the Black race in the Southern States, was by far the most exciting and all-absorbing one, at that time, on both sides, and was the main proximate cause which brought those principles of the Government into active play, resulting in the conflict of arms. *This relation of political and legal subordination of the Inferior to the Superior race, as it existed in 1860, in all the Seceding States, had at one time, be it constantly kept in mind, existed in all the States of the Union, and did so exist in all, save one, in 1787, when the present Articles of Union were entered into.*

Stephens wrote extensively about the true cause of Lincoln's War, but his writings have been ignored and suppressed by the Left.

By these Articles this relation was fully recognized, as appears from the solemn covenant therein made, that fugitives from service, under this system, as it then thus existed, escaping from one State into another, should, upon claim, be delivered up to the party to whom the service was due. This was one of the stipulations of the Compact upon which the Union was formed, as we have seen, and of which Judge [Joseph] Story said, on an important occasion, in delivering an opinion from the Bench of the Supreme Court of the United States, "it cannot be doubted that it constituted a fundamental article, without the adoption of which the Union could not have been formed."

These are all great facts never to be lost sight of in this investigation of the rightfulness of this most terrible war, and in determining correctly and justly upon which side the huge responsibility of its inauguration, and of the enormous wrongs, and most disastrous consequences attending its subsequent conduct, must, in the judgment of mankind, forever rest.[524]

It is not at all germane to [my] . . . purpose in this [discussion] . . . at this time, to inquire into the Right, or Wrong of the Institution of Slavery itself, as it thus existed in what were then [incorrectly and unfairly] known as the Slave States. Neither is it in the line of my argument now, to treat of the defects, or abuses of the system. Nor is it at all necessary, or pertinent to my present object, to trace from its inception to its culmination, the history or progress of that movement against it, which was organized for the purpose of bringing the questions it involved into the arena of Federal Councils, and within the range of Federal action. *Suffice it here barely to say, and assume as a fact what is known to us all so well, that, in 1860, a majority of the Northern States, having long previously of their own accord abolished this Institution, within their own limits respectively, had, also, by the action of their Legislatures, openly and avowedly violated that clause in the Constitution of the United States [i.e., the Fugitive Slave Clause], which provided for the rendition of fugitives of this class from service.*

To give a history of that movement to which I allude, to trace its progress from its origin, would require a volume of itself. A volume both interesting and instructive, might be devoted to it. This is what is known as the Abolition movement in this country, and this is what Mr. [Horace] Greeley is pleased to style the "American Conflict." But from entering into an investigation of that sort, I now forbear. It is in no way pertinent or essential to my purpose. Whoever feels an interest in the subject, will see it treated fully, truthfully, and ably by the master hand of Mr. George Lunt, of Boston, in his history of the "*Origin of the War.*"[525]

Stephens next lays out the Truth about so-called Southern "slavery" and the real cause of the War for Southern Independence:

Suffice it, therefore, for me, at present, on this subject, only to say, generally, that such a movement was started, such a conflict was begun at an early day after our present system of Government went into operation. As early as the 12th day of February, 1790, within twelve months after [George] Washington was inaugurated as President, a petition invoking the Federal authorities to take jurisdiction of this subject, with a view to the ultimate abolition of this Institution in the States respectively, was sent to Congress, headed by Dr. [Benjamin] Franklin. This movement, in its first step thus taken so early, was partially checked by the Resolution to which the house of

Representatives came, after the most mature consideration of the petition and its objects. That Resolution declared:

> "That Congress have no authority to interfere in the emancipation of slaves, or in the treatment of them within any of the States; it remaining with the several States alone to provide any regulations therein, which humanity and true policy may require."

This clear exposition of the nature of the Federal Government, and its utter want of power to take any action upon the subject, as sought for by the petitioners, checked, I say, for a time, this movement, or conflict so started and commenced. *The conflict, however, was only partially checked; it went on until in 1860, when those who so entered into this movement standing forth as the Abolition or Anti-Slavery Party under the [erroneous] name of Republican, but which in truth was the*

Stephens often referred to Liberals as "consolidationists" and his fellow Conservatives as "constitutionalists."

[Liberal] party of Centralism and Consolidation, organized upon the principle of bringing the Federal Powers to bear upon this Institution in a way to secure its ultimate Abolition in all the States, succeeded in the election of the two highest officers of the Government [Liberal President Abraham Lincoln and Liberal Vice President Hannibal Hamlin], pledged to carry out their principles, and to carry them out in open disregard of the decision of the Supreme Court, which highest Judicial Tribunal under the Constitution, had by solemn adjudication denied the power of the Federal Government to take such action as this Party and its two highest officers stood pledged to carry out. With all these questions, I repeat, I have nothing now to do, except to say that *the conflict from its rise to its culmination, was not a conflict between the advocates and opponents of the Institution itself. It seems to have been [socialist] Mr. [Horace] Greeley's leading object, throughout his work, to give this idea of the nature of the conflict, as I stated in the beginning. This, however, was in no sense the fact of the case. The [slavery] conflict, fierce and bitter as it was for seventy years, was a conflict between those who were for maintaining the Federal [Confederate] character of the Government, and those who were for centralizing*

all power in the Federal Head [in Washington, D.C.]. This was the conflict. *It was a conflict between the true [Conservative] supporters of the Federal [Confederate] Union of States established by the Constitution, and those [Liberals] whose object was to overthrow this Union of States, and by usurpations to erect a National Consolidation in its stead.*

. . . The same conflict arose upon divers other questions, also, at an early day. It exhibited itself in the discussions of the first Judiciary Act. In the financial measures submitted by Mr. [Alexander] Hamilton, the then Secretary of the Treasury. In the assumption of the State debts. In the first Apportionment Bill, which was vetoed on these grounds by [George] Washington, in 1792, and much more formidably it exhibited itself in the passage of the Alien and Sedition Acts, in 1798, under the elder Adams [John]. *This [big government Liberal] Party, as we have seen, then [wrongly] assumed the popular name of Federal, as it [wrongly] assumed the popular name of Republican in 1800. These latter measures of 1798 came near stirring up civil war, and would most probably have resulted in such a catastrophe, if the Party, so organized with such principles and objects, had not been utterly overthrown, and driven from power by the advocates of our true Federal [Confederate] system of Government, under the lead of [the Confederacy advocate] Mr. [Thomas] Jefferson, in 1800. It was after this complete defeat on these other questions, that the Centralists rallied upon this question of the Status of the Black race in the States, where it continued to exist, as the most promising one for them to agitate and unite the people of the Northern States upon, for the accomplishment of their sinister objects of National Centralization or Consolidation.*[526]

Stephens comments on the underhanded ploys instigated by Liberals (mainly in the North), who used slavery as a false issue to try and push through their big government agenda:

On this question, Mr. Greeley and other writers speak of only two Parties during the entire conflict. The *Pro-Slavery party*, and the *Anti-Slavery* or *Liberty party*. *The truth is there never was in the United States, or in any one of them, an organized Pro-Slavery party. No such antagonism, as he represents, ever existed in the Federal Councils. The antagonism on this question, which was clearly exhibited in the beginning, as appears from the Resolution of the House of Representatives referred to, was an antagonism growing out of Constitutional principles, and not any sort of antagonism growing out of the principles involved in the right or wrong of negro Slavery, as it then existed in the several States of the Union. It was an antagonism growing out of principles lying at the foundation of the common Government of the States.* Of those men, for instance, who voted for the Resolution referred to, in 1790 [which proposed that the central government be prohibited from interfering with the institution of slavery in the individual states], how many can be supposed to have been Pro-Slavery in their sentiments, or in favor of the Institution? Let us look into it. Here is the record of the vote. Amongst the prominent supporters of the Resolution, and on the list of those who voted for it, is the name of Roger Sherman, of Connecticut. Here is Benjamin Huntington, also of the same State. From Massachusetts, we see the names of Theodore Sedgwick, Elbridge Gerry, and Benjamin Goodhue. From New Hampshire, we see the name of Nicholas Oilman. From New Jersey, Elias Boudinot and Lambert Cadwallader. From Pennsylvania, Frederick A. Muhlenberg, Thomas Hartley, and Daniel Heister. These were all prominent men in the formation of the Constitution. *All from the Northern States. The vote shows, that not only a majority of the members from the Northern States voted for the Resolution, but that a majority of those who did vote for it, were from the Northern States.* Those from the South who voted against it, the debate shows so voted, because they did not think the petition should be considered, or acted upon at all, as it related to subjects not within their Constitutional jurisdiction. But how many of this majority of the Northern members who voted for it, can be reasonably supposed to have been Pro-Slavery in sentiment?

In their action in entertaining the petition, they intended only to show what they considered a due regard to the right of petition, and at the same time prove themselves true to the Constitution of their country. This the debate conclusively shows. So in all after times up to the election in 1860. *Those who resisted the action of the Abolitionists did so, because it was based upon revolutionary principles—principles utterly at war with those upon which the Union was established. As a striking illustration of this, Mr. [Thomas] Jefferson himself is well-known to have been as much opposed to the Institution of Slavery, as it then existed in the United States, as any man in either of them; and yet he headed the great party in opposition to this mode of effecting the object of those who desired its Abolition, as he had led the same party to success over the Centralists on other questions, in 1800. He utterly denied that the Federal Government could rightfully exercise any power with the view to the change of any of the Institutions of the States respectively.*

The same is true of all the prominent leaders of this party, as well as the great mass of the people composing it, from the days of Jefferson to those of General [Lewis] Cass and Mr. [Stephen A.] Douglas. Mr. [William] Pinkney and Mr. [Henry] Clay, *though Southern men as Mr. Jefferson was, were decidedly Anti-Slavery in their sentiments, and yet they ever acted with the party of Mr. Jefferson upon this question.* General Cass and Mr. Douglas were Northern men with sentiments equally averse to Slavery, and for the same reasons opposed the Abolition movement in the Federal Councils. Even Chief Justice [Roger B.] Taney, who delivered the opinion of the Supreme Court in the case referred to, was by no means individually Pro-Slavery in his

Conservative Stephens helped expose the Liberal lie about slavery being the cause of Lincoln's War.

sentiments. His views upon the Institution are understood to have been very similar to those of Mr. Pinkney and Mr. Clay. Out of the million and half, and more, of men in the Northern States who voted against Mr. [Abraham] Lincoln, in 1860, perhaps not ten thousand could be said, with truth, to be in favor of the Institution, or would have lived in a State where it existed. It was a subject with which they were thoroughly convinced they had nothing to do, and could have nothing to do under the terms of the Union by which the States were confederated, except to carry out and faithfully perform all the obligations of the Constitutional Compact in regard to it. In opposing the 'Liberty Party,' so-called, they enlisted under no banner of Slavery of any sort, but only arrayed themselves against that [Liberal] organization, which had virtually hoisted the banner of Consolidation. *The struggle or conflict, therefore, from its rise to its culmination, was between those who in whatever State they lived, were for maintaining our Federal [Confederate] system as it was established, and those who were for a consolidation of power in the Central Head.*

. . . *The great fact now to be considered in this investigation, is, that this Anti-Constitutional Party [i.e., the Republicans, the Liberals of the day], in 1860, came into power upon this question in the Executive branch of the Federal Government.*

This is the state of things which produced so much excitement and apprehension in the popular mind of the Southern States at that time. This Anti-Slavery Party had not only succeeded in getting a majority of the Northern States to openly violate their Constitutional faith in the avowed breach of the Compact, as stated; but had succeeded in electing a President and Vice President pledged to principles which were not only at war with the domestic Institutions of the States of the South, but which must inevitably, if carried out, ultimately lead to the absorption of all power in the Central Government, and end sooner or later in Absolutism or Despotism. These were the principles then brought into conflict, which, as stated, resulted in the conflict of arms.

The Seceding States feeling no longer bound by a Compact which had been so openly violated, and a majority of their people being deeply impressed with the conviction that the whole frame-work of the Constitution would be overthrown by this Party which would soon have control of the Executive Department of the Government, determined to withdraw from the Union, for the very reasons which had induced them to enter it in the beginning. Seven of these States, South Carolina, Georgia, Florida, Alabama, Mississippi, Louisiana, and Texas, did withdraw. Conventions of their people, regularly called by the proper authorities in each of these States respectively—Conventions representing the Sovereignty of the States similar in all respects to those which by Ordinances had ratified the Constitution of the United States—passed Ordinances resuming the Sovereign Powers therein delegated. These were the Secession Ordinances.... These Conventions also appointed Delegates, to meet in Montgomery, Alabama, on the 4th of February, 1861, with a view to form a new Confederation among themselves, upon the same essential basis of the Constitution of the United States.

It was not in opposition to the principles of that Government that they withdrew from it. They quit the Union to save the principles of the Constitution, and to perpetuate, on this Continent, the liberties which it was intended to secure and establish. Mr. [James] Buchanan was then President of the United States. He held that the Federal Government had no power to coerce a Seceding State to remain in the Union, but, strangely enough, at the same time held, that no State could rightfully withdraw from the Union. Mr. Lincoln came into power on the 4th of March, 1861. He held that the Federal Government did possess the Constitutional Power to maintain the Union of States by force, and it was in the maintenance of these views, the war was inaugurated by him.[527]

Anti-South proponents, pro-North writers, and liberals in general have long put forth the notion that the South started the American "Civil War." "Did not Confederate General Pierre G. T. Beauregard in command of the Confederate forces, so-called, at Charleston, South Carolina, fire upon Fort Sumter in that Harbor?" they ask. "Did he not compel Union Major Robert Anderson, the United States officer in command of that Fort, to capitulate and surrender? Was it not this outrage upon the American flag that caused such deep and universal excitement and indignation throughout the entire North?

Conservative Confederate General Pierre G. T. Beauregard of Louisiana.

Was it not this that caused the great meetings in New York, Boston and every Northern city? How can one maintain in the face of these notorious facts, that the war was begun by Mr. Lincoln, or the Federal authorities? Is it not as plain as day that the Insurgents, or Confederates launched this war?" Stephens knew the truth:

> My whole argument is based upon facts, and upon facts that can never be erased or obliterated. It is a fact that the first gun was fired by the Confederates. It is a fact that General Beauregard did, on the 12th of April, 1861, bombard Fort Sumter, before any blow had actually been struck by the Federal authorities. That is not disputed at all. That is a fact which I have no disposition to erase or obliterate in any way. That is a great truth which will live forever. *But did the firing of the first gun, or the reduction of Fort Sumter inaugurate or begin the war? That is a question to be first solved, before we can be agreed upon the fact as to who inaugurated the war; and in solving this question, you must allow me to say that in personal or national conflicts, it is not he who strikes the first blow, or fires the first gun that inaugurates or begins the conflict.* [English historian Henry] Hallam has well said that "*the aggressor in a war (that is, he who begins it,) is not the first who uses force, but the first who renders force necessary.*"
>
> Which side, according to this high authority, (that only announces the common sentiments of mankind,) was the aggressor in this instance? Which side was it that provoked and rendered the first blow necessary? The true answer to that question will settle the fact as to which side began the war.

I maintain that it was inaugurated and begun, though no blow had been struck, when the hostile [U.S.] fleet, styled the "Relief Squadron," with eleven ships, carrying two hundred and eighty-five guns and two thousand four hundred men, was sent out from New York and Norfolk, with orders from the authorities at Washington, to reenforce Fort Sumter peaceably, if permitted—"but forcibly if they must."

The war was then and there inaugurated and begun by the authorities at Washington. General Beauregard did not open fire upon Fort Sumter until this fleet was, to his knowledge, very near the harbor of Charleston, and until he had inquired of Major Anderson, in command of the Fort, whether he would engage to take no part in the expected blow, then coming down upon him from the approaching fleet. Francis W. Pickens, Governor of South Carolina, and General Beauregard, had both been notified that the fleet was coming, and of its objects, by a messenger from the authorities at Washington. This notice, however, was not given until it was near its destination. When Major Anderson, therefore, would make no such promise, it became necessary for General Beauregard to strike the first blow, as he did; otherwise the forces under his command might have been exposed to two fires at the same time—one in front, and the other in the rear.

. . . To understand this fully, let us see how matters stood in Charleston Harbor at the time.

The Confederate States, then seven in number, had, as stated, all passed Ordinances of Secession. All of them, in regularly constituted Conventions, had withdrawn all their Sovereign powers previously delegated to the United States. They had formed a new Confederation, with a regularly constituted Government, at Montgomery, Alabama, *as they had a perfect right to do*, if our past conclusions were correct, and these [no truthful person can] . . . assail. This new Confederation had sent a [peace] commission to the [Yankee] authorities at Washington . . . to settle all matters amicably and peacefully. *War was by no means the wish or desire of the [Confederate] authorities at Montgomery.* Very few of the public men in the Seceding States even expected war. All of them, it is true, held themselves in readiness for it, if it should be forced upon them against their wishes and most earnest protestations. This is abundantly and conclusively apparent from the speeches and addresses of their leading public men at the time. It is apparent from the resolutions of the State Legislatures, and the State Conventions, before, and in their acts of Secession. It is apparent and manifest from their acts in their new Confederation at Montgomery. It is apparent from the inaugural address of [Confederate] President [Jefferson] Davis. *It is apparent from the appointment of commissioners to settle all matters involved in the separation from their former Confederates honorably, peaceably, amicably, and justly. It is apparent and manifest from every act that truly indicates the objects and motives of men, or from which their real aims can be justly arrived at. Peace not only with the States from which they had separated, but peace with all the world, was the strong desire of the Confederate States.*

It was under these circumstances, that the Confederate commissioners were given to understand, that Fort Sumter would be peacefully evacuated. An assurance to this effect was given, though in an informal manner, by Mr. [William H.] Seward, the Secretary of State under Mr. Lincoln. *This pledge was most strangely violated by sending the armed squadron, as stated, to re-enforce and provision the Fort.* The information that this fleet had put to sea with such orders, reached General Beauregard, when it was already near the offing, as I have stated. He immediately communicated the fact, by telegraph, to the [Confederate] authorities at Montgomery [Alabama]. In reply, he received this order from the Secretary of War of the Confederate States Government [LeRoy P. Walker]:

"If you have no doubt of the authorized character of the agent who communicated to you the intention of the Washington Government to supply Fort Sumter by force, you will at once demand its evacuation; and if this is refused, proceed in such manner as you may determine, to reduce it."

Accordingly, on the 11th of April, [Confederate] General Beauregard made a demand on [U.S.] Major [Robert] Anderson, in command of the Fort, for its evacuation. In reply Major Anderson stated:

"I have the honor to acknowledge the receipt of your communication demanding the evacuation of this Fort, and to say in reply thereto, that it is a demand with which I regret that my sense of honor and my obligation to my Government prevent my compliance."

To this he added, verbally, to the messenger: "I will await the first shot, and, if you do not batter us to pieces, we will be starved out in a few days."

This written reply, as well as the verbal remark, were forthwith sent by General Beauregard to the [C.S.] Secretary of War [Walker] at Montgomery, who immediately returned the following response:

"Do not desire needlessly to bombard Fort Sumter. If Major Anderson will state the time at which, as indicated by himself, he will evacuate, and agree that, in the meantime, he will not use his guns against us, unless ours should be employed against Fort Sumter, you are authorized thus to avoid the effusion of blood. If this or its equivalent be refused, reduce the Fort, as your judgment decides most practicable."

This was communicated to [U.S.] Major Anderson. He refused to comply with the terms. He would not consent to any such arrangement.

The Conservative Confederate Cabinet, L-R: Judah P. Benjamin, Stephen R. Mallory, Christopher G. Memminger, Alexander H. Stephens, LeRoy P. Walker, Jefferson Davis, John H. Reagan, and Robert A. Toombs. At Fort Sumter Liberal Lincoln and his progressive henchmen deceived the South, purposefully luring the Confederacy into firing the first shot. This makes Liberals the instigators of the War, not Conservatives.

Whereupon, [C.S.] General Beauregard opened fire on the Fort at 4:30, on the morning of the 12th of April. The fire was returned. The bombardment lasted for thirty-two hours, when Major Anderson agreed to capitulate. General Beauregard exhibited no less of the magnanimity of the true soldier in the terms of capitulation, than he had of high military skill and genius in forming his plans, and in their execution for the reduction of the Fort. The entire [U.S.] garrison numbering eighty in all, officers and men, was permitted to be marched out with their colors and music. They were permitted to salute their flag with fifty guns. All private as well as company property was also allowed to be taken by those to whom it belonged. These were the same terms that General Beauregard had offered on the 11th, before he opened fire. As Providence ordered it, not a life was lost in this most memorable and frightful combat. The firing on both sides, at some times, particularly at night, was represented by those who witnessed it, as both "grand and terrific."

This was the first blow. It is true, the first gun was fired on the Confederate side. That is fully admitted. But all the facts show that, if force was thus first used by them, it was so first used only, because it was rendered necessary in self-defence on the part of those thus using it, and so rendered necessary by the opposite side. This first use of force, therefore, under the circumstances, cannot, in fact, be properly and justly considered as the beginning of the war.

What has been stated, also, shows how earnestly the [Confederate] authorities at Montgomery, had in every possible way, consistent with honor and safety, endeavored to avoid a collision of forces. *The whole question of the right or wrong, therefore, in striking this first blow, as well as the right or wrong of the war, depends upon the Constitutional points we have been discussing. If the Seceding States were right on these points, then this first blow was perfectly justifiable, even if it had not been given, as it was, to avert one then impending over them.*[528]

Stephens' Liberal friends were quick to respond to the South's view concerning the start of Lincoln's War. "Did the Fort not belong to the United States?" they responded. "Was it not the property of the United States? Were not the officers and men in it attached to the service of the United States? What right, therefore, had Confederate General Beauregard, or any body else, to attempt to prevent the United States Government from provisioning the garrison then holding it, and reenforcing it, if they thought proper? Was it not the duty of Mr. Lincoln to do it, as well as, his right?" Stephens was ready with his usual well informed reply:

Not if South Carolina had the Sovereign right to demand the possession of the Fort. Rights, whether civil, moral, or political, never conflict. If South Carolina had this Sovereign right to demand the possession of the place, which was within her jurisdiction, then Mr. Lincoln could have had no right to continue to hold it against this demand; nor was it his duty, in any sense, to attempt, even, to provision it by force, under the circumstances.

The Fort was within the jurisdiction of South Carolina. It was built specially for her protection, and belonged to her in part as well as to the other States jointly. On the 11ᵗʰ of January, Governor [Francis W.] Pickens, in behalf of the Sovereign Rights of the State, demanded its possession of Major Anderson for the use of the State. On his refusal to deliver it up, the Governor immediately sent Isaac W. Hayne, the Attorney General of the State, to Washington, and made a like demand for its possession of Mr. [James] Buchanan, the [U.S.] President, alleging that the possession of this Fort was necessary for the safety of the State for whose protection it had been erected. In this letter, Governor Pickens also stated, that a full valuation of the property would be accounted for, on settlement of the relations of South Carolina with the United States.

This whole question, relating to the right in this matter, and the side on which the right existed, depends, as I have said, upon the correctness of our conclusions on the points discussed. *If South Carolina, after the resumption of her delegated powers, was a separate, Sovereign State (which is one of our established truths), then, of course, she had a perfect right to demand the possession of any landed property whatever, lying within the limits of her jurisdiction, if she deemed it of importance for her public use and benefit.* This perfect right so to do, was subject to but one limitation, and that was the moral obligation to pay a fair and just compensation for the property so demanded for public use. There can be no question of the correctness of this principle. It is the foundation of the great right of Eminent domain, which ever accompanies Sovereignty. We have seen that this right of Eminent domain was never parted with by her, even under the Constitution. *South Carolina, then, even before Secession, and while she held herself to be*

Conservative U.S. President James Buchanan of Pennsylvania was for allowing the Southern states to peacefully secede.

bound by the Constitution, had a perfect right to demand of the United States Government the possession of this identical property, on paying a just compensation for it, if she had deemed it essential for her public interests. This Fort never could have been erected on her soil without her consent. . . . The title, therefore, of the United States to the land on which Fort Sumter was built, was in no essential respect different from the title of any other land-holder in the State. The tenure by which the United States claimed and held this property, differed in no essential respect from the tenure by which every other land-owner held similar property in the State; nor was this property of the United States, so purchased and held under grant from South Carolina, any less subject to the right of Eminent domain on the part of the State, than any other lands lying within her limits. If this was so even before Secession, (and no one can successfully assail the position,) then how much more clearly this right (by virtue of the principle of Eminent domain,) to demand the possession of this property for public use, for her own protection, appears after she had expressly resumed the exercise of all of her Sovereign powers? *This right to demand the possession of this Fort, therefore, being unquestionably perfect in her as a Sovereign State after Secession, whether it was before or not, she had transferred to the Confederate States. Hence, their right to demand the evacuation of Fort Sumter, was perfect, viewed either morally, or politically.*

. . . *The Confederate States had offered to come to a fair and just settlement with the United States, as to the value of this property, as well as all other public property belonging to all the States in common, at the time of their separation. This Fort, as well as all else that belonged to the United States, belonged in part to these seven Seceded States. They constituted seven of the United States, to which all this joint property belonged. All the Forts which lay within the limits of the Seceded States, had been turned over by these States, respectively, to the Confederacy. . . . The Confederate States, therefore, through their authorities, had a right to demand, and take possession of all of these Forts, so lying within their limits, for their own public use, upon paying a just compensation for them to their former associates of the United States, who still adhered to that Union.* These principles cannot be assailed. *The offer so to pay whatever should be found to be due upon a general and just account, had been made. Mr. Lincoln, therefore, had no right under the circumstances, to hold any of these Forts by force, after the demand for the possession had been made; much less was it his duty either morally, or politically, when it was known that the attempt would inevitably lead to a war between the States. This is my answer to [the Liberals'] . . . property view.*

. . . I do stand upon facts, and these are the incontestable facts of this case, which will forever perpetuate the truth of my assertion, that *upon the head of the Federal Government will forever rest the inauguration of this most terrible war which did ensue.*

No part of its responsibility rests upon the Southern States. They were the aggressors in no instance. They were ever true to their plighted faith under the Constitution. No instance of a breach of its mutual covenants can be ever laid to their charge. The open and palpable breach was committed by a number of their Northern Confederates [i.e., Yankee comrades]. No one can deny this. Those States at the North, which were untrue to their Constitutional engagements, claimed powers not delegated, and elected a Chief Magistrate pledged to carry out principles openly in defiance of the decision of the highest Judicial Tribunal known to the Constitution.

The Battle of Fort Sumter, April 12-14, 1861, the opening of Lincoln's War.

Their policy tended inevitably to a Centralized Despotism. It was under these circumstances that Secession was resorted to, as before stated; and, then, the war was begun and waged by the [liberal] North to prevent the exercise of this Right. All that the [conservative] Southern States did, was in defence, even in their firing the first gun.

[Here is how the Northern States repudiated, and thus violated, their constitutional obligations.] *They did what I say by passing State laws—'Personal Liberty Bills,' so-called—which effectively prevented the execution of that clause of the Constitution which provided for the rendition of fugitives from service.* Several of these States also refused to deliver fugitives from justice, when the crime charged was that of stealing or enticing away any person owing service to another. For, besides their personal liberty acts, which nullified, in the language of Mr. [Daniel] Webster, that provision of the Constitution for the rendition of slaves, the Governors of Maine, New York, and Ohio, had refused to deliver up fugitives from justice, who had been charged with a breach of the laws of the Southern States, in matters relating to the status of the Black race.

. . . As to [this] . . . fact, there can be no doubt. Here, for instance, is the law of Vermont upon the subject.

"Every person who may have been held as a slave, who shall come or who may be brought into this State, with the consent of his or her alleged master or mistress, or who shall come or be brought, or shall be in this State, shall be free.

"Every person who shall hold, or attempt to hold, in this State, in slavery, as a slave, any free person, in any form or for any time, however short, under the pretence that such person is or has been a slave, shall, on conviction thereof, be imprisoned in the State prison for a term not less than five years, nor more than twenty, and be fined not less than one thousand dollars, nor more than ten thousand dollars."

From this it clearly appears, that that State utterly refused to comply with her Constitutional obligations. She did more. She made it penal for any person to attempt to carry out this provision within her limits.

The acts of Massachusetts were not dissimilar. . . . But it is useless to go through with them. I have a document here which renders all that unnecessary. It is the speech of Judge [Salmon P.] Chase before the Peace Congress, so-called, in February, 1861.

So anxious were the people of the South to continue the Union under the Constitution, so desirous were they to stand by and perpetuate the principles of the Constitution, that even after South Carolina seceded, Virginia, the mother of States and Statesmen, she that took the lead in the separation from Great Britain and in the formation of our Federal Republic, as we have seen, made a great and strong effort still to save the Union by calling an informal Congress of the States to deliberate and see if no scheme could be devised to save the country from impending dangers and feuds. A number of States

sent deputies to this Congress. Amongst these deputies was Judge
Chase, then a distinguished leader of the [Liberal] Anti-Slavery Party,
so-called, subsequently Mr. Lincoln's Secretary of Treasury, and now
Chief Justice of the United States. *In that Peace Congress, so assembled,
Judge Chase, on the 6th of February, 1861, in all the candor of his nature,
declared most emphatically to the [conservative] Southern members, that the
[liberal] Northern States never would fulfil that part of their Constitutional
obligations.* His whole speech is exceedingly interesting as one of the
'footprints' of the momentous events of that day. Let me call your
special attention to these parts:

> [Chase said:] "The result of the national canvass which
> recently terminated in the election of Mr. Lincoln, has been
> spoken of by some as the effect of a sudden impulse, or of
> some irregular excitement of the popular mind; and it has
> been somewhat confidently asserted that, upon reflection
> and consideration, the hastily formed opinions which brought
> about that election will be changed. It has been said, also,
> that subordinate questions of local and temporary character
> have augmented the Republican [Liberal] vote, and secured
> a majority which could not have been obtained upon the
> national questions involved in the respective platforms of the
> parties which divide the country.
>
> "I cannot take this view of the result of the Presidential
> election. I believe, and the belief amounts to absolute
> conviction, that the election must be regarded as a triumph
> of principles cherished in the hearts of the people of the Free
> States. These principles, it is true, were originally asserted
> by a small party only. But, after years of discussion, they
> have, by their own value, their own intrinsic soundness,
> obtained the deliberate and unalterable sanction of the
> people's judgment.
>
> *Chief among these principles is the Restriction of Slavery within
> State limits; not war upon Slavery within those limits, but fixed
> opposition to its extension beyond them. Mr. Lincoln was the
> candidate of the people opposed to the extension of Slavery. We have
> elected him. After many years of earnest advocacy and of severe
> trial, we have achieved the triumph of that principle.* By a fair and
> unquestionable majority, we have secured that triumph. Do
> you think we, who represent this majority, will throw it

away? Do you think the people would sustain us if we undertook to throw it away? I must speak to you plainly, gentlemen of the South. It is not in my heart to deceive you. I therefore tell you explicitly, that if we of the North and West would consent to throw away all that has been gamed in the recent triumph of our principles, the people would not sustain us, and so the consent would avail you nothing. And I must tell you further, that *under no inducements, whatever, will we consent to surrender a principle which we believe to be so sound and so important as that of restricting Slavery within State limits*."

Liberal Yankee statesman Salmon P. Chase invented and vigorously promoted the Northern myth about the so-called "Southern slavocracy"—which never existed. Less than 5 percent of white Southern males owned slaves.

This part of the speech was in reference to the claim of power on the part of the Federal Government to prevent the people of the Southern States from going into the common Territories with their slaves, and which power the Supreme Court had decided the General Government had no right to exercise. [Judge Chase] . . . here deliberately asserted, that the Party which elected Mr. Lincoln would not regard this decision of the Supreme Court. But then Mr. Chase goes on to say:

> "Aside from the Territorial question—the question of Slavery outside of Slave States—I know of but one serious difficulty. I refer to the question concerning fugitives from service. The clause in the Constitution concerning this class

of persons is regarded by almost all men, North and South, as a stipulation for the surrender to their masters of slaves escaping into Free States. The people of the Free States, however, who believe that Slave-holding is wrong, cannot and will not aid in the reclamation, and the stipulation becomes, therefore, a dead letter. You complain of bad faith, and the complaint is retorted by denunciations of the cruelty which would drag back to bondage the poor slave who has escaped from it. You, thinking Slavery right, claim the fulfilment of the stipulation; we, thinking Slavery wrong, cannot fulfil the stipulation without consciousness of participation in wrong. Here is a real difficulty, but it seems to me not insuperable. It will not do for us to say to you, in justification of non-performance, 'the stipulation is immoral, and therefore we cannot execute it;' for you deny the immorality, and we cannot assume to judge for you. On the other hand, you ought not to exact from us the literal performance of the stipulation when you know that we

Slave traders in Washington, D.C., with the Capitol Building in the background. Both the American slave trade and American slavery got their start in the Northeast, under the auspices of Yankee Liberals.

cannot perform it without conscious culpability. A true solution of the difficulty seems to be attainable by regarding it as a simple case where a contract, from changed circumstances, cannot be fulfilled exactly as made. A court of equity in such a case decrees execution as near as may be. It requires the party who cannot perform to make compensation for non-performance. Why cannot the same principle be applied to the rendition of fugitives from service? We cannot surrender—but we can compensate. Why not then avoid all difficulties on all sides and show respectively good faith and good-will by providing and accepting compensation where masters reclaim escaping servants and prove their right of reclamation under the

Constitution? Instead of a judgment for rendition, let there be a judgment for compensation, determined by the true value of the services, and let the same judgment assure freedom to the fugitive. The cost to the National Treasury would be as nothing in comparison with the evils of discord and strife. All parties would be gainers."

Whatever may be thought of this as a proposed compromise to induce the Parties to remain in the Union, *no one can doubt its unequivocal declaration that the Non-Slave-holding States would not comply with their acknowledged obligations under the Constitution. It was a confession of one high in authority that that part of the Constitution was a dead letter, and, of course, if the Southern States would not agree to his offer, they were absolved from all further obligation to the Compact.* This is conclusive upon well settled principles of public law.

. . . This declaration that the Northern States would not comply with their Constitutional obligations, bear in mind, was made by the Chancellor of the Exchequer, under Mr. Lincoln. He spoke for the President and his Party. He spoke for that [Liberal Northern] Party which, after the [Conservative] Southern States had seceded, in the House, passed this Resolution:

"Resolved, That as our country, and the very existence of the best government ever instituted by man, are imperilled by the most causeless and wicked rebellion that the world has seen, and believing, as we do, that the only hope of saving this country and preserving this Government is by the power of the sword, we are for the most vigorous prosecution of the war until the Constitution and laws shall be enforced and obeyed in all parts of the United States; and to that end we oppose any armistice, or intervention, or mediation, or proposition for peace from any quarter, so long as there shall be found a Rebel in arms against the Government; and we ignore all party names, lines, and issues, and recognize but two parties in this war—patriots and traitors."

This Resolution passed the [U.S.] House, December 17, 1863, by a vote of ninety-four to sixty-five. The ninety-four votes all belonged to that [Liberal] party for which Judge [Salmon P.] Chase spoke. *Was there ever an instance in the history of the world of such inconsistency, or—no! I will withhold the word I was about to utter. But let me ask, if the Federal arms had been directed against those who resisted the enforcement of the Constitution and the laws of the United States, with the real purpose of preserving "the best Government ever instituted by man," was there a single one of those who voted for this Resolution, who would not justly have been the first subjects of slaughter? These are the men who still talk of "loyal States!" Who still have so much to say of 'loyal men!' Was ever noble word, when properly applied, so prostituted, as this is in its present use by this class of boasting patriots? . . . The [conservative] Southern States were ever loyal and true to the Constitution. This I maintain as a great truth for history. The only true loyalty in this country is fidelity to the principles of the Constitution! The openly 'disloyal,' or those avowedly untrue to the*

Truth-teller Stephens, a hero of the traditional South.

Constitution, were those [liberals in the North] who instigated, inaugurated, and waged this most unrighteous war against their Confederate neighbors! If I express myself with too much fervor on this point, you will please excuse me. I do, however, but express the thorough convictions of my judgment.[529]

Stephens never backed down from a debate over the Constitution, states' rights, slavery, secession, or the cause of Lincoln's War, and for good reason: he had the facts of history on his side:

> . . . there is nothing that [a Liberal] . . . can say on any of these subjects, in accordance with truth and fact, which can ruffle me in the least. It is truth when told to one's disadvantage which generally ruffles temper the quickest.
>
> . . . In this case, I know there is no truth, that can hurt, and as for bare epithets, or declamation, after I have heard with perfect equanimity all that [Northern Liberals] Mr. [Joshua R.] Giddings, Mr. [Owen] Lovejoy, and Mr. [Charles] Sumner have said about "Slavery," "the Slave Power," the "Slavery Oligarchy," the "Slave Driver," etc., I can promise you, in advance, that nothing that [the Liberals] . . . can say upon these subjects, or any other within the range of [these topics] . . . will ruffle me in the least.[530]

ROBERT E. LEE
ON LINCOLN'S WAR

WE NOW TURN TO THE words of Conservative Southerner Robert E. Lee, who, as commander-in-chief of all Confederate armies, was the highest ranked military officer in the South. As such he had access to the inner sanctum at the Confederate White House and was well versed on the causes for which the South and the North fought.

Lee wrote the following letter—which we touched on earlier, but will now quote in full—to Sir John Dalberg Acton (better known as Lord Acton), from Lexington, Virginia, on December 15, 1866. The General, who was President of Washington College (now Washington and Lee University) at the time, and which was thus nicknamed the "Headquarters of the Southern Confederacy" by his adoring students,[531] is responding to a letter from Lord Acton:

> Sir,—Although your letter of the 4th ulto. has been before me some days unanswered, I hope you will not attribute it to a want of interest in the subject, but to my inability to keep pace with my correspondence. As a citizen of the South I feel deeply indebted to you for the sympathy you have evinced in its cause, and am conscious that I owe your kind consideration of myself to my connection with it. The influence of current opinion in Europe upon the current politics

of America must always be salutary; and the importance of the questions now at issue in the United States, involving not only constitutional freedom and constitutional government in this country, but the progress of universal liberty and civilization, invests your proposition with peculiar value, and will add to the obligation which every true American must owe you for your efforts to guide that opinion aright.

Amid the conflicting statements and sentiments in both countries, it will be no easy task to discover the truth, or to relieve it from the mass of prejudice and passion, with which it has been covered by party spirit. I am conscious of the compliment conveyed in your request for my opinion as to the light in which American politics should be viewed, and had I the ability, I have not the time to enter upon a discussion, which was commenced by the founders of the constitution and has been continued to the present day. *I can only say that while I have considered the preservation of the constitutional power of the General Government to be the foundation of our peace and safety at home and abroad, I yet believe that the maintenance of the rights and authority reserved to the states and to the people, not only essential to the adjustment and balance of the general system, but the safeguard to the continuance of a free government.*

The "Old Rebel," Robert E. Lee.

I consider it as the chief source of stability to our political system, whereas the consolidation of the states into one vast republic, sure to be aggressive abroad and despotic at home, will be the certain precursor of that ruin which has overwhelmed all those that have preceded it. I need not refer one so well acquainted as you are with American history, to the State papers of Washington and Jefferson, the representatives of the federal and democratic parties, denouncing consolidation and centralization of power [that is, liberalism, socialism, communism], as tending to the subversion of State Governments, and to despotism. The New England states, whose citizens are the fiercest opponents of the Southern states, did not always avow the opinions they now advocate. Upon the purchase of Louisiana by Mr. Jefferson, they virtually asserted the right of secession through their prominent men; and in the convention which assembled at Hartford in 1814, they threatened the disruption of the Union unless the war should be discontinued.

The assertion of this right has been repeatedly made by their politicians when their party was weak, and Massachusetts, the leading state in hostility to the South, declares in the preamble to her constitution, that the people of that commonwealth "have the sole and exclusive right of governing themselves as a free sovereign and independent state, and do, and forever hereafter shall, exercise and enjoy every power, jurisdiction, and right which is not, or may hereafter be by them expressly delegated to the United States of America in congress assembled."

Such has been in substance the language of other State governments, and such the doctrine advocated by the leading men of the country for the last seventy years. Judge [Salmon P.] Chase, the present Chief Justice of the U. S., as late as 1850, is reported to have stated in the Senate, of which he was a member, that he "knew of no remedy in case of the refusal of a state to perform its stipulations," thereby acknowledging the sovereignty and independence of state action.

But I will not weary you with this unprofitable discussion. Unprofitable because *the judgment of reason has been displaced by the arbitrament of war*, waged for the purpose as avowed of maintaining the union of the states. *If, therefore, the result of the war is to be considered as having decided that the union of the states is inviolable and perpetual under the constitution, it naturally follows that it is as incompetent for the general government to impair its integrity by the exclusion of a state, as for the states to do so by secession; and that the existence and rights of a state by the constitution are as indestructible as the union itself.*

The legitimate consequence then must be the perfect equality of rights of all the states; the exclusive right of each to regulate its internal affairs under rules established by the constitution, and the right of each state to prescribe for itself the qualifications of suffrage. The South has contended only for the supremacy of the constitution, and the just administration of the laws made in pursuance of it. Virginia to the last made great efforts to save the union, and urged harmony and compromise. [Liberal African-American] Senator [Frederick] Douglass, in his remarks upon the compromise bill recommended by the committee of thirteen in 1861, stated that every member from the South, including [Conservative] Messrs. [Robert A.] Toombs and [Jefferson] Davis, expressed their willingness to accept the proposition of Senator [John J.] Crittenden from Kentucky, as a final settlement of the controversy, if sustained by the Republican [Liberal] party, and that the only difficulty in the way of an amicable adjustment was with the Republican party. Who then is responsible for the war?

Although the South would have preferred any honorable compromise to the fratricidal war which has taken place, she now accepts in good faith its constitutional results, and receives without reserve the amendment [the Thirteenth] which has already been made to the constitution for the extinction of slavery. That is an event that has been long sought, though in a different way, and by none has it been more earnestly desired than by citizens of Virginia. In other respects I trust that the constitution may undergo no change, but that it may be handed down to succeeding generations in the form we received it from our forefathers. The desire I feel that the Southern states should possess the good opinion of one whom I esteem as highly as yourself, has caused me to extend my remarks farther than I intended, and I fear it has led me to exhaust your patience. If what I have said should serve to give any information as regards American politics, and enable you to enlighten public opinion as to the true interests of this distracted country, I hope you will pardon its prolixity.

Conservative Southerner Lee believed in and fought for limited government and the constitutional rights of the states, not slavery.

In regard to your inquiry as to my being engaged in preparing a narrative of the campaigns in Virginia, I regret to state that I progress slowly in the collection of the necessary documents for its completion. I particularly feel the loss of the official returns showing the small numbers with which the battles were fought.—With sentiments of great respect, I remain your obt. servant, R. E. Lee.[532]

General Lee could have been speaking of the Liberals' version of Lincoln's War when he advised his daughter Mildred:

Read history, works of truth, not novels and romances. Get correct views of life and learn to see the world in its true light.[533]

Though he shunned the spotlight and did not author any books, the General himself was a truth-teller, one who had a profound appreciation for honest and objective historians. He once made the following remark:

> Everyone should do all in his power to collect and disseminate the truth, in the hope that it may find a place in history and descend to posterity.[534]

As General Lee was a Conservative and a deeply religious Christian, midway through the War he attributed the Confederacy's mounting losses to the fact, in part, that the patriotism of he and his soldiers was not "pure" enough; that is, not strong enough to preserve the Constitution, self-government, and states' rights against the violent and intrusive onslaught of liberalism into the South. On August 21, 1863, after the Gettysburg Campaign, Lee issued an order for a day of "fasting, humiliation and prayer," which included the follow statement:

> Soldiers! we have sinned against Almighty God. We have forgotten His signal mercies, and have cultivated a revengeful, haughty, and boastful spirit. We have not remembered that *the defenders of a just cause* should be pure in His eyes; that our times are in His hands, and we have relied too much on our own arms for the achievement of our independence. God is our only refuge and our strength. Let us humble ourselves before Him. Let us confess our many sins and beseech Him to give us a higher courage, *a purer patriotism*, and a more determined will; that He will convert the hearts of our enemies; that He will hasten the time when war, with its sorrows and sufferings, shall cease, and that He will give us a name and place among the nations of the earth.[535]

In October 1870, in the middle of the Liberals' second war on the South, sardonically known as "Reconstruction," Lee lay dying in his bed. His doctors attributed his coming death "in great measure to moral causes." One of these moral causes was "the bitterness of defeat aggravated by the bad faith and insolence of the victor"—that is, the liberal North.[536] A few months earlier, such treatment had prompted

General Lee to tell Texas Governor Fletcher Stockdale privately:

> Governor, if I had foreseen the use these people [Lee's standard term
> for Liberals, and in particular Yankee Liberals] designed to make of
> their victory, there would have been no surrender at Appomattox
> Courthouse. No, sir, not by me. Had I foreseen these results of
> subjugation, I would have preferred to die at Appomattox with my
> brave men, my sword in this right hand.[537]

General Lee leading a charge on the true enemy. Not
Yankees. Liberalism.

After the War Lee had much to say about the Liberal-dominated
U.S. government and its socialistically and communistically inclined
members in Washington, D.C. On July 9, 1866, he told Captain James
May of Illinois:

> . . . I must give you my special thanks for doing me the justice to
> believe that my conduct during the last five eventful years has been
> governed by my sense of duty. I had no other guide, *nor had I any other
> object than the defence of those [conservative] principles of American liberty
> upon which the constitutions of the several States were originally founded; and
> unless they are strictly observed, I fear there will be an end to Republican
> government in this country.* . . .[538]

In February 1867 he gave his opinion of the Liberal Party, the
Republicans—then known as the National Union Party (1864-
1868)—running the country from Washington:

The dominant party [that is, the liberal Yankee Republicans] cannot reign forever, and truth and justice will at last prevail.[539]

A little later that year Conservative Lee referred to the Liberal government and its anti-American and unconstitutional policies as "the evil that now hangs over our dear land,"[540] declaring:

I cannot think the course pursued by the dominant political party the best for the interests of the country, and therefore cannot say so or give it my approval. . . .[541]

In an 1868 letter to Union General William Starke Rosecrans, Lee made these comments:

At the close of the war, the Southern people laid down their arms and sought to resume their former relations to the government of the United States. Through their State conventions they abolished slavery and annulled their ordinances of secession; and they returned to their peaceful pursuits with a sincere purpose to fulfill all their duties under the Constitution of the United States which they had sworn to support. If their action in these particulars had been met in a spirit of frankness and cordiality, we believe that, ere this, old irritations would have passed away, and the wounds inflicted by the war would have been, in a great measure, healed.

As far as we are advised, the people of the South entertain no unfriendly feeling towards the government of the United States, but they complain that their rights under the Constitution are withheld from them in the administration thereof. *The idea that the Southern people are hostile to the negroes, and would oppress them, if it were in their power to do so, is entirely unfounded. They have grown up in our midst, and we have been accustomed from childhood to look upon them with kindness. The change in the relations of the two races [since the Thirteenth Amendment] has wrought no change in our feelings towards them. . . .*

The important fact that the two races are, under existing circumstances, necessary to each other, is gradually becoming apparent to both, and we believe that but for [the] influences [of Liberals, who have] exerted to stir up the passions of the negroes, the relations of the two races would soon adjust themselves on a basis of mutual kindness and advantage.

. . . The great want of the South is peace. The people earnestly desire

168 ⌒ LINCOLN'S WAR

tranquillity and a restoration of the Union. They deprecate disorder and excitement as the most serious obstacle to their prosperity. They ask a restoration of their rights under the Constitution. They desire relief from oppressive misrule [by the Liberals]. Above all, they would appeal to their countrymen for the re-establishment, in the Southern States, of that which has justly been regarded as the birthright of every American, the right of self-government. Establish these on a firm basis, and we can safely promise, on behalf of the Southern people, that they will faithfully obey the Constitution and laws of the United States, treat the negro population with kindness and humanity, and fulfil every duty incumbent on peaceful citizens, loyal to the Constitution of their country.[542]

In one of his last letters, this one to George W. Jones and dated March 22, 1869, General Lee wrote:

*I was not in favour of secession and was opposed to war. In fact I was for the Constitution and the Union established by our forefathers. No one now is more in favour of that Union and that Constitution, and as far as I know, it is that for which the South has all along contended; and if restored, as I trust they will be, I am sure there will be no truer supporters of that Union and that Constitution than the Southern people. . . . * Present my kindest regards to your brave sons who aided in our struggle for State rights and Constitutional government. *We failed, but in the good providence of God, apparent failure often proves a blessing.* I trust it may eventuate so in this instance.[543]

Today's traditional Southerners, and liberty-loving Conservatives everywhere, trust so as well.

We will close this chapter on the beloved Southern General Lee with the following anecdote. It illustrates the devotion that the "Old Rebel," as he called himself, as well as the average Confederate soldier, had for the Conservative Cause then being waged in the South. It was penned by Miss Elizabeth Ryall, "the daughter of an Ex-Confederate who has always cherished the cause of the Southern Confederacy and who eagerly sought information or incidents relative to the struggle her native Southland made to gain her independence." Here, Miss Elizabeth "remembers a touching scene enacted on the banks of the Potomac as related to her by her father, while that glorious Chieftain, Robert E. Lee was in Virginia":

On a beautiful autumn day while the two armies were confronting each other and only divided by this historic stream, General Lee accompanied only by a staff officer, was riding along the front, on "Traveler," and when he had reached an eminence which commanded a view of the country across the river, and which was occupied by the enemy, dismounted from his horse, and with his field-glasses peered long and earnestly, and involuntarily the glasses dropped from his hands—he came down on bended knees with his face turned to heaven and silently sought intercession with his God;—finally arising with tears streaming down his face, his manly form trembling with emotion, his voice choking and almost inaudible—"Adjutant," he said, "this is the most trying ordeal of my life. In that house on yonder hill I first met my wife, under its roof and on that veranda I wooed and won her love, under the shade of the trees my children have played, the enemy has discovered its commanding view to gain vantage ground and thus imperil the result of our success in the coming conflict—they must be dislodged at any cost, although the dearest spot on earth to me, it must and shall be done. Order those batteries to this point and have them to storm with shot and shell, if necessary, until not one vestige of the house is left."[544]

After reading this, can any intelligent individual seriously believe that General Lee—an ardent antebellum abolitionist who did not personally own any slaves and openly "hated slavery"[545]—was willing to make such personal sacrifices in order to preserve the peculiar institution?

Lee surveying the battlefield with some of his officers. No truer American patriot ever lived, yet today uneducated Liberals, and even some uninformed Conservatives, continue to call him a "traitor."

7

CONFEDERATE OFFICERS ON LINCOLN'S WAR

WE HAVE EXAMINED THE REAL cause, the real winner, and the real loser of Lincoln's War. Let us continue our study to uncover the unvarnished facts about the conflict with a presentism-free look at the thoughts and words of Confederate officers who lived through it. The importance of eyewitness accounts is obvious.

The *original* words of the Victorians of the "Civil War" period cannot be and have not been distorted, rewritten, perverted, or edited by the left-wing foes of authentic history. Yes, Liberals and other anti-American groups and movements have ignored them and have even tried to suppress them, carefully

Confederate General Albert Pike, like the author, a Conservative supporter of the Southern Cause and a Christian mystic.

hiding them from the public. But, thankfully, they have survived, for they were recorded long ago in 19th- and early 20th-Century articles, speeches, and books which have been forever preserved as part of America's historical record. It is these chronicles we will now peruse in our quest to uncover further confirmation regarding the real cause, the real winner, and the real loser of Lincoln's War on the American people and the Constitution.

In 1918 the celebrated Confederate clergyman Reverend James Hugh McNeilly of Nashville, Tennessee, wrote of the importance of establishing and recording the truth about the conflict and its brave conservative patriots for the benefit of future generations:

> Every true American soldier should go into this war [that is, World War I] resolved to keep untarnished the name and fame of his ancestry by his own worthy deeds. This is especially true of those who are heirs of the traditions of the Confederate soldiers of 1861 to 1865, in whose veins flows the blood of the men and women of that heroic period, and all the more because of *the malignant and persistent efforts to misrepresent and dishonor the memory of those who stood for four years of dreadful conflict for their constitutional rights. The cause, origin, and course of that war between the States, when truly recorded, will vindicate the Southern people as standing for liberty and justice.* It is ours to see that the history is truly written and falsehoods corrected. And we may be sure that time, with slow, unswerving step, will in the end overtake every false hood and trample it into the dust of forgetfulness. We may not write the final word as to *that great war of principles*, but we can gather and record the materials from which the future historian shall make up the authoritative verdict of history.[546]

That same year, 1918, Cornelius H. Fauntleroy of St. Louis, Missouri, made these comments:

> *Fighting for their constitutional rights, the Southerners who supported their Confederacy offered up their lives and their property without pay, stint, or hesitation for their cause. At the end of the war they faced widespread devastation, wholesale bankruptcy, and slavery for years under the carpet-bagger and negro régime. Where can such an enormous and heroic sacrifice of life and property for the sake of constitutional principle be found?*
> *The most distinctive and brilliant characteristic of the English-speaking*

Secession was not a "treasonous act" invented by the Southern Confederacy in 1860. When Antifederalist (Conservative) U.S. President Thomas Jefferson bought Louisiana in 1803, Massachusetts Liberals threatened to secede—only one of many times they did so.

peoples is their deathless love of constitutional principles and limitations. John Hampden, gentleman, as [British historian Thomas B.] Macaulay calls him, and not that bloody despot and hypocrite, Oliver Cromwell, was the hero of the rebellion against Charles I, for the latter's violation of the English Constitution. Hampden said: "I am a rich man and am easily able to pay the shilling tax which Charles Stuart has levied against me; but he has done so in violation of the Constitution of England without an act of Parliament, and I will not pay it, but will take up arms against him." He did so; and when King Charles I heard of his having been mortally wounded in the battle of Chalgrove Field, he sent his royal surgeon to attend him, but in vain. Few names stand as high in the temple of fame as that of Hampden. The American people in their war of independence [1775] started their revolution to vindicate their constitutional rights. *So did the Southern people in their War between the States [1861]. In no section of the United States have there existed reverence for and obedience to the Constitution as widespread and potent as in the Southern States.*

By the Southern people the Constitution has never been regarded as obsolete nor as "a scrap of paper" [as it was called by early American Liberals]. One of the strangest and most significant things in American history is the careful suppression by Northern writers of the assertion by the State of Massachusetts and by many of the leading men in the New England States of their right of secession and of the official declaration of open and unyielding resistance to the Federal government by members of the governments of other leading Northern States. These momentous facts of American history are also carefully excluded from the schools and many of the colleges from Boston to San Francisco.

When Thomas Jefferson, as President of the United States, purchased for the Federal government the vast Louisiana Territory in 1803, the legislature of Massachusetts passed the following resolution:

"Resolved, That the annexation of Louisiana to the Union transcends the constitutional power of the government of the United States. *It forms a new confederacy to which the States united by a former compact are not bound to adhere.*"[547]

In a 1918 article entitled "Service With the Shelby Grays," Nathan D. Bachman of Bristol, Tennessee, writes:

I have carefully, and I might say eagerly, read a great deal concerning the conditions that existed prior to 1861 and the real causes of the War between the States; and now that the issues involved have been settled and were settled by force of arms, I am thoroughly satisfied that *so long as we have in reality a republican [conservative] form of government in the United States of America the principles and governmental doctrines for which Confederate soldiers fought will live. Confederate soldiers were not "rebels"; they fought and contended for rights and privileges guaranteed by the Constitution, and the mere fact of our defeat should not be taken as evidence that our cause was not just. It was clearly a case in which "might triumphed over right."*[548]

Conservative Confederate surgeon Dr. Hunter H. McGuire of Virginia.

In 1907 Dr. Hunter Holmes McGuire, Chief Surgeon in Confederate General Stonewall Jackson's army (and the man who amputated Jackson's left arm just before he died), wrote the following "paper" on the real cause of Lincoln's War. It derives from an article rebutting the work of liberal Yankee historian John Fiske of Connecticut, whose terribly written, inaccurate, Northern-slanted "history" books the U.S. government was intentionally installing in Southern schools—an effort to turn Dixie's children against their noble conservative heritage:

We return to the most offensive doctrine of the books that we condemn, the charge that the Southern soldier fought for slave property. If this charge be just, let the truth be taught. It is false. The answer to it is on every page of our history, and the books that make the charge should not be used in our schools.

We all remember how many Virginians of 1861, knowing that the bloodthirst of [the English battles of] Naseby and Marston Moor was unslaked, yet weary of the blood-feud that had antedated the Revolution; tired of sectional strife recurring with every question of general interest; simply weary of quarrelling; convinced by the election of Lincoln that the quarrel never would end—went into the war in hope of conquering peace, and *before going gave their negroes leave to be free, if they chose.* The attitude of one or two prominent fighters with respect to slave property will be sufficient for our purpose.

The *Campaigns of Stonewall Jackson*, by Colonel G. F. E. Henderson, of the British Staff College, Camberley, England, should be read by every man, woman, and child in the South. It would help the Northern people to a knowledge of the truth. [In it] we find the following extract from a letter of General Robert E. Lee:

> "In this enlightened age," wrote the future general-in-chief of the Confederate army, "there are few, I believe, but will acknowledge that *slavery as an institution is a moral and political evil.* It is useless to expatiate on its disadvantages. *I think it is a greater evil to the white than to the colored race*, and while my feelings are strongly interested in the latter, *my sympathies are more deeply engaged for the former.* The blacks are immeasurably better off here than in Africa—morally, socially, and physically. The painful discipline they are undergoing is necessary for their instruction as a race, and, I hope, will prepare them for better things. How long their subjection may be necessary is known and ordered by a merciful Providence. *Their emancipation will sooner result from the mild and melting influence of Christianity than from the storms and contests of fiery controversy.* This influence, though slow, is sure. The doctrines and miracles of our Saviour have required nearly two thousand years to convert but a small part of the human race, and even among Christian nations what gross errors still exist!
>
> While *we see the course of the final abolition of slavery is still onward, and we give it the aid of our prayers and all justifiable means in our power*, we must leave the progress as well as the result in His hands who sees the end and who chooses to work by slow things, and with whom a thousand years are

but as a single day. The Abolitionist must know this, and must see that he has neither the right nor the power of operating except by moral means and suasion; if he means well to the slave he must not create angry feelings in the master. Although he may not approve of the mode by which it pleases Providence to accomplish its purposes, the result will nevertheless be the same; and the reason he gives for interference in what he has no concern holds good for every kind of interference with our neighbors when we disapprove of their conduct."

The army of Conservative Confederate General Stonewall Jackson included some 3,000 armed and uniformed black soldiers. Though according to the U.S. Census, Jackson, an avid abolitionist, had slaves in his household, contrary to Yankee myth he was not a true slave owner, for those who lived with him did so voluntarily. In 1855, six years before Lincoln's War, and ten years before the Thirteenth Amendment was ratified, Jackson founded and personally funded an all black Sunday School in Lexington, Virginia, where he himself sometimes taught. After his untimely death his many African-American friends donated money toward the erection of his memorial. You will never read these facts in any pro-North history book.

On the same page Colonel Henderson quotes from the lips of Mrs. [Stonewall] Jackson like opinions held by her husband. These are opinions expressed before the war. Do they indicate that Lee and Jackson fought to preserve slave property? *I myself know that at the beginning of the war General Lee, wise and far-seeing beyond his fellow-men, was in favor of freeing all the slaves in the South, giving to each owner a bond, to be the first paid by the Confederacy when its independence should be secured; and that Stonewall Jackson, while believing in the Scriptural right to own slaves, thought it would be politic in the white people to free them.*

He owned two—one a negro man, whose first owner, being in financial difficulties, was compelled to sell. The negro asked General Jackson to buy him, and let him work until he accumulated the money to pay the General back. He was a waiter in a hotel, and in a few years earned the money; gave it to Jackson, and secured his freedom. The other was a negress about to be sold and sent away from Lexington. She asked Jackson to buy her, which he did, and then offered to let her work as the man had done and secure her freedom. She preferred to stay with the General and his wife as a slave, and was an honest, faithful, and affectionate servant.

General Joseph E. Johnston never owned a slave. How much of the fighting spirit and purpose of the South was in the breast of Lee, Johnston, and Jackson? Do the facts recited indicate that the desire to retain slave property gave them nerve for the battle? *Does any man living know of a soldier in this State who was fighting for the negro or his value in money? I never heard of one.*

The Stonewall Brigade of the Army of Northern Virginia, was a fighting organization. I knew nearly every man in it, for I belonged to it for a long time; and I know that I am within proper bounds when I assert that *there was not one soldier in thirty who owned or ever expected to own a slave.* "The South fighting for the money value of the negro!" What a cheap and wicked falsehood!

MOTIVES OF ACTION

Finally, and this deserves a separate paragraph—with respect to the motives of action, we would be glad if [Yankee historian] Mr. [John] Fiske [who wrote a number of anti-South "histories"] or any other Northern author would relieve us of the mental confusion resulting from the contemplation of the facts that *Robert E. Lee set free all of his slaves long before the Sectional War began, and that U. S. Grant retained his as slaves until they were made free as one of the results of Lincoln's Emancipation Proclamation.*

Soldiers and gentlemen, we accepted in full faith and honesty the arbitrament of the sword. We are to-day all that may be honorably meant by the expression "loyal American citizens." But we are also loyal to the memory of our glorious dead, and the heroic living of the Confederacy, and we will defend them in our poor way from the false and foul aspersions of Northern historians as long as brain can think or tongue and pen can do their office. We desire that our children shall be animated by the same spirit.

Mr. Fiske furthermore teaches our children that, but for the war the South would have reopened the slave trade. He tells, without quotation of authorities, a certain story of slave ships landing their cargoes in the South. Those of us who were men in the later fifties will remember a rumor . . . that one or more ships, owned and commanded by Northern men, were engaged in the same work. The stories may or may not have been true.

Granted the truth; the fact that one or more Yankee slave-traders had returned to the sins of their fathers does not prove that 20,000,000 of them were about to do so; nor does the purchase of such cargoes by half a dozen Southern planters prove that 5,000,000 of them had determined thus to strengthen their working forces.

WHAT HE OVERLOOKS

In his work Mr. Fiske overlooks the fact that *the Confederate Government, at the first meeting of its Congress, incorporated into its Constitution a clause*

It was England's King George III who first forced slavery on the American colonies.

which forever forbade the reopening of the slave trade. I beg you to consider the following contrast: [The British King] George III forced the Virginia Governor to veto our Virginia act of 1769, prohibiting the further importation of slaves. Mr. Fiske tells us that "in Jefferson's first draft of the Declaration of Independence this act (of the King) was made the occasion of a fierce denunciation of slavery, but in deference to the prejudices of South Carolina and Georgia, the clause was struck out by Congress." The different impressions made on different authors by the same facts is to be observed. Mr. George Lunt, of Boston (*Origin of the Late War*), understood Mr. Jefferson to show that *the omission was very largely due to "the influence of the Northern maritime States."* Mr. Jefferson wrote the passage and describes the incident. To us, it appears from his account that this denunciation was of the King not less than—perhaps more than—of *this traffic to which we Virginians were so much opposed*. As to the omission of the passage, he gives Mr. Fiske's statement as to South Carolina and Georgia, but adds the following, which Mr. Fiske omits:

> "*Our Northern [liberal] brethren* also, I believe, felt a little tender under these censures, for though their people had very few slaves, yet *they had been pretty considerable carriers of them to others [that is, slave traders]*."

Of course, historians cannot say everything—must omit something. We could wish, however, that our author had displayed a less judicious taste in omissions.

Be it understood that we ourselves omit many things that we would say, but for the fact that we are only seeking to supply some of Mr. Fiske's omissions, and so establish our proposition that our children cannot get true pictures from this artist's brush, and that *his book ought not to be in our schools*.

UNHOLY COMBINATION

The Origin of the Late War, published by the Appleton's in 1866, but out of print for lack of Northern popularity, is a book pre-eminently, worthy of reading. Its author, Mr. George Lunt, of Boston, in Mr. Fiske's own State of Massachusetts, tells us that an unholy combination between Massachusetts Freesoilers and Democrats to defeat the Whigs, with no reference to any principle at all, sent [Charles] Sumner to Congress and materially contributed to the cause of the war, partly through the Preston [S.] Brooks incident, which Mr. Fiske so unfairly describes. "Slavery," this author observes, "was the cause of war, just as property is the cause of robbery."

If Mr. Fiske will read the Lincoln and Douglas debates of the time before the war; if he will lay aside preconceived opinion and read the Emancipation Proclamation itself, he will see that not even for Lincoln himself was slavery the cause of action, or its abolition his intent; that emancipation was simply a war measure, not affecting, as you know, the border States that had not seceded; even excluding from its operation certain counties of Virginia; simply intended to disable the fighting States, and more thoroughly to unite the rabid Abolitionists of the North in his own deadly purpose to overthrow the constitutional rights of the States.

Just after the battle of Sharpsburg, from which, as you remember, he dated his abolition proclamation, he very clearly indicated his view of the cause or purpose of the war on his part. "If I could save the Union," he said, "by freeing the slaves, I would do it; if I could save it by freeing one-half and keeping the other half in slavery, I would take that plan; if keeping them all in slavery would effect the object, then that would be my course."

Further, with respect to the provocation offered to the South that led to the war—so far as slavery was its cause—Mr. [Daniel] Webster,

Liberal statesman Daniel Webster of New Hampshire.

in his speech at Capon Springs in 1851, used these words: *"I do not hesitate to say and repeat that if the Northern States refuse willfully and deliberately to carry into effect that part of the Constitution which respects the restoration of fugitive slaves, the South would no longer be bound to keep the compact." Mr. Lunt and Mr. Webster were Massachusetts men, like Mr. Fiske. Mr. Webster was a great constitutional lawyer; Mr. Lincoln was President. Yet we do not learn from Mr. Fiske that any of these heresies or mistaken purposes had currency in Massachusetts or in the Union. He would teach all men that Mr. Lincoln claims immortality as the apostle of freedom. He is the co-worker with the orator of their absurd Peace Jubilee, who lately proclaimed that the flag of Washington was the flag of independence; the flag of Lincoln the flag of liberty.*

FALSE PICTURE

"Demands of slave-holders," "Concessions to slave-holders." These and the like are the expressions our author uses to paint a picture of an aggressive [conservative] South and a conciliatory [liberal] North. Through and through this author's work runs the same evidence of *preconception as to the causes of war*, and *predetermined purpose as to the effect his book is to produce*; the same consciousness of the necessity laid upon him and his co-laborers; the same *proof of his consequent inability to write a true history of the sectional strife; the same proof that his book is unfit to be placed in the hands of Southern children.*

. . . [As to the reason for the war, Fiske believes that] "slavery was the cause," but only in so far as the action of the South made it so, and by no means in consequence of any act done by the North or Northern men. That is the doctrine that [he thinks] we must teach our children.

[To him] even the John Brown raid is outside of the group of causes. [But we know that] that was beyond question an overt act of Northern men [and had nothing to do with Southern men]. Therefore, [in Civil War books written by Liberals] the [John Brown] incident is to be minimized in history and effect.

Those of you who remember the situation and possibly marched to Harper's Ferry on that occasion, will be surprised to note that Mr. Fiske says "he (Brown) intended to make an asylum in the mountains for the negroes, and that the North took little notice of his raid." There is no occasion for answering such a statement. We know that [ultra Liberal] Brown and those [radical Liberals] who sent him here, aiding him to buy his pikes, etc., purposed war, intending that his fort should be the headquarters of an insurrection of the negroes, and purposed that his pikes should be driven into the breasts of Virginia men and women. All of us remember the platform and pulpit denunciation of our people, the parading, the bell-tolling, and other clamorous manifestations of approval and sympathy which went through the North and convinced the people of Virginia that the long-threatened war of the North against the South had at last begun. In this sense, perhaps, [the John Brown Raid] . . . was not [one] of the causes of the war; it was the war.

I myself saw the demonstration of the Northern people on that occasion. Happening to be at that time living in Philadelphia, it was instantly plain to me that I was in an enemy's country. The southern students around me saw it as plainly as I did. It took but a dozen sentences to open the eyes of the least intelligent. It was only to say, "Come on, boys! Let's go!" and three hundred of us marched over on our side of the line. The war for us was on, and I know that the State of Virginia knew that was what the North meant. Just how Mr. Fiske enables himself to make the statement quoted, we cannot understand. We only see another proof that *his point of view distorts the picture* in his mind, *to such an extent that he ought not to be employed as a painter for us or our children.*

Much has been said of Mr. Fiske's elegant style. We will only observe that *the sugar-coating of a pill does not justify our administering poison.* The Trojan horse may have been a shapely structure, but in its belly were concealed the enemies of the city. It has been said, perhaps untruly, that the rounded period marks the unreliable historian. There have been notable examples of it. And it is certainly true that *an inconvenient fact* does sometimes give pain to a writer who is in the habit of testing his sentences by his ear.[549]

In 1914 educator, author, and former Confederate Captain John Anderson Richardson of Georgia did posterity a great service by publishing his book *Richardson's Defense of the South*. What follows is an excerpt from his chapter on "Who Caused the War?"

The thirteen original Colonies declared themselves "States in the same sense that Great Britain is a State." That meant they were sovereignties in the full sense. Therefore the compact they formed was one of sovereign States. [We will also note the] legal maxim: *"Everything is dissolved by the same means it is constituted."* To this we add the same well established legal truth [as given by Herbert Broom in his legal maxims] in these words: *"Nothing is so consonant to natural equity as that every contract should be dissolved by the same means that rendered it binding."*

The thirteen original States formed a compact among themselves by adopting ordinances ratifying the same Constitution, each in its own way, and at its own time and place. Thus they rendered the common Constitution "binding." In the same way, or "by the same means" the eleven seceding States of the South in 1860-61 "dissolved" this compact. They therefore acted within their legal rights and the United States Government had no more right to coerce them than she would have to coerce England for dissolving a compact between her and England. If we take the definition of a State as given by the thirteen original States, there is no evading the conclusion. Their definition is the only true one since they Constituted the States. Therefore the conclusion is inevitable.

If then *it is inevitably true that the eleven Southern States in 1860-61, had the legal and natural right to dissolve the compact just as they formed it*; and at the same time expressed a desire that their dissolution should be peaceful, who caused the war?

They not only "dissolved" the Union "by the same means by which they constituted it," but *they also sought by all honorable means to make their dissolution a peaceful one. This honest desire they declared both by words and acts. They immediately sent commissioners to Washington in the interest of peace and goodwill. These commissioners were encouraged to hope, only to be deceived.* Who then caused the war?

Not only did their words and acts most emphatically declare for a peaceful separation, but their unpreparedness for war most earnestly proclaimed their desires for peace. They were an agricultural people, inexperienced as to war.

They were without arms and the means of manufacturing them. In short they were without all the essentials of war except brave hearts and a conviction of right. Would such a people, under such circumstances, deliberately inaugurate war? Who then caused the war?

Conservative, Confederate Captain, and fervent Southern defender, John A. Richardson.

The real cause of the war lay in the [Liberals'] violation of the Constitution. It is confessed that our [country's] political organization was more or less complex. But its complexity was not at fault. It was its plain precepts that were violated.

1. The assumption by the dominant party [that is, the Republican or Liberal Party at the time] that the [tacit] silence of the Constitution [concerning secession] conferred authority upon the Federal Government was a plain violation of the Constitution. No reputable historian, North or South, denies this. Yet the silence of the Constitution was the main basis upon which Lincoln, in his inaugural, built his doctrine of restriction and coercion. But *restriction and coercion were unconstitutional.* Who caused the war?

2. Every Compromise was a violation of the Constitution. This cannot be denied. Each compromise was the result of aggression, and *it is an indisputable fact of history that all aggression came from the North [the Liberals]. Aggression, according to [Noah] Webster, means "the first attack." Every "first attack" upon the Constitution was made by the [liberal] North, and the [conservative] South, in consenting to a compromise through her love for the Union, also became violators of that instrument in a reluctant*

sense. On the part of the South it was a reluctant yielding of her rights to secure peace. On the part of the North it was pure and simple aggression to prevent the extension of slave territory. The South can truthfully assert that in no other way did she ever violate the Constitution. This is her proud boast: her impregnable defense against the false charges that she caused the war.

3. The refusal to obey the universally acknowledged decision of the Supreme Court was another and indisputable violation of the Constitution [by the Liberal Party]. All know that [big government Liberal] Lincoln rebelled against this decision in his celebrated Cooper Institute Speech; that he next led a great political party in rebellion against it; that he was elected president as an avowed enemy against it; that as such he was inaugurated president; and that as president his declared policy was against it. At first it was Lincoln and the Republican [Liberal] party who opposed the decision of this Court. After that subtle deceptive inaugural address to which we have referred, it was Lincoln, the Republican [Liberal] party and a practically united North. Who, then, caused the war?

4. The Constitution was violated—yea more, it was supplanted, it was rendered obsolete—by a false *"higher law,"* a "false common law"; and a false *"unwritten Constitution,"* etc. [fabricated out of thin air by Liberals]. As for the [conservative] South, she knew but one Constitution; the one common to all the States alike; the one ratified by all the States in the same manner,—by separate State Conventions; the one Constitution to which all the States alike had sworn eternal fidelity. The South knew of a "higher law" that existed when Adam and Eve walked together in the Garden of Eden; "a higher law" that existed in all succeeding ages; a "higher law" written on the tablets of human hearts, rendering more sacred and more binding the oaths of the States and of their citizens, to obey its God-given precepts; a "higher law" that uses human statutes and human governments, as "ordained of God," to advance and strengthen its influence and power among men; a higher law that was never designed by its divine author to supplant and render obsolete human statutes, human institutions and human governments: a "higher law" that gives aid and strength to human laws, *but never supplants them.*

The [conservative] South knew of "a common law" a rule of action "immemorially received and recognized by judicial tribunals"; a common law "which derives its authority from long usage, or established custom," not from the supposed change of convictions of men,—not from "the ignorance of foreigners" as to our Federal

Constitution; but a common law that reaches back "beyond the memory of man," and was therefore in full force when our fathers wrote the Constitution and which aided them in framing that "most wonderful" political document. This common law did not then render the Constitution obsolete. It established it. What credence then are we to give to the very remarkable claim that it changed its nature in 1860-61, and rendered the Constitution obsolete? *It was not the "Common Law," unchangeable by its very nature and definition, that then rendered our Constitution obsolete, and inaugurated what our own Supreme Court has pronounced to be the greatest "Civil War" of the world; but a so-called false common law, based on a presumed, not a verified, change of human opinions as to the real character of our Republican form of Government: a so-called common law was not in the least sense common, but sectional to the core.* Who then caused the war?

As to an "Unwritten Constitution" the [conservative] South was in absolute ignorance of it till its existence was proclaimed and it was defined by Francis Newton Thorpe in The Civil War from a Northern Standpoint. *Was it treason to disobey a Constitution of which one had never heard? This was the false charge made in the 1860s. Treason is rebellion against the Constitution that represents the Government it established. That Constitution,—that Government,—was the one formed, in Philadelphia in 1787. To this Constitution all history in unbroken evidence attests the fidelity of the South. Even the North admits this in calling the South of the Sixties "Eighteenth Century reactionists."* Who then caused the war?

The charge made to the world by the United States Government that the Southern States in their State conventions, and in their general Convention at Montgomery, were "Conspirators against the principles of the United States Government," was a declaration of war. For who has ever heard of a bona fide conspiracy against a reputable Government that did not call forth the strong arm of the Government to crush it? If that charge, as published to the world, was true the South deserved the avenging hand of war. If it was a false charge the South did not merit the sword and the torch.

The open, frank, earnest, and patriotic manner in which these States had protested against the infringements upon their Constitutional rights refutes the charge. When all protests had failed, and all efforts at compromise had proved futile, they met in conventions of their own. These Conventions were advertised, in advance, to the world; and the objects for which they were called were known of all men. Conspiracy is born in secret, but there were no secrets in any of these Conventions. They had grievances. These they met to discuss and to devise remedies. Their debates upon the question of secession were able, earnest, and spirited. All the speakers were a unit as to the right of secession, but a large minority, and among them some of the ablest statesmen of the South, did not believe in the policy of secession as the best remedy. Strange to say this fact lead Lincoln and his party to believe that the South was divided on the question of the legal right of secession.

In the Convention of the States which met at Montgomery there was the same open, manly, frank, and dignified discussion of questions of vital importance pertaining to their common interest. *All their proceedings were published to the world. They concealed nothing. The very Constitution this Convention devised and submitted to the States for ratification, is a standing refutation of the charge of conspiracy.* Of this [the Confederate] Constitution the Honorable Alexander H. Stephens speaks in these pertinent words:

> *"The whole document utterly negatives the idea which many have been active in endeavoring to put in the enduring form of history, that the Convention at Montgomery was nothing but a set of 'Conspirators' whose object was the overthrow of the principles of the Constitution of the United States, and the erection of a great 'slave oligarchy' instead of the free institutions thereby secured and guaranteed. This work of the Montgomery Convention with that of the provisional Government, will ever remain, not only a monument of the wisdom, forecast, and statesmanship of the men who constituted it, but an everlasting refutation of the charges which have been brought against them. These works together show clearly that their only leading object was to sustain, uphold, and perpetuate the fundamental principles of the Constitution of the United States."*

This [Confederate] Constitution was modeled after that of the United States. The preamble to each is substantially the same, almost in the identical words. No changes in the entire instrument were made except such as experience had dictated. *It stands also as an impregnable bulwark of defense against the often repeated charge that "the Confederacy was founded on slavery," that "its corner-stone was slavery."*

"Property in slaves, already existing, was recognized and guaranteed, just as it was in the Constitution of the United States." But the "extension of slavery," the cause of great complaint by Lincoln and his party, was more effectually prevented by the Constitution of the Confederacy than by that of the United States, as witnessed by the instruments themselves.

Black slaves on a plantation in 18th-Century Massachusetts, the birthplace of American slavery. The institution was constitutionally legal across the entire U.S. until the issuance of the Thirteenth Amendment in December 1865—eight months after the end of the Civil War. Up until that month an estimated 500,000 to 1,000,000 Northern slaves were owned by 315,000 Yankee slaveholders, including Union General Ulysses S. Grant. Obviously then, slavery could not have been the cause of the conflict. Despite these historical facts Liberals continue to blame the conservative South for both American slavery *and* the War.

In the 9th section of the Constitution of the United States are these words:

"The migration or importation of such persons as any of the States now existing shall think proper to admit, shall not be prohibited by the Congress prior to the year one thousand eight hundred and eight; but a tax or duty may be imposed on such importations not exceeding ten dollars for each person."

From the 9th section of the Confederate Constitution we quote as follows:

1. "The importation of negroes of the African race from any foreign country other than the slave-holding States or Territories of the United States of America, is hereby forbidden; and Congress is required to pass such laws as shall effectually prevent the same.

2. "Congress shall also have the power to prohibit the introduction of slaves from any State, not a member of, or Territory not belonging to this Confederacy."

These extracts speak for themselves. That form, the Federal [U.S.] Constitution, declares the "importation of slaves" shall not be prohibited prior to the year 1808"; and then follow "but a tax or duty may be imposed on such importations, not exceeding ten dollars for each person." What is the meaning of this clause? Does it not virtually annul the preceding clause by further legalizing the importation of slaves? If it does not further legalize the importation of slaves, what is the meaning of the right to impose "a tax or duty on such importations?" The fact cannot be denied that after 1808 [the U.S.] Congress still had the power to encourage the importation of slaves.

But what is the voice of the extract from the Confederate Constitution? Its clear-cut meaning is "The importation of negroes" from Africa "*is hereby forbidden,*"—positively forbidden; and [the C.S.] Congress was required to enforce this mandate of the States through their Constitution. This clause gives Congress but one discretion, that of admitting slaves from any State or Territory of the United States; and this one discretion is the language of friendship, not of war.

As the charge of "Conspiracy" was a declaration of war, so was that of "insurrection," of "rebellion" and of "treason." When the speaker and other members of the Burgesses cried "treason, treason," to the impassioned words of the fiery [Patrick] Henry they knew well the meaning of treason, and so did the bold and impetuous Henry as he finished his sentence: "May profit by their example. If this, be treason, make the most of it." So too the Colonies knew it meant war when they rebelled against Great Britain; and the seven long years of war were the result. When the cry of "conspiracy," "insurrection," "rebellion," and "treason" went forth from the White House, all the world knew it meant war, and only war; and the four succeeding years presented the bloodiest page of history. Who then caused the war?

Let us next consider the attitude of the Confederate States. Perhaps no better evidence can be produced than extracts from the inaugural address of Mr. [Jefferson] Davis as President of the

Provisional Government, delivered on the 18th of February, 1861. He says,

> "The declared purpose of the Compact of the Union from which we have withdrawn, was to 'establish justice, insure domestic tranquility, provide for the common defence, promote the general welfare and secure the blessings of liberty to our selves and posterity'; and *when in the judgment of the Sovereign States now composing this Confederacy, it had been perverted from the purpose for which it was ordained, and had ceased to answer the ends for which it was established, a peaceful appeal to the ballot-box declared that, so far as they were concerned, the Government created by that compact should cease to exist. In this, they merely asserted a right which the Declaration of Independency of 1776, had defined to be inalienable.*
>
> Of the time and occasion for its exercise they, as Sovereigns, were the final judges each of itself. *The impartial and enlightened verdict of mankind will vindicate the rectitude of our conduct, and He who knows the hearts of men, will judge of the sincerity with which we labored to preserve the Government of our fathers in its spirit. The right solemnly proclaimed at the birth of the States, and which has been affirmed in the Bills of Rights of States, subsequently admitted into the Union of 1789, undeniably recognizes in the people the power to resume the authority delegated for the purpose of Government. Thus the Sovereign States here represented, proceeded to form this Confederacy, and it is by abuse of language that their act has been denominated a Revolution. They formed a new alliance, but within each State its Government has remained, and the rights of persons and property have not been disturbed.* The agent through whom they communicated with foreign nations, is changed; but this does not necessarily interrupt their international relations."

Is there any declaration of war in words like these? Consider this: "They merely asserted a right which the Declaration of Independence of 1776, had declared to be inalienable," that is cannot or should not, be alienated, surrendered or transferred to another. Is the Declaration of Independence good authority? Then who can doubt the correctness of this position? If it cannot be doubted, who caused the war?

Consider these other words: "He who knows the hearts of men, will judge of the sincerity with which we labored to preserve the Government of our Fathers in its spirit." *History is full of the sacrifices made by the South, and of her efforts to preserve the Union. This assertion cannot be challenged. It greets the patriot's eye on every page of the history of the times.*

Again: "It is an abuse of language that their act has been denominated a Revolution. They formed a new alliance, but within

each State its Government has remained, and the rights of persons and property have not been disturbed. The agent through whom they communicated with foreign powers is changed; but this does not necessarily interrupt their international relations." With what dignity of speech does Mr. Davis here meet the charge of Mr. Lincoln that he leads a revolution against the Federal Government! The assertion of a revolution "is an abuse of language." *"They," the Southern States, have "formed a new alliance" as was their right according to the Declaration of Independence. The United States Government had been their "agent through whom they communicated with foreign nations," but now these States have met and appointed another agent for this purpose. If the Declaration of Independence be true this is not revolution. By it Massachusetts freed her slaves to the surprise of her citizens. For its truth every State in the Union vouches.* Then who caused the war? We quote further from this inaugural address [by Jefferson Davis]:

Liberal Lincoln incorrectly referred to the conservative Confederate Cause as a "revolution," the same word that Karl Marx and thousands of other socialists and communists used to describe it. Only radical Liberals consider the conservative principals of the Founding Fathers "revolutionary."

> "Sustained by the consciousness that the transition from the former Union to the present Confederacy, has not proceeded from a disregard on our part of just obligations, or any failure to perform any Constitutional duty; *moved by no interest or passion to invade the rights of others; anxious to cultivate peace and commerce with all the nations*, if we may not hope to avoid war, we may at least expect that posterity will acquit us of having needlessly engaged in it."

No bugle note of war is heard in these words: But there is a solemn protestation that the Confederate states have "not proceeded from a disregard of just obligations"; that they have "not failed to perform any Constitutional duty"; that they have not been "moved" by any "interest or passion to invade the rights of others"; and that they are "anxious to cultivate peace and Commerce with all nations." It is also a solemn declaration that if war is forced upon them, they "may at least expect that posterity will acquit" them of "having needlessly engaged in it." Who then caused the war? Again [from President Davis]:

> "An agricultural people, whose chief interest is the export of a commodity required in every manufacturing country, *our true policy is peace* and the freest trade which our necessities will permit. It is alike our interest, and that of all those to whom we would sell and from whom we would buy, that there should be the fewest practicable restrictions upon the interchange of commodities. There can be but little rivalry between ours and any manufacturing community such as the Northeastern States of the American Union. It must follow, therefore, that a mutual interest would invite good will and kind offices."

What sound of a war-like spirit is to be found in these words? Do they not assert, "Our true policy is peace"? Are they not emphatic in declaring, "There can be but little rivalry between ours and any manufacturing community such as the Northeastern States of the American Union ?" Do they not take for granted "that a mutual interest would invite good will and kind offices?" Who then caused the war? Again [President Davis]:

> "Through many years of controversy with our late associates, the [liberal] Northern States, we have vainly endeavored to secure tranquility and to obtain respect for the rights to which we are entitled. As a necessity, *not of choice*, we have resorted to the remedy of separation. . . . If a just perception of mutual interest shall permit us peaceably to pursue our separate political career, my most earnest desire will have been fulfilled."

What remotest indication of a threat of war is to be found in these words? In vain we "endeavored to secure tranquility." In vain we attempted to "obtain respect for the rights to which we were entitled." It was from "necessity, not choice," that we "resorted to the remedy of separation." The entire history of the long "controversy" sustains this assertion. *Mr. Davis's earnest desire for peace was that of all true Southerners*: "If a just perception of mutual interest shall permit us peaceably to pursue our separate career, my most earnest desire will have been fulfilled." Is the thunder of artillery heard in words like these? Again:

> "We have changed the Constituent parts, but not the system, of our Government. *The Constitution formed by our fathers is that of these Confederate States*, in their exposition of it; and in the judicial construction it has received, we have a light which reveals its true meaning."

Every syllable, yea every letter, in these words of Davis, breathes of devotion to the Constitution of our fathers. The [conservative] South's one great sin in the eyes of Lincoln and his [Liberal] party was her fidelity to that instrument. History has piled evidence upon evidence as to this fact till a mountain of testimony kisses the very skies. The South had no purpose, no desire, no motive, to make war upon the North. It was a libel upon her common sense, upon her self-interest, upon her normal condition to assert that she wished to commit aggression or to do anything wrong whatever to the Northern States or their people. Her only motive in quitting the Union was to preserve for herself "at least the principles of the Constitution." This is why she has been derided by a leading Northern historian as *"eighteenth century reactionists,"* that is, eighteenth century constitutionalists [Conservatives]. *This derision is her proudest appellation. For the principles of the eighteenth century Constitution, "the eighteenth century reactionists" gave the best blood of their veins.* Shut out by blockade from all ports of

Conservative Davis rightly declared that the Confederacy was not trying to destroy the U.S. government, but preserve it. It was Liberal Lincoln and the progressive Unionists who were trying to dismantle the government of the Founding Fathers.

the world, without war materials and the means of manufacturing them, the eighteenth-century Constitutionalists [Conservatives], less than 650,000 strong, successfully opposed for four long years more than 2,600,000 eighteenth-century anti-Constitutionalists [Liberals] with all the powers of well-organized Government at their back, and went not, then, down beneath the hail of lead and iron, and the keen edge of the Damascus blade, till death had made their serried columns mere picket lines; and not then till their slaves were proclaimed free and 200,000 of them armed in defense of the North; and not then till plunder and torch had done their most effective work; and not then in abjection, but as heroes invincible still.

Conscious of no wrong, but deeply sensible of right, they bent no knee. They stood erect, majestic, sublime, while the shadows of sorrow gathered about their heroic forms. They knew the meaning of victory upon many hard fought fields. As immortal victors they knew how to vanquish even defeat. And they did it as no other soldiers have ever done. *Too conservative* to violate the "18th century" Constitution, their *conservatism* has snatched victory from defeat, and *the world to-day is looking upon the restored South as the most glorious section of the Union*, and soon to be ranked as the best and most prosperous of all the world. [550]

On July 20, 1898, some 1,155 UCV camps met at the Auditorium in Piedmont Park, at Atlanta, Georgia. It was the first day of the Eighth Annual Meeting and Reunion of the United Confederate Veterans. One of the speakers, former Confederate General Charles E. Hooker of Mississippi, was introduced as the "orator of the day." According to the notes from the convention, "General Hooker was greeted with deafening applause, and received a splendid ovation, his fame as 'the Chrysostom of the South' having preceded him, and the old Veterans were anxiously waiting to catch the golden words as they fell from his lips."

After the audience finally sat back down, General Hooker offered the following remarks:

"Comrades! Soldiers of the Army and Navy of the Confederacy, Daughters of the Confederacy, Sons of Confederates, Ladies and Gentlemen.—Standing on the soil of a State which gave to the Confederacy so many intrepid soldiers, from the gallant Colonel [Francis Stebbins] Bartow, who fell at the first battle of Manassas, shot through the heart, down to the last charge of Lee's army, led by another Georgian, your own illustrious commander, General John B. Gordon; standing here, in the gateway city to the gulf, in hearing of the guns of Peachtree battle ground, and almost in sight of the line of Kennesaw mountain, so gallantly defended by General [Joseph E.] Johnston, and which he regretted he had ever given up, close to the battlefields, dyed with the blood of your heroic comrades,—I greet you as the survivors of the greatest war waged in all the annals of time.

It was a war, my comrades, waged not for conquest; not for pelf; not for ambition, but in maintenance of the great cardinal principle of home rule and community independence, which lies at the foundation of the government which our fathers builded, after the trials and tribulations and bloodshed of the seven years' war of the Revolution.

Conservative Confederate General Charles E. Hooker of South Carolina, "the Chrysostom of the South."

First, I shall speak of the cause of the war. Secondly, of the men who fought it. Thirdly, of its results.

When our fathers met at Independence Hall, in the City of Philadelphia, they made the solemn declaration *"That these colonies are and of right ought to be free and independent States."*

They fought the seven years' war of the Revolution to maintain that declaration. When they came to frame a government for the original thirteen States, fresh from the long conflict, to free the colonies from onerous, unjust and oppressive taxation, without representation, *they refused to concede the power of taxation to the central or Federal Government.*

The thirteen original States, in order to guard against any misconstruction of the compact of confederation between them, unanimously declared:

> *"That each State retains its sovereignty, freedom and independence, and any power, jurisdiction and right, which is not by this confederation expressly delegated to the United States, in Congress assembled."*

Nine years of experience under "the articles of confederation" between the original thirteen States showed that a Federal Government, without the power of taxation, was not self-sustaining.

A convention of the original thirteen States was called "to amend the articles of confederation." It met at Annapolis, in the State of Maryland, and recommended to Congress that a convention be called, composed of delegates from all the original thirteen States, to frame a new Constitution.

Congress acted on this recommendation and called a convention, composed of delegates from all the original thirteen States, which met at Philadelphia in 1787, and with George Washington as its president, adopted the Constitution of the United States which, being ratified by nine of the original thirteen States in sovereign convention assembled, went into effect in 1789, "as a Constitution between the States so ratifying the same."

This Constitution, and *the principle of home rule and community independence*, upon which it was founded, was very elaborately discussed in the general convention and then in the conventions of each one of the original thirteen States, when they met to ratify or reject it.

Article I, paragraph 7, of this Constitution provided "the ratification of the conventions of nine States shall be sufficient for the establishment of this Constitution between the State as ratifying the same."

Thus it wilt be seen that the refusal of four of the smallest, of the original thirteen States—with a meagre population—could have defeated the adoption of the Constitution.

Immediately after the ratification of the nine States necessary to adopt the Constitution, the whole of the nine States—with absolute unanimity—and I think at the instance of Massachusetts, adopted the following amendment to the Constitution:

"Article 9. The enumeration in the Constitution of certain rights, shall not be construed to deny or disparage others retained by the people. [This article became the Ninth Amendment.]

"Article 10. The powers not delegated to the United States by the Constitution, nor prohibited by it to the States, are reserved to the States respectively, or to the people." [This article became the Tenth Amendment.]

Thus, it will be seen, in the ratification of the Constitution by the original thirteen States, and in the adoption of amendments thereto, it will be seen that each State ratified for herself, by herself, and is bound only by her own ratification, to use the language of John C. Calhoun, the great and lucid interpreter of the Constitution. Article 5 of the Constitution, thus adopted, provides: "No State, without its consent, shall be deprived of its equal suffrage in the Senate." Mr. Calhoun justly says, "the Senate is the favorite of the Constitution." Delaware, the smallest State in the Union, with her 76,000 inhabitants, stands in the Senate on a perfect equality with New York, with her 5,000,000; all the votes of all the people of the other States in the Union cannot deprive her of this equality. No, there is no power on earth that can deprive her of this equality in the Senate, save and except by her own consent. Her vote alone, under the Constitution, can put a veto on all the other States; and all the people of all the other States.

Conservative pro-South advocate John C. Calhoun of South Carolina.

It is not true, as an historical fact, that the maintenance of slavery on one side, or its abolition on the other, was the cause and origin of the war. Its abolition was an incident to the war—and a very striking one—but not the cause of it.

The differences manifested in the very convention which adopted the Federal Constitution, and in the conventions of each one of the States ratifying it, and all the legislation introduced in Congress under it, shows that it

*originated in the differences of opinion as to how far the government created by
the Constitution was central or national, or how far it was federative in its
character.*

*This was the germ from which the conflict came. That slavery was seized
upon by the fanatics [Liberals] of the North to shower blows and hatred upon
the [conservative] Southern slave holders, I can well concede. But this did not
make it the cause of the war.*

When Mr. [William H.] Seward boasted in the Senate that the
North was about to take control of the government, Senator [James
Henry] Hammond, of South Carolina, said, in reply to him:

"Do not forget—It cannot be forgotten; it is written on the
highest page of human history that we, the slaveholders of
the South [Conservatives], took our country in her infancy;
and after ruling her for sixty out of seventy years of her
existence, we shall surrender her to you [Liberals] without
a stain upon her honor, boundless in prosperity, incalculable
in her strength—the wonder and the admiration of the
world. Time will show what you will make of her; but no
time can ever diminish our glory or your responsibility."

Yes, time has shown, and *our fathers, could they speak from the grave,
would ask: "Who is responsible for the destruction of the [conservative]
federative [republican] system of the government?*

When the seceding [Confederate] States had adopted a
Constitution, a complete counterpart of the [U.S.] Constitution of
1789, their first act was—as early as February 4th, before the
inauguration of Mr. Lincoln—to appoint a commission "for the
purpose of negotiating friendly relations between that government and
the Confederate States of America; and for the settlement of all
questions of disagreement between the two governments upon the
principles of right, justice, equity and good faith."

Two of these commissioners, Martin Crawford, of Georgia, and
John Forsythe, of Alabama, arrived in Washington the 5th day of
March, 1861, and on the 12th of March addressed a communication to
Mr. Seward, the then Secretary of State of the United States of
America, explaining their embassy. Mr. Seward declined to confer
with them officially, but through Judge [John Archibald] Campbell, of
Alabama, assured the commissioners of the Confederate States that the
government at Washington was friendly to a peaceful settlement; and

Liberal Union Major Robert Anderson of Kentucky.

further assured the commissioners that the "status in quo" in the harbor of Charleston should be observed, and that notice should be given to the commissioners before any change was made therein. Thus the commissioners were held in Washington until the 8th day of April following, when the public press communicated to them the fact that *the government of the United States was sending vessels of war from the port of New York laden with ammunition, provisions and troops to supply and reinforce the garrison in Fort Sumter*, in the harbor of South Carolina. Astonished at *this breach of plighted faith on the part of the government of the United States*, the commissioners from the Confederate, States demanded a reply to their official communication of the 12th of March previous. To this demand they received a reply on the 8th day of April, 1861, but bearing date March 15th, one month before, *refusing to hold any official communication with them*. On receipt of this reply the Confederate Commissioners retired from Washington.

The promises made to the Confederate Commissioners had been grossly violated; vessels of war had been sent to garrison and supply Fort Sumter.

[Union] Major [Robert] Anderson, in command of the forts in Charleston harbor, had abandoned Fort Moultrie, after spiking his guns, and taken refuge in Fort Sumter, then regarded as an impregnable fortress. When the Confederate Commissioners made their report to their government, Mr. Davis, the President of the Confederate States, in transmitting their report to the Confederate Congress, said:

> "The crooked paths of diplomacy can scarcely furnish an example so wanting in courtesy, in candor and directness as was the course of the United States government toward our commissioners in Washington."

What was done by the Confederate government was done in the open light of day, challenging the criticism of the world. Every effort was made to avoid the shedding of fratricidal blood.

Away, then, with the charge—the untruthful charge—that this war was a war waged by traitors, with treasonable design.

Let it never be forgotten! Let it be recorded in history! Let it be iterated and reiterated again and again as one of the indisputable facts of history that we surrendered with arms in our hands and on written terms of capitulation.

And here sits a living witness of the truth of what I say—our own illustrious commander, General John B. Gordon, who led the last charge of Lee's army, reduced by death on the battlefield, and disease, to less than ten thousand effective men, and who was present at the capitulation.

We are not left to assertion on this matter. Here is the last clause in the armistice agreed upon by U. S. Grant, commanding the armies of the United States, and Robert E. Lee, commanding the armies of the Confederacy:

> "Each officer and man shall be allowed to return to his home, not to be disturbed by United States authority so long as they observe their parole and the laws in force where they may reside."

The terms of capitulation agreed upon by W. T. Sherman, commanding the army of the United States in North Carolina, and Joseph E. Johnston, commanding the army of the Confederacy, are even more full and explicit. Clause six provides:

> "The executive authority of the United States government, not to disturb any of the people by reason of the late war, so long as they live in peace and quiet and abstain from acts of actual hostility and obey the laws in existence at the place of their residence."

These were the terms of capitulation and surrender after a four years' war in which each army had tested the bravery of the other on many a hotly contested battlefield.

These were not such terms as established governments mete out to traitors. When our great civic leader, Jefferson Davis, was made to suffer for all our sins, seized and shackled and confined in Fortress Monroe, and indicted for treason in the Federal Courts, at Richmond, Va., we, of

Mississippi felt it our duty to provide counsel for him, and under the authority of the State, the Governor of the State appointed General T. J. Wharton, Fulton Anderson and your humble speaker [Charles E. Hooker], then holding the office of Attorney General, of the State of Mississippi, to proceed to Washington and enter upon his defense. The friends of Mr. Davis had selected that brilliant Irish lawyer and great orator, Charles O'Connor, to be the leading counsel in the case.

He responded with generous enthusiasm to the request, and we joined him at Richmond.

Mr. O'Connor refused to receive any fee save the love and reverence of the entire people of the South.

Mr. Davis was brought up under guard from Fortress Monroe.

The whole population of Richmond turned out to pay to him their silent homage. As he bowed his proud head when he passed into the portal of the hotel where his guard conducted him, one brave and true Virginian, perched in one of the highest windows of the hotel, in shrill and piercing notes gave the command: "Hats off, Virginians!"

After the War well respected New York attorney Charles O'Connor was selected to head Jefferson Davis' defense against charges of treason. The case never went to trial, however, and Davis was eventually freed, even though he had repeatedly asked to be tried. Why was he exonerated? Because secession was legal in 1860 and no crime had been committed—by Davis or any other Confederate official. The Liberal-run U.S. government at the time thus spared itself years of legal troubles, as well as the humiliation of having to acknowledge that secession was a constitutional right, that its war on the conservative South had been illegal, pointless, and unjust, and worst of all, that countless thousands had died unnecessarily.

Instantly every head was uncovered, and every heart bowed in love and admiration of the lofty hero who had taken upon himself the sins of a whole people, and vicariously suffered for all with sublime abnegation of self, and with that indomitable power of will, which even in defeat and shackles, refused to acknowledge but one Master. *Mr. Davis was never tried, and he never asked for a pardon.*

Why was he not tried? If we were all traitors and guilty of treason, why did not the government try the chief traitor?

He was a prisoner, and like Paul, "in bonds, demanding a hearing." He was ironed and watched night and day under the unceasing gaze of his eternal guard, with instructions never to take their eyes off of him.

Why was he not tried?

No other reason can be given than that his prosecutors knew that his allegiance was due to his State, primarily, and that as a citizen of that State he was bound to obey her will, and yield obedience to her sovereign authority as expressed in her convention.

When Mr. Davis came to be indicted there was an effort at first to include General Robert E. Lee in the same indictment. When this came to the ears of General Ulysses S. Grant, it is due to him to say that he said: "No! this must not be. It would be to violate the terms of capitulation which I made with General Lee on the field of Appomattox when he surrendered with arms in his hands, and it would be to dishonor my parole."

This action was fully in keeping with the generous terms of surrender accorded to General Lee by the leader of the victorious army, and will ever be remembered by all true soldiers everywhere.

The miserable crew who would willingly have heaped dishonor on their own great and conquering leader, to wreak their spiteful vengeance on the great military leader of the Confederacy, were compelled to forego their nefarious and dishonorable plans.

Second, the men who fought it. *The personnel of the Confederate army was a remarkable one.*

It was composed of the descendants of the liberty-loving people who speak the English language. History tells us that when our Anglo-Saxon ancestors, at the battle of Hastings, fought in 1066, yielded to the prowess and numbers of William the Conqueror, of Normandy, he demanded hostages for the good faith of the Saxons; and Cedric, the Saxon, gave up his young and tender nephew, upon whose face the beard of manhood had not yet grown.

Tenderly warning his young kinsman against the blandishments of the Court of Normandy, then the gayest in Europe, the boy hostage replied to his uncle: "If when I return from the Court of Normandy, by the cut of my hair, or the fashion of my garb, you shall judge me Norman, you shall lay your hand upon my heart and feel England beat in every pulse." And *so it was with the Confederate. We were battling for the same eternal principles for which our forefathers fought at Bunker's Hill, the Cowpens and at Yorktown.*

The Confederate army was a volunteer army. We all went as privates, and from our ranks we chose our commanders up to and including the rank of Colonel.

It was the hardy endurance, the indomitable pluck and valor of the men in the ranks which forged the epaulettes that marked the rank of our Generals.

No one knew this better than our great military leader, Robert E.

The illustrious General Lee.

Lee! With touching pathos and earnest simplicity, he gave utterance to it in his farewell address to his army at Appomattox. We have always said if ever we had a war with a foreign foe we old Confederates would prove our fidelity to the common [U.S.] flag, and of what mettle we were made. Of all the plumes that waived in the front ranks at the battle of Santiago, in the present war, none glistened brighter than that which adorned the brow of our great old Confederate cavalry leader, glorious old Joe Wheeler. They may beat him for Congress in Alabama, but we will raise to him a monument whose foundations shall be laid broad and deep in the hearts of our whole people, and beneath his honored name we will place this simple inscription:

"He wore the gray, and he wore the blue,
"But was ever a soldier brave and true."

This is not the first time in the history of the English-speaking people, when the war of words has culminated in the wager of battle. When the rough and uncultured Barons met on the banks of the Runnmede they extorted from King John—false to his lionhearted brother, Richard, and the English people—the Magna Charta of human liberty. Thence we come down to the time when the red and the white rose struggled for pre-eminence, and yet a little later on, when our English-speaking ancestors made the declaration of rights, and yet a little later on when they passed the bill of rights, and yet a little later down the stream of history we come to the time when our own immediate English-speaking ancestors met at Independence Hall, in the City of Philadelphia, and declared *"that these colonies are and of right ought to be free and independent States."*

And they made them so.

Our Confederate people thought that their lives, property and sacred homes were endangered, and they resorted to the remedy which they believed was rightly theirs.

When assailed in their homes, and on their own soil, they defended themselves as their English-speaking ancestors were wont to do.

Of the [conservative] men who led us in the terrible conflict for four years, the English language furnishes no terms that can express our love. I have already, incidentally, spoken of our great civil leader, Jefferson Davis. It was my fortune to stand close to him from my earliest manhood. He gave me, while he was still a member of the lower House of Congress, my first letters of introduction to his friends in Mississippi. *He was jealous of the rights of his people under the Constitution and the laws made in pursuance thereof, and was always mindful of them himself.* When advised by his friends that his plantation and property was about to be swept away by the enemy, and urged to send troops to defend them, his reply was:

> "The President of the Confederacy cannot afford to use public means to protect private interests."

His aid, Governor [Francis Richard] Lubbock, of Texas, said of him:

> "From the day I took service with him to the moment we parted, I witnessed his unselfishness. He forgot himself, and displayed more self-abnegation than any other human being I have ever known."

When he [Davis] was about to bring suit for the recovery of his plantation, "Brierfield," he came to my home to consult me, and I said to him: "Why do you not allow Benjamin Montgomery (the confidential servant of his brother, Joseph E. Davis) to attorn to you, which he is more than willing to do," his reply was: "I cannot afford to do this. I am made one of the executors under my brother's will, and this would be unjust to the legatees under the will."

When he learned that his friends in Louisiana and Mississippi were creating a committee to raise a fund of $200,000, upon the interest of which he might live while he was writing his history of the Confederacy, he wrote to the committee to suspend their work for he would not receive the money if it was raised, accompanying it with the remark: "My people are poor and I cannot consent that they shall tax themselves for my benefit, even by their own voluntary action."

He achieved distinction as a military leader, a statesman, and an orator. *Such a man cannot die, but will live always in the hearts of the people who knew him best and loved him most.*

The Confederate flag gathered around it a galaxy of great [conservative] military leaders—Robert E. Lee, Albert Sydney Johnston, Joseph E. Johnston, [Pierre G. T.] Beauregard, [James] Longstreet, [Braxton] Bragg, [Leonidas] Polk, [Richard S.] Ewell, [William J.] Hardee, [John C.] Breckinridge, [Patrick R.] Cleburne, [Richard] Dick Taylor, [John Bell] Hood, [Sterling] Price, McCullough, [Paul Jones] Semmes, Daniel Harvey Hill, Ambrose Powell Hill, [George Edward] Pickett, [J. E. B.] Stuart, [Nathan] Bedford Forrest, [John Hunt] Morgan, [Turner] Ashby, Edward C. Walthall, Benjamin Humphries, Wade Hampton, Matthew [C.] Butler, Stephen D. Lee and Joe Wheeler.

Conservative Confederate General and Southern icon John Hunt Morgan of Alabama.

Neither time nor space will admit of naming a host of others equally entitled to their niche in the [South's conservative] temple of fame.

General Lee's touching and simple [antebellum] letter of resignation to his superior officer, [U.S.] General [Winfield] Scott, shows how strong was his love for the government he had served with such fidelity, and that he yielded only in obedience to that guiding star of his life—*duty*, the noblest word in the English language. He felt that his allegiance was due to his mother, [the state of] Virginia. Where she led, it was his duty to follow.

It was natural that we should look to Virginia, the home and tomb of great warriors and statesmen, for our leader. Virginia has been declared to be the mother of States and statesmen. No one who has stood on her lovely valleys, carpeted by the hand of the Master, and gazed on her lofty mountains, sometimes glassed in sunshine and sometimes covered with shadow, and sometimes the home of the storm god, could cease to wonder that a land so blessed by nature, and nature's God, should produce heroes among her men, and heroines among her women. Nobly, simply, bravely, did the grand old hero lead your armies, and when at last overcome by numbers, he capitulated on honorable terms, and in obedience to the terms of that capitulation, which he and every soldier under him honestly fulfilled and observed, he retired to the classic shades of Washington-Lee College, and devoted the remainder of his days to the education of the youth of the land he loved so well, and when the telegram flashed across the continent the sad news "that Robert E. Lee was no more," from his own immediate family circle, tied to him by the ties of blood and kindred, to the remotest citizen's breast was

"Linked the electric chain of that despair,
"Whose shock was as an earthquake's, and opprest
"The land which loved him so
"That none could love him best."

The wall of grief that came welling down from his own loved mountain sides, was caught up by the long swell of the Atlantic, and wafted to the distant shores of the old world, to come reverberating back on our ears "in all the languages, and the tongues, and the nations, under the heavens."

My heart prompts me to pay a tribute to each one of the illustrious Generals named, but time, space, and the proprieties of the occasion, do not permit it.

General Albert Sydney Johnston, though wounded unto death on the field of battle, refused to quit the field until loss of blood compelled him to fall into the arms of Governor [Isham G.] Harris, his aid and faithful friend, who pressed him to his heart with generous enthusiasm.

Stonewall Jackson fell by the unfortunate mistake of his own men. A brigade of men could not supply their loss to the great Commander General, Lee.

General [Nathan] Bedford Forrest was a natural warrior, bred in no school that taught the art of war, he taught war to his followers by his sublime courage and utter disregard of danger. Seriously wounded in one of his numerous battles, he received an order to hold his command in readiness to meet an expected raid from Memphis. Though not able to sit his horse, his answer was, "with one foot in the stirrup, I go to execute your order."

The Volunteer's State, and his comrades from other States, will yet do justice to his memory. General Pickett, in the memorable charge under Longstreet, at Gettysburg, on the 3rd day of July, 1863, has made his name immortal.

Conservative Confederate General George E. Pickett of Virginia.

Third, the results of the war. All are ready to admit, *as one of the results of the war, slavery has been forever abolished, and there is no regret expressed anywhere in the South.*

When the war was closed the vexed question of the rehabilitation of the seceded States had to be solved. The first effort was to appoint military satraps to act as Governors and rule the Southern States by the sword and the bayonet.

This was a miserable failure. Then came *the reconstruction acts, which did not reconstruct at all.* Then came the decision of the Supreme Court of the United States in *ex parte* Garland.

This court decided "that while this was an indissoluble Union, it was composed of indestructible States."

So it was discovered that the four years' war between the States had not destroyed the entity or sovereignty of the States. It had been asserted by some of the prominent men and journals that we could not live together in a Union where the States were "pinned together by bayonets," and the only method of rehabilitation was by the voluntary action of the seceding States by electing Senators and Representatives, and Georgia's glorious and true representatives, from Georgia, had declared that we were again "in the household of our fathers, and we were there to stay," and we did. We may be "pinned together by bayonets," but thank God, by nature's immutable law, the bayonets must be eaten up by rust and rot, but *there is nothing that can destroy the entity and sovereignty of the State, for the Supreme Court has declared "they are indestructible."*

So it may come to pass in the future that all the States will unite in thanking the conservative Confederate States for the glorious battle which they fought for preserving that which Mr. [John C.] Calhoun declared was "the breath of the nostrils of the government, the States."

So with this glorious result, we will not quarrel with the opprobrious epithet of "rebel" as applied by the valorous army of non-combatants who took part on neither side during the war. But it depends in what sense you apply the term "Rebel." If you mean by it rebellion against wrong, in vindication of that which is right, then you may apply the epithet to all the patriots of the war of the revolution. I was once riding through Arlington [Cemetery], that grand mausoleum which the government has provided for the burial of its' distinguished dead, with a Northern gentleman and two of his lady friends. We found the head of each Union soldier's grave marked with a marble slab, giving his name, if known, and his regiment and brigade. One of the ladies asked me if there were any Confederates buried in Arlington. I replied: "Yes, a few down in the remote corner of the cemetery, and that at the head of each one of these Confederate graves is a pine board with the word 'Rebel' written on it." They were polite enough to say they could hardly credit this, and asked to be driven to that part of the cemetery where the Confederates were buried. When they had seen with their own eyes they protested with great fervor against the outrage. I replied:

> "Well, I don't know, but what it was right that these boys
> who wore the ragged gray jackets of the Confederacy during

four years' war, between the States, should be buried in the soil which belonged to the second great 'Rebel' of America, Robert E. Lee, George Washington being the first."

We owe a great debt of gratitude to the women of the South for the example set us in enduring all the hardships and trials of the war.

They gave up father, husband, son, to the defense of country and home, and cheered the soldiers in the field with heroic endeavor to supply their every want. Ofttimes driven from home by a brutal soldiery, their homes consumed by fire, they would fly with their children, and their parting glances would disclose the lambent flames of the incendiary licking their house tops, and their ears were greeted by the sound of the crackling rafters as they crumbled into ashes on their hearthstones. Daughters of the Confederacy! Sons of Confederates! I hail your organizations with delight, and am gratified

The Confederacy was never officially closed down and her Constitution was never officially rescinded. Very fitting for a political concept that will never die: conservatism.

you are forming auxiliary associations to inherit the rich legacies of your sires and grand sires, of patriotic duties nobly discharged and unsullied by a single act that can bring the blush of shame to your cheeks.

We shall not be with you long and confidently leave to you the care and maintenance of the great memorial Battle Abbey, which the United Confederate Veterans have inaugurated, and which one of our comrades, living in a Northern State, has proposed to endow so munificently. Comrades of the Confederacy, let us kindle anew in our hearts the fervid devotion with which we sustained our country's cause for four long years, and let us take new heart and hope from the noble women who received us when we returned to our stricken homes, with nothing but our paroles, and whose loving hearts gave us new hope and inspired us with renewed thews and muscle, and brain, and blood to go forth and make our land blossom again as the rose.

Let us never fail to do just honor to our dead heroes, and provide, as far as in us lies, for the maintenance of the living. No! we can never forget them.

Memory! faithful memory! will wave its magic wand o'er the chill vaults of the sepulcher—the dead nation's sepulcher—her hundred battlefields, and the dead will start again into life, pale, pallid, passionless, as the seraphs, their sweet faces will beam again upon us. Indeed, and in truth, in the arms of our fancy may we again embrace those dear departed comrades who, while they lived, lived for us, and their country, and when they perished poured out their rich young lifeblood, a generous libation on that country's altar, and as their pale lips froze in death on many a distant battlefield, their last syllabled utterances perchance murmured our names.

May you all return safely to your homes with hearts cheered and revivified by another glorious reunion; and may He, whose all seeing eye watches the sparrow as it falls, and counts the unnumbered sands on the seashore, and weigheth the hills in scales, and the mountains in balances, and measureth the waters of the earth in the hollow of his hand, have you each and all in his holy keeping.[551]

The next day, July 21, 1898, the *Atlanta Constitution* published the following on General Hooker's speech:

GENERAL HOOKER SPEAKS ELOQUENTLY OF THE HISTORY OF THE CONFEDERACY
Declares, in a Magnificent Oration Delivered Before the Veterans, That *the South Fought Not for Slaves, But for Constitutional Liberty.*

The principal oration of the day, at the Auditorium yesterday, was by General [Charles E.] Hooker, of Mississippi, whose address is said to be one of the most eloquent ever heard at Confederate Reunions. General Hooker spoke for an hour and a half, and was often enthusiastically applauded. He graphically told the history of the Confederacy, and *gave potent facts to prove this war was not one for slavery, but for Constitutional rights. He paid a high tribute to the [conservative] heroes of the Old South, men and women, and told of how he and others volunteered to defend Jefferson Davis when he was arrested on the charge of treason, but never tried.* General Hooker is a magnetic speaker, and never fails to attract his hearers.[552]

A generation after Lincoln's War, Yankees, and American Liberals in general, were still questioning the patriotism of conservative Southerners, insinuating sedition, subversion, and worst of all "treason" toward the U.S. government. Along with these mean-spirited fictitious charges came the left-winger's age-old technique of stoking the fires of sectional, social, and racial discontent and division, which they disingenuously called "*Southern* racism"! In reality, most of what little white racism there was in the Victorian South can be traced directly to the Liberal Party, one of whose traditional sociopolitical ploys was, and still is, to purposefully stir up race riots in Dixie. [553]

The accusatory, smug, divisive, nosey, and judgmental tone of the Yankees' questions (the same Northern attitudes that sparked defiance in the antebellum South to begin with) was an insult to both the intelligence of Dixie's people and the memory of those who died fighting for the Southern Cause: conservatism—*self-government*, as inferred by the Declaration of Independence and as promised by the Articles of Confederation and the U.S. Constitution.

At the same 1898 UCV convention, Conservative Confederate General John B. Gordon brought these questions up and answered them this way:

> What is the meaning of these Confederate pageants? Are they due to any covert or sinister aims or in the remotest degree to self-seeking? Let our open sessions and public proceedings, which all the world is invited to inspect, furnish the answer. Do these reunions and the popular demonstrations which attend them draw their inspiration from the remotest suggestion of disloyalty to either of the tremendous results of our Civil War, that is, the freedom of the slaves and the eternal unity of the Republic?
>
> In answer to the first question—the position of the former slaves—*the South points to the impartial and equal justice meted out to the negro by the Southern Courts; to the negroes' reliance for security upon Southern sentiment and Southern honor; to the education of the negroes through taxation in Southern schools.*
>
> To the second question—her loyalty to the perpetual union of the States and the South has been making continuous answer from 1865 to this hour. She is answering to day by the presence and prowess of her heroic sons in the war with Spain. Her Fitzhugh Lee, her Joseph Wheeler, her one-legged [Matthew C.] Butler, her Thomas Lafayette Rosser, her George W. Gordon, her North Carolina Bagley, her

Kentucky [Bennett H.] Young, her Alabama Hobson, and her thousands of volunteers, who sprang to arms at their country's call, are now answering from the military camps, from the islands of the Philippines and from the miasmatic jungles of Cuba.

You, my Confederate comrades, would have been there also if your country had needed you. Many of us assembled here would have been there among the first, but for impaired health and shattered constitutions. But our sons and grandsons are there. With our prayers and blessings they have gone forth to represent us with single hearts and lofty aims.[554]

Conservative Confederate General John B. Gordon of Georgia.

On May 10, 1899, during the Ninth Annual Convention of the United Confederate Veterans at Charleston, South Carolina, Conservative Confederate General George Moorman of Louisiana delivered the "Memorial Address," honoring fallen Confederate patriots. His words included the following:

Standing with you to-day by the graves of our Beloved Dead, no discord should be fomented, nor dissensions permitted to disturb the tranquillity whose abode is here.

Time, the great healer, has waved his magic wand over those fateful scenes which have irresistibly borne us into this presence to-day; and, at his touch, bitterness and strife have long since vanished.

We will, therefore, leave those issues, and those questions to other times and to other themes, and dedicate the time set apart for this holy service in paying honor to the sacred dust of our departed Comrades, who lie here at the Cradle of the Confederacy, every one of whom merits that deathless inscription, "Around this Monument is buried all of heroism that could die."

For they need no vindication at our hands, and we are not here to offer apologies for them, neither will we indulge in fawning and hypocritical cant, because it would be an insult to their memory.

Every one of them is a martyr to the right as he conceived it, and his vindication was penned and his epitaph written by our first and only President before a sword was drawn from its scabbard, or a trigger pulled, or a lanyard placed in the vent of a Confederate gun.

With that perspicuity which always distinguished his papers and speeches above all others, Mr. Jefferson Davis, in his "Inaugural Address," delivered at Montgomery in February, 1861, said:

> "Through many years of controversy with our late associates, the [liberal] Northern States, we have vainly endeavored to secure tranquillity, and obtain respect for the rights to which we are entitled. As a necessity, not a choice, we have resorted to separation, and henceforth our energies must be devoted to the conducting of our own affairs, and perpetuating the [conservative] Confederacy we have formed. If a just perception of mutual interest shall permit us peaceably to pursue our separate political career, my most earnest desire will have been fulfilled. But if this be denied us, and the integrity and jurisdiction of our territory be assailed, it will but remain for us with a firm resolve to appeal to arms and invoke the blessings of Providence upon a just cause."

Was ever a cause more clearly stated? Was ever a more perfect vindication ever made for a people?[555]

At the same 1899 UCV convention, Colonel Bennett H. Young of Louisville, Kentucky, representing the Kentucky Division, made these comments:

> The State of Kentucky, in whose name and on whose behalf I speak on this pleasing occasion, made superb offerings to the cause of the South. Her sons, together with the soldiers of the Confederacy from Missouri and Maryland, were the only true rebels in the contest, through which the South passed; these left their homes and fought for the men and women of the South. No social or patriotic instinct drove them to war or caused them to cast in their lot with the people of the Confederacy. They came to fight for the Southland, because *the principles for which war was waged by the South were the principles of true liberty and were the great doctrines which were inculcated by the men who framed the Constitution of the United States.* 42,000 Kentuckians, in their young manhood, left Kentucky and tendered their service to the people of the South and half of these gave up their lives for the defence of the people for whom they had come to do battle, and scattered along the hillsides and valleys in Tennessee, Mississippi, Alabama and Georgia they lie sleeping their last sleep and their graves will ever remain as highest testimonial of pure and unselfish devotion to truth. [556]

These Confederate soldiers did not give their lives to "save slavery," a preposterous fiction invented by 19th-Century Liberals. It was to save the Founders' Constitutional government, which was formulated around conservative republican principles that date back to ancient Greece and Rome.

This convention also hosted Conservative Confederate Major Robert W. Hunter of Washington, D.C., representing Confederate Veteran Association of the District of Columbia Camp No. 171. During his speech he spoke tenderly of the conservative soldiers who fought in "our glorious struggle,"

> *the noblest cause for which mortals ever strove or heroes died*; of the missionary zeal we have shown in vindication of the truth as to the high motives which impelled the South to the unequal conflict of arms, and the unsurpassed heroism with which it was maintained, against *the exaggerations, fictions and distortions, which sectional vanity has put forth under the garb of history* . . .[557]

Another speaker who touched on the subject of the Southern Cause was Brant H. Kirk, representative of the Sons of Confederate Veterans from the Trans-Mississippi Department:

> My Fellow Patriots: It makes me exceedingly happy—gloriously happy—to behold such a grand panorama of Southern chivalry. I repeat it, it makes me gloriously happy. The grandest, a grander, nobler array never assembled under God's sun. We came to bring greetings to you from the Sons. We want to tell you that *we believe that the cause for which you fought from 1861 to 1865 was right.* (Applause.) Although now a "Lost Cause," *it is as dear to our hearts as then. We are not going around apologizing to any one for what you did.*
>
> On the other hand, we are gloriously proud of you, and we intend to hand down to our posterity the doctrines which you hold so dear in your breasts. Every hair upon your heads is dear to us. *It would take the eloquence of more than a Cicero's tongue to express how dearly the South loves its heroes. Every drop of blood coursing through your veins represents tons of chivalry. We love you because you fought for your rights, your homes and your firesides, your property and your constitutional rights.* (Applause.) *We believe that your [conservative] construction of the Constitution was eminently correct, and we want to promise you that, as you are leaving us one by one that, after you are gone, for ages, for generation's, yea, for centuries after you are gone, your influence and the righteous cause for which you fought will live.* We want to promise you further that we propose to organize in every State, every county, in every precinct in the United States, and we propose to meet every year, just as you have done for the past twenty years, and we are going to tell to the people of this country what you have done, and I believe that we will succeed in impressing even the far-off Yankees [Liberals] that we are right. (Much applause.)[558]

What follows is the "Report of the Historical Committee" of the United

Confederate Veterans, which was read on May 28, 1901, at the Eleventh Annual Meeting and Reunion of the UCV, held at Memphis, Tennessee. The report was written and read by Colonel J. W. Nicholson of Baton Rouge, Louisiana:

> One of the most favorable omens of our times is the catholicity with which thoughtful men, both North and South, now speak and write of the issues of the war between the States. True, *much intolerance still remains, especially with those who, from ignorance or prejudice, live only in the past*; but time, education, and intercourse between the North and South have broadened the views and mollified the feelings and prejudices of both sections. To this end we, your Historical Committee, have persistently labored from our organization, and we believe that our efforts have been more or less instrumental in promoting this commendable and promising result.
>
> *All that we have ever desired is the truth in reference to the war and the causes which led to it.* Our previous reports have been patriotic and liberal [that is, generous] in tone. While we have attempted to pay a just tribute to the devotion and heroism of Confederate soldiers, we have said nothing that would detract from the patriotism and gallant deeds of those who opposed them. The text-books which we have designated as acceptable include all reputable histories that are fair to the South and the North, whether written by Northern or Southern men, or published in the North or the South. *We have raised no objection to the splendid encomiums pronounced on the great statesmen and soldiers of the North, but we have protested against the omission in history of an honorable mention of Southern leaders, soldiers, and citizens.*
>
> The truth in reference to the war between the States does not require any section of the country to belittle the achievements, impugn the motives, or malign the characters of the citizens and soldiers of the other section. "Surely the time has come," as stated in a former report, "when the history of our great war can be taught throughout the country without holding either army up to shame, but with justice and charity towards all, imputing to both sides worthy motives, and dwelling with equal praise upon noble, self-sacrificing conduct, inspired by love of country, whether exhibited for the Nation or the State. Something will be found to condone and condemn on both sides, but very much more to honor and emulate."
>
> The chief and probably only impediment to the preparation and reception of such a history is prejudice. "Of all the obstacles," says

Mr. [Alexander H.] Stephens, "to the advancement of truth and human progress in every department of knowledge, in science, in art, in government, and in religion, in all ages and climes, not one on the list is more formidable, more difficult to overcome and subdue, than this horrible distortion of the moral as well as intellectual faculties."

Probably the generation now passing away will never completely outlive the prejudice engendered by the war, and the contentions and misapprehensions which led to it. Among the agencies to which we may confidently look for an impartial history of the war are the great Universities of the country, for the chief end of their creation is research, and the object of all research is truth. [Note: This last sentence was written before the majority of American universities were taken over by truth-hating, South-loathing Liberals. L.S.]. With the votary of science, literature, and history, "truth is more terrible than armies, more reliable than battalions, wiser than senates, greater than royalty, and sweeter than liberty." On the statements of writers and thinkers of this character posterity will make up its verdict, no matter what the partisans of our times may think, say, or do.

It is deemed advisable in the present report to make a brief statement of the real causes of the war as they are now regarded by impartial scholars and historians. Every thoughtful person would like to know the essential facts about the war, but many have neither the time nor the inclination to ferret them out of voluminous treatises. It is therefore believed that we could not render the country a greater or more acceptable service than to present a short, simple, and consecutive story of the struggle between the States. . . .

The estrangement between the North and South had its origin in physical and climatic conditions, and natural differences in life and social structure. The time was when both sections engaged chiefly in the pursuit of farming, and both employed slave labor. This homogeneity as to interests and labor was interrupted by the climatic conditions, which, in course of time, made commerce and manufactures, with free labor, profitable in the North, and agriculture, with slave labor, profitable in the South. Therefore, economic, and not moral, forces abolished slavery in the North and established it in the South. Thus natural conditions fixed upon the North and South distinct and diverging systems of interests and labor, and these played an important role in all the troubles that ensued.

[Jefferson Davis writes:] "At the time of the adoption of the Federal Constitution, African servitude existed in all the States that were parties to that compact, unless with the single exception of

Massachusetts [the state where both the American slave trade and American slave got their start in the 1600s],[559] in which it had, perhaps, very recently ceased to exist. The slaves, however, were numerous in the Southern and very few in the Northern States."

Right-leaning U.S. President James Madison of Virginia, "Father of the Constitution."

In the establishment of this government two doctrines as to its organic structure were suggested. On the one hand *Alexander Hamilton [who we would now refer to as a Liberal] advocated a strong central government to which the States should bear substantially the same subordinate relation that counties now do to a State.* On the other hand *Thomas Jefferson [who we would now refer to as a Conservative] advocated a Federation of all the States in such a manner that all would get together under one government, but each retain its separate sovereignty over all matters not specifically delegated to the Confederacy.*

[Professor H. C. Merwin of Boston Law School writes:] "The ideal basis of government, with Hamilton, was money, with Jefferson, the moral sense of man."

The new Constitution was terse in its provisions, and avoided details. It should be noted, however, that, as Mr. Blaine says, "the compromises on the slavery question inserted in the Constitution were among the essential conditions upon which the Federal government was organized."

Should the Constitution be construed in accordance with the doctrine of Hamilton or that of Jefferson? This was a burning question from the very beginning of Washington's administration, and it gave rise to that long and bitter struggle led by Hamilton on one side and by Jefferson on the other, which resulted in the election of Jefferson as President in 1800. Furthermore, "Jefferson served two terms," says Professor Merwin, "and he was succeeded first by [James] Madison and then by [James] Monroe, both of whom were his friends and disciples, and imbued with his [conservative] ideas. They, also, were re-elected. *For twenty-four years, therefore, Jefferson, and Jeffersonian Democracy predominated in the government of the United States, and the period was an exceedingly prosperous one. Not one of the dismal forebodings of the Federalists [the big government Liberals of the day] was fulfilled; and the practicability of popular government was proved.*"

As to the right of Secession, there is abundant evidence to show that the Constitution would never have been ratified by the States had they believed or even feared that a State, could, under no circumstances, withdraw from the Union. *"Indeed the doctrine that the States had not lost their individual sovereignty by entering the Union,"* says Professor Woodrow Wilson" [soon to become America's twenty-eighth president], *was accepted almost without question even by the courts, for quite thirty years after the formation of the government. Those who worked the theory out to its logical consequences described the sovereignty of the Federal government as merely an emanation from the sovereignty of the States. Every State or group of States which had a grievance against the national*

Liberal U.S. President John Quincy Adams of Massachusetts.

government bethought itself of the right to secede. The so-called Whiskey Rebellion in Pennsylvania had been symptomatic of disunion in that quarter; Virginia and Kentucky had plainly hinted at it in their protests against the Alien and Sedition laws; and New England had [been] more destructive of her own interests. She had talked of secession when the Embargo of 1807 and the war of 1812 had brought her commerce to a standstill. Josiah Quincy [III], of Massachusetts, had said in the House of Representatives, when it was considering the admission of the first State from the Great Louisiana purchase, 'It is my deliberate opinion that if this bill passes, the bonds of the Union are virtually dissolved; that the States which compose it are free from their moral obligations; and that, as it will be the right of all, so it will be the duty of some, to prepare definitely for separation—amicably, if they can, violently if they must;' and the House had seen nothing in the speech to warrant a formal censure."

In the face of these facts it is singular that Jefferson Davis and other Southern leaders should be denounced as "rebels" and "traitors." These opprobrious terms probably served a good purpose in rallying the unthinking masses to battle for the Union, but their use now is attributable only to ignorance or malignity. Truth is the end of all education, and the essence of all science and art, philosophy and religion, and without it history is a slander or a mockery, and should be condemned by every patriotic and self-respecting community.

"But by 1830," continues Professor Wilson, "conditions had changed in the North, and were to change in the immediate future with great and unprecedented speed; but the condition of the South, whether political or economic, had remained the same. *The [liberal] North was now beginning to insist upon a National government; the [conservative] South was continuing to insist upon the original understanding of the Constitution; that was all.*" These divergent political creeds were set forth and crystalized by the memorable debates between [Robert Y.] Hayne [of South Carolina] and [Daniel] Webster [of Massachusetts] (1830) and between Webster and [John C.] Calhoun [of South Carolina] (1833). *These debates brought out a distinct statement of the Constitutional principles upon which the North and South were to diverge.* The contentions of these intellectual giants are well known, and need not be repeated here. Suffice it to say, *"the ground which [Liberal] Webster took," says Professor Wilson, "was new ground; that which [Conservative] Hayne occupied, old ground." Indeed that for which Webster contended was virtually that on which [Liberal] Hamilton was defeated by those who helped to frame the Constitution.*

Now, let us examine briefly the conditions and forces which brought the [liberal] North more and more into sympathy with the doctrine of Hamilton, and also those which caused the [conservative] South to cling to the doctrine of Jefferson, or States' Rights.

First, as to the North [Liberals]. At the time of the adoption of the Constitution the United States consisted of thirteen States lying along the Atlantic coast. By 1861, it had grown in territory until the two great seas of the world washed its eastern and western boundaries. With this unaparalleled growth in territory there had been a corresponding development in population, commerce, and all the elements of national greatness. The great fundamental forces of that marvelous development tended to "the unification of the interests of all classes and section, and therefore, to *the nationalization of a government which was originally Confederate.*" The invention of steamboats, railroads, and the electric telegraph, annihilated distance, and brought all sections into commercial touch with each other. "Twenty States were added to the original thirteen, and almost all of them were actual creations of the Federal government, first, as Territories, then as States. Their populations came from all parts of the Union, and had formed communities which were arbitrary geographical units rather than natural political units. Not only that,

Liberal U.S. President Woodrow Wilson of Virginia.

but North of the Missouri compromise line the population of these new States had been swelled by immigration from abroad." Furthermore, *the chief employments of the North were commerce and manufacture.* Her wares were pushed across State lines without the annoyance or expense of duty, and her trading vessels, under the protection of the nation's flag, traversed every sea and touched every port. Thus *"upon the whole Northern and Northwestern section there had played those great economic forces and that aggressive spirit of commercialism which made steadily for the abolition of State lines as sovereignties, and for the development of the national spirit."*

Thus the course of events was a school in which the thinking men of the [liberal] North were educated to regard the Constitution not as a "legal document" to be binding in a fixed form for all time, but as "the skeleton frame of a living organism" to be expanded in the spirit of its creation with the growth and prosperity of the country. Probably the North had but a dim realization of these facts until the war came and with the watchword "Union" awoke the national spirit into full consciousness. *With the thoughtful men of the [liberal] North the inevitable trend of events had wrought out conditions not anticipated in the Constitution, and a conviction that an indissoluble union was the palladium of our political safety and prosperity, for the preservation of which they invaded the Southern States*, and fought with an energy, heroism, and devotion that will forever shed lustre on American arms.

Now let us notice the conditions in the [conservative] South. *Her chief employment was agriculture, and her citizens had that conservatism, patriotism, love of home and local institutions, which have in all ages and climes characterized farmers.* The Hon. William H. Seward said: "Farmers planted these colonies—all of them—and organized their governments. They were farmers who defied the British soldiery at Bunker Hill, and drove them back from Lexington. They were farmers who reorganized the several States and the Federal government, and established them all on the principles of equality and affiliation. . . . Our nation is rolling forward in a high career, exposed to shocks and dangers. It needs the utmost wisdom and virtue to guide it safely; it needs the steady and enlightened direction which of all others, *the farmers of the United States* can best exercise, because, being free-holders invested with equal rights of suffrage, they *are at once the most liberal [that is, egalitarian] and conservative element in the country.*"

Mr. Seward must have been reminded of the truthfulness of this beautiful tribute of his to the farmers, when, on boasting in the Senate that the North was about to take control of the government, Senator [James Henry] Hammond, of South Carolina, said, in reply to him: "Do not forget—it cannot be forgotten; it is written on the highest page of human history that we, the farmers of the South, took our country in her infancy; and after ruling her sixty out of seventy years of her existence, we shall surrender her to you without a stain upon her honor, boundless in her prosperity, incalculable in her strength, the wonder and admiration of the world. Time will show what you will make of her; but no time can ever diminish our glory or your responsibility." Probably Mr. Hammond had in mind the history of Rome; for it is well known that farmers laid the foundation of her prosperity, and her [conservative] government under their rule had a steady growth in all the elements of true and enduring greatness. It was [only] after it had passed out of their hands [and into the hands of empire-builders] that "the metropolis of the earth eventually became a sink of crime and pollution such as the world had never known."

"When I first entered upon the stage of public life," said [Conservative Thomas] Jefferson, "I came to a resolution never to engage, while in public office, in any kind of enterprise for the improvement of my fortune, nor to wear any other character than that of a farmer." This great statesman was not only a farmer, but he gloried in the name, simplicity, honesty, and patriotism of a farmer. Therefore, *the farmers of the South naturally found in Jefferson an exponent of their own views, sentiments, and principles, and, having shared in only a limited degree of the commercialism of the North, they had no occasion to depart from the wholesome and conservative doctrines which he inculcated.*

But the South adhered to the political school of Jefferson, not merely as a matter of principle but also of policy. The prosperity of Northern commerce

and manufacture depended largely upon a protective tariff. This tariff was highly injurious to the interests of the South, as it increased the cost of all her manufactured ware. Furthermore, there was a growing sentiment in the North [the birthplace of American slavery] in opposition to the institution of slavery. Hence, it can clearly be seen why the South adhered to the States Rights, or Jeffersonian school of politics. She knew that she was the weaker of the two sections in population and territorial domain, and that a central government would place her at the mercy of the stronger section. Therefore, her safety lay in entrenching herself behind the doctrine of States' Rights, and in preserving inviolate the

Liberal statesman William Henry Seward of New York.

Constitution as engrafted by the Fathers of the Republic.

Furthermore, this adherence to the Constitution and the principles underlying it was a school in which the thoughtful men of the South were educated to a respect and reverence for law, good order, justice, sincerity, estalished authority, and to high ideals of duty, home, and government. It was these molding forces that gave to the South her distinctive and pre-eminent order of civilization, and to which we are to ascribe the splendid morals of Southern soldiers and citizens, and the high character of Southern leaders. Washington, Jefferson, Madison, and all the Southern leaders down to Jefferson Davis, were products of this civilization, and hardly can the history of any country produce such another galaxy of statesmen so resplendent with all the elements of true greatness. Of Gen. Robert E. Lee, the immediate head of the Confederate Army, it has been said: "He was Caesar without his ambition, Frederick without his tyranny, Napoleon [Bonaparte] without his selfishness, and Washington without his reward."

The objects of the Union were to "establish justice, and insure domestic tranquility." Evidently these blessings could not be realized as long as one section persistently and prejudicially intermeddled with the affairs of the other. While the [conservative] South made no encroachments upon the right, or property of the [liberal] North, the latter on the assumption of "a higher law than the Constitution" [that is, the liberal political theory of "social justice"] grew more and more aggressive in trenching upon the rights of the former. For instance, the South made no attempt to prevent New England from carrying her mills into the territories which had been obtained by the common blood or treasury of both sections, but New England denied the South the right to carry her slaves into that territory, and yet slavery and mills were alike constitutional institutions. Again, the South made no attempt, as the North did, to enhance her own interests at the expense of the other section by means of a protective tariff on her products.

Therefore, as Professor Wilson says, *"The triumph of Mr. Lincoln was, in the eyes of the South, nothing less than the establishment in power of a party bent upon the destruction of the Southern system and the defeat of Southern interests, even to the point of countenancing and assisting servile insurrection. It seemed evident to the Southern men, too, that the North would not pause or hesitate because of constitutional guarantees. For twenty years Northern States had been busy passing personal liberty laws, intended to bar the operation of the Federal statutes concerning fugitive slaves, and to secure for all alleged fugitives legal privileges which the Federal statutes with held."*

In 1850 John C. Calhoun said, "If you who represent the stronger portion cannot agree to settle the great questions at issue on the broad principle of justice and duty, say so; and let the States we both represent agree to part in peace." "All that the South has ever desired," said Gen. R. E. Lee, "was that the Union as established by our fathers should be preserved, and that the government, as originally organized, should be administered in purity and truth." These two utterances give expression to the sentiments and principles which animated the Southern people in withdrawing from the Federal Union, and for which they fought for four years "over almost every foot of their territory, and, with the odds of 2,800,000 enlisted [Union] men against their 600,000 enlisted men, with their coasts blockaded and their rivers full of gunboats, protracted the struggle until half the soldiers were dead from the casualties of war."

"From a constitutional standpoint," says Professor Small, *of the Chicago University, the South was unquestionably right."* There are and will always be honest differences of opinion as to the doctrines of [Liberal] Hamilton and [Conservative] Jefferson; no one now knows which would ultimately have subserved the best interests of this country, but there is one thing of which we may be certain, namely, *every Confederate grave is a mute but eloquent protest against any departure on the part of the government from the precepts and examples of the founders of this Republic.*

The North [Liberals], by superior resources, conquered. What does this signify? *It signifies the triumph of national over local interests, the triumph of the evolutions of social conditions and commerce over constitutional guarantees, and we pray most devoutly that it may not prove in its ultimate consequence, a triumph of consolidation and monopoly over industrial and commercial freedom, a triumph of national aggression over the liberties of the American people.*

It is an injustice to both sections to speak of the war as the struggle over slavery. Slavery was merely "the straw that broke the camel's back." In 1828 a serious rupture of the government was threatened by the tariff issue, and this was long before the question of slavery had been injected into politics. Speaking of the debate between Webster and Hayne, Professor Wilson says: "It was the formal opening of the great controversy between the North and the South concerning the nature of the Constitution which bound them together. This controversy was destined to be stimulated by the subsequent course of events to greater and greater heat, more and more intense bitterness, until it should culminate in war."

Let us now notice briefly the part slavery played in the role of a stimulant.

At the time of the adoption of the Constitution a sentiment in opposition to slavery from a moral standpoint was springing up in both North and South. *Many of the leading Southern men advocated its abolition, and the [conservative] South [where the American abolition movement got its start],* [560] *following the example of all civilized countries, would in the course of time have abolished it, on her own motion, for certainly she was not inferior in intelligence and morals to all the civilized peoples of the world. Indeed, there have been but few, if any, men in the South since the war that would re-establish the system if they had the power to do so; which shows, as Mr. [Jefferson] Davis says, "that slavery could have been abolished without war." But there were three factors which checked for a time the growth of the abolition movement in the South. (1) The fear "of setting free a body of men so large, so ignorant, so unskilled in the moderate use of freedom; (2) the invention of the cotton gin, which multiplied the profitable use of slave labor for the production of the immense cotton crops which made the South rich; (3) the intermeddling of the North, not only in denouncing Southern slavery and slave-holders, but in persistently attempting to stifle it by national legislation.*

As an instance of the illiberality and fanaticism of Northern abolitionists [Liberals] we cite the facts: (1) In 1833 the British Parliament passed a bill abolishing slavery throughout the British Empire, by a purchase amounting to 20,000,000 pounds sterling; (2) in the same year (1833) the American Anti-Slavery Society held a convention at Philadelphia and adopted a series of principles, the very first of which was: *"We maintain that no compensation should be given to the planters emancipating their slaves."*

The *Nightingale*, one of hundreds of Yankee slave ships that engaged in the transatlantic slave trade between 1638 and 1861. There were no Southern slave ships, and the Confederacy banned the trade nearly five years before the North did, facts completely suppressed by Liberals.

Subsequently, in the language of Professor Wilson, "the whole course of the South was described (by these Northern fanatics) as one of systematic iniquity; Southern society was represented as built upon a wilful sin; the Southern people were held up to the world as those who deliberately despised the most righteous commands of religion. They knew they did not deserve such reprobation. They knew that their lives were honorable, their relations with their slaves humane, their responsibility for the existence of slavery among them remote." This agitation widened the breach between the two sections, and precipitated the struggle which had been brewing almost from the foundation of the government—a struggle in which the sons of the South defended their political rights and their personal honor with a heroism and a devotion that has no parallel in the annals of time.

But all the people of the [liberal] North did not participate in that abuse and misrepresentation of the characters, motives, and institutions of Southern people. It was only the political partisans and moral fanatics that poured into the ears of the masses *"statements which had no foundations in truth, preconceived opinions which were quoted as historical virtues, and a maudlin sentimentality that closed the avenues to the mind against logic and demonstration." There erroneous impressions were the more easily made and the more permanently implanted in consequence of the remoteness of the two sections from each other. There is nothing that so allays prejudice as social intercourse, and could the Northern people have visited us, and seen us and our institutions, we doubt not that the settlement of all differences would have been amicable.*

The passions and prejudices aroused by the war threatened to implant sectional animosities which time could never heal. But the American people belong to a race of strong passions, but not of sullen temper—a race of heroes, of warriors, and of statesmen. With such a race, passion and prejudice may for a while dethrone reason and outrage justice, but deep down in its heart are *indestructible chambers sacred to the memory and veneration of truth and liberty.* With the Anglo-Saxon race the embers of disinterestedness may smolder for a season, but sooner or later they will blaze forth and consume the dross by which they are stifled. We [conservative] Southern people once regarded [big government Liberal] Abraham Lincoln as one of the most despicable creatures that ever lived. Now, while we do not endorse the policy which he pursued, we honor him for his unquestioned sincerity, patriotism and ability. On the other hand, the people of the [liberal] North once regarded [small government Conservative] Jefferson Davis as the incarnation of selfishness and disloyalty. Now, wherever disabused of prejudices, they regard him, using the language of one of their ablest scholars, as one of "the purest, ablest, most patriotic and most consistent of American statesmen."

It was to this subordination of prejudice and narrowness to truth and duty that we are to ascribe the magnanimity of U. S. Grant and the lofty demeanor of R. E. Lee. It is to this that we are to ascribe that true historic talent which is now developing itself both at the North and the South, that spirit of fairness and truth which forms the essence of true Americanism.[561]

At the Twelfth Annual Meeting and Reunion of the UCV in 1902, Confederate General Stephen D. Lee read the following relevant paper written by John Henninger Reagan, Confederate Secretary of the Treasury under Jefferson Davis:

The war between the States, 1861 to 1865, measured by the size of the armies, by the number of battles fought, by the number of soldiers killed, wounded and missing, and by the amount and value of the property destroyed, was much the greatest war of modern times. *It grew out of great causes, and was not, as has been often alleged by those interested in perverting its history, a causeless war, brought about by ambitious political leaders of the Southern States.*

In the vindication of the truth of history I propose to state the principal causes which led to that war.

Conservative Confederate Postmaster-General John H. Reagan of Tennessee.

At the conclusion of the [Revolutionary] war which separated the American Colonies from the Crown of Great Britain, *the Colonies formed a Federal Government, to which they gave exclusive jurisdiction over all questions of foreign policy, and over questions involving interstate relations, reserving to the States exclusive jurisdiction over all questions relating to their local rights and duties.*

While this is clearly implied in the plan and constitution of the new Federal Government, *it is distinctly asserted in the tenth amendment to the Constitution*, which was adopted soon after the ratification of the Constitution, which reads as follows:

> "The powers not delegated to the United States by the Constitution, nor prohibited by it to the States, are reserved to the State respectively, or to the people."

In the formation of the Constitution, and adoption of the Federal Government, two very important and conflicting sets of opinions existed as to what the form and character of the Government should be. And these conflicting opinions became the more serious because entertained, on each side, by men of known patriotism, and of great ability. One party [the Federalists or Liberals] to this conflict of opinions doubted the capacity of the people for self-government, and favored a strong government, to be modeled somewhat on the plan of the British Constitution, omitting royalty and aristocracy, but to be made strong enough to control refractory States, to protect the lives, persons and property of the people, and to preserve peace and good order in society. The other party [the Antifederalists or Conservatives] to the conflict of opinion claimed that the American people had sufficient intelligence and virtue to enable them to organize and to so administer government as to successfully accomplish the same purposes. And *those who took this [conservative] view succeeded in getting it engrafted in the Constitution, placing the necessary limitations on the powers of the Federal Government, and preserving to the States and the people all the powers not so delegated.*

When the Federal Government was put in operation under the Constitution those representing the foregoing views classed themselves, respectively, as Federalists [that is, Liberals], led by [Liberal] Alexander Hamilton, and as Republicans (now Democrats) [that is, in 1787, Conservatives], led by [Conservative] Thomas Jefferson. *The [liberal] Federalists, who distrusted the capacity of the people for self-government and favored a strong government, on the one side, and the [conservative] Republicans, who believed in the capacity of the people for self-government, and who sought to preserve the rights of the States and the largest liberty of the people on the other side, continued the contest for the shaping and controlling of the character and policy of the Government, the*

Federalists aiming by a latitudinous construction of the Constitution to enlarge the powers of the Government, beyond what was prescribed by the letter of the Constitution, and thereby to abridge the rights of the several States, and thus, also, to endanger the liberties of the people.

The contests of opinion, on this vital question continued to divide the people continuously from the foundation of the Government until 1861-1865, when, as a result of the war, the Constitution was changed in important particulars, the doctrine of State rights was overthrown, and the rights of property in negro slaves was denied, and millions of dollars of what was then property was confiscated in plain and distinct violation of the Constitution.

This was one of the great questions which endangered the perpetuity of the Union.

Another cause of danger to the Union was the revenue policy of the Government. The Constitution provided for a tariff for revenue, for the support of the Government. The tariff policy was perverted [by Liberals] into a policy of protection, and fostering some industries at the expense of others, in plain violation of the Constitution, by taking the property of some of the people from them without compensating them for it, and giving to others who paid nothing for it,

These black slaves were owned by a wealthy African-American family in Louisiana. Some 25 percent of all free blacks in early American owned slaves, both black and white—more vital facts missing from our history books.

enriching some of the people and impoverishing others of them, by operation of unjust and unconstitutional legislation. This came near involving the country in a civil war about the year 1832, and give rise to the nullification measure of South Carolina.

The acquisition of foreign territory was another cause which threatened the perpetuity of the Union. The acquisition of the Louisiana territory, the acquisition of Florida, the admission of Missouri as a State, and the annexation of Texas, and the acquisition of the Mexican territory, caused much violent discussion, and threats by the New England States to secede from the Union, they assuming that these acquisitions increased the power of the agricultural States to the disadvantage of the manufacturing States. And when the United States, 1812-1814, became involved in the second war with Great Britain *the same New England States, in their opposition to it, threatened to secede from the Union.*

All these conflicts of opinion, were, in a large measure, sectional, as between the [liberal] Northern and [conservative] Southern States, and produced in the minds of patriotic citizens more or less anxiety for the safety of the Union and the preservation of the peace of the country.

To these causes of disturbance was added the protracted agitation of the slavery question, which threatened most dangerous results.

The question as to whether the States of the Union should be free, or slave, was a question for each State to decide for itself. And that had been the uniform practice. I shall show that it was the purpose of the abolitionists of the free States, where slavery did not exist, States which had no jurisdiction or authority over the subject of African slavery in the States where it did exist, to secure its abolition through the agency of a popular majority of the people of the United States, in plain violation of the Constitution which left to the several States the sole jurisdiction and authority over all their local institutions and domestic affairs, and that too, without compensation for them, though they were of the value of about three billions of dollars.

A review of this question is necessary to a proper understanding of what has been done in this country in relation to it.

A [Liberal] Northern, sectional anti-slavery party was organized,

Liberal Senator William L. Dayton of New Jersey.

and in the year 1856 placed in nomination for the office of President, [Liberal] John C. Frémont, of California, and for the office of Vice President, [Liberal] William L. Dayton, of New Jersey. These candidates received one hundred and fourteen electoral votes, all being from the free States of the North, though they were not elected, thus demonstrating its purely sectional character. Four years later, 1860, the anti-slavery party nominated [Liberal] Abraham Lincoln, for President [but not because he was anti-slavery, for he was only against the spread of slavery at the time], and [Liberal] Hannibal Hamlin, for Vice-President, and this ticket secured one hundred and eighty electoral votes, exclusively from the Northern free States, and was elected, demonstrating its sectional character; and showing that it commanded the support of a majority of the electoral college, and of the people of the United States. *This greatly alarmed the people of the Southern States.*

During and before the American revolution African slavery existed in all the American colonies; and the African slave trade [based in the Northeast] was carried on by the consent and policy of those colonies.

[Historian George] Bancroft says, *speaking of the colony of Virginia, "slavery was not introduced by the corporation, meaning colony, nor by the desire of the emigrants, but was introduced by the mercantile avarice of a foreign nation, and was riveted by the policy of England without regard to the interests or the wishes of the colony."* [Bancroft also says:] . . . *"slavery and the slave trade are older than the records of human society; they are found to have existed wherever the savage hunter began to assume the habits of pastoral or agricultural life,"* and with the exception of Australasia, they have extended to every portion of the globe. [He goes onto to say:] *"The traffic of Europe in negro slaves was fully established before the colonization of the United States, and had existed a half century before the discovery of America."*

Historian George Bancroft of Massachusetts.

Later slavery and the slave trade became offensive to the most enlightened nations of modern times, and this view was embraced by many of our own people. *After the people of the Northern States had got rid of their slaves by selling them to the planters of the Southern States, the opposition to it in those States grew until it was a controlling element in their policies.*

In addition to what was to be expected by the South from the two foregoing canvasses for President and Vice-President by the [Liberal] anti-slavery party, there were many other indications that its ultimate aim was to free the slaves of the South, breakup the social and industrial conditions of that section, with the vast sacrifice in property interests that would necessarily follow its consummation.

The Hon. Wm. H. Seward [a Liberal], who was one of the prominent candidates for the Presidency, and who was the most influential member of that party, and who became Secretary of State under President Lincoln, declared the slavery question presented "an irrepressible conflict." That could only mean that the agitation must continue until the people of the non-slave holding States could secure the abolition of slavery by unconstitutional means, for there was no other way to accomplish their purpose.

Later, [Liberal] Abraham Lincoln, afterwards President of the United States, declared, "that this country could not remain half free and half slave." That could only mean that the agitation must go on until the people of the States where slavery did not exist could secure its abolition in States where it did exist.

In the meantime war occurred, on this question, in Kansas, which called out the most angry feelings on both sides. And the notorious [Yankee Liberal] John Brown organized, in the Northern States, an armed company with which he invaded the State of Virginia, for the avowed purpose of inaugurating a war of races between the whites and blacks, carrying with it murder and arson. He and some of his associates were arrested, tried, condemned and hung for this great crime. And *as an indication of the temper of the Northern people [and in particular Northern socialists], instead of condemning the acts of these fellows, in many cases they draped their Churches in mourning for John Brown, and eulogized him as Saint and martyr.*

As further evidence of the aggressive determination of the [liberal] anti-slavery men to force a conflict with the South on this question, I call attention to the fact that *many of the Northern State legislatures, before the war, passed acts making it a penal crime for any of their officers or citizens to aid in the enforcement of the provisions of the provisions of the Constitution and the acts of Congress, which had the approval of the highest Court, for the rendition of fugitive; thus nullifying the Constitution and laws on this question, the members of the legislature violating their oaths to support the Constitution.*

And when [Conservative] Southern Members of Congress made appeals to the [Liberal] Northern members to aid them in sustaining the Constitution and in the protection of their rights they were met by the statement that *"we have the majority and you have to submit." I make this statement on personal knowledge. We were thus notified that a popular majority [a trait of a democracies; yet the U.S. was not and never has been a democracy] of all the people of all the States was to be substituted for the provisions of the Constitution which limits the powers of the Federal Government, and protects the rights of the several States [a trait of republics, our true form of government].*

It should be here stated that if African slavery was wrong, it was a national wrong, inherited from the Government which preceded ours, and was supported by the Constitution and laws and by the decisions of the Courts; and if it was to be abolished it should have been at the expense of the whole people. To this suggestion the anti-slavery men gave no heed.

The people of the South were thus compelled to face the question of submitting to the destruction of their property rights under a violated constitution, or of trying to secure the relief and protection they were entitled to by withdrawing from a Union hostile to them, and seeking the protection of friendly Governments.

Liberal U.S. President Zachary Taylor of Virginia, father of Confederate General Richard Taylor and Sarah Knox Taylor, the first wife of Confederate President Jefferson Davis.

The anti-slavery men [Liberals] had much to say about the sin and wickedness of slavery, and about the slaveholder's rebellion *as a means of inflaming the Northern mind.* In addition to what I have said about the universality of slavery, among the nations in the past, I may call attention to the fact of the existence of slaves and the slave trade among the ancient Israelites; a people under the immediate guidance of God; and the repeated injunctions of the Christ our Savior to servants to obey their masters.[562]

And to the fact that General Washington, who commanded our armies during the revolution, who was the President of the Convention which framed the Constitution, and who was twice elected President of the United States, was the owner of a greater number of slaves than any other citizen at that time, being the owner of about three hundred. That Mr. [Thomas] Jefferson, Mr. [James] Madison, Mr. [James] Monroe, General [Andrew] Jackson, Mr. [James K.] Polk and General [Zachary] Taylor were all slaveholders; and that a great number of devout Christian men and women were the owners of slaves. Are all these to be branded as criminals, as wicked and to be despised and their names cast into oblivion along with our violated Constitution and laws?

I am well aware of the sophistries, false statements and perversions of history employed by the victorious party [the Republicans or Liberals] for the purpose of ignoring these great facts, and upon which they base the charge that the ex-Confederates were rebels and traitors, and that through their ambitious leaders they brought about a causeless war. We must content ourselves with the consciousness, that in the Union we sought only the enforcement of the Constitution and laws, for the preservation of the rights of our States and for the protection of our people; that when we could not have these in the Union we attempted to withdraw our States from it, in order that we might enjoy our rights in peace under friendly Governments. And we can safely appeal to the final arbitrament of history as it shall be written, when the passions and prejudices of war shall have died out, for the vindication of our memories against the base and false charges of treason and rebellion.

While the cause for which we contended was [temporarily] lost [at Appomattox] we see the evidence, from year to year, that our people are as proud of the record they made for *their rights and for liberty*, as was ever any conqueror in the history of the past. And they are as proud of their success in restoring good government and prosperity to their people since the end of that disastrous war as they are of the grandeur of the struggle they made for independence.[563]

CONFEDERATE
WOMEN ON
LINCOLN'S WAR

CONSERVATIVE WOMEN, MAINLY FROM THE South, but also from every other state in the Union, have always been among the strongest and most vociferous supporters of the Sacred Cause for which the traditional South fought the progressive North: self-government, small government, limited government, constitutional government.

One of the most educated and ardent champion's of the Confederate Cause was Mildred Lewis Rutherford, a niece of Confederate Brigadier General Thomas Reade Rootes Cobb (the brother of Howell Cobb, president of the Confederate Provisional Congress), and Historian-General of the United Daughters of the Confederacy. She knew better than even the most highly

Conservative Southern historian Mildred Lewis Rutherford of Georgia.

"educated" liberal historians the real cause for which the South fought. In 1920 she presented one of her most magnificent essays, "Truths of

History," from which the following passages derive:

> *Had the cause of the South in 1865 prevailed, history would have been truthfully written by unprejudiced historians. The Southern statesmen who had been true to the Constitution could better have steered the "Ship of State'" than such men as Thad Stevens, Chas. Sumner, [William P.] Fessenden, Turnbull, Andrew Johnson and others.*

Conservative Howell Cobb of Georgia, President of the Confederate Provisional Congress and a relative of Mildred L. Rutherford.

It has taken the South many years to get off of that "Rock of Offense," the Reconstruction Period. *While the South was combating the destructive forces at work during this time—homes were being destroyed, domestic relations were being upset, property was being confiscated, politics was being corrupted, liberty of speech, and liberty of the press were being suppressed—the North was writing the history unmolested and we of the South have allowed this history written from the Northern viewpoint, with absolute ignorance of the South, to be taught in our schools all these years with an indifference that is truly appalling.*

We have allowed our leaders and our soldiers to be spoken of as "rebels." Secession was not rebellion.

We have allowed them to be called "traitors"—they could never convict one Southern man for the stand he took in 1861.

We have allowed our cause to be spoken of as a "Lost Cause."

The Cause for which the Confederate soldier fought was not a "Lost Cause." The late war [World War I] was fought to maintain the very same principle—*the non-interference with just rights.* The trouble in 1865 was that the South failed to maintain this principle by force of arms. *Being a Republic of Sovereign States and not a Nation she had the right to resent any interference with rights which had been guaranteed to her by the Constitution. The South never has abandoned the principle for which she fought nor ever will. By overwhelming arms, 2,850,000 to a small handful, comparatively speaking, 600,000, she was forced to surrender, and in surrendering she was forced to submit to the terms of parole which were that she should never secede again. This does not mean that the right to secede is not still in the Constitution,* but the promise has been made never to try it again, and she will keep that promise.

We have allowed the war to be called a Civil War because the North called it so when history was first written, and by allowing this we acknowledged that we were a Nation, not Sovereign States, and therefore had no right to secede. No wonder that the doctrine of State Rights has been so misunderstood!

It is with no thought of stirring up sectional strife, but rather with the desire of allaying sectional bitterness that I am anxious to have the truth known. *If the North does not know the South's side of history—and how can she know it if we do not tell it to the world—then the historians of the future will continue to misrepresent the South, and the South will continue to resent the misrepresentations.*[564]

The great underlying thought which animated the soldiers of the Confederacy was their profound regard for the principle of State self-government—they were not fighting to hold their slaves. Only a very small minority of the men who fought in the Southern army were slaveholders. It was the abolitionists of the [liberal] North who looked on the Constitution of the United States as a "scrap of paper," a "covenant with death and a league with hell," who demanded an anti-slavery Constitution, an anti-slavery Bible, and an anti-slavery God. George Lunt, in his Origin of the Late War, *says that such men at the North were in the minority.*

The movements for emancipation began early in the [conservative] South and were hindered by the intemperate and fanatical abuse of slaveholders by the abolitionists and also by the difficult problem of how to regulate the relations of the two races so radically different after emancipation. The South fought for the right to settle her own domestic affairs, free from any interference on the part of self-constituted advisers.[565]

The South should be as quick to resent an injustice to the North in history as she now resents an injustice to the South by the North. Already instances have come to notice where text books making false statements about the North have been rejected in Southern schools. Will not the North be as magnanimous?[566]

Liberal Union officer Donn Piatt of Ohio.

One of the many reasons we know that Lincoln's War was not about slavery was because its Liberal instigator and his party, the Republicans, the Liberal Party in the 1860s,[567] were not only apathetic toward blacks, but in many cases outwardly hostile and even racist. In 1904 one of our most able Southern writers, Elizabeth Avery Meriwether, penned the following comments, providing proof that kleptocratic Lincoln and his socialist- and communist-filled thugocracy would never have lifted a sword, let alone a finger, to abolish the "peculiar institution":

> *Those who best know Mr. Lincoln assert that he not only was indifferent to the future of the African race, but disliked negroes as a race, and had little or no faith in their capability of development.* At no period of his life was he in favor of bestowing upon them political or social equality with the white race. [Union] General Donn Piatt, a fervent Abolitionist, sounded Mr. Lincoln on this question. "I found," says Piatt,

"that *Mr. Lincoln could no more feel sympathy for that wretched race than he could for the horse he worked or the hog he killed.* Descended from the poor whites of the South, he inherited the contempt, if not the hatred, held by that class for the negro."

South-sympathetic Liberal Ward Hill Lamon of Virginia, friend of Lincoln.

In his *Life of Lincoln*, [Ward Hill] Lamon says, in 1846, in a speech, [Liberal] Mr. Lincoln

imputed to [Martin] Van Buren, a Democrat [Conservative], the great sin of having voted in the New York State Convention for negro suffrage with a property qualification. [Stephen A.] Douglas denied the imputation, but Lincoln proved it to the injury of Van Buren.

. . . *None of Mr. Lincoln's public acts, either before or after he became President, exhibit any special tenderness for the African race, or commiseration of their lot. On the contrary he invariably, in words and deeds, postponed the interest of the negro to the interest of the whites. When from political and military considerations he was forced to declare the freedom of the enemy's slaves, he did so with avowed reluctance; he took pains to have it known he was in no wise affected by sentiment. He never at any time favored the admission of negroes into the body of the electors in his State, or in the States of the South. He claimed that those negroes set free by the army were poor spirited, lazy and slothful; that they could only be*

made soldiers by force, and would not be ever willing laborers at all;
that they seemed to have no interest in the cause of their own race,
but were as docile in the service of the rebellion as the mule that
ploughed the fields or drew the baggage trains.

As a people, Lincoln thought negroes would only be
useful to those who were at the same time their masters, and
the foes of those who sought their good. *He wanted the negro*
protected as women and children are. He had no notion of extending
the privilege of governing to the negro. Lincoln always contended
that the cheapest way of getting rid of the negro was for the Nation
to buy the slaves and send them out of the country [a racist form of
deportation known then as "colonization"].

General Donn Piatt says:

"Lincoln well knew that the North was not fighting to free slaves,
nor was the South fighting to preserve slavery. In that awful conflict
slavery went to pieces."

Lincoln himself gives testimony on this slavery question. [His
friend William H.] Herndon said *when Lincoln issued the emancipation*
proclamation there was no heart in it. Every one remembers Lincoln's letter to
Greeley, in which he frankly declared that whatever he did for or with negroes,
he did to help him save the Union; that is, to conquer the South.

"My paramount object," wrote Lincoln to Greeley, "is to
save the Union, and *not either destroy or save slavery. If I could*
save the Union without freeing the slaves, I would do it. If I could
save the Union by freeing some and leaving others in slavery,
I would do it. If I could save it by freeing all, I would do
that. What I do about slavery and the colored race, I do
because I believe it helps to save the Union."

Yet this man had been put in office by a party [of liberals, socialists, and
communists] which hated and despised the Union. On another occasion
Lincoln wrote:

"I have no purpose to introduce political equality between the white
and black race. There is a physical difference between the two which
probably will forever forbid their living together on the same footing

of equality. I, as well as any other man, am in favor of the race to which I belong having the superior position. I have never said any thing to the contrary."

Simon Cameron, Lincoln's first Secretary of War, wrote General [Benjamin F.] Butler, then in New Orleans:

"President Lincoln desires the right to hold slaves to be fully recognized. The war is prosecuted for the Union, hence no question concerning slavery will arise."

Liberal politician Simon Cameron of Pennsylvania.

In his inauguration Lincoln said: *"I have no lawful right to interfere with slavery directly or indirectly; I have no inclination to do so."*

Mr. Wendell Phillips said that Lincoln was badgered into issuing the emancipation proclamation, and that after it was issued, Lincoln said it was the greatest folly of his life. That much lauded instrument speaks for itself. It plainly proves that its writer had not the least heart in the business of freeing slaves. Had he taken any joy in the work, would he have bestowed the boon of freedom only on those negroes still under the rule of the Confederacy, leaving

*the large number in those States and parts of States under his own control in
the bondage they were born in?*

When General Grant was Colonel of the Twenty-first Illinois
Infantry he expressed himself plainly on the negro question:

> "*The sole object of this war is to restore the union.* Should I be
> convinced it has any other object, or that the government
> designs using its soldiers to execute the wishes of the
> Abolitionists, I pledge to you my honor as a man and a
> soldier, *I would resign my commission and carry my sword to the
> other side.*"

On May 29, 1863, Mr. Martin F. Conway, Liberal Congressman
from Kansas, wrote to the New York *Tribune*, as follows:

> "The independence of the South is now an established fact.
> The war for the future becomes simply an instrument in the
> hands of the political managers to effect results to their own
> personal ends unfavorable to the cause of freedom. It is now
> assumed that the Union is the object paramount over every
> other consideration. Every institution is now of small
> importance. Slavery must give way, or not give way; must
> be strangled, or given new lease of life with increased power,
> just as the exigencies of the North may require. This has
> now become the doctrine of life-long Abolitionists. Gerrit
> Smith, [Asa] Raymond and other men want power and care
> for nothing else. *For the sake of power they would kill all the
> white people in the South, or take them to their arms. They would
> free all the slaves or make their bondage still more helpless; they
> would do anything wicked for the sake of power.*"

Never were truer words spoken or written than these by that
zealous Abolition Congressman Conway of Kansas. In Herndon's
suppressed *Life of Lincoln*, he said:

> "When Lincoln issued the proclamation to free the slaves
> there was no heart in the act."

One of the boldest Republican [Liberal] organs, in 1880, the
Lemars (Iowa) *Sentinel*, frankly betrays its party's real feeling toward

the negro race, as follows:

"As an office seeker, the negro has more brass [that is, impudence] in a square inch of his face, more rapaciousness for office, than his barbarian masters ever dared to possess. The Southern brigadier wants office and place, but he is willing to fight for them, or vote for them; at the drop of the hat he will shoot and cut for them; he does not whine like a whipped cur, or demand like a beggar on horseback, as the nigger does. Let the nigger first learn to vote before he asks for office. The brazen-jawed nigger is but a trifle less assuming, insolent and imperious in his demands than the lantern-jawed brigadiers; the educated nigger is a more capacious liar than his barbarian masters ever were, or dared to be.

"*The greatest mistake the Republican [Liberal] party ever made was taking the nigger at a single bound and placing on his impenetrable skull the crown of suffrage. It is a wrong to him and to us to let him wield the ballot. The nigger is necessarily an ignoramus. The free nigger, we repeat, is a fraud.*"[668]

In 1909 Southern historian Eugenia Dunlap Potts gave a series of speeches before the Lexington, Kentucky, Chapter of the UDC. The following is a pertinent excerpt concerning the reasons for the secession of the Southern states, which ignited Lincoln's fury and, ultimately, his call for the illegal and unnecessary invasion of the Confederacy:

The Tariff question caused excited sectional feeling. A tax on foreign goods for the sake of revenue only had satisfied everybody; but *a protective tariff was unpopular with the South.* The North, having manufactories, was glad to protect her infant industries. The South had no manufactories—only agricultural products, and her representatives combatted the measure with zeal. *This tariff bill has always caused opposition*, and a glance at the daily doings at Washington shows that it is still a bone of contention.

Mississippi was admitted as a state in 1817 with slaves; Illinois in 1818, free; and Alabama, in 1819, slave, making twenty-two states, eleven free, and eleven slave [optional] states—an equal division. In 1819 Florida was bought from Spain.

The greatest quarrel came when Missouri was talked of as a State.

The South wanted her left free to choose slave labor [or not]; the North feared that this would give the Southern legislators control of the Senate. There were numerous slaves in Missouri Territory, and she wanted to retain them as a State. So angry were the debaters, and so heated the feeling, that it was feared the country would go to pieces. This was as far back as 1819. Maine, cut off from Massachusetts, now wanted to come into the Union. As she would be a free labor State, the Southerners would not vote for her admission unless Missouri could have slaves; hence the Missouri Compromise Bill, of which we have all heard. Senator Jesse B. Thomas, of Illinois, proposed this compromise. The terms of it admitted Missouri with slaves, but prohibited slavery in any other portion of the Louisiana Purchase north of a certain specified latitude, which was the Southern boundary of Missouri. This quelled the matter for many years, but most of us have seen the celebrated steel engraving, where Henry Clay stands speaking on this question, and pouring oil on the troubled waters. His powerful oratory so often saved the country from dissension that he was termed the Great Pacificator.

Lincoln's racist apathy toward blacks and his negative views of abolition utterly disqualifies him for the title the "Great Emancipator." Like Liberals today he used African-Americans mainly as tools and weapons to achieve his leftist agenda: full governmental control.

The gifted triumver, Henry Clay from Kentucky, Daniel Webster from Massachusetts, and John C. Calhoun from South Carolina, had labored through years to reconcile the national vexed questions. All three died in the early fifties, and remembering the results of their mighty genius, there were many to say, ten years after that if they had lived there would have been no war, save perhaps another war of words in Congress. But their patriotic heads were laid low, and there were none to take their places. The two sources of dissension, slavery and the tariff, were always on hand to make a stormy session, so that a detailed history of the wrangling among the North, South and West would be a tedious transcription. What suited one section was adverse to the best interests of the others. *The [conservative] South abided strictly by the wording of the Constitution. The North was ever ready to put a liberal construction on its meaning, and naturally they took issue.*

In 1824 the Tariff question became so untenable that some of the Southern States rebelled outright, and protested through their legislatures against the measure as unconstitutional. Some favored secession; others advocated nullification, and this was what was done. They nullified the law and refused to stand by it. Clamor for State rights was heard on every side. But they did not take this step till they had waited two or three years for Congress to give relief by reducing the tariff. *In 1832 the crisis came; nullification was pronounced by South Carolina, and she forbade the collection of tariff duties in her own State. She also declared that if the United States used force, she would withdraw from the Union and organize a separate government.*

Andrew Jackson, who was President, determined to enforce the tariff law in the State, and asked Congress for the power to use the army to sustain the law. Volunteers had offered in South Carolina, and the country stood aghast at the prospect of civil war. Here again Henry Clay's eloquence saved the day. He proposed the measure of gradually reducing the tariff through a period of ten years till it would provide only for the expenses of the government. This removed the cause of trouble, so South Carolina rescinded her act of nullification.

The South had continually yielded up portions of her immense territory to the Union, and thus far there had been an equal balance of power in the legislative voting of the two sections. The annexation of Texas raised a stormy conflict. The South hoped for a division of this large tract into five slave [optional] states. *The North, as usual, wished to obtain the lion's share.* In 1835 Arkansas was admitted a slave State. In 1836 Michigan came in with free labor. After the Mexican War the retrospect [hindsight] showed that *since the Declaration of Independence the North had possessed herself of nearly three-fourths of all the territory added to the original states.* She fought the annexation of Texas because it would be [optionally] slave-holding.

In 1845 Florida was admitted with slave labor. In the same year Texas came in as a slave State. In 1846 Iowa came in with free labor; in 1848 Wisconsin, also free. When California applied for admission in 1850 there was such bitter antagonism that it was universally feared the Southern States would secede from the Union. Should she be a free state there would then be no other State to offset it with slaves.

It was finally decided to leave the choice to California herself.

Henry Clay was again at hand to effect a satisfactory compromise. In a former paper I have referred to the Fugitive Slave Law, whereby runaway slaves should be captured and sent back to their owners. But about a decade before the war, a great Abolition wave had begun to flood the country. *Thurlow Weed, William Lloyd Garrison, Parson [William G.] Brownlow, John Brown and Mrs. [Harriet Beecher] Stowe, by the power of tongue and pen and printing press, endeavored to stir up the North to the pitch of fanatical desperation, and the slaves to revolt against their masters. It was not for the sake of the Union. Perish the Union, if only the slaves were freed. Drive out the Southern States if they refused to abolish them. Their acts and their words were the extreme of anarchy and tyranny.*

John Brown of Connecticut: Yankee Liberal, South-loather, psychopath, murderer, deluded fanatic, violent meddler, and all-around progressive thug. To this day Brown is still worshiped by misguided Liberals and Conservatives.

Jealousy had long formed a vindictive element in their breasts. And how could the two sections be wholly fraternal? They had come from, not only different stocks of population, but from different creeds in religion and politics. There could be no congeniality between the [liberal] Puritan exiles who settled upon the cold, rugged and cheerless soil of New England, and the [conservative] Cavaliers who sought the brighter climate of the south, and who, in their baronial halls, felt nothing in common with roundheads and regicides.

In 1859 the tragic raid of John Brown at Harper's Ferry—his execution—and the startling effects of the open outbreak against slavery put the Southern States on guard. *When the next presidential election came on it was apparent from Mr. Lincoln's debates with Mr. Douglas, what the future policy of the government would be. When he therefore won the election, the south withdrew her representatives from Congress, and her states from the Union. Secession, so long threatened by both sections in turn, had come at last.* Everything had been done on the floor of the House to harmonize the issues, but without avail.

On December 20, 1860 South Carolina passed the ordinance of secession. On January 9, 1861, Mississippi followed; Florida, January 10; Alabama, January 11; Georgia, January 19; Louisiana, January 26; Texas, February 1; Virginia, April 17; Arkansas, May 6; North Carolina, May 20; Tennessee, June 8.

To sum up the Causes for the secession of the South:

1. The State had always been supreme: each was a distinct sovereignty, not subject to the general government in matters of their own home rule.

2. The interests of the South were injured by the burden of tax for the benefit of the North.

3. The Republican [Liberal] party had determined that slavery should not be admitted in the territories—the Republicans were in power, and foreseeing further interference in their rights, the [conservative] South [which saw slavery as a *pro-choice* issue] thought the time had come to form an independent government.

4. The [liberal] North refused to accept the compromise proposed by Senator John J. Crittenden of Kentucky, which might have averted the war. Nor would she consent to submit the matter to a vote of the people; hence there was no chance for harmony. *The aggressive measures of the North were such as no self-respecting State in the South could endure.*

It had come to be a habit in Congress, to insult the South because she held slaves [despite the bold fact that American slavery had begun in the North and was later imposed on the South by Yankees].[569] *Reason and right alike succumbed to prejudice and hatred, and the dissatisfied States, weary of wrong and oppression, sounded the note of separation;* and from every throat burst the refrain:

We are a band of brothers,

Native to the soil,
Fighting for the property,
We've gained by honest toil.
Hurrah! Hurrah! for Southern rights hurrah!
Hurrah! for the Bonnie Blue Flag
That bears a single star.[570]

In the following 1912 article, Mrs. Owen Walker, Historian of the Tennessee Division of the United Daughters of the Confederacy, reviews Volume 12 (and others) from the 13-volume history, *The Real America in Romance*, by famed lecturer and poet Edwin Markham. A Westerner (born in Oregon in 1852) who later died in New York City (in 1940), Markham unfortunately adopted the Liberals' false, slanderous, fact-free, disinformation-filled version of Lincoln's War. This gave his "Civil War history" a Northern, that is, a Liberal/Socialist slant, that greatly detracts from the entire work, and which Mrs. Walker here corrects. In the process she lays out the facts behind slavery, secession, and the cause of the War, while providing the Southern view of American history, one that has been completely eliminated from mainstream history books:

Mr. Markham has written a history of compelling interest. His method of presenting history by the aid of romance brings into bold relief the dramatic and picturesque features in which American history abounds. It also imparts to his narrative the vividness, vitality, and charm so painfully lacking in the ordinary history. The average student who finds history a dry and tedious subject will be so fascinated with these books that he will lay them down with reluctance. The periods of the discovery, exploration, and colonization of the New World, usually so insufferably dull, are here clothed with the alluring hues of mystery, romance, and adventure which really belonged to them.

The reader will also gain some knowledge of the sources of American history; some idea of the character of the old and rival civilizations which struggled for ascendancy upon American soil. He will see clearly that *to the victory of the Anglo-Saxon race he owes his citizenship in a republic founded upon ideals of freedom and self-government.*

His account of the early achievements of the American navy is unusually full and graphic. Nowhere, perhaps, can we find a more thrilling story of Texas's heroic struggle for independence, or a finer portrayal of the heroes of the Alamo and of San Jacinto. In these and other respects Mr. Markham's work is worthy of high praise.

But upon those subjects most vitally touching the birth and development of the nation and upon the sectional issues which have played such a large part in our history and the bloody conflict in which they culminated, we find that, in his opinions and general attitude of thought, *the writer belongs to the Northern school of American historians.* Still he shows a kindly, fraternal spirit toward the South, from his point of view, and makes us feel that he has the desire to be impartial.

Historian Edwin Markham of Oregon.

As *discussion stimulates research and tends to bring out the truth*, I venture to offer some criticisms of Mr. Markham's work in points relating to Southern history.

First [in Volume 9], I notice that he makes the story of the American Revolution too much of a New England story. He traces the spirit of revolution in New England from its source in the Navigation Acts to its flood-tide at Concord and Lexington, a period of fourteen years, relating the more striking incidents not only in detail, but with the accessories of fiction to heighten the effect. *The equally stirring and dramatic course of events in the Southern colonies during this period he covers in three brief sentences. By this means the patriot leaders of New England are made to occupy, not the center only, but practically the whole of the historic stage. Of Southern patriots he mentions only Philip Gadsden and Patrick Henry, and relates in detail not a single incident illustrating the popular feeling at the South during this period.*

Of the events which led to the battle of Alamance [May 16, 1771] and of the battle, he makes no mention. Nor does he give us any inkling of the fact that Virginia led the colonies in opposition to the Stamp Act through the adoption by the House of Burgesses of Henry's famous Five Resolutions. As to the effect of this act in rousing the spirit of resistance throughout the colonies, we have impartial testimony from high sources, Edmund Burke himself proclaiming it in the British Parliament.

Conservative statesman Samuel Adams of Massachusetts.

Mr. Markham states that Samuel Adams organized committees of correspondence which were "the first dawn-break of union." He neglects to state that Adams's committees were confined to Massachusetts, and that Virginia, at the instance of Richard Henry Lee, Thomas Jefferson, and Dabney Carr, acting in concert, created and set in motion a system of committees of intercolonial correspondence which resulted, first, in the Continental Congress, and later in union. [Historian George] Bancroft sums the matter up thus: *"Virginia laid the foundation of our union. Massachusetts organized a province. Virginia promoted a Confederacy."*

After 1775 the author is more balanced in his narrative and brings out much better the achievements of the South during the years of actual conflict, yet he does not fully reveal how largely the South fought her own battles at her own expense, at the same time contributing her full share of troops to the regular Continental armies.

Conservative American patriot
Henry Knox of Massachusetts.

His account of the hazardous expedition of George Rogers Clark, which wrested the great Northwest territory from the British, and of which Virginia afterwards made a princely gift to the nation; of the brilliant achievements of the Southern partisan leaders and their hands in Georgia and the Carolinas; of the battles and victories by which the bold frontiersmen held the Southwestern border intact against the constant pressure of savage hordes, crowning their services by the decisive battle of King's Mountain and saving the patriot cause in its darkest hour—is satisfactory, except that he does not bring out with sufficient clearness the fact that all these were services rendered by the South alone, at her own expense, and in addition to supplying her full quota of troops to the Continental armies. On the latter point Curry says: "According to General [Henry] Knox's report, the North sent to the army 100 men for every 227 of military age, as shown by the census of 1790, and the South 100 out of every 209." It is worth noting that *South Carolina furnished more troops in proportion to her military strength than any other State.*

Note the contrast in rewards for service. In 1848 the North had nearly twice as many Revolutionary pensioners as the South. New York alone had two-thirds as many as were in the whole South, though she furnished not one-seventh as many soldiers. What a noble spirit of manly independence animated these heroes of the South who were content to fight the battles of freedom for freedom's sake alone! This is the kind of manhood that makes a nation truly great.

It is apparent from these facts that New England cannot justly be accorded the lion's share of the credit in the War of Independence.

The key note of the author's position and feeling in regard to the War of the Eighteen-Sixties is found in his eloquent apostrophe to the [Confederate] Army of Northern Virginia near the close of Volume 12: "Judgment is a matter of the mind; courage is of the soul. Your judgment was false; your courage true; and souls are the immortal things after all." Accordingly, we find that he pays frequent and glowing tribute to the heroism, devotion, and endurance of the Confederate soldier, and to the military genius and skill of the great Confederate leaders, especially Lee and Jackson, while *he condemns the cause for which they fought.* On this subject, indeed, he is much at sea. His vision of deeper issues is much obscured by the slavery question. Not yet has the great truth dawned upon him that *the South seceded and fought, not primarily to preserve slavery for the African, but to preserve principles and rights which she regarded as essential to the freedom of the Anglo-Saxon.*

It is too early to say that her "judgment was false" in this respect. That depends upon the final outcome of centralized government in the United States. Her cause is not yet a "lost cause." Like her imperishable faith and courage, it has become the glorious birthright of her children, the clarion call of past and future which summons them to duty and to destiny. But it must now be achieved within the Union, not outside of it.

Mr. Markham makes no attempt to present an adequate picture of slavery conditions as they actually existed in the Old South. His strong touch is on the darkest side. He speaks of "the terrible traffic and the more terrible slave life 'down the river.'" He says: "No revival preacher's portrayal of hell contained more of menace than that simple, rather euphonious phrase 'down the river.'" He gives the South no credit for lifting the African savage to a higher plane of civilization; no credit for the fact that her slaves were the best cared for and happiest class of laborers in the world.

In speaking of the "Impending Crisis" (an antebellum book by Hinton Rowan Helper, of North Carolina), Mr. Markham says: "In this book Mr. Helper spoke some plain truths. Among them was the fact that slavery was the thing that was clogging the progress of the

South, was lowering the whole tone of its civilization, and would if left to itself work ultimate ruin."

The author does not here in plain terms institute a comparison between the civilizations of the North and the South; but the natural and just inference from his language is that Southern civilization where slavery existed was inferior to that of the North where it did not exist; that it was indeed on the road to "ultimate ruin." If it be true that the North held higher political and moral ideals, how did it happen that while the Northern leaders were abolishing chattel slavery in the South by the sword and by unconstitutional proclamations and legislation, at the very same time they were building by class legislation that deadly system of monopoly by the few and "industrial slavery" for the masses, which the best men of our day are now declaring to be far more iniquitous and oppressive than any conditions that ever existed through slavery in the South? How does it happen that we have from the same source, and still growing like Jack's bean stalk, a gigantic system of pension graft, alike corrupting and degrading to promoters and beneficiaries? What about the high "moral tone" of [Union General William T.] Sherman in Georgia and [Union General Philip H.] Sheridan in the Shenandoah Valley? And from what lofty virtues and enlightened statesmanship did the blessings of "reconstruction" flow?

Liberal Union General William T. Sherman of Ohio, still regarded as a war criminal in the conservative South.

Mr. Markham's paragraph on [Stowe's] *Uncle Tom's Cabin* lays the effect which the book had on Southern sentiment "at the door" of the proslavery politicians of the South. He admits that it made a "tremendous sensation" at the North. It had the same effect abroad. *In view of the fact that it held up the South to the scorn and condemnation of the whole civilized world, was not the sense of injury and outrage created in every Southern mind, proslavery or not, perfectly natural and inevitable? Stern justice demands that the responsibility be laid where it belongs—"at the door" of the book itself.*

Mr. Markham makes much of the nullification measures of South Carolina in 1828. But he does not tell us that Massachusetts was the pioneer State in passing nullification resolutions (1809), and that she passed such resolutions several times in her history, and as late as 1845. Nor does he mention the Nullification Acts of fourteen Northern States from 1850 to 1860 (Personal Liberty Bills).

He treats the subject of secession more fairly in that he does not omit mention of the secession agitations at the North, and he gives a full and explicit account of the Hartford Convention. Yet he certainly does not give an adequate idea of the real strength and frequent agitation of disunion principles in New England from the foundation of the government to 1814.

He admits that the right of a State to secede was "held as a part of the doctrine of freedom," that it was "insisted upon by the North and South alike." But *he thinks "it was regarded more as a theory than as a matter of vital fact." The fallacy of this reasoning is apparent. What sort of a "right" is it which is one in "theory" only?* The same principle could just as easily be applied to any part of "the doctrine of freedom" and be made to justify any infraction of it.

Mr. Markham takes the position that the South did not act "without precedent and authority in withdrawing from the Union," but maintains that while secession was really illegal and unconstitutional it had never been proved to be so. *The points at issue were settled by war, hence his logical position is that powder and shot "proved" secession to be "illegal and unconstitutional."*

Not only so, but *he goes a step farther into absurdity and says "that it [secession] was ethically wrong may be held to be demonstrated by the judgment of the Civil War." Is it possible that a point in ethics—the right or wrong of a question—can indeed be "demonstrated" at the cannon's mouth? It is strange that by such lame logic as this even liberal-minded Northern historians seek to convince themselves and others that the [conservative] South really violated the laws of God and man—here termed ethics and the Constitution—in seceding from the Union.*

Among the evidences of [the Liberal] party spirit in this volume is the sneering language employed to discredit the commissioners sent by the Confederate government to treat with the Washington authorities regarding forts, arsenals, etc. The object is to remove the onus of "broken faith" in regard to the evacuation of Fort Sumter from the Washington government. More offensive is the story of the "Knights of the Golden Circle," an old slander of Northern politicians, to the effect that a secret conspiracy against the United States government existed prior to the secession of the Southern States, and that it embraced "about five thousand of the wealthiest and most influential men of the South and of Cuba," with "great names in the councils . . . none higher in the land."

Among inaccuracies is the statement that "the South flung the gage" (declared war) by firing on Fort Sumter. [In reality] Lincoln did this when he announced that he had dispatched an armed fleet to provision the fort "by force if necessary." Another is that [Confederate General John Bell] Hood's army was "totally annihilated" at Nashville; while the battle of Franklin is not even mentioned nor the name of Tennessee's great cavalry leader, N. B. Forrest.

I repeat that, while this work has many merits and is on the whole probably the fairest yet issued from the Northern press, *the volume on the war between the North and the South needs thorough revision before it will be acceptable to Southern readers.* The spirit manifested by its publishers is such as to lead us to hope that this will be done.

Let it be understood that we do not ask for history with a Southern bias. We do not desire sectional glorification, but historic justice only. As sectionalism has in the past been the curse of our country, so it is now the bane of our history, which has thus far been written too much by one section to the great detriment of the other. True history means much to the future of our country. Enduring greatness cannot be built upon false foundations. True fraternal regard and a broad, unselfish patriotism cannot be nurtured upon one sided and unjust history; and believing that it is well to discuss differences with sincerity and kindly spirit and with truth as the sole aim, I submit this review.[571]

9

NORTHERNERS AND LIBERALS ON LINCOLN'S WAR

A S THIS BOOK HAS PROVEN and made abundantly clear, Lincoln's War was not truly a fight between South and North. It was merely a continuation of the ancient battle between conservatism and liberalism—those "two inherently and eternally antagonistic principles which underlie nearly, if not every, war fought on earth."[572] This is why informed and intelligent Yankees, and even many Liberals and foreigners, understood the real cause of the conflict and the legality of secession, and often spoke up for the South. What follows are a few examples of the many thousands of individuals that could be given:

THE RIGHT OF SECESSION

"If the states are interfered with they may wholly withdraw from the Union." — William Rawle, constitutional scholar from Pennsylvania.[573]

"Who is to be the final arbiter, the government or the States? Why, *to yield the right of the States to protect its own citizens would consolidate this government into a miserable despotism.*" — Senator Benjamin F. Wade of Ohio.[574]

"The Southern leaders ought not to have been treated as rebels. *Secession is not rebellion.*" — Goldwin Smith of Cornell University.[575]

"When the South drew the sword to defend the doctrine of States Rights and the institution of slavery [that is, the right to own or not own slaves], they certainly had on their side the Constitution and the laws of the land for the National Constitution justified the doctrine of States Rights. . . . *Is it not perfectly evident that there was a great rebellion, but the rebels were the men of the North, and the men who defended the Constitution were the men of the South, for they defended States Rights and slavery, which were distinctly entrenched within the Constitution?*" — Charles Beecher Stowe of New England.[576]

Radical socialist Horace Greeley of Massachusetts.

"Let the people be told why they wish to break up the Confederation, and let the act of secession be the echo of an unmistakable popular fiat. Then those who rush to carnage to try to defeat it would place themselves clearly in the wrong. . . . *If the Declaration of Independence justified the secession of 3,000,000 colonists in 1776, I do not see why the Constitution ratified by the same men should not justify the secession of 5,000,000 of the Southerners from the Federal Union in 1861. . . . We have repeatedly said, and we once more insist that the great principle embodied by Jefferson in the Declaration of Independence that government derives its power from the consent of the governed is sound and just, then if the Cotton States, the Gulf States or any other States choose to form an independent nation they have a clear right to do it.*" — Socialist Horace Greeley of New York.[577]

"Had [President James] Buchanan in 1860 sent an armed force to prevent the nullification of the Fugitive Slave Law, as Andrew Jackson threatened to do in 1833, there would have been a secession of fifteen Northern States instead of thirteen Southern States." — George Lunt of Massachusetts.[578]

"In the celebrated resolutions of 1789, *Mr. Madison and Mr. Jefferson declared that each State had an equal right to be its own judge.* If so, then, the right of secession by the South could have followed, and each State has the right to judge if the infraction is sufficient to warrant her withdrawal." — Benjamin J. Williams of Massachusetts.[579]

"The action of the Southern States in seceding from a Union which refused to recognize and protect their Constitutional rights meets with my most cordial approbation." — C. W. Cottom of Minnesota.[580]

"*The right to secede may be a revolutionary one, but it exists nevertheless; and we do not see how one party can have a right to do what another party has a right to prevent.* We must ever resist the asserted right of any State to remain in the Union and nullify or defy the laws thereof; to withdraw from the Union is another matter. And when a section of our Union resolves to go out, we shall resist any coercive acts to keep it in. *We hope never to live in a Republic where one section is pinned to the other section by bayonets.*" — Socialist Horace Greeley of New York.[581]

"*The South has an undeniable right to secede from the Union. In the event of secession, the City of New York, and the State of New Jersey, and very likely Connecticut will separate from New England when the black man is put on a pinnacle above the white.*" — The *New York Herald*, November 11, 1860.[582]

"The maintenance of the authority of the States over matters purely local is as essential to the preservation of our institutions as is the conservation of the supremacy of the Federal power in all matters entrusted to the nation by the Federal Constitution. *The power of the States to regulate their purely internal affairs of such laws as seem wise to the local authority is inherent and has never been surrendered to the general government.*" — George Lunt of Massachusetts.[583]

"If Congress can regulate matters entrusted to local authority, the power of the States may be eliminated and thus our system of government be practically destroyed."—Chief Justice William R. Day of Ohio, June 3, 1918.[584]

Moderate Conservative and Supreme Court Justice William R. Day of Ohio.

THE RESPONSIBILITY FOR THE "CIVIL WAR"

"We have no doubt Mr. Lincoln wants the [Confederate] Cabinet at Montgomery to take the initiative by capturing two forts in its waters, for it would give him the opportunity of throwing the responsibility of commencing hostilities [onto the South]. But the country and posterity will hold him just as responsible as if he struck the first blow." — The *New York Herald*, April 5, 1861.[585]

"Unless Mr. Lincoln's administration makes the first demonstration and attack, President Davis says there will be no bloodshed. With Mr. Lincoln's administration, therefore, rests the responsibility of precipitating a collision, and the fearful evils of protracted war." — The *New York Herald*, April 7, 1861.[586]

"There was not a man in the Cabinet that did not know that *an attempt to reinforce Fort Sumter would be the first blow of the war*." — Gideon Welles of Connecticut, U.S. Secretary of the Navy under Lincoln.[587]

Gideon Welles of Connecticut, Liberal
U.S. Secretary of the Navy under Lincoln.

"The first gun of the war was the gun put into that war fleet that sailed against Charleston. The first gun fired at Fort Sumter was the first gun in self-defense. This is the simple fact stripped of all nonsensical with which it has been surrounded by Abolitionists [radical Liberals]." — From Horton's History.[588]

"The attempt to reinforce Sumter will provoke war. The very preparation of such an expedition will precipitate war. I would instruct [Union Major Robert] Anderson to return from Sumter." — William H. Seward of New York, U.S. Secretary of State under Lincoln.[589]

"They [the Northern Liberal leaders under Lincoln] are bold, determined men. *They are striving to break up the Union under the pretense of preserving it. They are struggling to overthrow the Constitution while professing undying attachment to it, and a willingness to make any sacrifice to maintain it.* They are trying to plunge the country into a cruel war as the surest means of destroying the Union upon the plea of enforcing

the laws and protecting public property." — Illinois Senator Stephen
A. Douglas, February 2, 1861.[590]

Yankee Conservative and statesman
Stephen A. Douglas of Vermont.

"The aggressor in a war is not the first who uses force, but the first
who renders force necessary." — From Henry Hallam's *The
Constitutional History of England.*[591]

*"The South was invaded and a war of subjugation was begun by the Federal
government against the seceding States in amazing disregard of the foundation
principle of its existence and the South accepts the contest forced upon her with
a courage characteristic of this proud-spirited people. The North had no
Constitutional right to hold Fort Sumter in case the States seceded and to hold
it meant war." —* Benjamin J. Williams of Massachusetts.[592]

"The South claimed that she had the right to demand the forts, arsenals
and government property in her States, these were her sovereign
rights. If South Carolina had this sovereign right to demand the
surrender of the fort within her jurisdiction, and it belonged to South
Carolina as soon as she resumed her sovereign right, then President

Lincoln had no right to hold it against her demand nor to arm or provision it by force. The U.S. Government could not have erected it on South Carolina's soil without South Carolina's consent, and the action of Lincoln was that of centralized despotism. *Governor [Francis Wilkinson] Pickens sent Isaac W. Hayne, the Attorney General of South Carolina, to President [James] Buchanan saying that the fort was necessary for the protection of the State it was erected to protect—and that South Carolina was willing to pay a full valuation in settlement between the State and the government.*" — John Codman Ropes of Massachusetts.[593]

"*Here are a series of States girding the Gulf which think they should have an independent government: they have the right to decide this question without appealing to you or to me.*

"*Let the South go!* Let her go with flags flying and trumpets blowing! Give her her forts, her arsenals, and her sub-treasuries. Speed the parting guest! All hail dominion! Beautiful on the mountains are the feet of them who bring the glad tidings of disunion." — Wendell Phillips of Massachusetts.[594]

THE "SLAVERY WAS THE CAUSE OF THE WAR" MYTH

"I have no purpose directly or indirectly to interfere with the institution of slavery in the States where it exists. *I believe I have no lawful right to do so, and I have no inclination to do so.*" — U.S. President Abraham Lincoln, First Inaugural Address, March 4, 1861.[595]

Big government Liberal Abraham Lincoln: friend of socialists, worshiped by communists, idolized by anarchists, praised by dictators, revered by tyrants.

"If there be those who would not save the Union unless they could at the same time save slavery, I do not agree with them. If there be those who would not save the Union unless they could at the same time destroy slavery, I do not agree with them. *My paramount object in this struggle is to save the Union, and is not either to save or destroy slavery. . . .* If I could save the Union without freeing any slave, I would do it . . . What I do about slavery and the colored race, I do because I believe it helps save the Union." — U.S. President Abraham Lincoln to Horace Greeley, August 22, 1862.[596]

"The war is waged by the Government of the United States, not in the spirit of conquest or subjugation, nor for the purpose of overthrowing or interfering with the rights or institutions of the states, *but to defend and protect the Union.*" — U.S. Congress, July 22, 1861.[597]

"*The sole object of this war is to restore the union.* Should I be convinced it has any other object, or that the government designs using its soldiers to execute the wishes of the Abolitionists, I pledge to you my honor as a man and a soldier, I would resign my commission and carry my sword to the other side." — Union General Ulysses S. Grant.[598]

Liberal Union General and U.S. President Ulysses S. Grant of Ohio.

"*President Lincoln desires the right to hold slaves to be fully recognized.* The war is prosecuted for the Union, hence no question concerning slavery will arise." — Lincoln's U.S. Secretary of War Simon Cameron, in a letter to Union General Benjamin F. "the Beast" Butler.[599]

"To say that the South seceded and fought to hold her slaves is to accuse her of political imbecility." — English historian Percy Gregg.[600]

"The Union Army showed the greatest sympathy with [Yankee General George B.] McClellan for the bold protest against emancipation. Five States, Indiana, Illinois, Ohio, Pennsylvania, and New York went against Lincoln on this account. *While Lincoln felt he could free the slaves as a war measure, he knew the North would not approve of freeing them.*" — From Massachusetts historian Edward P. Channing's *A Short History of the United States.*[601]

Conservative New York Governor Horatio Seymour.

"Had not the Constitution provided for representation and taxation based on slave labor, and for the restoration of the fugitive slave there would have been no war. Slavery was only an incident out of which grew questions regarding State rights and rights of Territories seeking to become States. But whether slavery was here rightfully or wrongfully, it was here under the protection of the law and not subject to be taken away by violence or any insidious device of abstraction. . . . In presenting the causes which led to the war, it will be seen that slavery, though an occasion, was not in reality the cause of the war. . . . Disregard of the rights of the South led to an unnatural war, and the policy wrought an irreparable injury, if not absolute ruin of the unhappy race they [Yankees] professed to love." — George Lunt of Massachusetts.[602]

"Not war upon slavery within those limits, but fixed opposition to its extension beyond them. *Mr. Lincoln was the candidate of the people not for abolition but as opposed to the extension of slavery*." — Salmon P. Chase, Secretary of War under Lincoln.[603]

"The pretence that the 'abolition of slavery' was either a motive or justification for the war, is a fraud of the same character with that of 'maintaining the national honor.' Who, but such [Northern Liberal] usurpers, robbers, and murderers as they, ever established slavery? Or what government, except one resting upon the sword, like the one we now have [Liberal and former slave owner Ulysses S. Grant was then president of the U.S.], was ever capable of maintaining slavery? *And why did these men abolish slavery? Not from any love of liberty in general—not as an act of justice to the black man himself, but only 'as a war measure,' and because they wanted his assistance, and that of his friends, in carrying on the [Civil] war they had undertaken for maintaining and intensifying that political, commercial, and industrial slavery, to which they have subjected the great body of the people, both white and black. And yet these imposters now cry out that they have abolished the chattel slavery of the black man—although that was not the motive of the war—as if they thought they could thereby conceal, atone for, or justify that other slavery which they were fighting to perpetuate, and to render more rigorous and inexorable than it ever was before.* There was no difference of principle—but only of degree—between the slavery they boast they have abolished, and the slavery they were fighting to preserve; for all restraints upon men's natural liberty, not necessary for the simple maintenance of justice, are of the nature of slavery, and differ from each other only in degree." — Lysander Spooner of Massachusetts.[604]

UNCONSTITUTIONAL FORCE AGAINST THE SOUTH
"It would be contrary to the spirit of the American Government to use force to subjugate the South." — William H. Seward to *London Times* Correspondent, Mr. Russell, April 4, 1861.[605]

"Only a despotic and imperial government can coerce seceding States." — William H. Seward to Charles Francis Adams Sr., Minister to England, April 10, 1861.[606]

"To try to hold fifteen States to the Union is preposterous." — Edward Everett of Massachusetts.[607]

"There is no power under the Constitution to coerce a seceding State." — U.S. President James Buchanan to Edwin M. Stanton, Secretary of War.[608]

Ultra Liberal Senator Charles Sumner of Massachusetts.

"The day before Fort Sumter was surrendered two-thirds of the newspapers in the North opposed coercion in any shape or form, and sympathized with the South. Three-fifths of the entire American people sympathized with the South. Over 200,000 voters opposed coercion and believed the South had a right to secede. The Journal of Commerce fought coercion until the United States mail refused to carry its papers in 1861." — The *New York Herald*.[609]

"Nothing can possibly be so horrible, so wicked or so foolish as a war against the South." — Charles Sumner of Massachusetts.[610]

"If the incoming Administration shall attempt to carry out a line of policy which has been foreshadowed, and construct a scaffold for coercion another name for execution we will reverse the order of the French Revolution and save the blood of the people by making those who would inaugurate a 'Reign of Terror' the first victim of a national guillotine." — James S. Thayer of New York, January 21, 1861.[611]

In 1902 it was written of celebrated Yankee scholar, Judge Jeremiah S. Black of the Keystone State:

He was a Pennsylvanian; a man of the highest character, who loved his Country and the Constitution under which it was governed and had prospered; he was a great constitutional lawyer and jurist, a statesman of the first rank and above all *an honest man and a Christian gentleman*. He wielded a mighty pen in the cause of truth, and the splendid contributions he left behind him should be reproduced in popular form and be in the hands of every lover of this Country.[612]

The following 1877 "open letter" from Judge Black, Attorney General under President James Buchanan, to James A. Garfield (a Liberal who was embroiled in the 1872 Crédit Mobilier Scandal)[613] is one of Black's "splendid contributions." At the time Ulysses S. Grant was president and Garfield—a South-hating radical leftist who, during Lincoln's War, had advocated for the seizure and redistribution of Southern lands and the execution of "the leaders of the rebellion"[614]—was a member of the Congress of Ohio (he himself would be elected president of the U.S. in November 1880). Though lengthy, I include this letter—a reply to a speech sent to him by Garfield—for the tremendous light it sheds on the uneducated remarks made by members of the anti-South movement, as well as the true facts of history as observed by reliable and objective historians, such as Judge Black:

To Hon. James A. Garfield, Member of Congress from Ohio: I have read the speech you sent me. I am astonished and shocked. As the leader of your party [the Republican Party, the Liberal Party at the time], to whom the candidates have specially delegated the conduct of the pending campaign, you should have met your responsibilities in a very different way. I do not presume to lecture so distinguished a man upon his errors, but if I can prevent you, even to a small extent, from abusing the public credulity, it is my duty to try. Promising only my great anxiety to preserve the fraternal relations existing between us for many years, I follow the Horatian rule, and come at once to "the middle of things."

You trace back the origin of present parties to the earliest immigrations at Plymouth and Jamestown, and profess to find in the opposing doctrines then planted and afterward constantly cherished in Massachusetts and Virginia, the germs of those ideas which now make Democracy [that is, conservatism] and Abolitionism [that is, liberalism] the deadly foes of each other. The ideas so planted in

Massachusetts, were, according to your account, the freedom and equality of all races, and the right and duty of every man to exercise his private judgment in politics as well as religion. On the other hand, you set forth as irreconcilably hostile the doctrine of Virginia, "that capital should own labor, that the negro had no rights of manhood, and that the white man might buy, own and sell him and his offspring forever." Following these assertions with others, and linking the present with the long past, you employ the devices of your rhetoric to glorify the modern Abolitionist and to throw foul scorn, not merely on the Southern people, but on the whole Democracy of the Country.

This looks learned and philosophical, and it gives your speech a dignity seemingly above the reach of the ordinary demagogue. Happy is he who knows the causes of things; felicitous is the partisan member of Congress whose stump speech goes up the river of time to the first fountains of good and evil. But *your contrast of historical facts* is open to one objection, which I give you in a form as simple as possible when I say that *it is wholly destitute of truth*: This, of course, implies no imputation on your good faith. Your high character in the church as well as the State, forbids the belief that you would be guilty of willful misrepresentation.

Conservative Copperhead and statesman Jeremiah S. Black of Pennsylvania.

TOLERANCE IN NEW ENGLAND

The men of Massachusetts, so far from planting the right of private judgment, extirpated and utterly extinguished it, by means so cruel that no man of common humanity can think of them even now without disgust and indignation. I am surprised to find you ignorant of this. Did you never hear of the frightful persecutions they carried on systematically against Baptists and Quakers and Catholics? How they fined, imprisoned, lashed, mutilated, enslaved and banished everybody that claimed the right of free thought? How they stripped the most virtuous and inoffensive women, and publicly whipped them on their naked backs, only for expressing their conscientious convictions? Have you never, in all your reading, met with the story of Roger Williams? For merely suggesting to the public authorities of the colony that no person ought to be punished on account of his honest opinions, he was driven into the woods and pursued ever afterwards with a ferocity that put his own life and that of his friends in constant danger. In fact, *the cruelty of their laws against the freedom of conscience and the unfeeling rigor with which they were executed, made Massachusetts odious throughout the world.*

These great crimes of the Pilgrim Fathers ought not to be cast up to their children; for some of their descendants (I hope a good majority) are high-principled and honest men, sincerely attached to the liberal [that is, more tolerant] institutions planted in the more Southern latitudes of the Continent. But if you are right in your assertion that the Abolitionists [Liberals] derive their principles from the ideas entertained and planted at Plymouth, that may account for the course and brutal tyranny with which your party has, in recent times, trampled upon the rights of free thought and free speech.

SLAVERY IN MASSACHUSETTS

Nor are you more accurate in your declaration that the old Yankees planted the doctrine of freedom and equality, or opposed the domination of one race over another. Messrs. [John Gorham] Palfrey and [Charles] Sumner have said something to the effect that slavery never existed in Massachusetts, and you may have been misled by them. But either they were wholly ignorant of the subject, or else they spoke with that loose and lavish unveracity which is a common fault among men of their political sect. The Plymouth colony and the province of Massachusetts Bay were pro-slavery to the backbone. If you doubt this, I refer you to [George H.] Moore's History of Slavery in Massachusetts, where the evidence (consisting chiefly of records and documents perfectly authenticated) is produced and collated with a fullness and fairness which cannot be questioned. *The Plymouth immigrants planted precisely the doctrine which you ascribe to the Jamestown colonists; that is to say, they held that "the negro had no rights of manhood; that the white man might buy, own and sell him, and his offspring forever."* Practically and theoretically they maintained that human slavery in its most unmitigated form was a perfectly just, proper and desirable institution, entirely consistent with Christianity as they understood it, and founded on principles of universal jurisprudence. They insisted upon it as an established and settled rule of the law of nations that when one government or community or political organization made war upon its own subjects or the subjects of another, and vanquished them, the people of the beaten party had no rights to which the right of the conquerors was not paramount.

Conservative Copperhead George H. Pendleton of Ohio.

Whenever it was demonstrated by actual experiment that any people were too weak to defend their homes and families against an invader who visited them with fire and sword, they might lawfully be stripped of their property, and they, themselves, their wives and their children, might justly be held as slaves or sold into perpetual bondage. That was the idea they planted in their own soil, propagated among their contemporaries and transmitted to the Abolition

[Liberal] party of the present day. You have preached and practiced it in all your dealings with the [conservative] South. This absolute domination is what you mean, if you mean anything, when you talk about the "precious results of the war."

If the doctrines thus planted by the original settlers in Massachusetts be true, and if the "precious fruits" of it, which you are gathering with so much industry, be legitimate, it is a perfect justification of all the slavery that ever existed on this Continent. Your great examplars, from whom you acknowledge that you have derived your ideas of freedom, certainly thought, or professed to think so, and they carried it out to its logical consequences. *When an African potentate chose to fight with and subdue a weak tribe, inside or out of his own dominions, he sold the prisoners whom he did not think proper to kill, and the men of Massachusetts bought them without a question of his title. They kept them and worked them to death, or sold them again as their interest prompted—for they held that the right of domination, resulting from the application of brute force, was good in the hands of all subsequent purchasers, however remote from their original conquistador.*

THE MASSACHUSETTS SLAVE FRAUDS

They executed this theory to its fullest extent in their own wars with the Indians. *Without cause or provocation, and without notice or warning, they fell upon the Pequods, massacred many of them, and made slaves of the survivors, without distinction of age or sex. About seven hundred, including many women and children, were sent to the West Indies, and there sold on public account, the proceeds being put in the colonial treasury.* Eight score of these unfortunate people escaped from the butchery by flight, and afterward agreed to give themselves up on a solemn promise of the authorities that they should neither be put to death nor enslaved. The promise was broken with as little remorse as a modern Abolitionist [Liberal] would violate his oath to support the Constitution. The "precious results of the war" were not to be lost by an honest observance of their pledged faith, and the victims of this infamous treachery were all of them shipped to the Barbados, and sold or "swapped for Blackamoors." *This practice of enslaving their captives was uniform, covered all cases, included women and children, as well as fighting men.* When death put King Philip beyond their reach, they sent his wife and child with the rest to be sold into slavery. The Indians make bad slaves. They were hard to tame, they escaped to the forest, and had to be hunted down, brought back and branded. They never ceased to be sullen and disobedient. The Africans always, on the contrary, "accepted the situation," were easily domesticated, and bore the yoke without murmuring. For that reason, *it became a settled rule of public and private economy in Massachusetts to exchange their worthless Indians for valuable negroes, cheating their West India customers in every trade.*

Perhaps, it was here that your party got the germ of its honesty as well as its humanity. *They made war for no other object than to supply themselves with subjects for this fraudulent traffic.* In 1643, Emanuel Downing, the foremost lawyer in the colony and a leader of commanding influence, as well as high connection, made a written argument in favor of a war with the Narragansetts. He did not pretend that any wrong had been done, but he had a pious dread that

Puritans attacking and enslaving Indians in Massachusetts, a long tradition in early New England.

Massachusetts would be held responsible for the false religion of the Narragansetts. "I doubt," says he, "if it be not synne in us, having power in our hands, to suffer them to mayntayne the worship of the devil, which their pow-wowes often doe." This tenderness of conscience is very characteristic of the [Liberal] party which got the "germ of its ideas" from that source. But go a little further, and you will see with pleasure how exactly you have copied their doctrines. *"If," says he, "upon a just war, the Lord should deliver them into our hand, we might easily have men, women and children to exchange for Moors (negroes), which will be more gayneful pilladge for us than wee conceive, for I do not see how we can thrive until we get in a stock of slaves sufficient to do all our business."* This (except the spelling) might come from an Abolition caucus to-day.

YANKEE HUMANITY

They did get most of their Indians off, and supplied themselves with negroes in their place. The shameless in humanity with which the blacks were used made slavery in Massachusetts "the sum of all villainy." In the letter of Downing, already referred to, he says: "You know very well we shall mayntayne twenty Moores cheaper than one English servant." Think of reducing a West India negro in that intensely cold climate to the one-twentieth part of the food and clothing which a white menial was in the habit of getting. They must have been frozen and starved to death in great numbers. *When that happened, it was but the loss of an animal. The harboring of a slave woman, was, in 1646, pronounced by the highest authority to be the same injury as the unlawful detention of a beast.* In 1716, Sewell [Judge Samuel Sewall of Salem Witch Trial fame], the chief justice of the colony, said that negroes were rated with horses and hogs. Dr. [Jeremy] Belknap tells us that afterward, *when the stock enlarged and the market became dull, young negroes and mulattoes were sometimes given away like puppies.* This is the kind of "freedom," this the "equality of the races," which you learned from the ancient colonists. But they taught you more than that. *Their precept and example established the slavery of white persons as well as Indians and negroes. As their remorseless tyranny spared no age and no sex, so it made no distinction of color. Besides the cargoes of white heretics which were captured and shipped to them by their brethren in England, they took special delight in fastening their yoke on all who were suspected of heterodoxy.* One instance is worthy of special attention.

Lawrence Southwick and his wife were Quakers, and accused at the same time with many others of attending Quaker meetings, or "syding with Quakers," and "absenting themselves from the publick ordinances." The Southwicks had previously suffered so much in their persons and estates from this kind of persecution that they could no longer work or pay any more fines, and, therefore, the general court, by solemn resolution, ordered them to be banished on pain of death. Banishment, you will not fail to notice, was in itself equivalent to a lingering death, if the parties were poor and feeble; for it meant merely driving them into the wilderness to starve with hunger and cold. *Southwick and his wife went out and died very soon. But this is not all. This unfortunate pair had two children, a boy and a girl (Daniel and Provided), who, having healthy constitutions, would bring a good price in the slave market. The children were taken from the parents and ordered to be sold in the West Indies.*

It happened, however, that there was not a shipmaster in any port of the colony who would consent to become the agent of their exportation and sale. The authorities, being thus balked in their views of the main chance, were fain to be satisfied in another way; *they ordered the girl to be whipped; she was lashed accordingly, in company with several other Quaker ladies, and then committed to prison, to be further proceeded against. History loses sight of her there. No record shows whether they killed her or not.*

This is one case out of a great many. It is very interesting and instructive when taken in connection with your speech, for it shows the "germ of the idea" *which your party acted on when it kidnapped and imprisoned men and women by the thousands for believing in American liberty as guaranteed by the Constitution.* The Quakers and Baptists had no printed organs in that day through which their private judgment could be expressed, else you would no doubt have cases directly in point to justify your forcible suppression of two hundred and fifty newspapers.

Liberal U.S. President John Adams of Massachusetts, a Federalist.

A CHANGE OF LEADERS

Enmity to the right of private judgment comes down to the party of Plymouth ideas by consistent and regular succession. It is woven like a dirty stripe into the whole warp and woof of their history. *As soon as they got possession of the Federal Government* under [Federalist, that is, big government Liberal] John Adams *they began to use it as an engine for the suppression of free thought.* Their alien law gave the President power to banish or imprison, without trial, any foreigner whose opinions might be obnoxious to his supporters. Their sedition put every Democratic [that is, Conservative] speaker and writer under the heel of the administration. Their standing army was used, as it is now, to crush out their political opponents. If you come into Eastern Pennsylvania, and particularly into the good county of Berks, you will learn that the people there still think with indignation of that old reign of terror when Federal dragoons kidnapped, insulted and beat their fathers, chopped down their "liberty pole," broke to pieces the press of the *Reading Eagle*, and whipped its venerated editor in the market-house. The same spirit broke out again in the burning of nunneries and churches under Maria Monk, and under John Brown the whole country swarmed with spies and kidnappers. When you abandoned the harlot and rallied to the standard of the thief you changed your leader without changing your principles.

THE YANKEE SLAVE CODE

The slave code planted in Massachusetts was the earliest in America and the most cruel in all its provisions. It was pertinaciously adhered to for generations, and never repented of, or formally repealed. It was gradually abandoned, not because it was wrong, but solely because it was found, after long experiment, to be unprofitable. Their plan of keeping twenty negroes as cheaply as one white servant did not work well; for in that climate a negro thus used would infallibly die before his labor paid what he cost. They sold their stock whenever they could, but emancipation was forbidden by law, unless the owner gave security to maintain the slave and prevent him from becoming a public charge. To evade this law, those who had old or infirm negroes encouraged them to bring suits for their freedom, and then by sham demurrers, or other collusive arrangements, got judgments against themselves that the negroes were free and always had been. Females likely to increase the stock were advertised to be sold "for that fault alone." Young ones, because they were not worth raising, were given away like puppies of a superabundant litter. In this way domestic slavery by degrees got loose in practice, simply because it would not pay—but the principle on which one man may own another whom he subdues by superior strength or cunning was never abandoned, repudiated or denied. That principle was cherished, preserved and transmitted to you, their imitative and loving disciples, and you have applied it wherever you could as tyrannically as they did.

THE PURITAN'S "IDEA" OF WAR

You say that "war without an idea is simply brutality." I submit to your judgment, as a [Conservative] Christian man, whether war is redeemed of its brutality by such ideas as you and your [Liberal] political associates entertain of its purposes, objects and consequences. *In all your acts and measures, and by all your speeches and discussions, you express the idea that the logic of blows proves everything you choose to assert; that a successful invasion of one people by another has the effect of destroying all natural right to, and all legal guarantees for, the life, liberty and property of the people so invaded and conquered; that after a trial by battle the victor may enter up and execute what judgment he pleases against his adversary; that the crime which a weak community are guilty of when they attempt to defend their lives, their property and their families against invaders who come upon them to kill, destroy and subjugate them is so unpardonable that the whole body of the offenders taken collectively, and all individuals who partake even passively of the sin, may justly be devoted to death or such other punishment, by wholesale or retail, as the strong power shall see proper to inflict; that the conqueror, after the war is over, may insist that the helpless and unarmed people, whom he has prostrated, shall assist him by not merely accepting, but "adopting" (I use your own word) the measures intended to degrade and rob them, and thus make himself master of their soul as well as their bodies. All rights of men are resolved by this theory into the mights of men.*

I aver that this doctrine, in all its length and breadth, is false and pernicious. It is the foundation on which all slavery rests, and the excuse for all forms of tyranny. It has no support in any sound rule of public law, and has never been acknowledged by wise or virtuous governments in any age since the advent of Christ. You can find no authority for it, except in the examples of men whose names are given over to universal execration.

Indigenous African slavery: here, an African king handpicks a fellow African from a nearby village for enslavement. If the victim survives his brutal subjugation he may eventually be sold to a professional African, Arab, European, or Yankee slaver. All early American black slaves arrived having already been enslaved by their own countrymen.

. . . On the same principle Poland was partitioned, and Ireland plundered a dozen times. The King of Dahomey acted upon it when he sold his captives, and the men of Massachusetts indorsed it when they took them in exchange for captives of their own. *You and your confreres adopted it as a part of your political creed when, after the Southern people were thoroughly subdued, you denied them all rights of freemen, tore up their society, abrogated all laws which could protect them in person or property,*

broke their local governments in pieces, and put them under the domination of
notorious thieves, whom you forced them to accept as their absolute masters.

These results of the war are no doubt very precious. *The right to*
traffic in the flesh of Indians and negroes was precious to the Yankees and the
King of Dahomey. That was the fruit of their wars. But was it in either case
legitimate? Your great reverence for the founders of your [Liberal] political
school in Massachusetts, to say nothing of your respect for the authority of the
African princes, or your faith in the Koran, will probably impel you to stand
up in favor of the "ideas" which you have learned from them. But I think I can
maintain the Christian law of liberty in opposition to all your Mussulman
[Muslim] notions . . .

THE CANT OF THE PHARISEE

It would be very unjust to deny that a great many men, from the
earliest period of our history, were sincerely opposed to African
slavery, from motives of religion, benevolence and humanity. *This*
sentiment was strong in the South as well as the North, and by none was it
expressed with more fervor than by [Thomas] Jefferson himself, the great apostle
of Democracy [conservatism].

But this concession can hardly be made to the political abolitionists
[Northern Liberals and Socialists]. As an almost universal rule, the leaders of
that sect were ribald infidels [atheists], and their conventicles teemed with the
most shocking blasphemy. They were, by their own avowals, the most cruel
barbarians of any age. Servile insurrection and a general butchery of the
Southern people was a part of their programme from the beginning. The
leaders to whom they gave their highest admiration were the men whose feet
were the swiftest in running to shed innocent blood. Seward won their
affections in his early manhood by proposing measures from which civil war
would be sure to come, and in which he promised that negroes should be incited
to "rise in blackest insurrection." They applauded John Brown to the echo for
a series of the basest murders on record. They did not conceal their hostility to
the Federal and State Governments, nor deny their enmity to all laws which
protected the liberties of white men. The Constitution stood in their way, and
they cursed it bitterly; the Bible was quoted against them, and they reviled God
Almighty himself. I know that the mind of man, like his body, is
fearfully and wonderfully made; I understand all the difficulty of
analyzing human passions, and I admit we should not judge harshly of
motives; but *how these heartless oppressors of their own race could have any*
care for the freedom of the negro passes my comprehension. Unless you can
explain it otherwise, the judgment of history must inevitably be against the

sincerity of their anti-slavery professions. In the present aspect of the case, it seems impossible to believe that love of the negro was not assumed as a mere excuse for enslaving the white race, just as their ancestors put on the pretense of piety to gratify their appetite for the property and blood of better people than themselves. You must positively reconsider this subject before you undertake again to present the abolitionists to the world in the respectable character of fanatics. I think you will find that the crew of the Mayflower brought over and planted no "germ of an idea" which has flourished with more vigor than their canting hypocrisy.

The Pilgrim ship, *Mayflower*.

Here, let me say again, that the vices and wickedness of the Plymouth colonists are not to be visited on the heads of their children, according to the flesh. Among them, in every part of the country are great statesmen, brave soldiers, true servants of the church, and virtuous, patriotic Democrats [Conservatives], who are no more responsible for the crimes of their ancestors than a peaceable Scotchman is for the raids and robberies which in past generations were committed by his clan upon the English border. But you acknowledge that you get your political ideas from them—you boast that your party has no doctrine of public law and no notions of public duty which were not planted at Plymouth. Therefore, it is not only proper, but necessary, to show what those doctrines and ideas were.

A FUNDAMENTAL REPUBLICAN LIE

I pass now to a later period. You say that there were two radically different theories about the nature of our Government; "the [liberal]

North believing and holding that we were a nation, the [conservative] South insisting that we were only a confederation of sovereign States." It is not true that any such theoretical conflict ever existed between the sections. That the Articles of Confederation first and the Constitution afterwards united the States together for certain purposes therein enumerated, and thus made us a nation among nations was never denied that I know of by any party. But this national character was given to the general government by sovereign States who confederated together for that purpose. They bestowed certain powers on the new political corporation then created, and called it the United States of America [and nicknamed "The Confederate States of America"],[615] and they expressly reserved to themselves all the sovereign rights not granted in the charter. Democratic [Conservative] statesmen had no theory about it. They saw their duty written down in the fundamental law, they swore to perform it, and they kept their oaths. They executed the powers of the general Government in their whole constitutional vigor, for that, as Mr. Jefferson said, was "the sheet-anchor of our peace at home and our safety abroad," and they carefully guarded the rights of the States as the only security we could have for a just administration of our domestic affairs. This was universally assented to as right and true. No counter theory was set up. Difference of construction there might be, but all admitted that when the line of power was accurately drawn between the Federal Government and State sovereignty, the rights of one side were as sacred as those on the other. But *within the last two or three years [circa 1875] the low demagogues [radical Liberals and socialists] of your party have got to putting in their platforms the assertion that this is a nation and not a confederation.* What do they mean? What do you mean when you indorse and reproduce it? Do you deny that the States were sovereign before they united? Do you affirm that their sovereignty was wholly merged in the Federal Government when they assented to the Constitution? *Is the Tenth Amendment a mere delusion?* Do you mean to assert that the States have not now, and never had, any rights at all except what are conceded to them at the mercy of the "nation"? No doubt this new article was inserted in the creed of the Abolitionists, because they supposed it would give a sort of plausibility to their violent intervention with the internal affairs of the States. But *it is so false, so shallow, and so destitute of all respectable authority, that it imposes upon nobody.*

SECESSION A YANKEE PRODUCT

As a part of this conflict of theories, and resulting from it, you describe the South as "insisting that each State had a right, at its own discretion, to break the Union, and constantly threatening secession, where the full rights of slavery were not acknowledged." *In fact and in truth secession, like slavery, was first planted in New England. There it grew and flourished and spread its branches far over the land, long before it was thought of in the South, and long before "the full rights of slavery" were called in question by anybody. The anti-Democrats [the Liberals at the time] of that region, in former as well as in later times, totally misunderstood the purposes for which this Government was made.*

They regarded it as a mere commercial machine, by which they could make much "gaynefull pilladge," if allowed to run it their own way. When they were disappointed in this by certain perfectly just and constitutional regulations of their trade, which the common defense and general welfare made necessary, they immediately fell to plotting the dismemberment of the Union. Before 1807 they organized a conspiracy with the British authorities in Canada for the erection of New England into a separate republic under British protection. Not long afterwards [Federalist, that is, Liberal] Josiah Quincy [III], whose fidelity to the [Liberal] party which elected him was never doubted, formally announced in Congress the intention of his State to leave the Union, "peaceably if she could, forcibly if she must." Their hatred of the Union deepened, and their determination to break it up grew fiercer, as the resolution of the Democrats [Conservatives] to maintain the independence of the country became

Federalist (big government Liberal) Josiah Quincy III of Massachusetts.

stronger. *When the war of 1812 began they were virtually out of the Union, and remained out during the whole of that desperate struggle, not only refusing all assistance to carry it on, but helping the enemy in every possible way. It was while England had her tightest grasp on the throat of the nation that the Hartford Convention was called to dismember it; and this Mr. Jefferson says, they would have accomplished but for the battle of New Orleans and the peace of Ghent.*

John Quincy Adams in 1839, and Abraham Lincoln in 1847,

made elaborate arguments in favor of the legal right of a State to go out [secede]. The later abolitionists did not attempt to conceal their rancorous hostility to the Union. "No union with slaveholders" was one of their watchwords, and down to the opening of the war its destruction was the avowed object of their machinations.

There is one conclusive proof of your enmity to the Union, and that is *your unwavering opposition to the Constitution which held the States together.* You know as well as I do how absurd it is to suppose that any man or party can support the Union, and at the same time trample on the Constitution; and you certainly are not ignorant that *you and your [Liberal] predecessors, from the earliest times, have been anti-constitutional in all your proclivities. Contemptuous disregard of constitutional obligations is not now the mere germs of a doctrine; it is a part of your settled creed. Before the war, and since, you have trodden under foot every provision contained in the great charter of our liberties. I do not speak at random. I challenge you to designate a single constitutional right of the States, or of individuals, which you have not at some time, or in some way, deliberately violated.*

LAWLESSNESS AND "LOYALTY"

This contempt for the Constitution, this practical denial that an oath to support it is sacred, implies a disregard of all laws, human and divine, and when adopted, it left nothing to guide you except the propensities, evil or good, of your natural hearts. Many of you (and notably yourself [James A. Garfield]) contracted no individual guilt, because you were too proud for petty larceny, too benevolent for large-handed robbery, and too full of kindness to break wantonly into the tabernacle of human life.

But *generally the principles of the [radically liberal] ultra-Abolitionists (if they ever had any) became so wholly perverted that they saw nothing wrong in the worst offenses that could be committed against their political opponents. In their eyes, theft and murder not only lost their felonious character, but became meritorious, if the victims lived south of Mason and Dixon's line. When John Brown stole horses in the State of Missouri, he was taking his lawful booty; when he sneaked into a quiet Virginia village on a Sunday night and assassinated defenseless citizens, he was a hero; and when he died a felon's death on the scaffold, to which he was justly condemned, he became a martyr.*

THE DEMOCRATS OF THE NORTH

You persist in misunderstanding the anti-bellum attitude of the Northern Democracy [that is, Northern Conservatives]. We [Conservatives here in Pennsylvania] stood steadfastly by the Union against all attempts of the [liberal] New England party to break it up by secession. *We sustained the Constitution against the ferocious assaults of the Abolitionists [extreme Liberals]; we labored earnestly to save Republican [Conservative] institutions from the destruction with which they were threatened by you; and as long as the Southern people acted with us, we gratefully accepted their aid in the good work.*

Your averment that the Democratic [Conservative] party desired the aggrandizement of slavery, and "yielded their consciences" on that subject to the South, is grossly unjust, if you mean to charge them with anything more than a willingness to protect the Southern, as well as the Northern and Middle States in the exercise of their constitutional rights. We had disposed of slavery within our own jurisdiction [in Pennsylvania] according to our sense of sound policy and justice. But we had made an express compact with the other States to leave the entire control of their domestic affairs to themselves. We kept our covenant, simply because it would have been gross dishonesty to break it. The Abolitionists took a different view, and refused to keep faith. They swore as solemnly as we did to observe the terms of the bargain, but according to their code it was a sin not to violate it. The fact is true that we did not think it right to cut the throats, or shoot, or strangle the men or women of the South for believing in negro slavery; but that is no justification of your assertion that we yielded our consciences to them.

Again: You charge us (the Northern Democracy) [Northern Conservatives], with having given bad advice to the Southern people. This consisted, you say, in assuring them that if they seceded we would take their part against any attempt to force them back again into the Union. This is a gross error, and you will see it when I recall your attention to the facts. *In all our exhortations to Southern men against secession we were met by the expression of their fear that the Abolitionists intended, in any event, to invade and slaughter them. Some reason for this apprehension was given by the fierce threats of your leading men, and especially by your almost universal admiration of Brown for his raid into Virginia.* Certain Democrats (and very good [Conservative] men, too,) did then declare that a lawless expedition intended for purposes of mere

Conservative Copperhead and New York Mayor Fernando Wood.

pillage could not and should not be started in the North, without such opposition as would effectually stop it. But this was before secession, and it was intended to prevent that movement, not to encourage it.

You cannot, with any show of justice, deny that devotion to the Union was one of the strongest feelings in the heart of the Northern Democracy [Northern Conservatives]. We had always deprecated a separation from the Southern States with so much earnestness that one of the opprobrious epithets you bestowed on us was that of "Union savers." This was not a mere sentiment of admiration or gratitude to the great Southern men who had led us through the perils of the Revolution, settled our institutions, and given our country its high place in the estimation of the world. We felt all this! but we felt much more. The preservation of the Union was to us an absolute necessity. It was indispensable to the security of our lives, our personal liberty and our plainest rights of property. How true this was at all times, and especially in 1860, you will, see if you reflect a moment on our situation at that time.

THE ADVENT OF RADICALISM

The Abolitionists [radical Liberals] were coming into power. I need not say by what combination of imposture or accident they got it. All the Northern States as well as the Federal Government fell into their hands. *No doubt their dislike of Southern people was very great; but Northern Democrats [Northern Conservatives] were objects of their special malignity.* Long before that time, and ever since, this sentiment has been expressed in words and acts too plain to be misunderstood. You show how strong it is in your own heart when you tell Southern [Conservative] men (and you do tell them so in this very speech) that you honor them ten thousand times more than Democrats [Conservatives] of the North. Remember, in addition to this, that *the leading Abolitionists acknowledged no law which might stand in the way of their interests or their passions. Against anybody else the Constitution of the country would have been a protection. But they disregarded its limitations, and had no scruples about swearing to support it with a predetermination to violate it.*

We had been well warned by all the men best entitled to our confidence—particularly and eloquently warned by Mr. [Henry] Clay and [Daniel] Webster—that if ever the Abolitionists got a hold upon the organized physical force of the country they would govern without law, scoff at the authority of the courts and throw down all the defences of civil liberty.

But if the South had not seceded we might have made a successful defense of our Constitution though the powers of the Government were in the hands of its enemies. With the aid of the Southern people, if they had been true to their duty, we could have organized an opposition so formidable in its moral and political power that you would scarcely have dared to assault us. No wonder that we were "Union savers;" for to us the Union meant personal liberty, free thought, an independent press, *habeas corpus,* trial by jury, the impartial administration of justice—*all those great legal institutions which our forefathers had shed so much of blood to build up.*

The South deserted us at the crisis of our fate, and left us in our weakness to the mercy of the most unprincipled tyrants [Liberals and Socialists] that ever betrayed a public trust. Secession was not mere folly and madness; it was something much worse. We could not but feel that we were deeply wronged. There was no remedy for the dire calamities with which we were threatened except in bringing the seceded States back to their places in the Union. Our convictions of legal duty, our exasperated sense of injury and a proper care for our best interests, all impelled us to join the new administration in the use of such force as might be found necessary to execute the laws in every part of the country. [Note: This particular paragraph voices the view of a *Northern* Conservative; but it was not the view of Victorian *Southern* Conservatives—and it still is not.]

THE WAR OF THE PHARISEE

But the Abolitionists [Liberals, Socialists, revolutionaries, etc.] wanted a war for the destruction of the Union, for the overthrow of the Constitution, for the subversion of free government, and for the subjugation of the whole country to that "higher law" which imposes no restraint upon the rapacity and malice of the ruling power. To such a war the national conscience was opposed. The soul of every respectable officer in the army and navy revolted at it, and every virtuous man in private life felt it to be an unspeakable outrage. To those who doubted before, the disaster of Bull Run [the Battle of Manassas to Confederates] made it plain that the war could not be successfully carried on unless it was put upon principles consistent with the usages of Christendom and the safety of our own institutions. Therefore it was that on the 22nd of July, 1861, Congress, with almost perfect unanimity, passed a resolution through both houses declaring in the most explicit words that the war should be conducted to preserve the Constitution, and not to revolutionize it. I give you here the words of the resolution itself, from the Congressional Globe:

"Resolved, That the present deplorable civil war has been forced upon the country by the disunionists of the Southern States, now in arms against the constitutional Government, and in arms around the capital; that in this national emergency, Congress, banishing all feeling of mere passion or resentment, will recollect only its duty to the whole country; that this war is not waged on their part in any spirit of oppression, or for any purpose of conquest or subjugation or purpose of overthrowing or interfering with the rights or established institutions of those States, but to defend and maintain the supremacy of the Constitution, and to preserve the Union with all the dignity, equality and rights of the several States unimpaired; and that as soon as these objects are accomplished the war ought to cease."

The Battle of First Manassas, Virginia, July 21, 1861, pitted Conservative Confederate Generals Joseph E. Johnston and Pierre G. T. Beauregard against Liberal Union General Irvin McDowell.

Confiding in this assurance, Democrats [Conservatives] from every Northern State rushed to the front by the hundred thousand; the border States of the South gave in their formal adhesion to the Government, and our great military leaders drew their swords with alacrity in support of the free institutions to which they had shown their fidelity so often before. With what base perfidy this solemn pledge was broken I need not tell you, for this speech shows that you know it well. You expressly declare that so far from sustaining the Government you revolutionized it. Instead of a war for the Union, you claim that it put the States out of the Union, and you had a right to keep them out as long as you pleased or admit them to their places on any terms, however degrading, which you choose to dictate. *Instead of restoring the supremacy of the Constitution all your politicians held, and so far as I know from their public declarations still hold, that the victory of the Federal forces abolished the Constitution not only in the South but in the North, and therefore they were not bound to observe its limitations, either in their legislative, judicial or executive measures. Instead of bringing back the States with their rights unimpaired, according to your promise, you crippled, enslaved, subjugated and disfranchised them. Instead of using the war power for the just and lawful purposes to which you were pledged, you converted it into a black Republican job to put the rights of all the people permanently under the feet of an unprincipled party* [then the Republicans, or Liberals].

I submit this part of the case to your consideration. I ask you to say whether you can find in the whole history of the human race another instance of similar perfidy on a scale so large. The baseness of the Massachusetts authorities in selling the surrendered Pequods into slavery, after a solemn promise to the contrary, was but the "germ of an idea" on which you acted in the fullness of its growth. Their act was in its nature and character nearly as bad as it could be; but only eight score of helpless people suffered by it; *the victims of your treachery are counted by millions.*

THE CORRUPTION OF THE PHARISEE

The offenses which you [Liberals] are now [1877] engaged in committing upon the public treasury are the natural sequence of your crimes against popular liberty. Universal experience proves that power usurped will always be dishonestly used. Seeing that *the Abolitionists [extreme Leftists] were led by men whom no oath could hold to the Constitution, and whom no pledge could bind to an observance of its principles,* we had no right to expect a decent regard for justice in their administration of the national finances. I do not mean that the masses of your party were, or are now, destitute of common integrity. But that was overruled by the political doctrines of their leaders. Having once set aside the established law of the land they had no standard by which they could measure the moral conduct of themselves or others, and *they became incapable of seeing the difference between right and wrong in public affairs. The "higher law" threw the reins loose on the neck of all evil passions. It not only abrogated the Constitution, but the Decalogue as well, and the eighth commandment was nullified with the rest.*

You [Liberals] have consequently made ours the corruptest government on this side of Constantinople. Perhaps you will say this is a mere general assertion. But I am ready to maintain the truth of it against all opposers. *You may take the rottenest monarchy in Europe, go over its history for a hundred years, and produce the worst act you can find of fraudulent spoliation upon its people, and if I do not show something worse committed here under the auspices of the party now in power, I will give up the case.*

I am speaking of the Government—of [Liberal] officials who rule us for their pleasure and plunder us for their personal profit—and it is no answer to quote Mr. Lord's speech before the Senate on the trial of [William W.] Belknap. His eulogy was on the virtue and intelligence of the people, and he argued from that the duty of their servants to behave with integrity. He certainly did not mean to whitewash the Administration. If he had meant to do so he could not have succeeded, for there was not wash enough in his bucket to go over the twenty-thousandth part of the job.

An 1873 cartoon satirizing the Crédit Mobilier scandal under Liberal U.S. President Ulysses S. Grant, considered the second most corrupt administration in American history after Lincoln's.

While you were hunting for certificates of character among the speeches of the impeachment managers, why did you overlook that of [Grant's Attorney General] Mr. [Ebenezer Rockwood] Hoar? He said in effect (for I cite him from memory) that the one production in which our country excels all others in the world is corruption of its government. There was the testimony of a candid witness belonging to your own party, who knew whereof he affirmed and spoke directly to the point.

But it is useless to cite the evidence of individuals upon great public facts that are felt and seen and known of all men. *Nothing ever was more notorious than the general disregard of all sound principle by this [the Liberal Grant] Administration. No people on earth are now suffering so much from extravagant taxation, and nowhere does so small a portion of the taxes go to legitimate public purposes, or so much to the rulers themselves and the rings they choose to favor. Industry is crushed as it never was before. Labor no longer works for itself, since all and more than all of its surplus profits are exacted and consumed by the hangers-on of the Government. Now, although we call ourselves freemen or freedmen, we are, to all intents and purposes, slaves, so long as you continue to make us hand over to you the earnings of our labor; for the essence of slavery consists in compelling one man, or class of men, to work for another without equivalent. We are determined to relieve ourselves from this intolerable bondage, as far as we can, legally and peaceably, and, if you do not help us, you must at least cease to mock us by pretending to be an anti-slavery man upon principle.*

A PHARISEE'S BRAVADO

You tell us that the Republican [Liberal] party "will punish its own rascals." The newspaper report of your speech says that this was greeted with laughter from the Republican side of the House. Certainly, it sounds like the broadest of jokes. If you meant it in earnest, please to say what you found this claim of impartial justice upon. You will hardly prove it by showing that [Liberal Benjamin H.] Bristow and [Union officer Bluford] Wilson succeeded, with much tribulation, in convicting certain manufacturers of crooked whisky, and thereby got themselves turned out of office. It is vain to deny that there is, and has been, a general system of dishonesty pervading all ranks of the civil service, which, so far from being punished, is protected, encouraged and rewarded by the highest authorities. You have set your faces like a flint against all investigations tending to expose rascality. Proof of that, if proof were wanting, would be found in your own denunciation of the present Congress for pushing its inquiries into those regions where venality and corruption might otherwise have dwelt in safety.

In all your Southern measures you have shown a positive abhorrence of honest government. You forced into all places of power men whose characters were notoriously bad, and maintained them while they perpetrated the most shameless robberies. You resisted every effort of the oppressed people to throw them off, and when those efforts were successful in some of the States, you mourned the fall of the felons with sincere lamentation. Just look at the crew of godless wretches by whom Louisiana has been almost desolated! In the face of a constitutional interdict, your [Grant] administration at Washington repeatedly interfered to shield them from justice, and to uphold them in the possession of power to which they had no manner of legal claim. At this moment they are preying upon the prostrate people of the State, under the protection of Federal bayonets. Is that what you call punishing your own rascals?

You may answer that the white people of Louisiana, being conquered, are rightfully enslaved, according to the principles planted at Plymouth, and, therefore, it is not for the like of them to invoke the protection of law and justice. I will, therefore, call your attention to another case to which Dahomeian rule does not apply, and in which the failure of the Republican [Liberal] party to punish its own rascals has been equally signal; I mean the frauds of the Union Pacific Railroad Company and the Crédit Mobilier.

"THE MOST UNKINDEST CUT OF ALL"

You will pardon me, I am sure, for referring to this affair; you are the last man upon whom I would make a personal point, and I could not do it here if I would try; for the conviction I have often expressed remains unchanged, that your integrity was not stained by such connection as you had with that business. But we both know that it was the most gigantic fraud that the history of modern times discloses. The magnitude of the iniquity almost exceeds belief. The entire amount of the booty already taken from the public and stowed away in the pockets of the perpetrators cannot be less than one hundred million dollars, and every six months they make a new demand, which is honored at the treasury by an additional payment. I am told that a late attorney general counts one hundred and eight millions as the sum which the United States will lose in solid cash, directly taken out of the Treasury. I am not sure that this calculation is accurate, but it cannot be very far wrong, and it is not equal to one-half of the whole steal, for it does not include the value of the road itself, nor the land grants, nor the proceeds of the bonds to which the lien of the United States was postponed, nor the equipment bonds. As this swindle was the largest, so it was one of the most inexcusably base. It was perpetrated at a time when the nation was swamped with debt, when the people were loaded with taxes, and when the most rigid economy was imperatively required. All circumstances, as well as the direct evidence, show that it was no sudden act of thoughtless imprudence, but was wilfully, deliberately and corruptly pre-arranged and determined. There is nothing to mitigate it; you cannot defend it even by waving the bloody shirt [a political ploy used, mainly by Liberals, to incite anger against the South over the Civil War, slavery, etc.].

How did the Republican [Liberal] party "punish its own rascals" in this case? Not a hair on the head of any rascal was touched. *On the contrary, they were promoted, honored and advanced; the most guilty of them are now, as they were before, the very darlings of the party.* Even that is not the worst of it. These swindlers are periodically swelling the colossal proportions of their crime by taking out of the treasury additional millions which they claim as the "precious results" of their original fraud. They have no better title to them than a wolf has to the mutton he slaughters by moonlight. The legal remedy against these exactions is so plain that ignorance alone could hardly miss it. But your officers have found out the way not to do it. They permit the Government to lie down and be robbed semi-annually by a corporation which [New York prosecutor Samuel J.] Tilden would long ago have disarmed of its power, and whose criminal abettors he would have swept into the penitentiary by scores.

An 1876 political banner for the Democratic (Conservative) presidential ticket: Samuel J. Tilden and Thomas A. Hendricks. In the most disputed election in U.S. history, they lost to Republican (Liberals) Rutherford B. Hayes and William A. Wheeler.

HAYESISM ALIAS GRANTISM

I repeat that I do not blame you as an active accomplice in this wickedness. But you ought to have come out from the evil and corrupt fellowship as soon as you saw how evil and corrupt it was. You owed it to yourself, your church and your country to break off at once from [liberal] political associates capable of such indefensible conduct. But your acceptance of the doctrines planted at Plymouth by the Yankees blinded your judgment, and made your conscience inaccessible to the principles planted in Jerusalem by the "people first called Christians at Antioch."

You would have us believe that [Liberal politician Rutherford B.] Hayes, if elected, would reform abuses and give us a pure administration. Your statement, and that of other gentlemen equally reliable, make it certain that Mr. Hayes bears an irreproachable character in all his private relations. I do not doubt his possession of that negative honesty which it is a disgrace to want. I accord him those tame household virtues which entitle him to the respect of his neighbors and the confidence of his family; but he can no more stem the torrent of Republican [Liberal] corruption than he can swim against the rapids of Niagara.

His whole history shows that he would not even make an effort to do so. He has been most happily called "a man of tried subserviency." A reformer in these times must be made of stern material. He must have no connection with, and be under no obligation to, the authors of the abuses which need reform. Above all things, he must not have consented expressly or impliedly to the commission of the public wrongs which his duties as a reformer would require him to punish. When he comes to oppose wickedness in high places the consciousness that he, himself, is in *pari delicto* ["in equal fault"] will make even a strong man as nerveless as infancy.

To show how hard it would be for a man like Mr. Hayes to resist the worst orders of his own party, I must cite a case directly in point, and certainly within your recollection as well as mine. In the case of [Ex parte] Milligan [which maintained the Lincoln had breached the Constitution by suspending the right of *habeas corpus*], you made an eloquent and powerful speech before the Supreme Court for those free principles, which I, at the same time, supported in my weaker way. You showed the indestructible right of every citizen to a legal trial; you proved that *Magna Charta* did not perish on the battlefield; you demonstrated by irresistible logic that the Constitution was supreme after the war as it was before; you spurned with lofty contempt the brutal idea that law was extinguished by the victory of the forces called out to defend it; and you closed with that grand peroration on the Goddess of Liberty, which, if spoken at Athens in the best days of her "fierce Democratic," would have "shook the arsenal and fulminated over Greece." These were not the words of a paid advocate, for you had volunteered in the case; nor the sudden emotions of a neophyte, for you had read and pondered the case well. You spoke the deliberate conclusions of your mind, and there is no doubt in your heart of hearts you believe them to be true this day.

Liberal U.S. President Rutherford B. Hayes of Ohio.

Yet when the Reconstruction law was proposed you suffered yourself to be whipped in, surrendered your conscience to your [Liberal] party, and voted against your recorded convictions, for a measure that nullified every provision of the Constitution, whereby ten millions of people were deprived of rights which you knew to be sacred and inalienable.

If this was the case, what subserviency may not be expected from Mr. Hayes, when the party lash comes to be laid on his back? You are his superior in every quality that holds a man true to public duty. You have been carefully schooled in the morality of the New Testament, you have lived all your life in the full blaze of the gospel, you are gifted with a logical acumen which few can boast, and with moral courage far above the average. If you fell down before the Moloch [a Pagan god] of Abolitionism, and gave up all principle at once, what act of worship will Hayes deny to that grim idol?

HOISTED BY HIS OWN PETARD

Speaking of Reconstruction, and seeing your broad accusations of treason, I am tempted to ask if you are sure that you, yourself, and your associates did not commit that crime.

In March, 1867, the then existing Government of the Union was supreme all over the country, and every State had a separate government of its own for the administration of its domestic concerns. That Government was entitled then, if it ever was, to the universal obedience of all citizens, and you, its officers, had taken a special oath of fidelity to it. *Nevertheless, you made a deliberate arrangement, not only to withdraw your support from it, but to overthrow it totally in ten of the States; and this you did by military force. In all the South you levied war against the nation and against the defenseless States, destroyed the free governments of both, and substituted in their place an untempered and absolute despotism.*

Now, suppose you had been indicted for this, how could you have escaped the condemnation of the law? I know your excuses, and I can understand your claims to mercy; but what legal defense could you have made consistent with your own argument and the decision of the court in the [Ex parte] Milligan case?

I cannot describe to you how unpleasant is the sensation produced by your professions of a desire for peace. Why do you not give us peace if you are willing, we shall have it? You need but to cease hostilities and the general tranquility will be restored. You refuse to do that because peace would endanger your party ascendency. To maintain your plunderers in power you have uniformly resorted to the bayonet—you have made civil war the chronic condition of the country—wherever you have displaced liberty, fraternity and equality, and given nothing instead but infantry, artillery and cavalry. You are at this moment openly engaged in preparing your battalions for armed intervention in the struggle of the people with the carpet-baggers.

What makes this worse is your closing declaration that you will take no step backward. There is to be no repentance, no change of policy, and consequently no peaceful or honest government. "Onward," you say, is the word. Onward—to what? To more war, more plunder, more oppression, more universal bankruptcy, heavier taxes and still worse frauds on the public treasury? — J. S. Black.

[General Stephen D. Lee, who read Black's letter at a Confederate gathering:] "I extract [the following by Judge Black] from *Letters to Henry Wilson* [Liberal vice president under President Grant]":

[To Henry Wilson:] Mr. [James] Buchanan being a [Conservative] man of this class, I submit the question whether his prejudices against perjury (unreasonable as you may think them) are not entitled to some little respect.

Apart from the religious obligation of his oath, *he loved the Constitution of his country on its own account, as the best government the world ever saw.* I do not expect you to sympathize with this feeling; your affections are otherwise engaged. But can you not make allowance for his attachment to *that great compact which was framed by our forefathers to secure union, justice, peace, State independence and individual liberty for ourselves and our posterity?*

Statue of Conservative Confederate General Stephen Dill Lee, Vicksburg, Mississippi.

Another thing: All his [Conservative] predecessors governed their conduct by similar notions of fidelity to the Constitution. In peace and in war, in prosperity and disaster, through all changes, in spite of all threats and provocations *they had kept their oaths, and assumed no ungranted power.* It was the most natural thing in the world for Mr. Buchanan to follow the example of such men as Washington, Madison, and Jackson, rather than the precepts of those small but ferocious [Liberal] politicians who thought their own passions and interests a "higher law" than the law of the country.

Again: *All his [Buchanan's] advisers—not I alone, but all of them—expressed the clear and unhesitating opinion that his view of the law on the subject of coercing States was right.* His legal duty being settled, not one among them ever breathed a suggestion that he ought to violate it.

But the [Liberal] Lincoln Administration did not stop here. That Cabinet voted six to one in favor of surrendering Fort Sumter—Mr. [Francis P.] Blair [Sr.] being the only dissentient. The President, if he did not yield to the majority, must have wavered a considerable time; the Secretary of State was so sure of him, that he caused the South Carolina authorities to be informed that the fort would be given up. You will not deny these facts, but you will continue, as heretofore, to say that the [Conservative] Buchanan Administration weakly and wickedly favored secession, while that of [Liberal] Lincoln was firmly and faithfully opposed. The man who involves himself in such inconsistencies, whether from want of information, want of judgment, or want of veracity, is not qualified to write on an historical subject.

I have given more time and space than I intended to this part of your paper. But I am addressing a man of peculiar character. To a person whose moral perceptions are healthy and natural, I could make my defense in a breath. But being required to apologize for not violating a sworn duty, some circumlocution is necessary.

[General Stephen D. Lee:] "In conclusion, I have the pleasure of presenting the following extract from the same author [Judge Black], and most pertinent in this connection. I take it from his reply to Charles Francis Adams' speech on the 'Character of William Seward'":

By Mr. [Gideon] Welles's paper it is distinctly made known that *Mr. Seward, as soon as he came into office, concocted a scheme for the surrender of Fort Sumter into the hands of the Secessionists; that he drew General Scott into it, and tried to get the President's assent also; that the President having declined to surrender, and determined to re-enforce the place, a confidential friend and protege of Mr. Seward notified his confederates in the South of the movement about to be made; that the whole plan and arrangement of the Administration for the relief of the fort was brought to nothing by a series of secret, deceptive, and underhand manoeuvres which Mr. Seward carried on without the knowledge of the War or Navy Department; and that, while he was thus betraying his associates, he wrote to Secessionists that his faith pledged to them would be fully kept. These accusations seem to be proved by overwhelming evidence.*

Conservative newspaperman and political advisor Francis P. Blair Sr. of Virginia.

When the troubles were at their worst, certain Southern gentlemen, through [Conservative] Judge [Archibald] Campbell, of the Supreme Court (of the U.S.), requested me to meet [Liberal] Mr. Seward and see if he would not give them some ground on which they could stand with safety inside of the union. I consented, and we met at the State Department. The conference was long and earnest. I cannot, within these limits, set forth even the substance of it. He [Seward] seemed conscious of his power, and willing to use it in the interests of peace and union, as far as he could without the risk of offending his own party. What could he do? Many propositions were discussed, and rejected as being either impractical or likely to prove useless, before *I told him what I felt perfectly sure would stop all controversy at once and forever, I proposed that he should simply pledge himself and the incoming administration to govern according to the constitution, and upon every disputed point of constitutional law to accept that exposition of it which had been or might be given by the judicial authorities. He started at this, became excited, and violently declared he would do no such thing.*

"That," *said he,* "is treason; that would make me agree to the Dred Scott case."

In vain I told him [Seward] that he was not required to admit the correctness of any particular case, but merely to submit to it as the decision of the highest tribunal, from which there could be no appeal except to the sword.

You will see that if such a pledge as this had been given and kept, the war could not have taken place; it would have left nothing to fight about; and the decent men [Liberals] of the Anti-Slavery party would have lost nothing by it *which they pretended to want*, for even the Dred Scott case had enured to their practical benefit. . . . *I had never before heard that treason was obedience to the Constitution as construed by the courts.*

[General Stephen D. Lee:] "The foregoing letter and these extracts here presented above are from Judge Jeremiah S. Black, Attorney General in the Cabinet of President Buchanan."[616] [End of letter. L.S.]

If we were to change the dates and modernize the language slightly, Judge Black's words could just as easily apply to 21st-Century Liberals as those from the 19th Century. The only difference is that today's leftists are even more criminal minded, more aggressive, more racist (practicing both ethnomasochism and ethnosadism),[617] more self-deluded, more underhanded, and more unethical than their Victorian predecessors—the same group that instigated the "Civil War" on the American people and their Constitution to begin with.

Let us end this chapter with the following relevant article by the aforementioned Yankee Benjamin J. Williams of Lowell, Massachusetts. It was published in the Lowell *Sun* on June 5, 1886, following former Confederate President Jefferson Davis' triumphant tour of the South in May of that year:

Editor of the *Sun*, Dear Sir: The demonstrations in the South in honor of Mr. Jefferson Davis, the ex-President of the Confederate States, are certainly of a remarkable character and furnish matter for profound consideration. Mr. Davis, twenty-one years after the fall of the Confederacy, suddenly emerging from his long retirement, journeys among his people to different prominent points, there to take part in public observances more or less directly commemorative, respectively, of the cause of the Confederacy and of those who strove and died for it; and everywhere he receives from the people the most overwhelming manifestations of heartfelt affection, devotion, and reverence, exceeding even any of which he was the recipient in the time of his power; such manifestations as no existing ruler in the world can obtain from his people, and such were never before given to a public man—old, out of office, with no favors to dispense, and disfranchised. Such homage is significant, startling. *It is given, as Mr. Davis himself has recognized, not to him alone, but to the cause whose chief representative he is. And it is useless to attempt to deny, disguise, or evade the conclusion that there must be something great and noble and true in him and in the cause to evoke this homage.*

As for Mr. Davis himself, the student of American history has not yet forgotten that it was his courage, self-possession, and leadership that in the very crisis of the battle of Buena Vista [during the Mexican-American War, February 1847] won for his country her proudest victory upon foreign fields of war, that as Secretary of War in Mr. [Franklin] Pierce's administration he was its master spirit, and that he was the recognized leader of the United States Senate at the time of the secession of the Southern States. For his character there let it be stated by his enemy but admirer, Massachusetts's own Henry Wilson: "The clear-headed, practical, dominating Davis." This was said by him in a speech made during the war, while passing in review the Southern Senators who had withdrawn from their States. When the seceding States formed their new Confederacy, in recognition of Mr. Davis's varied and predominant abilities, he was unanimously chosen its chief magistrate. And from the hour of his arrival at Montgomery to assume that office, when he spoke the memorable words, "We are determined to make all who oppose us smell Southern powder and feel Southern steel," all through the Confederacy's four year's unequal struggle for independence down to his last appeal as its chief, in his defiant proclamation from Danville after the fall of Richmond, "Let us not despair, my countrymen, but meet the foe with fresh defiance and with unconquered and unconquerable hearts," he exhibited

America's greatest Conservative, Confederate President Jefferson Davis of Kentucky, known proudly in the South as "the Patriot of Patriots."

everywhere and always the same proud and unyielding spirit, so expressive of his sanguine and resolute temper, which no disasters could subdue, which sustained him even when it could no longer sustain others, and which, had it been possible, would of itself have assured the independence of the Confederacy. And when at last the Confederacy had fallen, literally overpowered by unmeasurably superior numbers and means, and Mr. Davis was a prisoner, subjected to the grossest indignities, his proud spirit remained unbroken; and *never since the subjugation of his people has he abated in the least his assertion of the cause for which they struggled. The seductions of power or interest may move lesser men, that matters not to him; the cause of the Confederacy as a fixed, moral, and constitutional principle, unaffected by the triumphs of physical force, he asserts to-day as unequivocally as when he was seated in its executive chair at Richmond, in apparently irreversible power with its victorious legions at his command.*

Now, when we consider all this, what Mr. Davis has been and, most of all, what he is to-day in the moral greatness of his position, can we wonder that his people turn aside from timeservers and self-seekers and from all the commonplace chaff of life and render to him that spontaneous and grateful homage which is his due?

And we cannot indeed wonder when we consider the cause for which Mr. Davis is so much to his people. Let Mr. Davis himself state it, for no one else can do it so well. In his recent address at the laying of the corner stone of the Confederate monument at Montgomery he said:

> "I have come to join you in the performance of a sacred task—to lay the foundation of a monument at the cradle of the Confederate government—which shall commemorate the gallant sons of Alabama who died for their country and *whose sires won in the War of the Revolution the State sovereignty, freedom, and independence which were left by them as an inheritance to their posterity forever.*"

This is a true statement of the case. It is also a complete justification of the Confederate cause to all who are acquainted with the origin and character of the American Union and the principles of State rights upon which it was founded.

When the original thirteen colonies threw off their allegiance to Great Britain, they became independent States, "independent of her and of each other," as the great Luther Martin expressed it in the Federal Convention. This independence was at first a revolutionary one, but afterwards, by its recognition by Great Britain, it became legal. The recognition was of them separately, each by name, in the treaty of peace which terminated the War of the Revolution. And that

this separate recognition was deliberate and intentional, with the distinct object of recognizing the States as separate sovereignties and not as one nation, will sufficiently appear by reference to the sixth volume of Bancroft's *History of the United States*. The articles of

"Beauvoir," the Mississippi home of President Davis.

confederation between the States declared that *"each State retains its sovereignty, freedom, and independence."* And the Constitution of the United States, which immediately followed, was first adopted by the States in convention, each State casting one vote, as a proposed plan of government; and then ratified by the States separately, *each State acting for itself in its sovereign and independent capacity*, through a convention of its people.

And it was by this ratification that the Constitution was established, to use its own words, "between the States so ratifying the same." It is, then, *a compact between the States as sovereigns*, and the Union created by it is a Federal partnership of States, the Federal government being their common agent for the transaction of the Federal business within the limits of the delegated powers.

. . . It appears, then, from this review of the origin and character of the American Union that when the Southern States, deeming the constitutional compact broken and their own safety and happiness in imminent danger in the Union, withdrew therefrom and organized their new Confederacy, they but asserted, in the language of Mr. Davis, "the rights of their sires, won in the War of the Revolution, the State sovereignty, freedom, and independence which were left to us as an inheritance to their posterity forever;" and *it was in defense of this high and sacred cause that the Confederate soldiers sacrificed their lives. There was no need for war. The action of the Southern States was legal and constitutional, and history will attest that it was reluctantly taken in the last extremity, in the hope of thereby saving their whole constitutional rights and liberties from destruction by Northern aggression, which had just culminated in triumph at the presidential election by the union of the North as a section against the South.* But the North, left in possession of the old government of the Union, flushed with power and angry lest its destined prey should escape, found a ready pretext for war.

Immediately upon secession, by force of the act itself, the jurisdiction of the seceding States, respectively, over the forts, arsenals, and dockyards with their limits, which they had before ceded to the Federal government for Federal purposes, reverted to and reinvested in them respectively. They were, of course, entitled to immediate repossession of these places, essential to their defense in the exercise of their reassumed powers of war and peace, leaving all questions of mere property value apart for separate adjustment. In most cases the seceding States repossessed themselves of these places without difficulty; but in some of them forces of the United States still kept possession. Among these last was Fort Sumter, in the harbor of Charleston. South Carolina in vain demanded the peaceful possession of this fortress, offering at the same time to arrange for the value of the same as property, and sent commissioners to Washington to treat with the Federal government for the same as well as for the recognition of her independence. But *all her attempts to treat were repulsed or evaded [by the Liberal Lincoln Administration], as likewise were those subsequently made by the [Conservative] Confederate government.*

Of course the Confederacy could not continue to allow a foreign power to hold possession of a fortress dominating the harbor of her chief Atlantic seaport; and the Federal government having sent a powerful expedition with reënforcements for Fort Sumter, the Confederate government at last proceeded to reduce it. The reduction, however, was a bloodless affair; while the captured garrison received all the honors of war, and were at once sent North with every attention to their comfort and without even their parole being taken.

But forthwith President Lincoln at Washington issued his call for militia to coerce the seceding States. The cry rang all over the North that the flag had been fired upon; and amidst the tempest of passion which that cry everywhere raised the Northern militia responded with alacrity, *the South was invaded, and a war of subjugation, destined to be the most gigantic which the world has ever seen, was begun by the Federal government against the seceding States in complete disregard of the foundation principle of its own existence, as affirmed in the Declaration of Independence, that "governments derive their just powers from the consent of the governed," and as established by the War of the Revolution for the people of the States respectively.*

Fort Sumter as it looked on April 14, 1861, after the evacuation of U.S. troops.

The South accepted the contest thus forced upon her with the eager and resolute courage characteristic of her proud-spirited people. But the Federal government, though weak in right, was strong in power; for it was sustained by the mighty and multitudinous North. In effect, the war became one between the States—between the Northern States, represented by the Federal government [Liberals], upon the one side and the Southern States, represented by the Confederate government [Conservatives], upon the other—the border Southern States being divided.

The odds in numbers and means in favor of the North were tremendous. Her white population of nearly twenty millions was fourfold that of the strictly Confederate territory; and from the border Southern States and communities of Missouri, Kentucky, East

Tennessee, West Virginia, Maryland, and Delaware she got more men and supplies for her armies than the Confederacy got for hers. Kentucky alone furnished as many men to the Northern armies as Massachusetts. In available money and credit the advantage of the North was vastly greater than in population, and it included the possession of all the chief centers of banking and commerce. Then she had the possession of the old government, its capital, its army and navy, and mostly its arsenals, dockyards, and workshops, with all their supplies of arms and ordnance and military and naval stores of every kind and the means of manufacturing the same. Again, the North, as a manufacturing and mechanical people, abounded in factories and workshops of every kind immediately available for the manufacture of every species of supplies for the army and navy; while the South, as an agricultural people, were almost wanting in such resources.

Finally, in the possession of the recognized government, the North was in full and free communication with all nations, and had full opportunity, which she improved to the utmost, to import and bring in from abroad not only supplies of all kinds but men as well for her service; while the South, without a recognized government and with her ports speedily blockaded by the Federal navy, was almost entirely shut up within herself and her own limited resources.

Among all these advantages possessed by the North the first, the main, and decisive was the navy. Given her all but this and they would have been ineffectual to prevent the establishment of the Confederacy. That arm of her strength was at the beginning of the war in an efficient state, and it was rapidly augmented and improved. By it, the South being almost without naval force, the North was enabled to sweep and blockade her coasts everywhere, and so, aside from the direct distress inflicted, to prevent foreign recognition, to capture one after another her seaports, to sever and cut up her country in every direction through its great rivers, to gain lodgments at many points within her territory from which numerous destructive raids were sent out in all directions, to transport troops and supplies to points where their passage by land would have been difficult or impossible, and finally to cover, protect, and save, as by the navy was so often done, the defeated and otherwise totally destroyed armies of the North in the field. But for the navy Grant's army was lost at Shiloh; but for it on the Peninsula, in the second year of the war, McClellan's army, notwithstanding his masterly retreat from his defeats before Richmond, was lost to a man, and the independence of the

Confederacy established.

After a glorious four years' struggle against such odds as have been depicted during which independence was often almost secured, when successive levies of armies amounting in all to nearly three millions of men had been hurled against her, the South, shut off from all the world, wasted, rent, and desolate, bruised and bleeding, was at last overpowered by main strength; outfought, never, for from first to last she everywhere outfought the foe.

The Confederacy fell, but she fell not until she had achieved immortal fame. Few great established nations in all time have ever exhibited capacity and direction in government equal to hers, sustained as she was by the iron will and fixed persistence of the extraordinary man who was her chief; and few have ever won such a series of brilliant victories as that which illuminates forever the annals of her splendid armies; while *the fortitude and patience of her people, and particularly of her noble women, under almost incredible trials and sufferings, have never been surpassed in the history of the world.*

Such exalted character and achievement were not all in vain. *Though the Confederacy fell as an actual physical power, she lives, illustrated by them, eternally in her just cause, the cause of constitutional liberty.* And Mr. Davis's Southern tour is nothing less than a virtual moral triumph for that cause and for himself as its faithful chief, manifesting to the world that *the cause still lives in the hearts of the Southern people and that its actual resurrection may yet come.*

Here in the North, that is naturally presumptuous and arrogant in her vast material power, and where consequently but little attention has in general been given to the study of the nature and principles of constitutional liberty as connected with the rights of States, there is, nevertheless, an increasing knowledge and appreciation of the Confederate cause, particularly here in the New England States, whose position and interests in the Union are in many respects peculiar, and perhaps require that these States, quite as much as those of the South, should be the watchful guardians of the State sovereignty. *Mingled with this increasing understanding and appreciation of the Confederate cause naturally comes also a growing admiration of its devoted defenders*; and the time may yet be when the Northern, as well as the Southern, heart will throb reverently to the proud words upon the Confederate monument at Charleston: "These died for their State."[618]

10

AMERICANISM: THE INDESTRUCTIBLE CAUSE

T HOUGH THIS BOOK IS BRIEF, it has proven a great Truth; a Truth that has been known to traditional Southerners and educated non-Southerners for 150 years, but which is still being suppressed by those most heavily invested in its concealment: Liberals.

And what is that Truth?

The cause of Lincoln's War was not slavery, the North did not win, and the South did not lose. The cause was the Liberals' lust for power and their dictatorial urge to control the American people, their minds, their money, and their government, and the Conservatives' refusal to allow their constitutional liberties to be stolen from them—in particular by those with no regard for American law, Christian morality, or accepted Western tradition.

In 1865 Liberals achieved their nefarious goal of installing big government at Washington, D.C., largely because Conservatives obeyed the law,[619] while they themselves freely used illegal and unethical methods, including a "total war" approach, all in stark contradiction to the will of the people, the U.S. Constitution, and international law. As we have seen, they were greatly assisted and motivated along by hundreds of socialists and communists, many who were European immigrants who fled to the U.S. after their failed revolution in 1848, inevitably finding their way into Lincoln's administration and armies.

In the process what I call the "Cult of Liberalism" won and the Founding Fathers' ideal of Americanism lost.

What is Americanism? Confederate Vice President Alexander H. Stephens defined it this way:

> True Americanism, as I have learned it, is like true Christianity—disciples in neither are confined to any nation, clime, or soil whatsoever. Americanism is not the product of the soil; it springs not from the land or the ground; it is not of the earth, or earthy; it emanates from the head and the heart; it looks upward, and onward and outward; *its life and soul are those grand ideas of government which characterize our institutions, and distinguish us from all other people; and there are no two features in our system which so signally distinguish us from all other nations as free toleration of religion and the doctrine of expatriation—the right of a man to throw off his allegiance to any and every other State, prince or potentate whatsoever, and by naturalization to be incorporated as a citizen into our body politic. Both these principles are specially provided for and firmly established in our constitution.*[620]

America's second most important Conservative: Confederate Vice President Alexander H. Stephens.

This is why the North did not win and the South did not lose Lincoln's War. Liberals and the innately progressive concept of socialism were the victors. The American people and the inherently conservative concept of Americanism were the losers.

But only temporarily!

There will always be freedom lovers (those who prefer self-government), and there will always be freedom haters (those who prefer national government). Thus, despite the Liberals', Socialists,' and Communists' victory at Appomattox in April 1865, the "War" between Americanism, traditionalism, and conservatism (good) on the one side, and socialism, progressivism, and liberalism (evil) on the other, it is not over—and it will never be over.

It is the archetypal battle that has been fought between the light and the darkness, and among nearly every people and country in the world, since the beginning of human civilization. The American Civil War, Lincoln's War, was merely one more Conservative-Liberal conflict among the thousands that have already taken place and the untold number that will continue well into the future.

Thus, as we showed earlier, it is true, just as the liberal (Republican) journal, the *Globe-Democrat* of St. Louis printed in its April 9, 1900, issue, that:

> Lincoln, Grant and the Union armies gave a victory to Hamiltonism [liberalism] when it subjugated the Confederates [the Democrats or Conservatives] in the South. This is strictly true; it was a victory over . . . [conservatism] by . . . [liberalism]. The cardinal doctrines of [conservatism] . . . are the enlargement of the power of the States [that is, states' rights]. All the prodigious energies of the war could not extinguish these. The lesson of the war was extreme and extraordinary, and yet in a sense ineffective.[621]

"Ineffective"? How so? Because, contrary to Yankee mythology, the "Lost Cause" was not lost. It was merely beaten back for a brief moment. Thus, the sovereignty of the states did not "die at Appomattox," as Salmon P. Chase arrogantly declared over a century ago,[622] for it continues on under the Tenth Amendment, which will endure for as long as the U.S. Constitution does.

There are two facts that are vital to a true understanding of Lincoln's War: 1) *all* governments are, by nature, innately conservative, and 2) a perfectly equalitarian government, one of the primary goals of liberalism, is a utopian fantasy.[623] These are the main reasons the Founding Fathers established the U.S.A. on *conservative* principles rather than on liberal ones. As Samuel Augustus Steel of South Carolina declared in 1914, "the South was right," and thus a conservative not a liberal government is the only proper one for America—most of whose citizens cherish personal freedom above all else. This is why the South fought, and it is why the conservative South was right and the liberal North was wrong. Wrote Steel that year:

I believed in the beginning of the war, though only a child, that the South was right, and I believe it now. And I believe further that if this government lasts a hundred years longer, and continues to be a nation of free people, it will be because the principles of political liberty, for which the South contended, survive the shock of that tremendous revolution. For this reason, if for no other, the position of the South should be understood.[624]

As we complete our study of the causes and consequences of Lincoln's War, let us end on a positive note with a verse by the celebrated Confederate clergyman Father Abram Joseph Ryan of Alabama, which poetically describes the belief of conservative, freedom-loving patriots everywhere. That belief is that our Confederate ancestors did not die in vain, but gave their lives for the most worthy cause of all: personal liberty under small constitutional government:

Conservative Confederate clergyman Reverend Abram Joseph Ryan.

There is grandeur in graves,
	there is glory in gloom,
For out of the gloom future
	brightness is born,
And after the night comes
	the sunrise of morn.
And the graves of the dead,
	with the grass
	overgrown,
Shall yet form the footstool
	of Liberty's throne.
And each single wreck in the
	warpath of Might
Shall yet be a rock in the
	Temple of Right.[625]

I can think of no one better to give the last word to than the man I consider America's greatest and most inspiring political figure: Confederate President Jefferson Davis, who fought his entire life for the noble cause of conservatism.

In the following comments, written in 1881, he mentions "the principle for which we contended," which uneducated Liberals of course claim was slavery. While this book has thoroughly debunked this false charge, let us consider Davis' own words: 1) in February 1861, two months *before* Lincoln's War began, he told his wife Varina that if there was a fight with the North it would mean the end of slavery;[626] 2) Davis was discussing full Southern emancipation before Lincoln's War even ended.[627]

The Confederate National Flag—whatever its form and design—was the banner of the American Conservative Movement, 1861-1865, and it should be forever honored and recognized as such.

In any case, the peculiar institution had been *permanently* abolished by the Thirteenth Amendment 16 years earlier, much to the joy of all Southerners. For it was the South where the American abolition movement had begun, where (up until 1830) abolition was the most ardently supported, and where the first voluntary emancipation in what would become the U.S. took place in 1655.[628]

Let us bear these facts in mind as we read the sagacious sentiments of small government Conservative President Davis; words that should be memorialized in granite wherever the love of freedom still thrives:

> The principle for which we contended is bound to reassert itself, though it may be at another time and in another form. . . . The contest is not over, the strife is not ended. It has only entered on a new and enlarged arena. The champions of constitutional liberty must spring to the struggle . . . until the Government of the United States is brought back to its constitutional limits, and the tyrant's plea of "necessity" is bound in chains strong as adamant [diamond].[629]

The End

NOTES

1. Woods, p. 47.

2. Burns, pp. 549, 553. As their name indicates, though mainly progressive, fusionists embraced bits and pieces from various other political parties.

3. Benson and Kennedy, pp. 145-146.

4. See Jones, TDMV, pp. 144, 200-201, 273.

5. J. M. McPherson, ALATSAR, pp. 23-24.

6. J. M. McPherson, ALATSAR, pp. 5-6.

7. See Seabrook, TAHSR, passim. See also Stephens, ACVOTLW, Vol. 1, pp. 10, 12, 148, 150-151, 157-158, 161, 170, 192, 206, 210, 215, 219, 221-222, 238-240, 258-260, 288, 355, 360, 370, 382-384, 516, 575-576, 583, 587; Vol. 2, pp. 28-30, 32-33, 88, 206, 258, 631, 648; Pollard, LC, p. 178; J. H. Franklin, pp. 101, 111, 130, 149; Nicolay and Hay, ALCW, Vol. 1, p. 627.

8. Rutherford, TOH, p. ix.

9. Muzzey, Vol. 2, p. 140.

10. Stephens, ACVOTLW, Vol. 2, p. 33.

11. "Post-truth politics" is a political environment in which public opinion is shaped by emotion and personal belief rather than objective facts. We can thank the Liberal-controlled media, with its aggressive and largely uneducated bastion of socialists, communists, and anarchists, for this form of intellectual dishonesty.

12. Minutes of the Twelfth Annual Meeting, April 1902, p. 75.

13. Muzzey, Vol. 2, pp. 38, 78.

14. Meriwether, p. 93.

15. Meriwether, p. 93.

16. Thompson, pp. 11-12.

17. Rove, pp. 336, 372.

18. See Muzzey, Vol. 2, pp. 274-293; Boyd, passim; Bryan, passim.

19. Magliocca, p. 106.

20. Muzzey, Vol. 2, p. 140.

21. Muzzey, Vol. 2, p. 290. My paraphrasal. For more on the election of 1896, see Boyd, pp. 501-554.

22. See e.g., Seabrook, TQJD, pp. 30, 38, 76.

23. See e.g., J. Davis, RFCG, Vol. 1, pp. 55, 422; Vol. 2, pp. 4, 161, 454, 610. Besides using the term "Civil War" himself, President Davis cites numerous other individuals who use it as well.

24. See e.g., Confederate Veteran, March 1912, Vol. 20, No. 3, p. 122.

25. Minutes of the Eighth Annual Meeting, July 1898, p. 87.

26. J. M. McPherson, ALATSAR, p. 6.

27. Seabrook, EYWTAASIW, p. 539.

28. Seabrook, AL, p. 73. Emphasis added.

29. Seabrook, AL, pp. 74, 378. Emphasis added.

30. Rutherford, TOH, p. 14. Emphasis added.

31. Seabrook, AL, p. 71.

32. Meriwether, p. 219.

33. For more on Grant as a slave owner, see Seabrook, CFF, pp. 156-158.

34. Rutherford, TOH, pp. 13-14.

35. Tilley, FTHLO, p. 10.

36. Seabrook, CFF, pp. 24, 278-284, 303. See also Muzzey, Vol. 1, p. 521.

37. Muzzey, Vol. 1, p. 611.

38. For more on Lincoln's crimes, see Seabrook, AL, Chapter 11.

39. Seabrook, CFF, pp. 16, 37, 317.

40. Seabrook, CFF, p. 27.

41. F. Moore, Vol. 4, p. 201. Emphasis added.

42. ORA, Ser. 2, Vol. 3, p. 153.

43. Minutes of the Twelfth Annual Meeting, April 1902, p. 11.

44. To his great credit, Virginian John Tyler (1790-1862), America's tenth president, was the only man of that office, former or future, to either join the Confederacy or serve in the Confederate government. Though he did not fight in Lincoln's "Civil War" (being too old at the time), he served as a member of the Provisional Congress of the Confederacy. He was later elected to the Confederate House of Representatives, but passed away before taking his

seat. Tyler was an example of the overt anti-South bias that has long permeated the U.S. government: because of his devotion to the Confederate Cause, Northerners in his day regarded him as a traitor, his death in 1862 was ignored in Washington, and an official U.S. memorial was not placed over his grave until 1915, fifty-three years after he died. DeGregorio, s.v. "John Tyler" (pp. 158-159). In total, six men who would become U.S. presidents fought in the War for Southern Independence; unfortunately for history, all got it wrong by siding with liberal tyrant Lincoln and the North: Benjamin Harrison, James A. Garfield, Ulysses S. Grant, Rutherford B. Hayes, Chester A. Arthur, and William McKinley.

45. Tyler, TLATOTT, Vol. 2, p. 567. Emphasis added.

46. Strode, Vol. 2, p. xvii. There were some Southerners who claimed that secession and Lincoln's War originated over slavery; that slavery was in danger of being abolished. At the time, however, Southern slavery was not in danger (from outside forces, at least; in the South slavery was in more danger from the abolitionist majority), and no one, not even Lincoln, truly believed this view (indeed, slavery was more prosperous than ever in 1860—see Fogel and Engerman, pp. 38-106). In truth, those few Southerners, like Confederate Vice President Alexander Stephens, who declared that slavery was the "cornerstone" of the South, were engaging in a clever but reckless political ploy, one used to try and agitate other Southerners in the tariff conflicts with the North. C. Adams, p. 4. If slavery had truly been the "cornerstone of the Confederacy," then Lincoln's War would have ended with his Final Emancipation Proclamation on January 1, 1863. See Parker, p. 343.

47. Forrest ended up sparing the life of this very lucky Yank. See Seabrook, ARB, p. 485.

48. Garraty and McCaughey, p. 244; Faust, s.v. "slavery."

49. Napolitano, p. 75.

50. Channing, p. 165.

51. McElroy, pp. 444-447.

52. Website: http://buchanan.org/blog/the-new-intolerance-3878.

53. Kelly, Harbison, and Belz, Vol. 2, p. xxiii.

54. Rosenbaum and Brinkley, s.v. "American System"; DeGregorio, s.v. "John Quincy Adams"; Simpson, p. 75; Weintraub, pp. 48-49.

55. Seabrook, TAHSR, p. 11.

56. Seabrook, EYWTAASIW, p. 1014.

57. Cornish, p. 276.

58. Page Smith, p. 308.

59. Rutherford, TOH, p. 14.

60. Rutherford, TOH, p. 68.

61. Dana, p. 86.

62. C. Adams, p. 134.

63. Henderson, Vol. 2, p. 411.

64. Leech, p. 291.

65. Lincoln formally dismissed Porter from military service in January 1863, over problems at the Battle of Second Manassas, on August 29, 1862. As usual, Lincoln acted incorrectly. In 1879, fourteen years after his death, more intelligent individuals prevailed: Porter's dismissal was revoked and he was reinstated in the Federal army. J. S. Bowman, CWDD, s.v. "10 January 1863"; "21 January 1863."

66. Donald, L, p. 385.

67. B. Thornton, p.176. My paraphrasal.

68. Murphy, p. 86. For more on Greeley and socialism see Sotheran, passim.

69. Barrow, Segars, and Rosenburg, BC, p. 45. My paraphrasals.

70. E. L. Jordan, p. 141. My paraphrasal.

71. Wiley, LBY, p. 281. My paraphrasal.

72. Barrow, Segars, and Rosenburg, BC, p. 45. My paraphrasal.

73. Donald, L, p. 385.

74. J. H. Wilson, p. 169.

75. R. M. Reid, p. 2; Barney, pp. 127-128. My paraphrasal.

76. Cornish, pp. 87, 269.

77. Garraty and McCaughey, p. 254.

78. Current, TC, s.v. "African-Americans in the Confederacy."

79. Nicolay and Hay, ALCW, Vol. 2, p. 398.

80. Voegeli, p. 102; L. H. Johnson, p. 134; Jimerson, p. 96.

81. L. H. Johnson, p. 134.

82. Durden, p. 133.

83. Barrow, Segars, and Rosenburg, BC, p. 4; Mullen, p. 31.

84. L. H. Johnson, p. 134.

85. Horn, DBN, p. 74. Thanks, in great part to Lincoln, neither the U.S. military or the federal civil service were desegregated until 1948. It was President Harry Truman's Executive Order 9981 that finally put an official end to Lincoln's institutionalized white military racism. Adams and Sanders, p. 269. Sadly, Truman's integration policy was not implemented immediately: it was not until half way through the Korean War (1950-1953) that American forces became officially integrated for the first time since the Revolutionary War. Thus the Vietnam War (1959-1975) became the first conflict in which whites and blacks served as equals from beginning to end. Buckley, p. xx. This is the pitiful legacy of the so-called "Great Emancipator," a man who failed to do a single thing during his presidency to promote, create, or maintain racial equality within his military.

86. ORA, Ser. 3, Vol. 3, p. 252.

87. Cornish, p. 46.

88. Wiley, SN, pp. 322-323; Mullen, p. 25.

89. See Cornish, pp. 181-196.

90. Douglass, LTFD, p. 303.

91. Barney, pp. 146-147.

92. S. K. Taylor, p. 51.

93. Quarles, pp. 200-201.

94. Page Smith, p. 308.

95. Though 5,000 white Union officers eventually commanded all-black troops, only "about one hundred" blacks ever held Union officer commissions during Lincoln's War, and this despite the apathy, protests, and even outright opposition of Lincoln and his War Department. Cornish, pp. 214-215.

96. Alotta, p. 27. Lincoln paid his black soldiers $7 a month; he paid his white soldiers $13 a month. Quarles, p. 200.

97. E. M. Thomas, p. 297.

98. Seabrook, AL, p. 479, passim.

99. Seabrook, AL, p. 470.

100. Seabrook, EYWTAASIW, p. 707.

101. Seabrook, GTBTAY, p. 48.

102. Muzzey, Vol. 1, p. 526.

103. DiLorenzo, LU, pp. 24, 25.

104. Nicolay and Hay, ALCW, Vol. 2, p. 6.

105. Beard and Beard, Vol. 2, p. 65.

106. Seabrook, AL, p. 250.

107. Rutherford, TOH, p. 71.

108. Seabrook, AL, p. 492.

109. For the truth about American slavery, see Seabrook, EYWTAASIW, passim.

110. Seabrook, EYWTATCWIW, p. 45.

111. Rutherford, TOH, p. 71.

112. Seabrook, AL, p. 253.

113. Seabrook, AL, p. 239.

114. Muzzey, Vol. 1, p. 620.

115. Seabrook, AL, p. 256.

116. Seabrook, AL, p. 256.

117. Muzzey, Vol. 1, p. 595.

118. Rutherford, TOH, p. 76

119. Muzzey, Vol. 1, p. 596.

120. Rutherford, TOH, p. 76

121. Seabrook, TGYC, p. 187.

122. Minutes of the Ninth Annual Meeting, May 1899, pp. 199-200.

123. For more on this topic, see Seabrook, EYWTATCWIW, pp. 30-32, passim.

124. For more on Lincoln's crimes, see Seabrook, AL, Chapter 11.

125. Minutes of the Ninth Annual Meeting, May 1899, pp. 200-201. Emphasis added.

126. Hartzell, p. 1.

127. Nicolay and Hay, ALCW, Vol. 1, p. 556.

128. Seabrook, AL, p. 358, passim.

129. Rutherford, TOH, p. 15.

130. Seabrook, AL, p. 421.

131. Seabrook, AL, p. 421.

132. Seabrook, AL, pp. 421-422. Emphasis added.

133. We will note here that 19th-Century conservatives did not think slavery was "right" or that it "ought to be extended." This is leftist propaganda. They merely wanted the individual states to be able to decide for themselves whether to allow slavery or not, without interference from the Federal government. Thus they were pro-choice on the matter.

134. Nicolay, p. 166. Unfortunately Stephens kept Lincoln's letter private. If he had made it public it might have prevented or at least slowed the coming bloodbath, allowing time for nonviolent (diplomatic) solutions to be put forth. See Muzzey, Vol. 1, p. 527.

135. Seabrook, L, p. 406. Emphasis added.

136. Seabrook, L, pp. 420-421. Emphasis added.

137. Seabrook, AL, p. 241.

138. Seabrook, AL, p. 241. Emphasis added.

139. Ransom, p. 97.

140. Seabrook, AL, p. 242.

141. Seabrook, AL, p. 242.

142. Nicolay and Hay, ALCW, Vol. 1, p. 218.

143. Nicolay and Hay, ALCW, Vol. 1, p. 197. Emphasis added.

144. Nicolay and Hay, ALCW, Vol. 1, p. 257. Lincoln is here quoting his opponent Stephen A. Douglas, but is agreeing with him, as his words before and after this statement confirm.

145. Seabrook, AL, pp. 242-243.

146. America's history of black racism and black racial separatism is nearly as long as that of whites. Former Northern slave, Frederick Douglass, for example, once said "I saw in every white man an enemy . . ." Douglass, NLFD, p. 109. Black racism toward Caucasians was particularly strong during the 1800s: many African-Americans at this time were revolted by the sight of white skin, a vestige of the native African belief that "only black skin is beautiful." Blassingame, p. 25. Early American black nationalism, some of which grew out of a revulsion toward white racism, was expedited by a black Massachusetts Quaker named Paul Cuffe, who financed the emigration of nearly forty other blacks to Sierra Leone in 1815. Garraty and McCaughey, p. 145. In 1877, a number of blacks actually sought out the American Colonization Society (a Northern white supremacist organization to which Lincoln belonged), asking for help in resettling them in Liberia. Adams and Sanders, p. 228. In the 1920s, a black-sponsored "Back to Africa" movement emerged. Its founder, Jamaican-born black nationalist Marcus Garvey, promoted the ideas of black pride, economic independence from whites, and the establishment of a black-only state in Africa. Unfortunately for supporters of the Back to Africa movement, Garvey was later convicted of fraud, imprisoned, and eventually deported. Rosenbaum, s.v. "Garvey, Marcus Moziah." Even earlier, in the 19th Century, African-American abolitionist Martin Delany advocated a separation of the races, with an emphasis on black separatism specifically. Rosenbaum, s.v. "Delaney, Martin Robinson." Delany and Garvey were not the first, nor the last, American blacks to push for black separatism. The idea continues today among numerous African-American groups, many with extreme racist ideologies. Rosenbaum and Brinkley, s.v. "Back to Africa"; "Colonization." Like Lincoln and most other 19th-Century white Northerners, the majority of today's black racists are against interracial marriage and for racial separation. Needless to say, white separatist Lincoln, a lifelong champion of the idea of American apartheid and a former chapter leader of the American Colonization Society in Illinois, would have fully supported the Back to Africa movement. See Seabrook, L, pp. 584-633.

147. Nicolay and Hay, ALCW, Vol. 1, p. 231.

148. Lincoln was referring to "nearly all *Northern* white people." He repeatedly demonstrated that he knew almost nothing about how Southern whites felt toward blacks.

149. See DiLorenzo, LU, p. 101.

150. Trumbull, p. 13. Emphasis added.

151. *The Congressional Globe*, 36th Congress, 1st Session, No. 4, p. 58; Carey, p. 181. Emphasis added.

152. F. L. Riley, PMHS, Vol. 6, p. 233.

153. Lincoln himself was often referred to, not as a Southerner or a Northerner, but as a "Westerner."

154. Nicolay and Hay, ALCW, Vol. 1, p. 196. Emphasis added.

155. Basler, ALHSAW, pp. 382-383.

156. Rosenbaum, s.v. "Mexican War." See also Buckley, p. 67.

157. DeGregorio, s.v. "James K. Polk" (p. 170).

158. The idea of white American, even world, domination (Manifest Destiny) was nothing new to Lincoln, the racist dictator who used violence to control the Northern states and force a sovereign nation (the Confederacy) into a Union which by then it had come to abhor. No doubt he would have agreed with William H. Seward, his Secretary of State who, in 1867, said: "Give me fifty, forty, thirty more years of life, and I will engage to give you the possession of the American continent and the control of the world." Farrar, p. 113.

159. *The American Annual Cyclopedia*, 1862, Vol. 2, p. 351. Emphasis added.

160. The rancorous relationships Lincoln had with his fellow Republicans (Liberals) once prompted someone to ask him how he felt about having abolitionists in his party. That's not a problem, he replied, "as long as I'm not tarred with the abolitionist brush." Seabrook, AL, p. 265.

161. Nicolay and Hay, ALCW, Vol. 2, pp. 287-288. Emphasis added.

162. Denney, p. 251; C. Eaton, HSC, p. 93; Hinkle, p. 125.

163. Rutherford, TOH, pp. 13-14.

164. R. S. Phillips, s.v. "Emancipation Proclamation."

165. R. L. Mode, p. 31.

166. According to a September 11, 1863, letter from Lincoln to Tennessee Governor Andrew Johnson: "All of Tennessee is now clear of armed insurrectionists." Nicolay and Hay, ALCW, Vol. 2, p. 405.

167. Cromie, p. 248.

168. It was Tennessean Andrew Johnson, acting as military governor of that state from 1862 to 1864, who persuaded Lincoln to leave Tennessee out of the Final Emancipation Proclamation, which essentially allowed slavery to continue in the state unhindered. DeGregorio, s.v. "Andrew Johnson" (p. 251).

169. Muzzey, Vol. 2, p. 140.

170. J. Davis, RFCG, Vol. 2, pp. 475-476.

171. Palmer and Colton, p. 543.

172. Muzzey, Vol. 1, p. 595.

173. Donald, L, p. 363; Leech, p. 155.

174. Quarles, pp. 115-116.

175. Leech, p. 151; Black, p. 165; Muzzey, Vol. 1, 594. Lincoln later stripped Frémont of his command for freeing slaves in his assigned military area. Why? It was not a "military necessity" yet, Lincoln said. Seabrook, L, pp. 318-320.

176. Quarles, pp. 113-114.

177. Black, p. 165; Wiley, SN, pp. 296-298; Leech, pp. 305-306.

178. W. S. Powell, p. 144. See Nicolay and Hay, ALCW, Vol. 2, pp. 442-444.

179. Muzzey, Vol. 1, p. 600.

180. See Current, LNK, pp. 223, 239, 240, 241.

181. Harwell, p. 307.

182. DiLorenzo, LU, p. 55.

183. Website: www.lysanderspooner.org/letters/SESP012260.htm.

184. Muzzey, Vol. 1, p. 598.

185. Donald, L, p. 385.

186. Rosenbaum and Brinkley, s.v. "Lincoln and Douglas."

187. Current, LNK, pp. 242-243.

188. Nicolay and Hay, ALCW, Vol. 2, p. 270. See also Hacker, p. 583; Wiley, SN, p. 195.

189. Hacker, p. 580.

190. Nicolay and Hay, ALCW, Vol. 2, p. 1.

191. Muzzey, Vol. 1, p. 598.

192. Quarles, pp. 132-133.

193. W. Phillips, p. 456.

194. Meriwether, p. 9.

195. Julian, p. 234. Emphasis added.

196. The "twenty millions" mentioned by Greeley refers only to white Northerners. As the South's 8 million whites were even more anxious to abolish slavery, he should have named his article "The Prayer of 28 millions."

197. Brockett, pp. 308, 309, 311. Emphasis added.

198. Nicolay and Hay, ALCW, Vol. 2, pp. 227-228. Emphasis added.

199. Seabrook, AL, p. 381.

200. See Christian, passim.

201. Grissom, p. 131; Stonebraker, p. 46.

202. Bennett, BTM, p. 37.

203. C. Johnson, pp. 81-84.

204. Bennett, BTM, pp. 37-38.

205. J. C. Perry, p. 174.

206. Greenberg and Waugh, p. 376.

207. See Foner, FSFLFM, pp. 87-88. See also Hacker, p. 581; Quarles, p. xiii; Weintraub, p. 70; Cooper, JDA, p. 378; Rosenbaum and Brinkley, s.v. "Civil War"; C. Eaton, HSC, p. 93; Hinkle, p. 125.

208. J. C. Perry, p. 175.

209. Lincoln admitted that he nullified the emancipation proclamations of his officers because, as he put it, there was no "indispensable necessity." Nicolay and Hay, ALCW, Vol. 2, p. 508. The nation's 4,000,000 slaves (North and South) must have wondered what he meant by this.

210. Muzzey, Vol. 1, p. 510.

211. Nicolay and Hay, ALCW, Vol. 1, p. 252.

212. Seabrook, EYWTAASIW, passim. Emphasis added.

213. Long and Long, pp. 593-594.

214. Seabrook, CFF, p. 217.

215. Rutherford, TOH, p. 95.

216. See Tyler, LTT, Vol. 2, p. 567.

217. Seabrook, AL, p. 73. Emphasis added.

218. Minutes of the Ninth Annual Meeting, May 1899, pp. 200-201.

219. Confederate Veteran, December 1918, Vol. 26, No. 12, p. 509. Emphasis added.

220. Muzzey, Vol. 1, p. 524.

221. Crocker, pp. 20, 31.

222. Seabrook, AL, p. 76.

223. Spooner, NT, No. 6, p. 54. Emphasis added.

224. Also see Pollard, LC, p. 154.

225. Seabrook, AL, p. 77.

226. Muzzey, Vol. 2, p. 132.

227. Pollard, LC, pp. 131-132.

228. Fogel and Engerman, pp. 247-251.

229. Fogel, p. 87.

230. Fogel and Engerman, p. 249.

231. Fogel, pp. 87-88. Sadly, Lincoln's War destroyed much of the South's wealth. As just one example, it took Dixie another 100 years (into the 1960s) to reduce her income gap to the level she had enjoyed in 1860. Fogel, p. 89.

232. Current, TC, s.v. "Plantation."

233. Fogel, p. 436.

234. Fogel, pp. 414-415.

235. Collier and Collier, p. 71.

236. Hacker, p. 593.

237. Benson and Kennedy, p. 58.

238. For more on the Yankee slave trade, see Seabrook, EYWTAASIW, passim.

239. "American Disunion," Charles Dickens, *All the Year Round*, December 21, 1861, p. 299. Emphasis added.

240. Ashe, p. 24.

241. Nicolay and Hay, ALCW, Vol. 2, p. 63. Emphasis added.

242. Nicolay and Hay, ALCW, Vol. 2, pp. 60-61.

243. Seabrook, AL, p. 80.

244. Seabrook, AL, p. 80.

245. Perkins, Vol. 2, pp. 598-601.

246. Zinn, p. 185.

247. Seabrook, AL, p. 265.

248. Muzzey, Vol. 1, p. 532.

249. Seabrook, AL, pp. 269-270.

250. Seabrook, S101, p. 67.

251. Seabrook, TQAHS, p. 329. Emphasis added.

252. Seabrook, EYWTAASIW, pp. 260-264.

253. E. J. McManus, BBITN, pp. 6-7.

254. C. Adams, pp. 4, 58.

255. Seabrook, EYWTAAAIW, pp. 193-194.

256. This is false, and it is the same argument Lincoln and the Liberals used to try and sway public opinion against the South. The Union was not "destroyed" by the secession of the Southern states, because the Union is the U.S. Constitution, not the states or their "union."

257. The conservative South did not "overthrow the Constitution." As we will see, the Liberal North did.

258. The Union was "not dissolved" when the Southern states seceded. It continued under the leadership of Abraham Lincoln. A new Union was created, however, by the seceding Southern states, and called the Confederate States of America, the same name applied to the U.S. by many early Americans and foreigners. For more on this topic, see Seabrook, C101, passim.

259. Rhodes, Vol. 3, pp. 405-407. Emphasis added.

260. See Seabrook, AL, pp. 210-212.

261. Rhodes, Vol. 3, pp. 405-407.

262. Seabrook, C101, p. 90.

263. See Seabrook, TAHSR, passim. See also Stephens, ACVOTLW, Vol. 1, pp. 10, 12, 148, 150-151, 157-158, 161, 170, 192, 206, 210, 215, 219, 221-222, 238-240, 258-260, 288, 355, 360, 370, 382-384, 516, 575-576, 583, 587; Vol. 2, pp. 28-30, 32-33, 88, 206, 258, 631, 648; Pollard, LC, p. 178; J. H. Franklin, pp. 101, 111, 130, 149; Nicolay and Hay, ALCW, Vol. 1, p. 627.

264. See supra, pp. 9-13.

265. Muzzey, Vol. 1, pp. 528, 551.

266. Simpson, pp. 69, 74.

267. Coit, pp. 170, 175.

268. Rozwenc, p. 50.

269. Seabrook, EYWTAASIW, p. 533. Let us note here that the U.S. is not a "democracy" and never has been: as this was not the intention of the Founders, the word appears nowhere in our 18th- or 19th-Century official government documents. Because it aligns with left-wing ideology, however, early liberal-minded enemies of confederation began pushing the false idea that "the U.S. is a democracy" on the public. Continually reinforced into modern times, it is held by many Americans into the present day, with even many liberal mainstream historians still referring to the U.S. as a "democratic republic" (see e.g., Smelser, TDR). The U.S., however, remains a republic (a government based on law) rather than a democracy (a government based on majority rule), despite the misleading moniker "Democrats" and the blatant attempts by the Left to rewrite history and trick the public.

270. Thorpe, p. v.

271. For more on this topic see Seabrook, TQJD, passim; Seabrook, TAHSR, passim; Seabrook, TQAHS, passim.

272. DeGregorio, s.v. "John Quincy Adams" (p. 97).

273. Nicolay and Hay, ALCW, Vol. 1, p. 299.

274. Seabrook, AL, p. 47.

275. Like all Liberals, Lincoln liked the idea of the government bailing out mismanaged, bankrupt, and corrupt businesses, an idea then known as "internal improvements," but which we now more honestly refer to as "corporate welfare." See e.g., Lincoln's comment on, and support of, the internal improvement idea in Nicolay and Hay, ALCW, Vol. 1, p. 8.

276. Simpson, p. 75.

277. Rosenbaum and Brinkley, s.v. "American System."

278. Weintraub, pp. 48-49.

279. Today we would refer to the Federalists and Hamiltonians as Democrats; in other words, Liberals.

280. Woods, p. 34.

281. A. Cooke, ACA, p. 140.

282. Seabrook, AL, p. 48.

283. See Seabrook, AL, s.v. "Confederalist," p. 17.

284. Today we would refer to the Antifederalists or Jeffersonians as Conservative Republicans, or in some cases Libertarians.

285. Crallé, Vol. 2, p. 224.

286. Coit, p. 249.

287. Seabrook, C101, passim.

288. Shorto, p. 124.

289. Muzzey, Vol. 2, p. 87.

290. Mish, s.v. "republic."

291. Hacker, pp. 247, 264.

292. Bernhard, p. 18.

293. Hacker, p. 583.

294. Bernhard, p. 18.

295. DeGregorio, s.v. "George Washington" (pp. 8-9).

296. Modern socialists also dislike the Declaration of Independence, in this case because it promotes the "bourgeois" idea of "private property and its logical corollaries, competitive industry and individual liberty." Hillquit, SITAP, p. 79.

297. Rutherford, TOH, p. ix.

298. Seabrook, AL, pp. 27, 68.

299. Seabrook, AL, pp. 67-68.

300. See Muzzey, Vol. 2, pp. 40, 59.

301. Rutherford, TOH, pp. 42-43.

302. For the facts about the South, the North, the KKK, and Reconstruction, see Seabrook, NBFATKKK, passim.

303. See Benson and Kennedy, passim.

304. Seabrook, HJDA, p. 68.

305. See DiLorenzo, LU, pp. 149-155.

306. Seabrook, EYWTATCWIW, pp. 120-121.

307. Biagini, p. 76.

308. Borchard, passim.

309. Maltsev, p. 285.

310. Seabrook, AL, pp. 506-507.

311. Benson and Kennedy, pp. 158-159.

312. Seabrook, L, pp. 113-114.

313. Seabrook, TGYC, p. 60.

314. Basler, TCWOAL, Vol. 1, pp. 112, 278-279, 438-439, 441; Vol. 2, pp. 115, 251, 371.

315. Benson and Kennedy, p. 161.

316. Avrich, p. 18.

317. Sotheran, p. 293.

318. J. M. McPherson, BCOF, p. 138. For more on Greeley and socialism see Sotheran, passim.

319. Benson and Kennedy, p. 71.

320. J. H. Wilson, pp. xi, 182-193.

321. Benson and Kennedy, pp. 172-174, 186-188.

322. Muzzey, Vol. 2, p. 11.

323. McPherson, ALATSAR, pp. 5-6.

324. Mendel, p. 586.

325. Kamman, pp. 41, 61. See also p. 43.

326. Warner, GIB, s.v. "Max Weber."

327. Warner, GIB, s.v. "Francis Channing Barlow"; Welch, passim.

328. Blackburn, p. 25.

329. Basler, TCWOAL, Vol. 5, p. 272.

330. Basler, TCWOAL, Vol. 5, p. 272.

331. Warner, GIB, s.v. "Alexander Sandor Asboth."

332. Friedman, p. 132.

333. Warner, GIB, s.v. "Alexander Schimmelfennig."

334. Marcus, Vol. 3, p. 21. The German spelling of his surname is Busch.

335. Warner, GIB, s.v. "Franz Sigel."

336. Reichstein, pp. 92-95, passim.

337. McNitt, p. 225.

338. Warner, GIB, s.v. "Albin Francisco Schoepf."

339. Roba, pp. 1, 9; Benson and Kennedy, p. 146.

340. Warner, GIB, s.v. "Peter Joseph Osterhaus." See also Townsend, passim.

341. Bonansinga, passim.

342. After the War socialist Salomon continued to work for the U.S. government under the administrations of Presidents Hayes, Garfield, and Arthur. Warner, GIB, s.v. "Friedrich Salomon."

343. Warner, GIB, s.v. "Julius Stahel"; s.v. "Louis (Ludwig) Blenker." Like many other anti-American European leftists, Stahel was buried in Arlington Cemetery.

344. Warner, GIB, s.v. "Carl Schurz."

345. Neilson, s.v. "Schurz, Carl."

346. Muzzey, Vol. 2, p. 107.

347. Schurz, Vol. 2, pp. 393-396.

348. Hillquit, HOSITUS, p. 170.

349. See Benson and Kennedy, pp. 51-73, 285.

350. Fraysse, p. 141. In English the name of the newspaper is *Illinois State Advertiser*.

351. Benson and Kennedy, pp. 58-59.

352. J. M. McPherson, ALATSR, p. 24.

353. C. Miller, p. 157.

354. Sotheran, p. 95.

355. Sotheran, p. 95.

356. Mussey, Vol. 2, p. 108.

357. Benson and Kennedy, pp. 145-146.

358. Mendel, pp. 583-584.

359. Hillquit, HOSITUS, p. 56.

360. Fourierism, named after French socialist Charles Fourier, is a type of "utopian socialism" that led to the founding of numerous failed communes, such as Brook Farm in West Roxbury, Massachusetts, which thrived from 1841 to 1847. His "ideal communities" were known as "phalansteries." Mendel, p. 580.

361. Sotheran, p. 192.

362. Hartzell, p. 1.

363. Basler, TCWOAL, Vol. 4, p. 283.

364. Simon, Vol. 9, p. 645.

365. Stevenson, pp. 104, 117-118, 121, 193.

366. Stevenson, p. 193.

367. Silverman, pp. 38-40.

368. McAfee, p. 33; DePalma, p. 135.

369. Rowan, pp. 5, 354-361.

370. Spingola, p. 428.

371. Roba, p. 10.

372. Spingola, p. 428.

373. Browder, p. 5.

374. McCarty is incorrect. The word socialist was coined in 1833; the word socialism in 1839. See Mish, s.v. "socialist"; s.v. "socialism."

375. McCarty, title page. Emphasis added.

376. McCarty, p. 4. Emphasis added.

377. McCarty, p. 14. Emphasis added.

378. McCarty, p. 15.

379. For more on the many similarities between Lincoln and Hitler, see Seabrook, CFF, pp. 287-291.

380. Marx and Engels, p. 45.

381. Seabrook, AL, pp. 282, 300, 507.

382. Marx and Engels, p. 45.

383. Seabrook, CFF, p. 288.

384. Marx and Engels, p. 45.

385. Thornton and Ekelund, p. 99.

386. Muzzey, Vol. 1, p. 607.

387. Marx and Engels, p. 45.

388. Thornton and Ekelund, p. 99.

389. Muzzey, Vol. 2, p. 28.

390. Marx and Engels, pp. 45-46.

391. Thornton and Ekelund, p. 99.

392. Marx and Engels, p. 46.

393. Seabrook, AL, p. 530. My paraphrasal.

394. Marx and Engels, p. 46.

395. Morse, s.v. "Education in the United States."

396. See Seabrook, AL, pp. 495-504.

397. See e.g., Marx and Engels, pp. 33, 44, 49; Hillquit and Ryan, pp. vi-vii. Says socialist Morris Hillquit: "The majority of socialists find it difficult, if not impossible, to reconcile their general philosophic views with the doctrines and practices of dogmatic religious creeds." Hillquit and Ryan, p. 261.

398. Morse, s.v. "Education in the United States." Note: The Department of Education was briefly combined with an even larger communistic body, the disastrous, bloated, governmental boondoggle known as The Department of Health, Education, and Welfare. But it has since grown so oversized that it has been made an agency in its own right, and is now an autonomous entity once again: The Department of Education.

399. See supra, pp. 9-13.

400. Meriwether, pp. 91-95, 135-137. Emphasis added.

401. Rutherford, TOH, pp. 27-28. Emphasis added.

402. Rutherford, TOH, p. 28. Emphasis added.
403. Rutherford, TOH, pp. 27-28. Emphasis added.
404. Rutherford, TOH, p. 28.
405. Rutherford, TOH, p. 28.
406. Rutherford, TOH, p. 29.
407. Rutherford, TOH, p. 29.
408. Rutherford, TOH, p. 29. Emphasis added.
409. Rutherford, TOH, pp. 29-30. Emphasis added.
410. Seabrook, CFF, pp. 284-285.
411. Seabrook, CFF, p. 285.
412. For more on this topic, see Seabrook, CFF, pp. 212-213.
413. Seabrook, CFF, pp. 285-286.
414. Seabrook, CFF, p. 286.
415. Marx and other early uneducated socialists often idiotically referred to Davis as a "dictator." Benson and Kennedy, p. 263.
416. Confederate Veteran, December 1918, Vol. 26, No. 12, p. 508. Emphasis added.
417. Confederate Veteran, June 1918, Vol. 26, No. 6, p. 240. Emphasis added.
418. Meriwether, p. 137.
419. Muzzey, Vol. 1, p. 519.
420. Muzzey, Vol. 1, pp. 532-533.
421. Kane, p. 179.
422. Hacker, p. 584.
423. Napolitano, p. 235.
424. J. S. Bowman, ECW, s.v. "Reconstruction."
425. Garraty and McCaughey, p. 253.
426. L. H. Johnson, pp. 181-182.
427. See, e.g., K. C. Davis, p. xx.
428. Tocqueville, Vol. 1, p. 383. See also Vol. 1, pp. 384-385.
429. Lyell, Vol. 2, p. 57.
430. Tocqueville, Vol. 1, pp. 357-358. Emphasis added.
431. Seabrook, EYWTAAAATCWIW, pp. 62-64.
432. J. H. Franklin, p. 58.
433. Muzzey, Vol. 2, pp. 17, 21.
434. Rutherford, TOH, p. 91. Emphasis added.
435. See C. Johnson, pp. 31, 37-39, 236.
436. Seabrook, TAHSR, pp. 404, 479, 536, 571-572, 578.
437. Muzzey, Vol. 2, p. 96.
438. Christian, p. 3. Emphasis added.
439. For current news on the conservative fight against the big government that Lincoln helped install, see Website: www.breitbart.com.
440. Foley, p. 684; Weintraub, p. 44.
441. Seabrook, AL, p. 510.
442. Muzzey, Vol. 2, p. 84.
443. Muzzey, Vol. 2, p. 22.
444. Muzzey, Vol. 1, p. 613.
445. Seabrook, C101, p. 86.
446. Muzzey, Vol. 1, p. 614.
447. Meriwether, p. 191.
448. Seabrook, TQREL, p. 217. Emphasis added.
449. Weintraub, p. 143.
450. December 2, 2008, "Your World With Neil Cavuto," FOX News.
451. Ferrara, p. 11.
452. Website: www.gop.gov/indepth/balancethebudget/charts.
453. J. S. Brady, p. 53; H. Smith, p. 154.
454. Ellis, AS, p. 352.

455. Technically speaking the American "Civil War" did not end on April 9, 1865, with Lee's surrender. President Johnson attempted to *legally* terminate the conflict by issuing a Peace Proclamation on April 2, 1866. However, because the edict left out Texas, on August 20, 1866, he issued a second Peace Proclamation, this one that included the Lone Star State. It is this date that marks the official end to Lincoln's War. Benedict, pp. 44-45; Muzzey, Vol. 2, p. 3.
456. Hamilton, Madison, and Jay, p. 21.
457. This is a combination of my views and those found in Bailyn, Dallek, Davis, Donald, Thomas, and Wood, p. 6.
458. Palmer and Colton, p. 543.
459. Benson and Kennedy, p. 59.
460. Rosenbaum and Brinkley, s.v. "Civil War."
461. Bailyn, Dallek, Davis, Donald, Thomas, and Wood, p. 4.
462. See e.g., Napolitano, pp. 221-241.
463. Napolitano, pp. 131-138.
464. DeGregorio, s.v. "Franklin D. Roosevelt" (p. 498).
465. Weintraub, p. 116.
466. Weintraub, pp. 121, 123.
467. Thornton and Ekelund, p. 99.
468. Muzzey, Vol. 2, p. 85.
469. Thornton and Ekelund, p. 99.
470. Muzzey, Vol. 2, p. 95.
471. Hacker, pp. 1125-1126.
472. Seabrook, TAHSR, pp. 378, 386, 415, 420.
473. For more on the Confederate Constitution, see Seabrook, TCOTCSOAE, passim.
474. Collier and Collier, p. 245.
475. Seabrook, TAHSR, pp. 329, 605, 619.
476. Foley, p. 276.
477. DiLorenzo, HC, p. 197.
478. Gragg, p. 97.
479. Cartmell, p. 16.
480. Seabrook, AL, pp. 275-281.
481. Seabrook, AL, p. 182.
482. Minutes of the Ninth Annual Meeting, May 1899, p. 115.
483. For the Southern view from 1863, see Durden, p. 37.
484. Christian, p. 3. Emphasis added.
485. Long and Long, pp. 593-594.
486. ORA, Ser. 4, Vol. 3, p. 792. Emphasis added.
487. Napolitano, p. 8; Palmer and Colton, p. 543.
488. Thornton and Ekelund, pp. 98-99.
489. Website: www.lewrockwell.com/orig/mencken2.html. Emphasis added.
490. A. Cooke, ACA, p. 214. Contrary to Northern mythology, Lincoln's Gettysburg Address was not received with rapt attention, constant cheers, tear swollen eyes, and thunderous applause. Lincoln's own reaction to its reception tells it all: ". . . that speech fell on the audience like a wet blanket. I am distressed about it." Lamon, RAL, p. 173. "It is a flat failure and the people are disappointed," Lincoln told his friend Ward Hill Lamon. Christian, p. 27. Neither was it of much interest to either the media or the public at large. Indeed, "at the time almost no attention was paid to this address, it being relegated to the inner pages of the newspapers." Encyc. Brit., s.v. "Lincoln, Abraham."
491. M. Davis, p. 170.
492. By "true Americans" I am referring to Conservatives and Libertarians, for they are the only political groups which continue to adhere (however loosely in some cases) to the Jeffersonian concepts upon which the U.S. was originally constructed by the Founders, particularly the Southern Founding Fathers.
493. Seabrook, CFF, pp. 27, 42; Seabrook, C101, pp. 108-109.
494. Minutes of the Ninth Annual Meeting, May 1899, pp. 29, 38, 39, 88.
495. Muzzey, Vol. 1, p. 575.
496. Confederate Veteran, May 1918, Vol. 26, No. 5, pp. 204-205. Emphasis added.
497. Confederate Veteran, June 1918, Vol. 26, No. 6, p. 273.
498. Confederate Veteran, July 1918, Vol. 26, No. 7, p. 312. Emphasis added.
499. Confederate Veteran, December 1918, Vol. 26, No. 12, p. 510.

500. Meriwether, p. 162.

501. Seabrook, TQJD, p. 43.

502. Seabrook, TQJD, p. 43. Emphasis added.

503. Seabrook, TQJD, p. 43. Emphasis added.

504. Seabrook, TQJD, pp. 43-44. Emphasis added.

505. Seabrook, TQJD, p. 44. Emphasis added.

506. Seabrook, TQJD, pp. 44-45. Emphasis added.

507. Seabrook, TQJD, p. 45.

508. Seabrook, TQJD, pp. 45-46.

509. Seabrook, TQJD, p. 46. Emphasis added.

510. Seabrook, TQJD, p. 46.

511. Seabrook, TQJD, pp. 46-47. Emphasis added.

512. Seabrook, TQJD, p. 47. Emphasis added.

513. Seabrook, TQJD, pp. 47-48. Emphasis added.

514. Seabrook, TQJD, p. 48.

515. Seabrook, TQJD, p. 48. Emphasis added.

516. Seabrook, TQJD, p. 48.

517. Seabrook, TQJD, pp. 48-49. Emphasis added.

518. Seabrook, TQJD, p. 49. Emphasis added.

519. Seabrook, TAHSR, pp. 616-617. Emphasis added.

520. Seabrook, TAHSR, p. 617.

521. Seabrook, TAHSR, pp. 617-619. Emphasis added. Note that Stephens is using the word "nation" slightly differently from the way it is used by Conservatives today.

522. Seabrook, TAHSR, pp. 619-620. Emphasis added.

523. For the truth about American slavery, see Seabrook, EYWTAASIW, passim.

524. Seabrook, TAHSR, pp. 620-622. Emphasis added.

525. Seabrook, TAHSR, pp. 622-623. Emphasis added.

526. Seabrook, TAHSR, pp. 623-624. Emphasis added.

527. Seabrook, TAHSR, pp. 624-627. Emphasis added.

528. Seabrook, TAHSR, pp. 627-631. Emphasis added.

529. Seabrook, TAHSR, pp. 631-637. Emphasis added.

530. Seabrook, TAHSR, pp. 637-638. Emphasis added.

531. Riley, p. 22.

532. Riley, pp. 237-241. Emphasis added.

533. Riley, p. 160.

534. Riley, p. 160.

535. Riley, p. 188. Emphasis added.

536. Riley, p. 211.

537. Seabrook, TQREL, p. 213.

538. Seabrook, TQREL, pp. 216-217. Emphasis added.

539. Seabrook, TQREL, p. 219.

540. Seabrook, TQREL, p. 220.

541. Seabrook, TQREL, p. 221.

542. Seabrook, TQREL, pp. 221-224. Emphasis added.

543. Seabrook, TQREL, p. 224. Emphasis added.

544. Ridley, p. 564.

545. Muzzey, Vol. 1, p. 546.

546. Confederate Veteran, January 1918, Vol. 26, No. 1, p. 7. Emphasis added.

547. Confederate Veteran, February 1918, Vol. 26, No. 2, p. 57. Emphasis added.

548. Confederate Veteran, February 1918, Vol. 26, No. 2, p. 71. Emphasis added.

549. McGuire and Christian, pp. 20-27. Emphasis added.

550. Richardson, pp. 322-332. Emphasis added.

551. Minutes of the Eighth Annual Meeting, July 1898, pp. 28-40. Emphasis added. The following was appended to the original article: "NOTE.—The orator General Hooker was greeted by applause at the conclusion of nearly every sentence of this magnificent oration, and it was so urgent that notice is omitted at points where it occurred in the body of the oration, as it would mar its beauty.—Adjutant General."

552. Minutes of the Eighth Annual Meeting, July 1898, pp. 40-41. Emphasis added.

553. Muzzey, Vol. 2, p. 13. One of the purposes of Liberal Lincoln's Emancipation Proclamation, for example, was to encourage black insurrections in the South in an effort to destabilize the Confederacy. This shocking unpresidential, unconstitutional directive—which purposefully threatened the lives of white Southern men, women, and children—came with the promise that the U.S. government "will do no act or acts to repress such persons, or any of them, in any efforts they may make for their actual freedom." See Nicolay, p. 344. We will note that Lincoln's murderous plan utterly failed. Not one slave riot occurred in the South during his entire War, and for obvious reasons. For more on this topic, see Seabrook, EYWTAASIW, passim.

554. Minutes of the Eighth Annual Meeting, July 1898, pp. 26-27. Emphasis added.

555. Minutes of the Ninth Annual Meeting, May 1899, p. 61.

556. Minutes of the Ninth Annual Meeting, May 1899, p. 86. Emphasis added.

557. Minutes of the Ninth Annual Meeting, May 1899, p. 92. Emphasis added.

558. Minutes of the Ninth Annual Meeting, May 1899, p. 143. Emphasis added.

559. For the truth about American slavery, see Seabrook, EYWTAASIW, passim.

560. See Seabrook, S101, passim; Seabrook, EYWTAASIW, passim.

561. Minutes of the Eleventh Annual Meeting, May 1901, pp. 61-71. Emphasis added.

562. For more on this topic, see Seabrook, EYWTAASIW, pp. 400-419.

563. Minutes of the Twelfth Annual Meeting, April 1902, pp. 74-80. Emphasis added.

564. Rutherford, TOH, pp. vii-viii.

565. Rutherford, TOH, pp. viii-ix.

566. Rutherford, TOH, p. xi.

567. See supra, pp. 9-13.

568. Meriwether, pp. 217-220.

569. For more on Yankee slavery, see Seabrook, EYWTAASIW, passim.

570. Potts, pp. 21-25.

571. Confederate Veteran, May 1912, Vol. 20, No. 5, pp. 249-251.

572. Meriwether, p. 91. My paraphrasal.

573. Rutherford, TOH, p. 3. Emphasis added.

574. Rutherford, TOH, p. 4. Emphasis added.

575. Rutherford, TOH, p. 4. Emphasis added.

576. Rutherford, TOH, p. 6. Emphasis added.

577. Rutherford, TOH, p. 4. Emphasis added.

578. Rutherford, TOH, pp. 4-5.

579. Rutherford, TOH, p. 5. Emphasis added.

580. Rutherford, TOH, p. 5.

581. Rutherford, TOH, pp. 5-6. Emphasis added.

582. Rutherford, TOH, p. 6. Emphasis added.

583. Rutherford, TOH, p. 7. Emphasis added.

584. Rutherford, TOH, p. 7.

585. Rutherford, TOH, p. 7.

586. Rutherford, TOH, p. 7. Emphasis added.

587. Rutherford, TOH, p. 8. Emphasis added.

588. Rutherford, TOH, p. 8.

589. Rutherford, TOH, p. 9.

590. Meriwether, p. 152. Emphasis added.

591. Hallam, Vol. 2, p. 169. Emphasis added.

592. Rutherford, TOH, p. 10. Emphasis added.

593. Rutherford, TOH, p. 11. Emphasis added.

594. Rutherford, TOH, p. 11. Emphasis added.

595. Seabrook, AL, p. 73. Emphasis added.

596. Seabrook, AL, pp. 378-379. Emphasis added.

597. Seabrook, AL, p. 71. Emphasis added.

598. Meriwether, p. 219. Emphasis added.

599. Rutherford, TOH, p. 14. Emphasis added.

600. Rutherford, TOH, p. 14. Emphasis added.

601. Rutherford, TOH, p. 14. Emphasis added.

602. Rutherford, TOH, pp. 14-15. Emphasis added.

603. Rutherford, TOH, p. 15. Emphasis added.

604. Seabrook, AL, p. 187.

605. Rutherford, TOH, p. 19.

606. Rutherford, TOH, p. 19.

607. Rutherford, TOH, p. 19.

608. Rutherford, TOH, p. 19. Emphasis added.

609. Rutherford, TOH, p. 19. Emphasis added.

610. Rutherford, TOH, p. 19. Emphasis added.

611. Rutherford, TOH, p. 19.

612. Official Report of C. H. Tebault, p. 31.

613. Muzzey, Vol. 2, pp. 57-58.

614. J. M. McPherson, ALATSAR, p. 4.

615. For more on this topic, see Seabrook, C101, passim.

616. Official Report of C. H. Tebault, pp. 1-31.

617. I define ethnomasochism as self-racism, or more specifically, as gaining pleasure from the hatred of one's own race, and ethnosadism as other-racism, or more specifically, as gaining pleasure from hating other races. Seabrook, CFF, p. 312; Seabrook, EYWTAAAATCWIW, p. 371; Seabrook, NBFATKKK, pp. 55, 169.

618. Southern Historical Society Papers, pp. 119-126. Emphasis added.

619. See Muzzey, Vol. 1, p. 603.

620. Seabrook, TAHSR, p. 41. Emphasis added.

621. Meriwether, p. 137.

622. Kilpatrick, p. 3.

623. Muzzey, Vol. 2, p. 81.

624. Steel, p. 3.

625. Meriwether, p. 271.

626. Confederate Veteran, December 1918, Vol. 26, No. 12, p. 509. Emphasis added.

627. Harwell, p. 307.

628. Seabrook, EYWTAASIW, pp. 549-645.

629. Seabrook, TQJD, pp. 102, 106.

"It is history that teaches us to hope."

Robert E. Lee

BIBLIOGRAPHY

Note: My pro-South readers are to be advised that the majority of the books listed here are anti-South in nature (some extremely so), and were written primarily by liberal elitist, socialist, communist, and Marxist authors who loath the South, and typically the United States and the U.S. Constitution as well. Despite this, as a scholar I find these titles indispensable, for an honest evaluation of Lincoln's War is not possible without studying both the Southern and the Northern versions. Still, it must be said that the material contained in these works is largely the result of a century and a half of Yankee myth, falsehoods, cherry-picking, slander, anti-South propaganda, outright lies, and junk research, as modern pro-North writers merely copy one another's errors without ever looking at the original 19th-Century sources. This type of literature, filled as it is with both misinformation and disinformation, is called "scholarly" and "objective" by pro-North advocates. In the process, the mistakes and lies in these fault-ridden, historically inaccurate works have been magnified over the years, and the North's version of the "Civil War" has come to be accepted as the only legitimate one. Indeed, it is now the only one known by most people. That over 95 percent of the titles in my bibliography fall into the anti-South category is simply a reflection of the enormous power and influence that the pro-North movement—our nation's cultural ruling class—has long held over America's educational system, libraries, publishing houses, and media (paper and electronic). My books serve as a small rampart against the overwhelming tide of anti-South Fascists, Liberals, and political elites, all who are working hard to make sure you never learn the Truth about Lincoln and his War on the Constitution and the American people.

Adams, Charles. *When in the Course of Human Events: Arguing the Case for Southern Secession.* Lanham, MD: Rowman and Littlefield, 2000.

Adams, Francis D., and Barry Sanders. *Alienable Rights: The Exclusion of African Americans in a White Man's Land, 1619-2000.* 2003. New York, NY: Perennial, 2004 ed.

Alotta, Robert I. *Civil War Justice: Union Army Executions Under Lincoln.* Shippensburg, PA: White Mane, 1989.

Ashe, Captain Samuel A'Court. *A Southern View of the Invasion of the Southern States and War of 1861-1865.* 1935. Crawfordville, GA: Ruffin Flag Co., 1938 ed.

Ashworth, John. *Slavery, Capitalism, and Politics in the Antebellum Republic.* 2 vols. New York, NY: Cambridge University Press, 2007.

Astor, Gerald. *The Right to Fight: A History of African Americans in the Military.* Cambridge, MA: Da Capo, 2001.

Avrich, Paul. *Anarchist Portraits.* Princeton, NJ: Princeton University Press, 1988.

Baepler, Paul (ed.). *White Slaves, African Masters: An Anthology of American Barbary Captivity Narratives.* Chicago, IL: University of Chicago Press, 1999.

Bailey, Hugh C. *Hinton Rowan Helper: Abolitionist-Racist.* Tuscaloosa, AL: University of Alabama Press, 1965.

Bailey, Thomas A. *A Diplomatic History of the American People.* 1940. New York, NY: Appleton-Century-Crofts, 1970 ed.

Bailyn, Bernard, Robert Dallek, David Brion Davis, David Herbert Donald, John L. Thomas, and Gordon S. Wood. *The Great Republic: A History of the American People.* 1977. Lexington, MA: D. C. Heath and Co., 1992 ed.

Baker, George E. (ed.). *The Works of William H. Seward.* 5 vols. 1861. Boston, MA: Houghton, Mifflin and Co., 1888 ed.

Ballagh, James Curtis. *White Servitude in the Colony of Virginia: A Study of the System of Indentured Servitude in the American Colonies.* Whitefish, MT: Kessinger Publishing, 2004.

Bancroft, Frederic. *The Life of William H. Seward.* 2 vols. New York, NY: Harper and Brothers, 1900.

——. *Slave-Trading in the Old South.* Baltimore, MD: J. H. Furst, 1931.

Bancroft, Frederic, and William A. Dunning (eds.). *The Reminiscences of Carl Schurz.* 3 vols. New York, NY: McClure Co., 1909.

Barney, William L. *Flawed Victory: A New Perspective on the Civil War.* New York, NY: Praeger Publishers, 1975.

Barrow, Charles Kelly, J. H. Segars, and R. B. Rosenburg (eds.). *Black Confederates.* 1995. Gretna, LA: Pelican Publishing Co., 2001 ed.

——. *Forgotten Confederates: An Anthology About Black Southerners.* Saint Petersburg, FL: Southern Heritage Press, 1997.

Basler, Roy Prentice (ed.). *Abraham Lincoln: His Speeches and Writings.* 1946. New York, NY: Da Capo Press, 2001 ed.

—— (ed.). *The Collected Works of Abraham Lincoln.* 9 vols. New Brunswick, NJ: Rutgers University Press, 1953.

Beard, Charles A., and Mary R. Beard. *The Rise of American Civilization.* 1927. New York, NY: MacMillan, 1930 ed.

Bedford, Henry F., and Trevor Colbourn. *The Americans: A Brief History.* 1972. New York, NY: Harcourt Brace Jovanovich, 1980 ed.

Benedict, Michael Les. *The Impeachment and Trial of Andrew Johnson.* New York, NY: W. W. Norton and Co., 1973.

Bennett, Lerone, Jr. *Before the Mayflower: A History of Black America.* 1961. Harmondsworth, UK: Penguin, 1993 ed.

——. *Forced Into Glory: Abraham Lincoln's White Dream.* Chicago, IL: Johnson Publishing Co., 2000.

Benson, Al, Jr., and Walter Donald Kennedy. *Lincoln's Marxists.* Gretna, LA: Pelican, 2011.

Benton, Joel (ed.). *Greeley on Lincoln: With Mr. Greeley's Letters to Charles A. Dana and a Lady Friend.* New York, NY: The Baker and Taylor Co., 1893.

Bernhard, Winfred E. A. (ed.). *Political Parties in American History - Vol. 1: 1789-1828.* New York, NY: G. P. Putnams' Sons, 1973.

Biagini, Eugenio F. *Liberty, Entrenchment and Reform: Popular Liberalism in the Age of Gladstone, 1860-1880.* 1992. Cambridge, UK: Cambridge University Press, 2002 ed.

Black, Robert W., Col. *Cavalry Raids of the Civil War.* Mechanicsburg, PA: Stackpole, 2004.

Blackburn, Robin. *Marx and Lincoln: An Unfinished Revolution.* London, UK: Verso, 2011.

Blassingame, John W. *The Slave Community: Plantation Life in the Antebellum South.* 1972. New York, NY: Oxford University Press, 1974 ed.

Bonansinga, Jay. *Pinkerton's War: The Civil War's Greatest Spy and the Birth of the U.S. Secret Service.* Guilford, CT: Lyons Press, 2012.

Borchard, Gregory A. *Abraham Lincoln and Horace Greeley.* Carbondale, IL: Southern Illinois University Press, 2011.

Bowman, John S. (ed.). *The Civil War Day by Day: An Illustrated Almanac of America's Bloodiest War*. 1989. New York, NY: Dorset Press, 1990 ed.

——. *Encyclopedia of the Civil War* (ed.). 1992. North Dighton, MA: JG Press, 2001 ed.

Boyd, James P. *Parties, Problems, and Leaders of 1896: An Impartial Presentation of Living National Questions*. Chicago, IL: Publishers' Union, 1896.

Brady, Cyrus Townsend. *Three Daughters of the Confederacy*. New York, NY: G. W. Dillingham, 1905.

Brady, James S. (ed.). *Ronald Reagan: A Man True to His Word - A Portrait of the 40th President of the United States In His Own Words*. Washington D.C.: National Federation of Republican Women, 1984.

Brockett, Linus Pierpont. *The Life and Times of Abraham Lincoln, Sixteenth President of the United States*. Philadelphia, PA: Bradley and Co., 1865.

Browder, Earl. *Lincoln and the Communists*. New York, NY: Workers Library Publishers, Inc., 1936.

Bryan, William Jennings. *The First Battle: A Story of the Campaign of 1896*. Chicago, IL: W. B. Conkey Co., 1896.

Buckley, Gail. *American Patriots: The Story of Blacks in the Military from the Revolution to Desert Storm*. New York, NY: Random House, 2001.

Burns, James MacGregor. *The Vineyard of Liberty*. New York, NY: Alfred A. Knopf, 1982.

Carey, Matthew, Jr. (ed.). *The Democratic Speaker's Hand-Book*. Cincinnati, OH: Miami Print and Publishing Co., 1868.

Cartmell, Donald. *Civil War 101*. New York, NY: Gramercy, 2001.

Cash, W. J. *The Mind of the South*. 1941. New York, NY: Vintage, 1969 ed.

Catton, Bruce. *The Coming Fury* (Vol. 1). 1961. New York, NY: Washington Square Press, 1967 ed.

——. *Terrible Swift Sword* (Vol. 2). 1963. New York, NY: Pocket Books, 1967 ed.

——. *A Stillness at Appomattox* (Vol. 3). 1953. New York, NY: Pocket Books, 1966 ed.

Channing, Steven A. *Confederate Ordeal: The Southern Home Front*. 1984. Morristown, NJ: Time-Life Books, 1989 ed.

Christian, George L. *Abraham Lincoln: An Address Delivered Before R. E. Lee Camp, No. 1 Confederate Veterans at Richmond, VA, October 29, 1909*. Richmond, VA: L. H. Jenkins, 1909.

Coe, Joseph. *The True American*. Concord, NH: I. S. Boyd, 1840.

Coffin, Charles Carleton. *Abraham Lincoln*. New York, NY: Harper and Brothers, 1893.

Coit, Margaret L. *John C. Calhoun: American Portrait*. Boston, MA: Sentry, 1950.

Collier, Christopher, and James Lincoln Collier. *Decision in Philadelphia: The Constitutional Convention of 1787*. 1986. New York, NY: Ballantine, 1987 ed.

Collins, Elizabeth. *Memories of the Southern States*. Taunton, UK: J. Barnicott, 1865.

Conner, Frank. *The South Under Siege, 1830-2000: A History of the Relations Between the North and the South*. Newnan, GA: Collards Publishing Co., 2002.

Conway, Moncure Daniel. *Testimonies Concerning Slavery*. London, UK: Chapman and Hall, 1865.

Cooke, Alistair. *Alistair Cooke's America*. 1973. New York, NY: Alfred A. Knopf, 1984 ed.

Cooke, John Esten. *A Life of General Robert E. Lee*. New York, NY: D. Appleton and Co.,

1871.

Cooley, Henry S. *A Study of Slavery in New Jersey.* Baltimore, MD: Johns Hopkins University Press, 1896.

Cooper, William J., Jr. *Jefferson Davis, American.* New York, NY: Vintage, 2000.

——. (ed.). *Jefferson Davis: The Essential Writings.* New York, NY: Random House, 2003.

Cornish, Dudley Taylor. *The Sable Arm: Black Troops in the Union Army, 1861-1865.* 1956. Lawrence, KS: University Press of Kansas, 1987 ed.

Crallé, Richard Kenner. (ed.). *The Works of John C. Calhoun.* 6 vols. New York: NY: D. Appleton and Co., 1853-1888.

Craven, John J. *Prison Life of Jefferson Davis.* New York: NY: Carelton, 1866.

Crawford, Samuel Wylie. *The Genesis of the Civil War: The Story of Sumter, 1860-1861.* New York, NY: Charles L. Webster and Co., 1887.

Crocker, H. W., III. *The Politically Incorrect Guide to the Civil War.* Washington, D.C.: Regnery, 2008.

Cromie, Alice Hamilton. *A Tour Guide to the Civil War: The Complete State-by-State Guide to Battlegrounds, Landmarks, Museums, Relics, and Sites.* 1964. Nashville, TN: Rutledge Hill Press, 1990 ed.

Cromwell, John Wesley. *The Negro in American History: Men and Women Eminent in the Evolution of the American of African Descent.* Washington, D.C.: American Negro Academy, 1914.

Current, Richard N. *The Lincoln Nobody Knows.* 1958. New York, NY: Hill and Wang, 1963 ed.

——. (ed.) *The Confederacy (Information Now Encyclopedia).* 1993. New York, NY: Macmillan, 1998 ed.

Dana, Charles A. *Recollections of the Civil War: With the Leaders at Washington and in the Field in the Sixties.* 1898. New York, NY: D. Appleton and Co., 1902 ed.

Davis, Jefferson. *The Rise and Fall of the Confederate Government.* 2 vols. New York, NY: D. Appleton and Co., 1881.

Davis, Kenneth C. *Don't Know Much About the Civil War: Everything You Need to Know About America's Greatest Conflict But Never Learned.* 1996. New York, NY: Harper Collins, 1997 ed.

Davis, Michael. *The Image of Lincoln in the South.* Knoxville, TN: University of Tennessee Press, 1971.

Davis, Varina. Jefferson Davis: *Ex-President of the Confederate States of America - A Memoir by His Wife.* 2 vols. New York, NY: Belford Co., 1890.

DeGregorio, William A. *The Complete Book of U.S. Presidents.* 1984. New York, NY: Barricade, 1993 ed.

Denney, Robert E. *The Civil War Years: A Day-by-Day Chronicle of the Life of a Nation.* 1992. New York, NY: Sterling Publishing, 1994 ed.

DePalma, Margaret C. *Dialogue on the Frontier: Catholic and Protestant Relations, 1793-1883.* Kent, OH: The Kent State University Press, 2004.

DiLorenzo, Thomas J. *The Real Lincoln: A New Look at Abraham Lincoln, His Agenda, and an Unnecessary War.* Three Rivers, MI: Three Rivers Press, 2003.

——. *Lincoln Unmasked: What You're Not Supposed to Know About Dishonest Abe.* New York, NY: Crown Forum, 2006.

——. *Hamilton's Curse: How Jefferson's Archenemy Betrayed the American Revolution—and What*

It Means for America Today. New York, NY: Crown Forum, 2008.

Donald, David Herbert. *Lincoln Reconsidered: Essays on the Civil War Era*. 1947. New York, NY: Vintage Press, 1989 ed.

——. (ed.). *Why the North Won the Civil War*. 1960. New York, NY: Collier, 1962 ed.

——. *Lincoln*. New York, NY: Simon and Schuster, 1995.

Douglass, Frederick. *Narrative of the Life of Frederick Douglass: An American Slave*. 1845. New York, NY: Signet, 1997 ed.

——. *The Life and Times of Frederick Douglass, From 1817 to 1882*. London, UK: Christian Age Office, 1882.

Dunning, William Archibald. *Reconstruction: Political and Economic, 1865-1877*. New York, NY: Harper and Brothers, 1907.

Durden, Robert F. *The Gray and the Black: The Confederate Debate on Emancipation*. Baton Rouge, LA: Louisiana State University Press, 1972.

Eaton, Clement. *A History of the Southern Confederacy*. 1945. New York, NY: Free Press, 1966 ed.

Efford, Alison Clark. *German Immigrants, Race, and Citizenship in the Civil War Era*. Cambridge, UK: Cambridge University Press, 2013.

Elliot, Jonathan. *The Debates in the Several State Conventions on the Adoption of the Federal Constitution, As Recommended by the General Convention at Philadelphia in 1787*. 5 vols. Philadelphia, PA: J. B. Lippincott, 1891.

Elliott, E. N. *Cotton is King, and Pro-Slavery Arguments: Comprising the Writings of Hammond, Harper, Christy, Stringfellow, Hodge, Bledsoe, and Cartwright, on this Important Subject*. Augusta, GA: Pritchard, Abbott and Loomis, 1860.

Ellis, Joseph J. *American Sphinx: The Character of Thomas Jefferson*. 1996. New York, NY: Vintage, 1998 ed.

——. *Founding Brothers: The Revolutionary Generation*. 2000. New York, NY: Vintage, 2002 ed.

Eltis, David. *The Rise of African Slavery in the Americas*. Cambridge, UK: Cambridge University Press, 2000.

Emerson, Bettie Alder Calhoun. *Historic Southern Monuments: Representative Memorials of the Heroic Dead of the Southern Confederacy*. New York, NY: Neale Publishing Co., 1911.

Emerson, Ralph Waldo. *The Complete Works of Ralph Waldo Emerson*. 12 vols. 1878. Boston, MA: Houghton, Mifflin and Co., 1904 ed.

——. *Journals of Ralph Waldo Emerson*. 10 vols. Edward Waldo Emerson and Waldo Emerson Forbes, eds. Boston, MA: Houghton, Mifflin and Co., 1910.

——. *The Journals and Miscellaneous Notebooks of Ralph Waldo Emerson*. 16 vols. Cambridge, MA: Belknap Press, 1975.

Emison, John Avery. *Lincoln Über Alles: Dictatorship Comes to America*. Gretna, LA: Pelican Publishing Co., 2009.

Encyclopedia Britannica: A New Survey of Universal Knowledge. 1768. Chicago, IL/London, UK: Encyclopedia Britannica, 1955 ed.

Farrar, Victor John. *The Annexation of Russian America to the United States*. Washington D.C.: W. F. Roberts, 1937.

Faust, Patricia L. (ed.). *Historical Times Illustrated Encyclopedia of the Civil War*. New York, NY: Harper and Row, 1986.

Ferrara, Peter J. *America's Ticking Bankruptcy Bomb: How the Looming Debt Crisis Threatens the American Dream—And How We Can Turn the Tide Before It's Too Late*. New York, NY: Harper Collins, 2011.

Fogel, Robert William. *Without Consent or Contract: The Rise and Fall of American Slavery*. New York, NY: W. W. Norton, 1989.

Fogel, Robert William, and Stanley L. Engerman. *Time On the Cross: The Economics of American Negro Slavery*. Boston, MA: Little, Brown, and Co., 1974.

Foley, John P. (ed.). *The Jeffersonian Cyclopedia*. New York, NY: Funk and Wagnalls, 1900.

Foner, Eric. *Free Soil, Free Labor, Free Men: The Ideology of the Republican Party Before the Civil War*. New York, NY: Oxford University Press, 1970.

——. *Reconstruction: America's Unfinished Revolution, 1863-1877*. 1988. New York, NY: Harper and Row, 1989 ed.

Foner, Philip S., and Robert James Branham (eds.). *Lift Every Voice: African American Oratory, 1787-1900*. Tuscaloosa, AL: University of Alabama Press, 1998.

Foote, Shelby. *The Civil War: A Narrative, Fort Sumter to Perryville, Vol. 1*. 1958. New York, NY: Vintage, 1986 ed.

——. *The Civil War: A Narrative, Fredericksburg to Meridian, Vol. 2*. 1963. New York, NY: Vintage, 1986 ed.

——. *The Civil War: A Narrative, Red River to Appomattox, Vol. 3*. 1974. New York, NY: Vintage, 1986 ed.

Ford, Paul Leicester (ed.). *The Works of Thomas Jefferson*. 12 vols. New York, NY: G. P. Putnam's Sons, 1904.

Franklin, John Hope. *Reconstruction After the Civil War*. Chicago, IL: University of Chicago Press, 1961.

Frayssé, Olivier. *Lincoln, Land, and Labor, 1809-1860*. 1988. Urbana, IL: University of Illinois Press, 1994 ed.

Friedman, Jean E. *Abraham Lincoln and the Virtues of War: How Civil War Families Challenged and Transformed Our National Values*. Santa Barbara, CA: Praeger, 2015.

Garraty, John A., and Robert A. McCaughey. *A Short History of the American Nation*. 1966. New York, NY: Harper Collins, 1989 ed.

Gower, Herschel, and Jack Allen (eds.). *Pen and Sword: The Life and Journals of Randal W. McGavock*. Nashville, TN: Tennessee Historical Commission, 1959.

Gragg, Rod. *The Illustrated Confederate Reader: Extraordinary Eyewitness Accounts by the Civil War's Southern Soldiers and Civilians*. New York, NY: Gramercy Books, 1989.

Graham, John Remington. *A Constitutional History of Secession*. Gretna, LA: Pelican Publishing Co., 2003.

——. *Blood Money: The Civil War and the Federal Reserve*. Gretna, LA: Pelican Publishing Co., 2006.

Greenberg, Martin H., and Charles G. Waugh (eds.). *The Price of Freedom: Slavery and the Civil War - Vol. 1: The Demise of Slavery*. Nashville, TN: Cumberland House, 2000.

Greene, Lorenzo Johnston. *The Negro in Colonial New England, 1620-1776*. New York, NY: Columbia University Press, 1942.

Greenhow, Rose O'Neal. *My Imprisonment and the First Year of Abolition Rule at Washington*. London, UK: Richard Bentley, 1863.

Grissom, Michael Andrew. *Southern By the Grace of God*. 1988. Gretna, LA: Pelican

Publishing Co., 1995 ed.

Hacker, Louis Morton. *The Shaping of the American Tradition*. New York, NY: Columbia University Press, 1947.

Hallam, Henry. *The Constitutional History of England*. 3 vols. Paris, France: Baudry's European Library, 1841.

Hamblin, Ken. *Pick a Better Country: An Unassuming Colored Guy Speaks His Mind About America*. New York, NY: Touchstone, 1997.

Hamilton, Alexander, James Madison, and John Jay. *The Federalist: A Collection of Essays by Alexander Hamilton, James Madison, and John Jay*. New York, NY: The Co-operative Publication Society, 1901.

Hamilton, Neil A. *Rebels and Renegades: A Chronology of Social and Political Dissent in the United States*. New York, NY: Routledge, 2002.

Handlin, Oscar (ed.). *Readings in American History - Vol. 1: From Settlement to Reconstruction*. 1957. New York, NY: Alfred A. Knopf, 1970 ed.

Hartzell, Josiah. *The Genesis of the Republican Party*. Canton, OH: n.p., 1890.

Harwell, Richard B. (ed.). *The Confederate Reader: How the South Saw the War*. 1957. Mineola, NY: Dover, 1989 ed.

Hattaway, Herman, and Archer Jones. *How the North Won: A Military History of the Civil War*. 1983. Champaign, IL: University of Illinois Press, 1991 ed.

Hawthorne, Julian (ed.). *Orations of American Orators*. 2 vols. New York, NY: Colonial Press, 1900.

Hawthorne, Julian, James Schouler, and Elisha Benjamin Andrews. *United States, From the Discovery of the North American Continent Up to the Present Time*. 9 vols. New York, NY: Co-operative Publication Society, 1894.

Henderson, George Francis Robert. *Stonewall Jackson and the American Civil War*. 2 vols. London, UK: Longmans, Green, and Co., 1919.

Herbert, Hilary A. *Why the Solid South? or, Reconstruction and Its Results*. Baltimore, MD: R. H. Woodward and Co., 1890.

Hillquit, Morris. *History of Socialism in the United States*. 1903. New York, NY: Funk and Wagnalls, 1910 ed.

——. *Socialism in Theory and Practice*. New York, NY: Macmillan, 1909.

Hillquit, Morris, and John A. Ryan. *Socialism: Promise or Menace?* New York, NY: Macmillan, 1914.

Hinkle, Don. *Embattled Banner: A Reasonable Defense of the Confederate Battle Flag*. Paducah, KY: Turner Publishing Co., 1997.

Hofstadter, Richard. *The American Political Tradition, and the Men Who Made It*. New York, NY: Alfred A. Knopf, 1948.

——. (ed.) *Great Issues in American History: From Reconstruction to the Present Day, 1864-1969*. 1958. New York, NY: Vintage, 1969 ed.

Horn, Stanley F. *Invisible Empire: The Story of the Ku Klux Klan, 1866-1871*. 1939. Montclair, NJ: Patterson Smith, 1969 ed.

——. *The Decisive Battle of Nashville*. 1956. Baton Rouge, LA: Louisiana State University Press, 1991 ed.

Howe, Irving (ed.). *Essential Works of Socialism*. New York, NY: Bantam, 1970.

Johnson, Clint. *The Politically Incorrect Guide to the South (and Why It Will Rise Again)*. Washington, D.C.: Regnery, 2006.

Johnson, Ludwell H. *North Against South: The American Iliad, 1848-1877.* 1978. Columbia, SC: Foundation for American Education, 1993 ed.

Johnstone, Huger William. *Truth of War Conspiracy, 1861.* Idylwild, GA: H. W. Johnstone, 1921.

Jones, John William. *The Davis Memorial Volume; Or Our Dead President, Jefferson Davis and the World's Tribute to His Memory.* Richmond, VA: B. F. Johnson, 1889.

Jordan, Ervin L. *Black Confederates and Afro-Yankees in Civil War Virginia.* Charlottesville, VA: University Press of Virginia, 1995.

Julian, George Washington. *Speeches on Political Questions.* New York, NY: Hurd and Houghton, 1872.

Kamman, William Frederic. *Socialism in German American Literature.* Philadelphia, PA: Americana Germanica Press, 1917.

Kane, Joseph Nathan. *Facts About the Presidents: A Compilation of Biographical and Historical Data.* 1959. New York, NY: Ace, 1976 ed.

Katcher, Philip. *The Civil War Source Book.* 1992. New York, NY: Facts on File, 1995 ed.

——. *Brassey's Almanac: The American Civil War.* London, UK: Brassey's, 2003.

Kautz, August Valentine. *Customs of Service for Non-Commissioned Officers and Soldiers (as Derived from Law and Regulations and Practised in the Army of the United States).* Philadelphia, PA: J. B. Lippincott and Co., 1864.

Kelly, Alfred H., Winfred A. Harbison, and Herman Belz. *The American Constitution: Its Origins and Development* (Vol. 2). 1965. New York, NY: W.W. Norton, 1991 ed.

Kilpatrick, James Jackson. *The Sovereign States: Notes of a Citizen of Virginia.* 1957. Charles Town, WV: Old Line Press, 2007 ed.

Lamon, Ward Hill. *The Life of Abraham Lincoln: From His Birth to His Inauguration as President.* Boston, MA: James R. Osgood and Co., 1872.

——. *Recollections of Abraham Lincoln: 1847-1865.* Chicago, IL: A. C. McClurg and Co., 1895.

Lancaster, Bruce, and J. H. Plumb. *The American Heritage Book of the Revolution.* 1958. New York, NY: Dell, 1975 ed.

Lang, J. Stephen. *The Complete Book of Confederate Trivia.* Shippensburg, PA: Burd Street Press, 1996.

Langer, William L. (ed.). *Perspectives in Western Civilization.* New York, NY: American Heritage, 1972.

Lanning, Michael Lee. *The African-American Soldier: From Crispus Attucks to Colin Powell.* 1997. New York, NY: Citadel Press, 2004 ed.

Lapsley, Arthur Brooks (ed.). *The Writings of Abraham Lincoln.* 8 vols. New York, NY: The Lamb Publishing Co., 1906.

Leech, Margaret. *Reveille in Washington, 1860-1865.* 1941. Alexandria, VA: Time-Life Books, 1980 ed.

Long, Everette Beach, and Barbara Long. *The Civil War Day by Day: An Almanac, 1861-1865.* 1971. New York, NY: Da Capo Press, 1985 ed.

Lunt, George. *The Origin of the Late War: Traced From the Beginning of the Constitution to the Revolt of the Southern States.* New York, NY: D. Appleton and Co., 1866.

Lyell, Charles. *A Second Visit to the United States of North America.* 2 vols. London, UK: John Murray, 1850.

Magliocca, Gerard N. *The Tragedy of William Jennings Bryan: Constitutional Law and the Politics of Backlash*. New Haven, CT: Yale University Press, 2011.

Maltsev, Yuri N. (ed.). *Requiem for Marx*. Auburn, AL: Ludwig von Mises Institute, 1993.

Marcus, Jacob Rader. *United States Jewry, 1776-1985*. 3 vols. Detroit, MI: Wayne State University Press, 1993.

Marx, Karl, and Frederick Engels. *Manifesto of the Communist Party*. Chicago, IL: Charles H. Kerr and Co., 1906.

McAfee, Ward M. *Religion, Race, and Reconstruction: The Public School in the Politics of the 1870s*. Albany, NY: State University of New York Press, 1998.

McCarty, Burke (ed.). *Little Sermons in Socialism by Abraham Lincoln*. Chicago, IL: The Chicago Daily Socialist, 1910.

McElroy, Robert. *Jefferson Davis: The Unreal and the Real*. 1937. New York, NY: Smithmark, 1995 ed.

McGuire, Hunter, and George L. Christian. *The Confederate Cause and Conduct of the War Between the States*. Richmond, VA: L. H. Jenkins, 1907.

McManus, Edgar J. *A History of Negro Slavery in New York*. Syracuse, NY: Syracuse University Press, 1966.

——. *Black Bondage in the North*. Syracuse, NY: Syracuse University Press, 1973.

McMaster, John Bach. *Our House Divided: A History of the People of the United States During Lincoln's Administration*. 1927. New York, NY: Premier, 1961 ed.

McMurry, Richard M. *John Bell Hood and the War For Southern Independence*. 1982. Lincoln, NE: University of Nebraska Press, 1992 ed.

McNitt, Frank (ed.). *Navaho Expedition: Journal of a Military Reconnaissance From Santa Fe to New Mexico, to the Navaho Country*. 1964. Norman, OK: University of Oklahoma Press, 2003 ed.

McPherson, James M. *Battle Cry of Freedom: The Civil War Era*. New York, NY: Oxford University Press, 1988.

——. *Abraham Lincoln and the Second American Revolution*. 1991. New York, NY: Oxford University Press, 1992 ed.

Mendel, Arthur P. (ed.). *Essential Works of Marxism*. New York, NY: Bantam, 1961.

Meriwether, Elizabeth Avery (pseudonym, "George Edmonds"). *Facts and Falsehoods Concerning the War on the South, 1861-1865*. Memphis, TN: A. R. Taylor and Co., 1904.

Miller, Cristanne. *Reading in Time: Emily Dickinson in the Nineteenth Century*. Amherst, MA: University of Massachusetts Press, 2012.

Minutes of the Eighth Annual Meeting and Reunion of the United Confederate Veterans, Atlanta, GA, July 20-23, 1898. New Orleans, LA: United Confederate Veterans, 1907.

Minutes of the Ninth Annual Meeting and Reunion of the United Confederate Veterans, Charleston, SC, May 10-13, 1899. New Orleans, LA: United Confederate Veterans, 1907.

Minutes of the Twelfth Annual Meeting and Reunion of the United Confederate Veterans, Dallas, TX, April 22-25, 1902. New Orleans, LA: United Confederate Veterans, 1907.

Mish, Frederick C. (ed.). *Webster's Ninth New Collegiate Dictionary*. Springfield, MA: Merriam-Webster, 1984.

Mode, Robert L. (ed.). *Nashville: Its Character in a Changing America*. Nashville, TN:

Vanderbilt University, 1981.

Moore, Frank (ed.). *The Rebellion Record: A Diary of American Events*. 12 vols. New York, NY: G. P. Putnam, 1861.

Moore, George H. *Notes on the History of Slavery in Massachusetts*. New York, NY: D. Appleton and Co., 1866.

Morse, Joseph Laffan (ed.). *Funk and Wagnalls New Encyclopedia*. 1971. New York, NY: Funk and Wagnalls, 1973 ed.

Mullen, Robert W. *Blacks in America's Wars: The Shift in Attitudes From the Revolutionary War to Vietnam*. 1973. New York, NY: Pathfinder, 1991 ed.

Murphy, Jim. *A Savage Thunder: Antietam and the Bloody Road to Freedom*. New York, NY: Margaret K. McElderry, 2009.

Muzzey, David Saville. *The United States of America: Vol. 1, To the Civil War*. Boston, MA: Ginn and Co., 1922.

——. *The American Adventure: Vol. 2, From the Civil War*. 1924. New York, NY: Harper and Brothers, 1927 ed.

Napolitano, Andrew P. *The Constitution in Exile: How the Federal Government has Seized Power by Rewriting the Supreme Law of the Land*. Nashville, TN: Nelson Current, 2006.

Neilson, William (ed.). *Webster's Biographical Dictionary* (first ed.). Springfield, MA: G. and C. Merriam Co., 1943.

Nicolay, John George. *A Short Life of Abraham Lincoln*. 1902. New York, NY: The Century Co., 1911 ed.

Nicolay, John George, and John Hay (eds.). *Abraham Lincoln: Complete Works*. 12 vols. New York, NY: The Century Co., 1907.

Official Report of C. H. Tebault, M. D., Surgeon General, United Confederate Veterans. From the Minutes of the Twelfth Annual Meeting and Reunion of the UCV, April 1902. New Orleans, LA: United Confederate Veterans, 1907.

ORA (full title: *The War of the Rebellion: A Compilation of the Official Records of the Union and Confederate Armies*. 70 vols. Washington, D.C.: Government Printing Office, 1880.

ORN (full title: *Official Records of the Union and Confederate Navies in the War of the Rebellion*). 30 vols. Washington, D.C.: Government Printing Office, 1894.

Owsley, Frank Lawrence. *King Cotton Diplomacy: Foreign Relations of the Confederate States of America*. 1931. Chicago, IL: University of Chicago Press, 1959 ed.

Oxford English Dictionary. 1928. Oxford, UK: Oxford University Press, 1979 ed.

Padover, Saul K. (ed.). *Karl Marx on America and the Civil War*. New York, NY: McGraw-Hill, 1972.

Page, Thomas Nelson. *Robert E. Lee, Man and Soldier*. New York, NY: Charles Scribner's Sons, 1911.

Palin, Sarah. *Going Rogue: An American Life*. New York, NY: HarperCollins, 2009.

Palmer, R. R., and Joel Colton. *A History of the Modern World*. 1950. New York, NY: Alfred A. Knopf, 1965 ed.

Parker, Bowdoin S. (ed.). *What One Grand Army Post Has Accomplished: History of Edward W. Kinsley Post, No. 113*. Norwood, MA: Norwood Press, 1913.

Perkins, Henry C. *Northern Editorials on Secession*. 2 vols. D. Appleton and Co., 1942.

Perry, James M. *Touched With Fire: Five Presidents and the Civil War Battles That Made Them*. New York, NY: Public Affairs, 2003.

Perry, John C. *Myths and Realities of American Slavery: The True History of Slavery in America*.

Shippenburg, PA: Burd Street Press, 2002.

Phillips, Robert S. (ed.). *Funk and Wagnalls New Encyclopedia*. 1971. New York, NY: Funk and Wagnalls, 1979 ed.

Phillips, Ulrich Bonnell. *American Negro Slavery: A Survey of the Supply, Employment and Control of Negro Labor as Determined by the Plantation Régime*. New York, NY: D. Appleton and Co., 1929.

Phillips, Wendell. *Speeches, Letters, and Lectures*. Boston, MA: Lee and Shepard, 1894.

Piatt, Donn. *Memories of the Men Who Saved the Union*. New York, NY: Belford, Clarke, and Co., 1887.

Pollard, Edward Alfred. *The Lost Cause*. New York, NY: E. B. Treat and Co., 1867.

Potts, Eugenia Dunlap. *Historic Papers on the Causes of the Civil War*. Lexington, KY: Lexington Chapter, UDC, 1909.

Powell, William S. *North Carolina: A History*. 1977. Chapel Hill, NC: University of North Carolina Press, 1988 ed.

Quarles, Benjamin. *The Negro in the Civil War*. 1953. Cambridge, MA: Da Capo Press, 1988 ed.

Ransom, Roger L. *Conflict and Compromise: The Political Economy of Slavery, Emancipation, and the American Civil War*. Cambridge, UK: Cambridge University Press, 1989.

Reichstein, Andreas. *German Pioneers on the American Frontier: The Wagners in Texas and Illinois*. Denton, TX: University of North Texas Press, 2001.

Reid, Richard M. *Freedom for Themselves: North Carolina's Black Soldiers in the Era of the Civil War*. Chapel Hill, NC: University of North Carolina Press, 2008.

Rhodes, James Ford. *History of the United States from the Compromise of 1850 to the Final Restoration of Home Rule at the South in 1877*. 7 vols. 1895. New York, NY: Macmillan Co., 1907 ed.

Richardson, John Anderson. *Richardson's Defense of the South*. Atlanta, GA: A. B. Caldwell, 1914.

Ridley, Bromfield Lewis. *Battles and Sketches of the Army of Tennessee*. Mexico, MO: Missouri Printing and Publishing Co., 1906.

Riley, Franklin L. (ed.). *General Robert E. Lee After Appomattox*. New York, NY: Macmillan, 1922.

Roba, William. *German-Iowa Studies: Selected Essays*. New York, NY: Peter Lang, 2004.

Rosenbaum, Robert A. (ed). *The New American Desk Encyclopedia*. 1977. New York, NY: Signet, 1989 ed.

Rosenbaum, Robert A., and Douglas Brinkley (eds.). *The Penguin Encyclopedia of American History*. New York, NY: Viking, 2003.

Rouse, Adelaide Louise (ed.). *National Documents: State Papers So Arranged as to Illustrate the Growth of Our Country From 1606 to the Present Day*. New York, NY: Unit Book Publishing Co., 1906.

Rove, Karl. *The Triumph of William McKinley: Why the Election of 1896 Still Matters*. New York, NY: Simon and Schuster, 2015.

Rowan, Steven (ed.). *Memoirs of a Nobody: The Missouri Years of an Austrian Radical, 1849-1866*. St. Louis, MO: Missouri Historical Society Press, 1997.

Rowland, Dunbar (ed.). *Jefferson Davis, Constitutionalist: His Letters, Papers, and Speeches*. 10 vols. Jackson, MS: Mississippi Department of Archives and History,1923.

Rozwenc, Edwin Charles (ed.). *The Causes of the American Civil War*. 1961. Lexington,

MA: D. C. Heath and Co., 1972 ed.

Rubenzer, Steven J., and Thomas R. Faschingbauer. *Personality, Character, and Leadership in the White House: Psychologists Assess the Presidents.* Dulles, VA: Brassey's, 2004.

Ruffin, Edmund. *The Diary of Edmund Ruffin: Toward Independence: October 1856-April 1861.* Baton Rouge, LA: Louisiana State University Press, 1972.

Rushdoony, Rousas John. *The Nature of the American System.* Nutley, NJ: Craig Press, 1965.

Rutherford, Mildred Lewis. *Truths of History: A Fair, Unbiased, Impartial, Unprejudiced and Conscientious Study of History.* Athens, GA: n.p., 1920.

Ryan, Abram Joseph. *Poems: Patriotic, Religious, Miscellaneous.* 1880. Baltimore, MD: The Baltimore Publishing Co., 1888 ed.

Schurz, Carl. *The Reminiscences of Carl Schurz.* 3 vols. London, UK: John Murray, 1907-1909.

Seabrook, Lochlainn. *Abraham Lincoln: The Southern View.* 2007. Franklin, TN: Sea Raven Press, 2013 ed.

——. *A Rebel Born: A Defense of Nathan Bedford Forrest.* 2010. Franklin, TN: Sea Raven Press, 2011 ed.

——. *Everything You Were Taught About the Civil War is Wrong, Ask a Southerner!* 2010. Franklin, TN: Sea Raven Press, revised 2014 ed.

——. *The Quotable Jefferson Davis: Selections From the Writings and Speeches of the Confederacy's First President.* Franklin, TN: Sea Raven Press, 2011.

——. *The Quotable Robert E. Lee: Selections From the Writings and Speeches of the South's Most Beloved Civil War General.* Franklin, TN: Sea Raven Press, 2011.

——. *Lincolnology: The Real Abraham Lincoln Revealed In His Own Words.* Franklin, TN: Sea Raven Press, 2011.

——. *The Unquotable Abraham Lincoln: The President's Quotes They Don't Want You To Know!* Franklin, TN: Sea Raven Press, 2011.

——. *Honest Jeff and Dishonest Abe: A Southern Children's Guide to the Civil War.* Franklin, TN: Sea Raven Press, 2012.

——. *The Constitution of the Confederate States of America Explained: A Clause-by-Clause Study of the South's Magna Carta.* Franklin, TN: Sea Raven Press, 2012.

——. *The Great Impersonator: 99 Reasons to Dislike Abraham Lincoln.* Spring Hill, TN: Sea Raven Press, 2012.

——. *The Alexander H. Stephens Reader: Excerpts From the Works of a Confederate Founding Father.* Spring Hill, TN: Sea Raven Press, 2013.

——. *The Quotable Alexander H. Stephens: Selections From the Writings and Speeches of the Confederacy's First Vice President.* Spring Hill, TN: Sea Raven Press, 2013.

——. *Give This Book to a Yankee: A Southern Guide to the Civil War for Northerners.* Spring Hill, TN: Sea Raven Press, 2014.

——. *Everything You Were Taught About American Slavery War is Wrong, Ask a Southerner!* Spring Hill, TN: Sea Raven Press, 2015.

——. *Slavery 101: Amazing Facts You Never Knew About America's "Peculiar Institution."* Spring Hill, TN: Sea Raven Press, 2015.

——. *Confederacy 101: Amazing Facts You Never Knew About America's Oldest Political Tradition.* Spring Hill, TN: Sea Raven Press, 2015.

——. *The Great Yankee Coverup: What the North Doesn't Want You to Know About Lincoln's War!*

Spring Hill, TN: Sea Raven Press, 2015.

——. *Confederate Flag Facts: What Every American Should Know About Dixie's Southern Cross.* Spring Hill, TN: Sea Raven Press, 2016.

——. *Nathan Bedford Forrest and the Ku Klux Klan: Yankee Myth, Confederate Fact.* Spring Hill, TN: Sea Raven Press, 2016.

——. *Everything You Were Taught About African-Americans and the Civil War is Wrong, Ask a Southerner!* Spring Hill, TN: Sea Raven Press, 2016.

——. *The Unholy Crusade: Lincoln's Legacy of Destruction in the American South.* Spring Hill, TN: Sea Raven Press, 2017.

Shorto, Russell. *Thomas Jefferson and the American Ideal.* Hauppauge, NY: Barron's, 1987.

Shotwell, Walter G. *Life of Charles Sumner.* New York, NY: Thomas Y. Crowell and Co., 1910.

Silverman, Jason H. *Lincoln and the Immigrant.* Carbondale, IL: Southern Illinois University Press, 2015.

Simon, John Y. (ed.). *The Papers of Ulysses S. Grant.* 9 vols. Carbondale, IL: Southern Illinois University Press, 1982.

Simpson, Lewis P. (ed.). *I'll Take My Stand: The South and the Agrarian Tradition.* 1930. Baton Rouge, LA: University of Louisiana Press, 1977 ed.

Smelser, Marshall. *American Colonial and Revolutionary History.* 1950. New York, NY: Barnes and Noble, 1966 ed.

——. *The Democratic Republic, 1801-1815.* New York, NY: Harper and Row, 1968.

Smith, Adam. *An Inquiry into the Nature and Causes of the Wealth of Nations.* 1778. Edinburgh, Scotland: Thomas Nelson, 1843 ed.

Smith, Emma Peters, David Saville Muzzey, and Minnie Lloyd. *World History: The Struggle for Civilization.* Boston, MA: Ginn and Co., 1946.

Smith, Hedrick. *Reagan: The Man, The President.* Oxford, UK: Pergamon Press, 1980.

Smith, John David (ed.). *Black Soldiers in Blue: African American Troops in the Civil War Era.* Chapel Hill, NC: University of North Carolina Press, 2002.

Smith, Page. *Trial by Fire: A People's History of the Civil War and Reconstruction.* New York, NY: McGraw-Hill, 1982.

Sotheran, Charles. *Horace Greeley and Other Pioneers of American Socialism.* 1892. New York, NY: Mitchell Kennerley, 1915 ed.

Southern Historical Society Papers, Vol. 14, January-December, 1886. Richmond, VA: Rev. J. William Jones, 1886.

Spargo, John. *Karl Marx: His Life and Work.* New York, NY: B. W. Huebsch, 1910.

Spingola, Deanna. *The Ruling Elite: A Study in Imperialism, Genocide and Emancipation.* Bloomington, ID: Trafford, 2011.

Spooner, Lysander. *No Treason* (only Numbers 1, 2, and 6 were published). Boston, MA: Lysander Spooner, 1867-1870.

Steel, Samuel Augustus. *The South Was Right.* Columbia, SC: R. L. Bryan Co., 1914.

Stephens, Alexander Hamilton. *Speech of Mr. Stephens, of Georgia, on the War and Taxation.* Washington, D.C.: J & G. Gideon, 1848.

——. *A Constitutional View of the Late War Between the States; Its Causes, Character, Conduct and Results.* 2 vols. Philadelphia, PA: National Publishing, Co., 1870.

——. *Recollections of Alexander H. Stephens: His Diary Kept When a Prisoner at Fort Warren, Boston Harbour, 1865.* New York, NY: Doubleday, Page, and Co., 1910.

Stevenson, Louise L. *Lincoln in the Atlantic World*. New York, NY: Cambridge University Press, 2015.

Stonebraker, J. Clarence. *The Unwritten South: Cause, Progress and Results of the Civil War - Relics of Hidden Truth After Forty Years*. Seventh ed., n.p., 1908.

Strode, Hudson. *Jefferson Davis: American Patriot*. 3 vols. New York, NY: Harcourt, Brace and World, 1955, 1959, 1964.

Taylor, Susie King. *Reminiscences of My Life in Camp With the 33rd United States Colored Troops Late 1st S. C. Volunteers*. Boston, MA: Susie King Taylor, 1902.

The American Annual Cyclopedia and Register of Important Events of the Year 1861. New York, NY: D. Appleton and Co., 1868.

The American Annual Cyclopedia and Register of Important Events of the Year 1862. New York, NY: D. Appleton and Co., 1869.

The American Annual Cyclopedia and Register of Important Events of the Year 1863. New York, NY: D. Appleton and Co., 1864.

The Congressional Globe, Containing Sketches of the Debates and Proceedings of the First Session of the Twenty-Eighth Congress (Vol. 13). Washington, D.C.: The Globe, 1844.

The Congressional Globe: The Official Proceedings of the First Session of the Thirty-Sixth Congress. Washington, D.C.: John C. Rives, 1859.

Thomas, Emory M. *The Confederate Nation: 1861-1865*. New York, NY: Harper and Row, 1979.

Thompson, Holland. *The New South: A Chronicle of Social and Industrial Evolution*. New Haven, CT: Yale University Press, 1920.

Thornton, Brian. *101 Things You Didn't Know About Lincoln: Loves and Losses, Political Power Plays, White House Hauntings*. Avon, MA: Adams Media, 2006.

Thornton, Gordon. *The Southern Nation: The New Rise of the Old South*. Gretna, LA: Pelican Publishing Co., 2000.

Thornton, John. *Africa and Africans in the Making of the Atlantic World, 1400-1800*. 1992. Cambridge, UK: Cambridge University Press, 1999 ed.

Thornton, Mark, and Robert B. Ekelund, Jr. *Tariffs, Blockades, and Inflation: The Economics of the Civil War*. Wilmington, DE: Scholarly Resources, 2004.

Thorpe, Francis Newton. *The History of North America, Vol. 15: The Civil War From the Northern Standpoint*. Philadelphia, PA: George Barrie and Sons, 1906.

Tilley, John Shipley. *Lincoln Takes Command*. 1941. Nashville, TN: Bill Coats Limited, 1991 ed.

——. *Facts the Historians Leave Out: A Confederate Primer*. 1951. Nashville, TN: Bill Coats Limited, 1999 ed.

Tocqueville, Alexis de. *Democracy in America*. 2 vols. 1836. New York, NY: D. Appleton and Co., 1904 ed.

Toland, John. *Adolf Hitler*. 1976. New York, NY: Ballantine, 1987 ed.

Tourgee, Albion W. *A Fool's Errand By One of the Fools*. London, UK: George Routledge and Sons, 1883.

Townsend, Mary Bobbitt. *Yankee Warhorse: A Biography of Major General Peter Osterhaus*. Columbia, MO: University of Missouri Press, 2010.

Trumbull, Lyman. *Speech of Honorable Lyman Trumbull, of Illinois, at a Mass Meeting in Chicago, August 7, 1858*. Washington, D.C.: Buell and Blanchard, 1858.

Tyler, Lyon Gardiner. *The Letters and Times of the Tylers*. 3 vols. Williamsburg, VA:

N.P., 1896.

——. *Propaganda in History*. Richmond, VA: Richmond Press, 1920.

——. *The Gray Book: A Confederate Catechism*. Columbia, TN: Gray Book Committee, SCV, 1935.

Voegeli, Victor Jacque. *Free But Not Equal: The Midwest and the Negro During the Civil War*. Chicago, IL: University of Chicago Press, 1967.

Warner, Ezra J. *Generals in Gray: Lives of the Confederate Commanders*. 1959. Baton Rouge, LA: Louisiana State University Press, 1989 ed.

——. *Generals in Blue: Lives of the Union Commanders*. 1964. Baton Rouge, LA: Louisiana State University Press, 2006 ed.

Weintraub, Max. *The Blue Book of American History*. New York, NY: Regents Publishing Co., 1960.

Welch, Richard F. *The Boy General: The Life and Careers of Francis Channing Barlow*. Kent, OH: Kent State University Press, 2003.

Wiley, Bell Irvin. *Southern Negroes: 1861-1865*. 1938. New Haven, CT: Yale University Press, 1969 ed.

——. *The Life of Johnny Reb: The Common Soldier of the Confederacy*. 1943. Baton Rouge, LA: Louisiana State University Press, 1978 ed.

——. *The Plain People of the Confederacy*. 1943. Columbia, SC: University of South Carolina, 2000 ed.

——. *The Life of Billy Yank: The Common Soldier of the Union*. 1952. Baton Rouge, LA: Louisiana State University Press, 2001 ed.

Wilson, James Harrison. *The Life of Charles A. Dana*. New York, NY: Harper and Brothers, 1907.

Woodburn, James Albert. *The Life of Thaddeus Stevens*. Indianapolis, IN: Bobbs-Merrill, 1913.

Woods, Thomas E., Jr. *The Politically Incorrect Guide to American History*. Washington, D.C.: Regnery, 2004.

Woodson, Carter G. (ed.). *The Journal of Negro History* (Vol. 4). Lancaster, PA: Association for the Study of Negro Life and History, 1919.

Woodward, William E. *Meet General Grant*. 1928. New York, NY: Liveright Publishing, 1946 ed.

Woodworth, Steven E. *Jefferson Davis and His Generals: The Failure of Confederate Command in the West*. Lawrence, KS: University Press of Kansas, 1990.

Wright, John D. *The Language of the Civil War*. Westport, CT: Oryx, 2001.

Zinn, Howard. *A People's History of the United States: 1492-Present*. 1980. New York, NY: HarperCollins, 1995.

INDEX

MEET THE AUTHOR

LOCHLAINN SEABROOK, a Kentucky Colonel and the winner of the prestigious Jefferson Davis Historical Gold Medal for his "masterpiece," *A Rebel Born: A Defense of Nathan Bedford Forrest*, is an unreconstructed Southern historian, award-winning author, Civil War scholar, Bible authority, and traditional Southern Agrarian of Scottish, English, Irish, Dutch, Welsh, German, and Italian extraction.

A child prodigy, Seabrook is today a true Renaissance Man whose occupational titles also include encyclopedist, lexicographer, musician, artist, graphic designer, genealogist, photographer, and award-winning poet. Also a songwriter and a screenwriter, he has a 40 year background in historical nonfiction writing and is a member of the Sons of Confederate Veterans, the Civil War Trust, and the National Grange.

Due to similarities in their writing styles, ideas, and literary works, Seabrook is often referred to as the "new Shelby Foote," the "Southern Joseph Campbell," and the "American Robert Graves" (his English cousin).

Above, Colonel Lochlainn Seabrook, award-winning Civil War scholar and unreconstructed Southern historian. America's most popular and prolific pro-South author, his many books have introduced hundreds of thousands to the truth about the War for Southern Independence. He coined the phrase "South-shaming" and holds the world's record for writing the most books on Nathan Bedford Forrest: nine.

He coined the phrase "South-shaming" and holds the world record for writing the most books on Nathan Bedford Forrest: nine. Seabrook is also the first Civil War scholar to connect the early American nickname for the U.S., "The Confederate States of America," with the Southern Confederacy that arose eight decades later, and the first to note that in 1860 the party platforms of the two major political parties were the opposite of what they are today (Victorian Democrats were Conservatives, Victorian Republicans were Liberals).

The grandson of an Appalachian coal-mining family, Seabrook is a seventh-generation Kentuckian, co-chair of the Jent/Gent Family Committee (Kentucky), founder and director of the Blakeney Family Tree Project, and a board member of the Friends of Colonel Benjamin E. Caudill. Seabrook's literary works have been endorsed by leading authorities, museum curators, award-winning historians, bestselling authors, celebrities, noted scientists, well respected educators, TV show hosts and producers, renowned military artists, esteemed Southern organizations, and distinguished academicians from around the world.

Seabrook has authored over 50 popular adult books on the American Civil War, American and international slavery, the U.S. Confederacy (1781), the Southern Confederacy (1861), religion, theology and thealogy, Jesus, the Bible, the Apocrypha, the Law of Attraction, alternative health, spirituality, ghost stories, the paranormal, ufology, social issues, and cross-cultural studies of the family and marriage. His Confederate biographies, pro-South studies, genealogical monographs, family histories, military encyclopedias, self-help guides, and etymological dictionaries have received wide acclaim.

Seabrook's eight children's books include a Southern guide to the Civil War, a biography of Nathan Bedford Forrest, a dictionary of religion and myth, a rewriting of the King Arthur legend (which reinstates the original pre-Christian motifs), two bedtime stories for preschoolers, a naturalist's guidebook to owls, a worldwide look at the family, and an examination of the Near-Death Experience.

Of blue-blooded Southern stock through his Kentucky, Tennessee, Virginia, West Virginia, and North Carolina ancestors, he is a direct descendant of European royalty via his 6th great-grandfather, the Earl of Oxford, after which London's famous Harley Street is named. Among his celebrated male Celtic ancestors is

Robert the Bruce, King of Scotland, Seabrook's 22nd great-grandfather. The 21st great-grandson of Edward I "Longshanks" Plantagenet), King of England, Seabrook is a thirteenth-generation Southerner through his descent from the colonists of Jamestown, Virginia (1607).

The 2nd, 3rd, and 4th great-grandson of dozens of Confederate soldiers, one of his closest connections to Lincoln's War is through his 3rd great-grandfather, Elias Jent, Sr., who fought for the Confederacy in the Thirteenth Cavalry Kentucky under Seabrook's 2nd cousin, Colonel Benjamin E. Caudill. The Thirteenth, also known as "Caudill's Army," fought in numerous conflicts, including the Battles of Saltville, Gladsville, Mill Cliff, Poor Fork, Whitesburg, and Leatherwood.

Seabrook is a direct descendant of the families of Alexander H. Stephens, John Singleton Mosby, William Giles Harding, and Edmund Winchester Rucker, and is related to the following Confederates and other 18th- and 19th-Century luminaries: Robert E. Lee, Stephen Dill Lee, Stonewall Jackson, Nathan Bedford Forrest, James Longstreet, John Hunt Morgan, Jeb Stuart, Pierre G. T. Beauregard (approved the Confederate Battle Flag design), George W. Gordon, John Bell Hood, Alexander Peter Stewart, Arthur M. Manigault, Joseph Manigault, Charles Scott Venable, Thornton A. Washington, John A. Washington, Abraham Buford, Edmund W. Pettus, Theodrick "Tod" Carter, John B. Womack, John H. Winder, Gideon J. Pillow, States Rights Gist, Henry R. Jackson, John Lawton Seabrook, John C. Breckinridge, Leonidas Polk, Zachary Taylor, Sarah Knox Taylor (first wife of Jefferson Davis), Richard Taylor, Davy Crockett, Daniel Boone, Meriwether Lewis (of the Lewis and Clark Expedition) Andrew Jackson, James K. Polk, Abram Poindexter Maury (founder of Franklin, TN), Zebulon Vance, Thomas Jefferson, Edmund Jennings Randolph, George Wythe Randolph (grandson of Jefferson), Felix K. Zollicoffer, Fitzhugh Lee, Nathaniel F. Cheairs, Jesse James, Frank James, Robert Brank

(Photo © Lochlainn Seabrook)

Vance, Charles Sidney Winder, John W. McGavock, Caroline E. (Winder) McGavock, David Harding McGavock, Lysander McGavock, James Randal McGavock, Randal William McGavock, Francis McGavock, Emily McGavock, William Henry F. Lee, Lucius E. Polk, Minor Meriwether (husband of noted pro-South author Elizabeth Avery Meriwether), Ellen Bourne Tynes (wife of Forrest's chief of artillery, Captain John W. Morton), South Carolina Senators Preston Smith Brooks and Andrew Pickens Butler, and famed South Carolina diarist Mary Chesnut.

Seabrook's modern day cousins include: Patrick J. Buchanan (Conservative author), Cindy Crawford (model), Shelby Lee Adams (Letcher Co., Kentucky, photographer), Bertram Thomas Combs (Kentucky's 50th governor), Edith Bolling (wife of President Woodrow Wilson), and actors Andy Griffith, George C. Scott, Robert Duvall, Reese Witherspoon, Lee Marvin, Rebecca Gayheart, and Tom Cruise.

Seabrook's screenplay, *A Rebel Born*, based on his book of the same name, has been signed with acclaimed filmmaker Christopher Forbes (of Forbes Film). It is now in pre-production, and is set for release in 2017 as a full-length feature film. This will be the first movie ever made of Nathan Bedford Forrest's life story, and as a historically accurate project written from the Southern perspective, is destined to be one of the most talked about Civil War films of all time.

Born with music in his blood, Seabrook is an award-winning, multi-genre, BMI-Nashville songwriter and lyricist who has composed some 3,000 songs (250 albums), and whose original music has been heard in film (*A Rebel Born, Cowgirls 'n Angels, Confederate Cavalry, Billy the Kid: Showdown in Lincoln County, Vengeance Without Mercy, Last Step, County Line, The Mark*) and on TV and radio worldwide. A musician, producer, multi-instrumentalist, and renown performer—whose keyboard work has been variously compared to pianists from Hargus Robbins and Vince Guaraldi to Elton John and Leonard Bernstein—Seabrook has opened for groups such as the Earl Scruggs Review, Ted Nugent, and Bob Seger, and has performed privately for such public figures as President Ronald Reagan, Burt Reynolds, Loni Anderson, and Senator Edward W. Brooke. Seabrook's cousins in the music business include: Johnny Cash, Elvis Presley, Billy Ray and Miley Cyrus, Patty Loveless, Tim McGraw, Lee Ann Womack, Dolly Parton, Pat Boone, Naomi, Wynonna, and Ashley Judd, Ricky Skaggs, the Sunshine Sisters, Martha Carson, and Chet Atkins.

Seabrook lives with his wife and family in historic Middle Tennessee, the heart of Forrest country and the Confederacy, where his conservative Southern ancestors fought valiantly against Liberal Lincoln and the progressive North in defense of Jeffersonianism, constitutional government, and personal liberty.

LochlainnSeabrook.com

If you enjoyed this book you will be interested in Colonel Seabrook's other popular related titles:

☞ EVERYTHING YOU WERE TAUGHT ABOUT THE CIVIL WAR IS WRONG, ASK A SOUTHERNER!
☞ EVERYTHING YOU WERE TAUGHT ABOUT AMERICAN SLAVERY IS WRONG, ASK A SOUTHERNER!
☞ CONFEDERATE FLAG FACTS: WHAT EVERY AMERICAN SHOULD KNOW ABOUT DIXIE'S SOUTHERN CROSS
☞ CONFEDERACY 101: AMAZING FACTS YOU NEVER KNEW ABOUT AMERICA'S OLDEST POLITICAL TRADITION

Available from Sea Raven Press and wherever fine books are sold

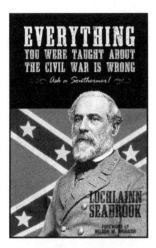
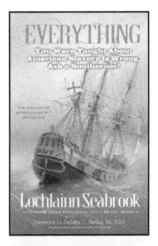

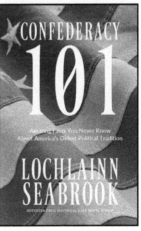

ALL OF OUR BOOK COVERS ARE AVAILABLE AS 11" X 17" POSTERS, SUITABLE FOR FRAMING.

SeaRavenPress.com • NathanBedfordForrestBooks.com

CPSIA information can be obtained
at www.ICGtesting.com
Printed in the USA
LVHW112056300419
615313LV00003B/73/P